INTERNATIONAL MONETARY FUND

WORLD ECONOMIC OUTLOOK

Countering the Cost-of-Living Crisis

2022
OCT

Cover and Design: IMF CSF Creative Solutions Division
Composition: AGS, An RR Donnelley Company

Cataloging-in-Publication Data

Joint Bank-Fund Library

Names: International Monetary Fund.
Title: World economic outlook (International Monetary Fund)
Other titles: WEO | Occasional paper (International Monetary Fund) | World economic and financial surveys.
Description: Washington, DC : International Monetary Fund, 1980- | Semiannual | Some issues also have thematic titles. | Began with issue for May 1980. | 1981-1984: Occasional paper / International Monetary Fund, 0251-6365 | 1986-: World economic and financial surveys, 0256-6877.
Identifiers: ISSN 0256-6877 (print) | ISSN 1564-5215 (online)
Subjects: LCSH: Economic development—Periodicals. | International economic relations—Periodicals. | Debts, External—Periodicals. | Balance of payments—Periodicals. | International finance—Periodicals. | Economic forecasting—Periodicals.
Classification: LCC HC10.W79

HC10.80

ISBN 979-8-40021-843-9 (English Paper)
979-8-40022-121-7 (English ePub)
979-8-40022-128-6 (English Web PDF)

The *World Economic Outlook* (WEO) is a survey by the IMF staff published twice a year, in the spring and fall. The WEO is prepared by the IMF staff and has benefited from comments and suggestions by Executive Directors following their discussion of the report on September 29, 2022. The views expressed in this publication are those of the IMF staff and do not necessarily represent the views of the IMF's Executive Directors or their national authorities.

Recommended citation: International Monetary Fund. 2022. *World Economic Outlook: Countering the Cost-of-Living Crisis.* Washington, DC. October.

Errata
October 17, 2022

At publication on October 11, certain tables in this report failed to incorporate the gross domestic product data for Italy that was available before the report's deadline for data submission. As a result, the data row for Italy has been corrected where appropriate in the following tables:

Table 1.1. (pages 9–10)
Annex Table 1.1.1. (page 42)
Annex Table 1.1.6. (page 47)
Statistical Appendix Table A2. (page 126)
Statistical Appendix Table A3. (page 128)
Statistical Appendix Table B1. (page 2)

Additionally, certain tables in this report included incorrect projections for gross domestic product in US dollars for China and the world, and current account balance in percent of GDP for China. These projections have been corrected in the following tables:
Annex Table 1.1.2. (page 43)
Statistical Appendix Table A1. (page 125)
Statistical Appendix Table A12. (page 144)

This version of the report now contains the proper data in the above tables.

Publication orders may be placed online, by fax, or through the mail:
International Monetary Fund, Publication Services
P.O. Box 92780, Washington, DC 20090, USA
Tel.: (202) 623-7430 Fax: (202) 623-7201
E-mail: publications@imf.org
www.imfbookstore.org
www.elibrary.imf.org

CONTENTS

Tables

Online Tables—Statistical Appendix

Figures

ASSUMPTIONS AND CONVENTIONS

A number of assumptions have been adopted for the projections presented in the *World Economic Outlook* (WEO). It has been assumed that *real effective exchange rates* remained constant at their average levels during July 22, 2022, to August 19, 2022, except for those for the currencies participating in the European exchange rate mechanism II, which are assumed to have remained constant in nominal terms relative to the euro; that established *policies of national authorities* will be maintained (for specific assumptions about fiscal and monetary policies for selected economies, see Box A1 in the Statistical Appendix); that the average price of oil will be $98.19 a barrel in 2022 and $85.52 a barrel in 2023; that the *three-month government bond yield* for the United States will average 1.8 percent in 2022 and 4.0 percent in 2023, for the euro area will average –0.2 percent in 2022 and 0.8 percent in 2023, and for Japan will average –0.1 percent in 2022 and 0.0 percent in 2023; and that the *10-year government bond yield* for the United States will average 3.2 percent in 2022 and 4.4 percent in 2023, that for the euro area will average 0.9 percent in 2022 and 1.3 percent in 2023, and that for Japan will average 0.2 percent in 2022 and 0.3 percent in 2023. These are, of course, working hypotheses rather than forecasts, and the uncertainties surrounding them add to the margin of error that would, in any event, be involved in the projections. The estimates and projections are based on statistical information available through September 26, 2022.

The following conventions are used throughout the WEO:

- . . . to indicate that data are not available or not applicable;
- – between years or months (for example, 2021–22 or January–June) to indicate the years or months covered, including the beginning and ending years or months; and
- / between years or months (for example, 2021/22) to indicate a fiscal or financial year.
- "Billion" means a thousand million; "trillion" means a thousand billion.
- "Basis points" refers to hundredths of 1 percentage point (for example, 25 basis points are equivalent to ¼ of 1 percentage point).
- Data refer to calendar years, except in the case of a few countries that use fiscal years. Please refer to Table F in the Statistical Appendix, which lists the economies with exceptional reporting periods for national accounts and government finance data for each country.
- For some countries, the figures for 2021 and earlier are based on estimates rather than actual outturns. Please refer to Table G in the Statistical Appendix, which lists the latest actual outturns for the indicators in the national accounts, prices, government finance, and balance of payments for each country.

What is new in this publication:

- For Algeria, starting with the October 2022 WEO, total government expenditure and net lending/borrowing include net lending by the government, which mostly reflects support to the pension system and other public sector entities.
- Ecuador's fiscal sector projections, which were previously omitted because of ongoing program review discussions, are now included.
- Tunisia's forecast data, which were previously omitted because of ongoing technical discussions pending potential program negotiations, are now included.
- Turkey is now referred to as Türkiye.
- For Sri Lanka, certain projections for 2023–27 are excluded from publication owing to ongoing discussions on sovereign debt restructuring, following the recently reached staff-level agreement on an IMF-supported program.
- For Venezuela, following methodological upgrades, historical data have been revised from 2012 onward. Nominal variables that were omitted from publication in the April 2022 WEO are now included.

In the tables and figures, the following conventions apply:

- Tables and figures in this report that list their source as "IMF staff calculations" or "IMF staff estimates" draw on data from the WEO database.
- When countries are not listed alphabetically, they are ordered on the basis of economic size.
- Minor discrepancies between sums of constituent figures and totals shown reflect rounding.
- Composite data are provided for various groups of countries organized according to economic characteristics or region. Unless noted otherwise, country group composites represent calculations based on 90 percent or more of the weighted group data.
- The boundaries, colors, denominations, and any other information shown on maps do not imply, on the part of the IMF, any judgment on the legal status of any territory or any endorsement or acceptance of such boundaries.

As used in this report, the terms "country" and "economy" do not in all cases refer to a territorial entity that is a state as understood by international law and practice. As used here, the term also covers some territorial entities that are not states but for which statistical data are maintained on a separate and independent basis.

FURTHER INFORMATION

Corrections and Revisions

The data and analysis appearing in the *World Economic Outlook* (WEO) are compiled by the IMF staff at the time of publication. Every effort is made to ensure their timeliness, accuracy, and completeness. When errors are discovered, corrections and revisions are incorporated into the digital editions available from the IMF website and on the IMF eLibrary (see below). All substantive changes are listed in the online table of contents.

Print and Digital Editions

Print

Print copies of this WEO can be ordered from the IMF bookstore at imfbk.st/512000.

Digital

Multiple digital editions of the WEO, including ePub, enhanced PDF, and HTML, are available on the IMF eLibrary at http://www.elibrary.imf.org/OCT22WEO.

Download a free PDF of the report and data sets for each of the charts therein from the IMF website at www.imf.org/publications/weo or scan the QR code below to access the WEO web page directly:

Copyright and Reuse

Information on the terms and conditions for reusing the contents of this publication are at www.imf.org/external/terms.htm.

DATA

This version of the *World Economic Outlook* (WEO) is available in full through the IMF eLibrary (www.elibrary.imf.org) and the IMF website (www.imf.org). Accompanying the publication on the IMF website is a larger compilation of data from the WEO database than is included in the report itself, including files containing the series most frequently requested by readers. These files may be downloaded for use in a variety of software packages.

The data appearing in the WEO are compiled by the IMF staff at the time of the WEO exercises. The historical data and projections are based on the information gathered by the IMF country desk officers in the context of their missions to IMF member countries and through their ongoing analysis of the evolving situation in each country. Historical data are updated on a continual basis as more information becomes available, and structural breaks in data are often adjusted to produce smooth series with the use of splicing and other techniques. IMF staff estimates continue to serve as proxies for historical series when complete information is unavailable. As a result, WEO data can differ from those in other sources with official data, including the IMF's *International Financial Statistics*.

The WEO data and metadata provided are "as is" and "as available," and every effort is made to ensure their timeliness, accuracy, and completeness, but these cannot be guaranteed. When errors are discovered, there is a concerted effort to correct them as appropriate and feasible. Corrections and revisions made after publication are incorporated into the electronic editions available from the IMF eLibrary (www.elibrary.imf.org) and on the IMF website (www.imf.org). All substantive changes are listed in detail in the online tables of contents.

For details on the terms and conditions for usage of the WEO database, please refer to the IMF Copyright and Usage website (www.imf.org/external/terms.htm).

Inquiries about the content of the WEO and the WEO database should be sent by mail, or online forum (telephone inquiries cannot be accepted):

World Economic Studies Division
Research Department
International Monetary Fund
700 19th Street, NW
Washington, DC 20431, USA
Online Forum: www.imf.org/weoforum

PREFACE

The analysis and projections contained in the *World Economic Outlook* are integral elements of the IMF's surveillance of economic developments and policies in its member countries, of developments in international financial markets, and of the global economic system. The survey of prospects and policies is the product of a comprehensive interdepartmental review of world economic developments, which draws primarily on information the IMF staff gathers through its consultations with member countries. These consultations are carried out in particular by the IMF's area departments—namely, the African Department, Asia and Pacific Department, European Department, Middle East and Central Asia Department, and Western Hemisphere Department—together with the Strategy, Policy, and Review Department; the Monetary and Capital Markets Department; and the Fiscal Affairs Department.

The analysis in this report was coordinated in the Research Department under the general direction of Pierre-Olivier Gourinchas, Economic Counsellor and Director of Research. The project was directed by Petya Koeva Brooks, Deputy Director, Research Department, and Daniel Leigh, Division Chief, Research Department.

The primary contributors to this report are Silvia Albrizio, Jorge Alvarez, Philip Barrett, Mehdi Benatiya Andaloussi, John Bluedorn, Christian Bogmans, Benjamin Carton, Christopher Evans, Allan Dizioli, Niels-Jakob Hansen, Florence Jaumotte, Christoffer Koch, Toh Kuan, Dirk Muir, Jean-Marc Natal, Diaa Noureldin, Augustus J. Panton, Andrea Pescatori, Ervin Prifti, Alexandre Sollaci, Martin Stuermer, Nico Valckx, Simon Voigts, and Philippe Wingender.

Other contributors include Michael Andrle, Gavin Asdorian, Jared Bebee, Rachel Brasier, Moya Chin, Yaniv Cohen, Federico Díez, Wenchuan Dong, Angela Espiritu, Rebecca Eyassu, Ziyan Han, Jinjin He, Youyou Huang, Eduard Laurito, Jungjin Lee, Li Lin, Li Longj, Yousef F. Nazer, Cynthia Nyanchama Nyakeri, Emory Oakes, Myrto Oikonomou, Clarita Phillips, Carlo Pizzinelli, Rafael Portillo, Evgenia Pugacheva, Tianchu Qi, Yiyuan Qi, Aneta Radzikowski, Max Rozycki, Muhammad Ahsan Shafique, Nicholas Tong, Yarou Xu, Jiaqi Zhao, and Canran Zheng.

Joseph Procopio from the Communications Department led the editorial team for the report, with production and editorial support from Michael Harrup, and additional assistance from Lucy Scott Morales, James Unwin, Harold Medina (and team), The Grauel Group, and TalentMEDIA Services.

The analysis has benefited from comments and suggestions by staff members from other IMF departments as well as by Executive Directors following their discussion of the report on September 29, 2022. However, estimates, projections, and policy considerations are those of the IMF staff and should not be attributed to Executive Directors or to their national authorities.

FOREWORD

As storm clouds gather, policymakers need to keep a steady hand.

The global economy continues to face steep challenges, shaped by the lingering effects of three powerful forces: the Russian invasion of Ukraine, a cost-of-living crisis caused by persistent and broadening inflation pressures, and the slowdown in China.

Our latest forecasts project global growth to remain unchanged in 2022 at 3.2 percent and to slow to 2.7 percent in 2023—0.2 percentage points lower than the July forecast—with a 25 percent probability that it could fall below 2 percent. More than a third of the global economy will contract this year or next, while the three largest economies—the United States, the European Union, and China—will continue to stall. In short, the worst is yet to come, and for many people 2023 will feel like a recession.

Russia's invasion of Ukraine continues to powerfully destabilize the global economy. Beyond the escalating and senseless destruction of lives and livelihoods, it has led to a severe energy crisis in Europe that is sharply increasing costs of living and hampering economic activity. Gas prices in Europe have increased more than four-fold since 2021, with Russia cutting deliveries to less than 20 percent of their 2021 levels, raising the prospect of energy shortages over the next winter and beyond. More broadly, the conflict has also pushed up food prices on world markets, despite the recent easing after the Black Sea grain deal, causing serious hardship for low-income households worldwide, and especially so in low-income countries.

Persistent and broadening inflation pressures have triggered a rapid and synchronized tightening of monetary conditions, alongside a powerful appreciation of the US dollar against most other currencies. Tighter global monetary and financial conditions will work their way through the economy, weighing demand down and helping to gradually subjugate inflation. So far, however, price pressures are proving quite stubborn and a major source of concern for policymakers. We expect global inflation to peak in late 2022 but to remain elevated for longer than previously expected, decreasing to 4.1 percent by 2024.

In China, the frequent lockdowns under its zero COVID policy have taken a toll on the economy, especially in the second quarter of 2022. Furthermore, the property sector, representing about one-fifth of economic activity in China, is rapidly weakening. Given the size of China's economy and its importance for global supply chains, this will weigh heavily on global trade and activity.

The external environment is already very challenging for many emerging market and developing economies. The sharp appreciation of the US dollar adds significantly to domestic price pressures and to the cost-of-living crisis for these countries. Capital flows have not recovered, and many low-income and developing economies remain in debt distress. The 2022 shocks will re-open economic wounds that were only partially healed following the pandemic.

Downside risks to the outlook remain elevated, while policy trade-offs to address the cost-of-living crisis have become acutely challenging. The risk of monetary, fiscal, or financial policy miscalibration has risen sharply at a time when the world economy remains historically fragile and financial markets are showing signs of stress.

Increasing price pressures remain the most immediate threat to current and future prosperity by squeezing real incomes and undermining macroeconomic stability. Central banks around the world are now laser-focused on restoring price stability, and the pace of tightening has accelerated sharply. There are risks of both under- and over-tightening. Under-tightening would entrench further the inflation process, erode the credibility of central banks, and de-anchor inflation expectations. As history repeatedly teaches us, this would only increase the eventual cost of bringing inflation under control. Over-tightening risks pushing the global economy into an unnecessarily harsh recession. As several prominent voices have argued recently, over-tightening is more likely when central banks act in an uncoordinated fashion. Financial markets may also struggle to cope with an overly rapid pace of tightening. Yet, the costs of these policy mistakes are not symmetric. Misjudging yet again the stubborn persistence of inflation could prove much more detrimental to future macroeconomic stability by gravely undermining the hard-won credibility of central banks. As economies start slowing down, and financial fragilities emerge, calls for a pivot toward looser monetary conditions will inevitably become louder. Where necessary, financial policy should ensure that markets remain stable, but central banks around the world need to keep a steady hand with monetary policy firmly focused on taming inflation.

These challenges do not imply that a large downturn is inevitable. In many countries, including the United States, the United Kingdom, and the euro area, labor markets remain tight, with historically low unemployment rates and high levels of vacancies. Chapter 2 of this report documents how the current environment—despite rapidly rising prices and wages—may still avert a wage-price spiral, unless inflation expectations become de-anchored.

Formulating the appropriate fiscal policy given the juxtaposed cost-of-living, energy, and food crises has become an acute challenge for many countries. I shall mention a few important principles. First, for countries where the pandemic is now firmly receding, it is time to rebuild fiscal buffers. As the pandemic vividly illustrated, fiscal space is essential for dealing with crises. Countries with more fiscal room were better able to protect households and businesses. Second, fiscal policy should not work at cross-purposes with monetary authorities' efforts to quell inflation. Doing otherwise will only prolong the fight to bring inflation down, risk de-anchoring inflation expectations, increase funding costs, and stoke further financial instability, complicating the task of fiscal as well as monetary and financial authorities, as recent events illustrated. Third, the energy crisis, especially in Europe, is not a transitory shock. The geopolitical re-alignment of energy supplies in the wake of Russia's war against Ukraine is broad and permanent. Winter 2022 will be challenging for Europe, but winter 2023 will likely be worse. Fiscal authorities in the region need to plan and coordinate accordingly. Fourth, price signals are essential to help curb demand and stimulate supply. Price controls, untargeted subsidies, or export bans are fiscally costly and lead to excess demand, undersupply, misallocation, rationing, and black-market premiums. History teaches us they rarely work. Fiscal policy should instead aim to protect the most vulnerable through targeted and temporary transfers. If some aggregate fiscal support cannot be avoided, especially in countries hardest hit by the energy crisis, it is important to embed policy in a credible medium-term fiscal framework. Fifth, fiscal policy can help economies adapt to a more volatile environment and bounce back from adversity by investing in expanding productive capacity: human capital, digitalization, green energy, and supply chain diversification can make economies more resilient when the next crisis comes. Unfortunately, these simple principles are not uniformly guiding current policy, and the risk of outsized, poorly targeted, and broadly stimulative fiscal packages in many countries is not negligible.

For many emerging markets, the strength of the dollar is causing acute challenges, tightening financial conditions, and increasing the cost of imported goods. The dollar is now at its highest level since the early 2000s. So far, this appreciation appears mostly driven by fundamental forces, such as the tightening of monetary policy in the United States and the energy crisis. The appropriate response in most countries is to calibrate monetary policy to maintain price stability, while letting exchange rates adjust, conserving valuable foreign exchange reserves for when financial conditions really worsen.

As the global economy is headed for stormy waters, financial turmoil may well erupt, prompting investors to seek the protection of safe-haven investments, such as US Treasuries, and pushing the dollar even higher. Now is the time for emerging market policymakers to batten down the hatches. Eligible countries with sound policies should urgently consider improving their liquidity buffers by requesting access to precautionary instruments from the Fund. Looking ahead, countries should also aim to minimize the impact of future financial turmoil through a combination of preemptive macroprudential and capital flow measures, where appropriate, in line with our Integrated Policy Framework. Too many low-income countries are in or close to debt distress. Progress toward orderly debt restructurings through the Group of Twenty's Common Framework for the most affected is urgently needed to avert a wave of sovereign debt crisis. Time may soon be running out.

Finally, the energy and food crises, coupled with extreme summer temperatures, starkly remind us of what an uncontrolled climate transition would look like. Much action is needed to implement climate policies that will ward off catastrophic climate change.

As discussed in Chapter 3, these policies may have some modest adverse implications for activity and inflation in the near term that pale in comparison to the catastrophic costs of doing nothing. Importantly, these costs rise sharply the more we delay the green transition. The message is clear: a timely and credible transition, in addition to being critical for our planet's future, also helps macroeconomic stability.

Progress on climate policies, as well as on debt resolution and other targeted multilateral issues, will prove that a focused multilateralism can, indeed, achieve progress for all and succeed in overcoming geo-economic fragmentation pressures.

Pierre-Olivier Gourinchas
Economic Counsellor

EXECUTIVE SUMMARY

The global economy is experiencing a number of turbulent challenges. Inflation higher than seen in several decades, tightening financial conditions in most regions, Russia's invasion of Ukraine, and the lingering COVID-19 pandemic all weigh heavily on the outlook. Normalization of monetary and fiscal policies that delivered unprecedented support during the pandemic is cooling demand as policymakers aim to lower inflation back to target. But a growing share of economies are in a growth slowdown or outright contraction. The global economy's future health rests critically on the successful calibration of monetary policy, the course of the war in Ukraine, and the possibility of further pandemic-related supply-side disruptions, for example, in China.

Global growth is forecast to slow from 6.0 percent in 2021 to 3.2 percent in 2022 and 2.7 percent in 2023. This is the weakest growth profile since 2001 except for the global financial crisis and the acute phase of the COVID-19 pandemic and reflects significant slowdowns for the largest economies: a US GDP contraction in the first half of 2022, a euro area contraction in the second half of 2022, and prolonged COVID-19 outbreaks and lockdowns in China with a growing property sector crisis. About a third of the world economy faces two consecutive quarters of negative growth. Global inflation is forecast to rise from 4.7 percent in 2021 to 8.8 percent in 2022 but to decline to 6.5 percent in 2023 and to 4.1 percent by 2024. Upside inflation surprises have been most widespread among advanced economies, with greater variability in emerging market and developing economies.

Risks to the outlook remain unusually large and to the downside. Monetary policy could miscalculate the right stance to reduce inflation. Policy paths in the largest economies could continue to diverge, leading to further US dollar appreciation and cross-border tensions. More energy and food price shocks might cause inflation to persist for longer. Global tightening in financing conditions could trigger widespread emerging market debt distress. Halting gas supplies by Russia could depress output in Europe. A resurgence of COVID-19 or new global health scares might further stunt growth. A worsening of China's property sector crisis could spill over to the domestic banking sector and weigh heavily on the country's growth, with negative cross-border effects. And geopolitical fragmentation could impede trade and capital flows, further hindering climate policy cooperation. The balance of risks is tilted firmly to the downside, with about a 25 percent chance of one-year-ahead global growth falling below 2.0 percent—in the 10th percentile of global growth outturns since 1970.

Warding off these risks starts with monetary policy staying the course to restore price stability. As demonstrated in Chapter 2, front-loaded and aggressive monetary tightening is critical to avoid inflation de-anchoring as a result of households and businesses basing their wage and price expectations on their recent inflation experience. Fiscal policy's priority is the protection of vulnerable groups through targeted near-term support to alleviate the burden of the cost-of-living crisis felt across the globe. But its overall stance should remain sufficiently tight to keep monetary policy on target. Addressing growing government debt distress caused by lower growth and higher borrowing costs requires a meaningful improvement in debt resolution frameworks. With tightening financial conditions, macroprudential policies should remain on guard against systemic risks. Intensifying structural reforms to improve productivity and economic capacity would ease supply constraints and in doing so support monetary policy in fighting inflation. Policies to fast-track the green energy transition will yield long-term payoffs for energy security and the costs of ongoing climate change. As Chapter 3 shows, phasing in the right measures over the coming eight years will keep the macroeconomic costs manageable. And last, successful multilateral cooperation will prevent fragmentation that could reverse the gains in economic well-being from 30 years of economic integration.

CHAPTER 1

GLOBAL PROSPECTS AND POLICIES

Inflation and Uncertainty

The world is in a volatile period: economic, geopolitical, and ecological changes all impact the global outlook. Inflation has soared to multidecade highs, prompting rapid monetary policy tightening and squeezing household budgets, just as COVID-19-pandemic-related fiscal support is waning. Many low-income countries are facing deep fiscal difficulties. At the same time, Russia's ongoing war in Ukraine and tensions elsewhere have raised the possibility of significant geopolitical disruption. Although the pandemic's impact has moderated in most countries, its lingering waves continue to disrupt economic activity, especially in China. And intense heat waves and droughts across Europe and central and south Asia have provided a taste of a more inhospitable future blighted by global climate change.

Amid these volatile conditions, recent data releases confirm that the global economy is in a broad-based slowdown as downside risks—including risks highlighted in the July 2022 *World Economic Outlook* (WEO) *Update*—materialize, although with some conflicting signals. The second quarter of 2022 saw global real GDP modestly contract (growth of –0.1 percentage point at a quarterly annualized rate), with negative growth in China, Russia, and the US, as well as sharp slowdowns in eastern European countries most directly affected by the war in Ukraine and international sanctions aimed at pressuring Russia to end hostilities. At the same time, some major economies did not contract—euro area growth surprised on the upside in the second quarter, led by growth in tourism-dependent southern European economies. Forward-looking indicators, including new manufacturing orders and sentiment gauges, suggest a slowdown among major economies (Figure 1.1). In some cases, however, signals conflict—with some indicators showing output weakness amid labor market strength.

An important factor underpinning the slowdown in the first half of this year is the rapid removal of monetary accommodation as many central banks seek to moderate persistently high inflation (Figure 1.2). Higher interest rates and the associated rise in borrowing costs, including mortgage rates, are having their desired effect in taking the heat out of domestic demand, with the housing market showing the earliest and most evident signs of slowdown in such economies as the US. Monetary policy tightening has been generally—although not everywhere—accompanied by a scaling back of fiscal support, which had previously propped up households' disposable incomes. Broadly speaking, nominal policy rates are now above pre-pandemic levels in both advanced and emerging market and developing economies. With elevated inflation, real interest rates have generally not yet reverted to pre-pandemic levels. Tightening financial conditions in most regions, with the notable exception of China (October 2022 *Global Financial Stability Report*), reflected in a strong real appreciation of the US dollar

This has also driven up yield spreads—the difference between countries' US dollar– or euro-denominated government bond yield and US or German government bond yields—for debt-distressed lower- and middle-income economies (Figure 1.3). In sub-Saharan Africa, yield spreads for more than two-thirds of sovereign bonds breached the 700 basis point level in August 2022—significantly more than a year ago. In eastern and central Europe, the effects of the war in Ukraine have exacerbated the shifting global risk appetite.

Beyond monetary policy alone, China's COVID-19 outbreaks and mobility restrictions as part of the authorities' zero-COVID strategy and Russia's invasion of Ukraine have also pulled down economic activity. China's lockdowns have imposed sizable constraints domestically and gummed up already strained global supply chains. The war in Ukraine and deepening cuts to supplies of gas to Europe have amplified preexisting stresses in global commodity markets, driving natural gas prices higher once more (Figure 1.4). European economies—including the largest, Germany—are exposed to the impact of the gas supply cuts. Continued uncertainty over energy supplies has contributed to slower real economic activity in Europe, particularly in manufacturing, dampening consumer and, to a lesser extent, business confidence (Figure 1.1). However, a strong recovery in the tourism-dependent southern economies helped

Figure 1.1. Leading Indicators Show Signs of Slowdown
(Indices)

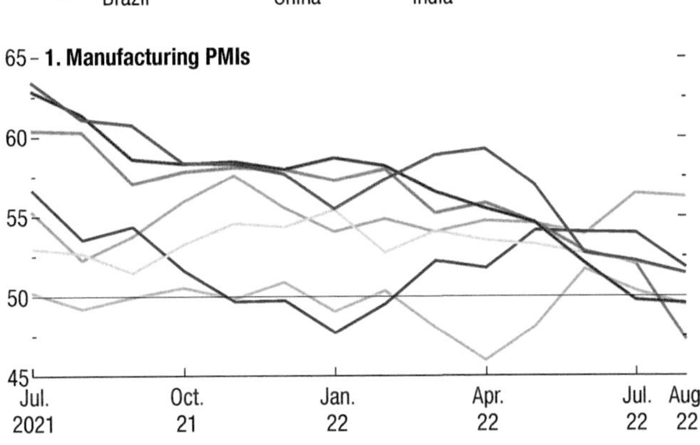

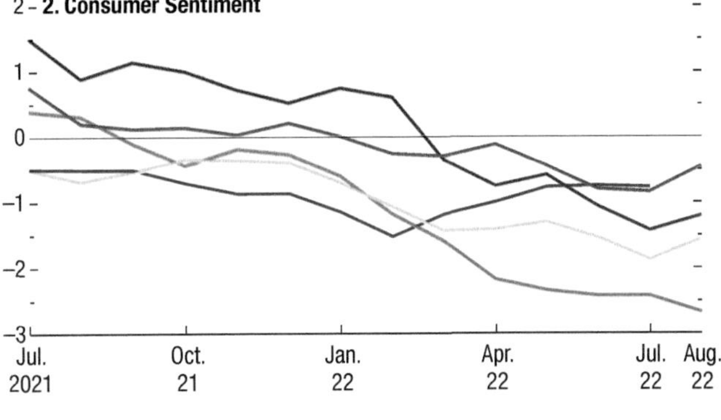

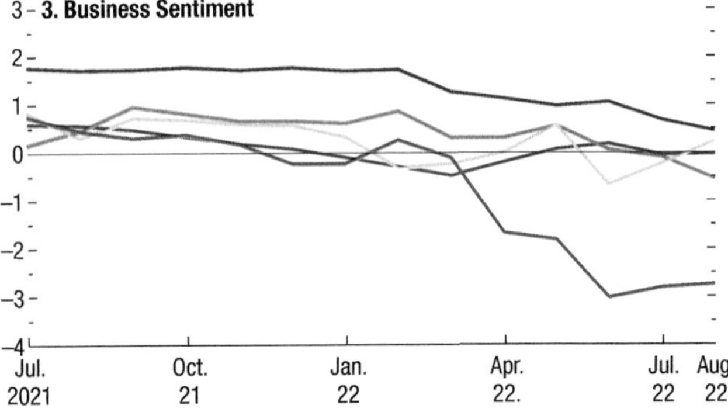

Sources: Haver Analytics; and IMF staff calculations.
Note: For panel 1, purchasing managers' indices (PMIs) greater than 50 denote expansion. In panels 2 and 3, values are normalized *z*-scores.

Figure 1.2. Change in Monetary Policy Cycle among G20 Economies
(Number of increases and cuts in policy rates)

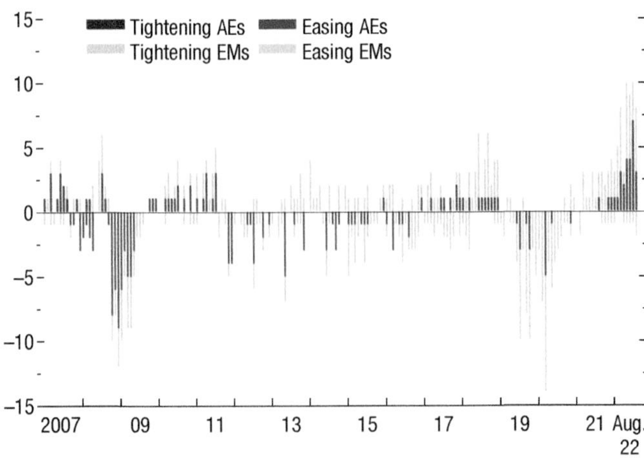

Sources: Bloomberg Finance L.P.; and IMF staff calculations.
Note: AEs = advanced economies; EMs = emerging market economies.

deliver better-than-anticipated overall growth in the first half of 2022.

Food prices—a prime driver of global inflation so far this year—have provided a rare slice of good news, with futures prices falling (Figure 1.4) and the Black Sea grain deal giving some hope of improved supply in coming months. More generally, some signs show that commodity prices might be starting to ease off as global demand slows, helping to moderate inflation. However, recent extreme heat waves and droughts are a stark reminder of the near-term threat from climate change and its likely impact on agricultural productivity (Figure 1.5).

Although a slight rebound is forecast for the second half of the year, full-year growth in 2022 will likely fall far short of average pre-pandemic performance and the strong growth rebound in 2021. In 2022, the world economy is predicted to be 3.2 percent larger than in 2021, with advanced economies growing 2.4 percent and emerging market and developing economies growing 3.7 percent. The world economy will expand even more slowly in 2023, at 2.7 percent, with advanced economies growing 1.1 percent and emerging market and developing economies 3.7 percent.

Three key factors critically shape this economic outlook: monetary policy's stance in response to elevated inflation, the impact of the war in Ukraine, and the ongoing impact of pandemic-related lockdowns and supply chain disruptions. The following sections discuss each of these forces in turn before presenting the outlook in detail.

Central Banks Tackle Stubbornly High Inflation

Since 2021, inflation has risen faster and more persistently than expected. In 2022, inflation in advanced economies reached its highest rate since 1982. Although inflation is a broad phenomenon, affecting most economies across the world (Figure 1.6), it has the most

Figure 1.3. EMDE Sovereign Spreads
(Basis points)

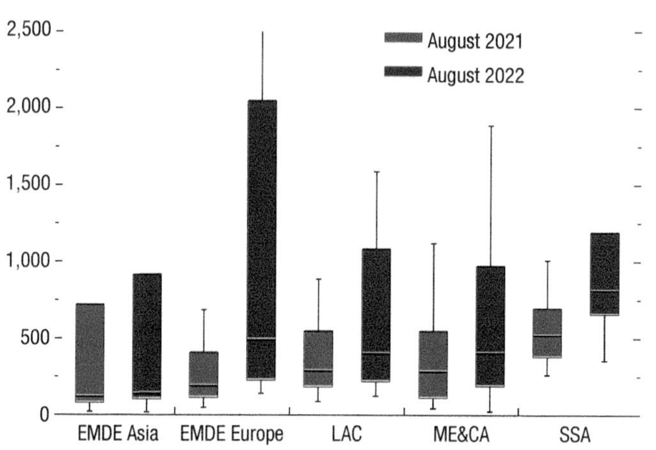

Sources: Bloomberg Finance L.P.; and IMF staff calculations.
Note: For each region, box denotes upper quartile, median, and lower quartile of the members, and whiskers show maximum and minimum values within the boundary of 1.5 times interquartile range from upper and lower quartiles. *Y*-axis is cut off at 2,500 basis points. EMDE = emerging market and developing economy; LAC = Latin America and the Caribbean; ME&CA = Middle East and Central Asia; SSA = sub-Saharan Africa.

Figure 1.4. Wholesale Food and Fuel Prices Expected to Moderate
(Index, January 2019 = 100)

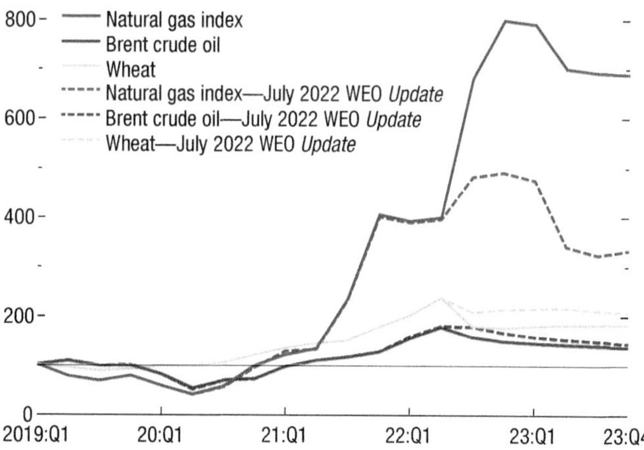

Source: IMF staff calculations.
Note: Natural gas index comprises European, Japanese, and US natural gas price indices. WEO = *World Economic Outlook.*

Figure 1.5. Mean Land Temperature
(Degrees Celsius; departures from 1960–91 normal)

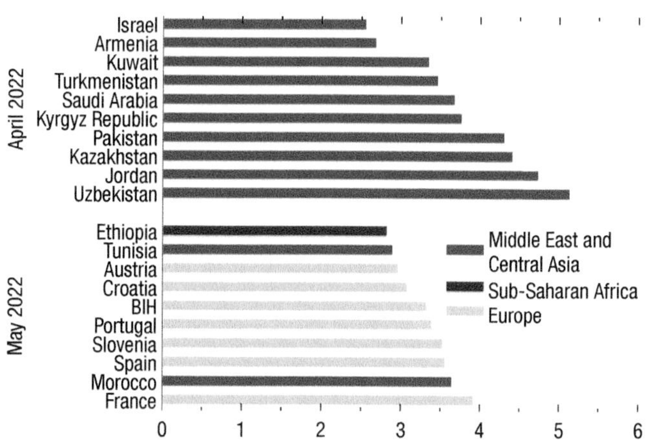

Sources: Osborn and others (2021); and IMF staff calculations.
Note: Figure shows deviation from 1960 to 1991 normal monthly temperatures and hottest 10 countries by month. BIH = Bosnia and Herzegovina.

Figure 1.6. Core Inflation and Its Distribution across Countries
(Annualized percent)

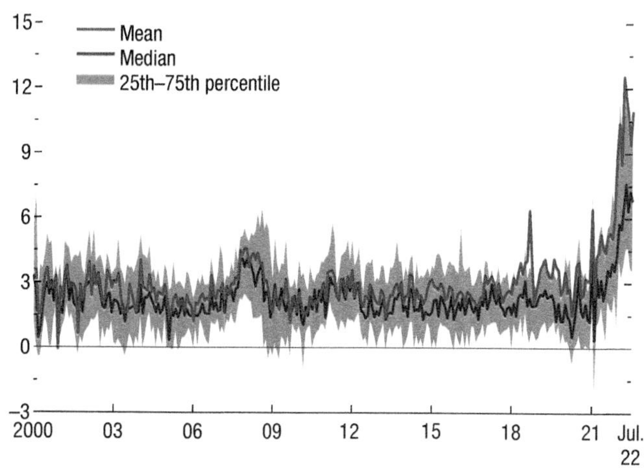

Sources: Haver Analytics; and IMF staff calculations.
Note: The set of economies includes ARG, BRA, CAN, CHE, CHL, CHN, COL, CZE, DEU, DNK, ESP, FRA, GBR, HKG, HUN, IDN, IND, ISR, ITA, JPN, KOR, MEX, MYS, NOR, PER, PHL, POL, RUS, SGP, SWE, THA, TUR, TWN, USA, and ZAF. The group represents 89.4 percent of advanced economy GDP, 75 percent of emerging market and developing economy GDP, and 81 percent of world GDP based on purchasing-power-parity weights. Economy list uses International Organization for Standardization (ISO) country codes.

Figure 1.7. Inflation Hits the Poorest Hardest
(Percent, 2022)

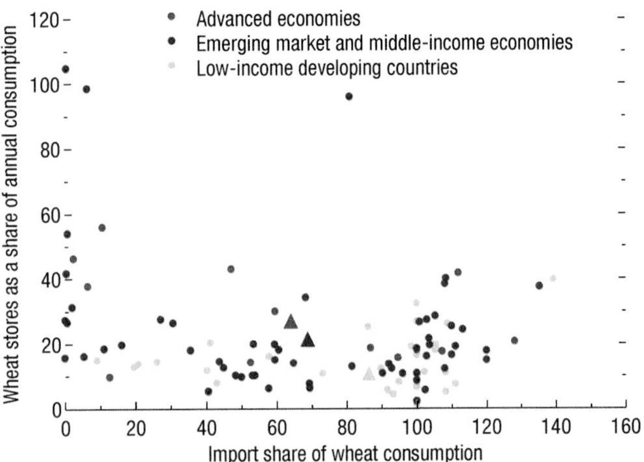

Sources: Food and Agriculture Organization of the United Nations; US Department of Agriculture, Foreign Agricultural Service; and IMF staff calculations.
Note: Data reflect storage-level estimates at the end of the first quarter of 2022 and projected consumption levels for 2022. Import share can exceed 100 because of stock building and reexport. Triangles show country group averages.

Figure 1.8. Rebalancing of Demand: Goods versus Services
(Percent deviation from pre–COVID-19 averages)

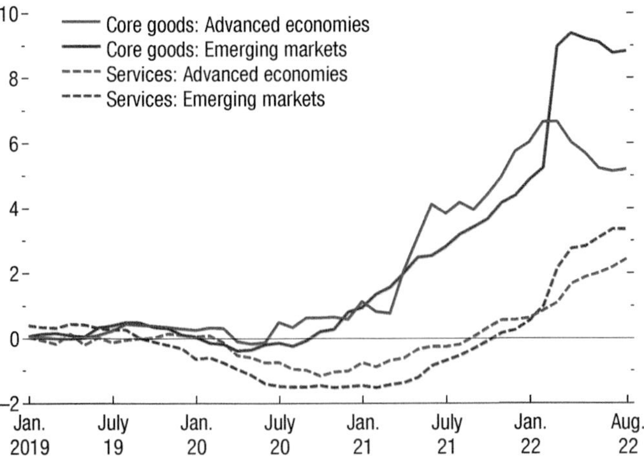

Sources: Haver Analytics; and IMF staff calculations.
Note: Lines show the difference between the year-over-year percent change in price indices each month and the average observed during 2018 and 2019 for each sector. Core goods exclude energy and food. Countries are aggregated using purchasing-power-parity weights. Advanced economies comprise Australia, Canada, the euro area, Japan, Korea, and the United States. Emerging markets comprise Brazil, Chile, Colombia, Indonesia, Malaysia, Mexico, Russia, and South Africa.

severe impact on lower-income groups in developing economies. In these countries, up to half of household consumption expenditure is on food, meaning that inflation can have particularly acute impacts on human health and living standards (Figure 1.7). Despite a slight decline in the consumer price index in July and August, US inflation reached one of its highest levels in about 40 years, with prices in August 8.3 percent higher than those one year earlier. Euro area saw inflation reach 10 percent in September, while the UK saw annual inflation of 9.9 percent. Emerging market and developing economies are estimated to have seen inflation of 10.1 percent in the second quarter of 2022 and face a peak inflation rate of 11.0 percent in the third quarter: the highest rate since 1999. The reverberations of last year's strong demand recovery and a continued rebalancing of demand toward services such as travel (Figure 1.8) have driven up inflation. Although futures prices have fallen, the delayed pass-through of past increases in food and energy prices from global commodity markets to consumer prices may continue to drive inflation yet higher in the short term. In Europe, a significant impact from war-related energy shocks compounds these effects, whereas in Asia, a more moderate impact on food prices is helping to keep inflation from rising as much as elsewhere (Figure 1.9).

An important recent development is that although volatile headline shocks to items such as energy and food prices still account for much of inflation, they are no longer the overwhelmingly dominant drivers. Instead, underlying inflation has also increased—as measured by different gauges of core inflation—and is likely to remain elevated well into the second half

Figure 1.9. Inflation Driven by Food and Fuel
(Annualized percent)

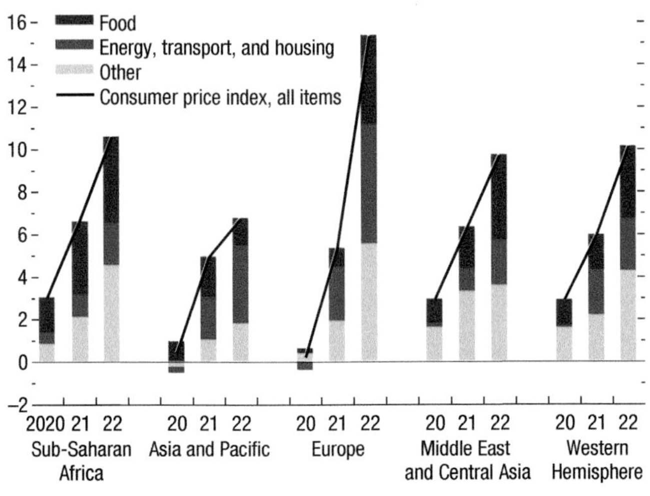

Sources: IMF, Consumer Price Index database; and IMF staff calculations.
Note: Figure shows inflation contributions from broad categories. Contributions are computed first by country, annualized over available months in cases in which data are partial (for example, for 2022). The figure shows both the median contributions and aggregate inflation rate for each region.

of 2022. Global core inflation, measured by excluding food and energy prices, is expected to be 6.6 percent on a fourth-quarter-over-fourth-quarter basis, reflecting the pass-through of energy prices, supply chain cost pressure, and tight labor markets, especially in advanced economies. In contrast, the cooling of economic activity in China has also eased core inflation. On average, nominal wages take time to increase in response to inflation, leading real wages to decline and acting as a dampener on demand (see Chapter 2). Yet despite some pockets of uncertainty, long-term inflation expectations have generally remained stable in most major economies.

High inflation in 2021 and 2022 has surprised many macroeconomic forecasters, including IMF staff. Upside inflation surprises have occurred for most economies but have been especially widespread among advanced economies. The simple question is, Why? While our understanding is still evolving, forecasters likely underestimated the impact of the strong economic recovery in 2021—supported by fiscal intervention in advanced economies—coinciding with strained supply chains and tight labor markets (Box 1.1). Across advanced economies, forecast errors are related to the size of COVID-19–related fiscal stimulus packages. The correlation of output and inflation forecast errors is positive in both 2021 and 2022, but the relationship was stronger in 2021 than it has been so far in 2022. That errors were in the same direction suggests that excess demand has been a dominant factor, particularly in 2021, as some large economies may have been at the steeper end of the aggregate supply curve. The declining cross-country correlation in 2022 hints at an increased role for supply shocks, related to clogged supply chains and, more recently, the war in Ukraine. Headline inflation forecast errors have been larger for eastern European economies in 2022, consistent with the war in Ukraine driving up headline inflation. More generally, forecast errors for the noncore part of inflation (mainly reflecting food and energy prices), which can reflect supply shocks, have contributed more to unexpected increases in inflation in 2022 than in 2021. Core inflation forecast errors in China and developing Asia have been negative and relatively small so far this year, consistent with the slowdown in real activity.

Public debate has also included discussion of the role of business markups—the price-to-marginal-cost ratio—during the pandemic as a potential driver of inflation. Markups have risen steadily over several years, prompting intense debate. Yet their recent dynamics do not suggest that markups are contributing in any sizable way to the current inflationary environment (Box 1.2). Elevated markups in fact make persistent wage-price spirals less likely, since they provide flexible buffers between general wage and general price increases (see Chapter 2 and in particular, Box 2.1). And despite historically tight labor markets in advanced economies, incipient wage-price spirals are not yet on the horizon.

The rise in US inflation has attracted especially intense attention, as it came earlier than in other advanced economies and surprised many economists. One factor explaining the surprise was unexpected adverse shocks from the disruption of supply chains and the rise in energy prices. The effects of those shocks appear to have passed through to underlying inflation. Another reason that economists' expectations missed the high-inflation episode was that economists typically measured labor market tightness using the unemployment rate, which has historically had a relatively flat relationship with inflation and did not decline below pre-pandemic levels. Meanwhile, other measures of labor market tightness, including the ratio of vacancies to unemployed workers and the intensity of on-the-job search, unexpectedly rose to historic highs and better explain the rise in inflation (Ball, Leigh, and Mishra, forthcoming).

To prevent inflation from becoming entrenched, central banks have rapidly lifted nominal policy rates. The Federal Reserve has increased the federal funds target rate by 3 percentage points since early 2022 and has communicated that further rises are likely. The Bank of England has raised its policy rate by 2 percentage points since the start of the year despite projecting weak growth. The European Central Bank has raised its policy rate by 1.25 percentage points this year. But because inflation has outstripped these increases, with a few exceptions, real policy rates remain below pre-pandemic levels (Figure 1.10). Differences in the paths of monetary policy normalization are due in part to core inflation rising rapidly in some advanced economies, most notably in the US, before it did in others. Real activity and financial markets have responded to the removal of monetary accommodation, with tentative signs of cooling housing markets, especially in the US, and of slowing momentum in labor markets. Interest rates and spreads have also risen in many countries and across the yield curve, inducing volatility in financial markets.

The Federal Reserve has raised interest rates more aggressively than the European Central Bank in part because of differences in underlying inflation dynamics and economic conditions to date. Core inflation rose

Figure 1.10. Real Short-Term Rates Are Rising
(Percent)

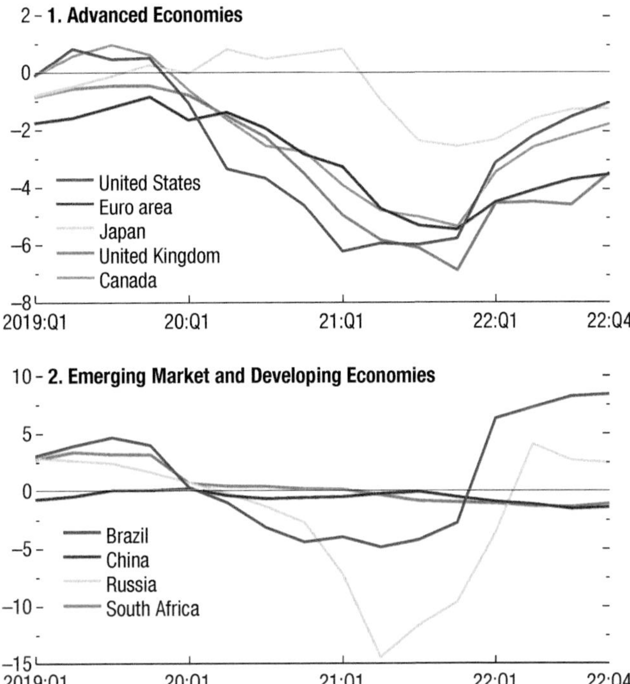

Source: IMF staff calculations.
Note: Projection for the euro area is estimated using projections for 16 individual euro area countries. Real rate computed as short-term nominal interest rate less core inflation one year ahead.

Figure 1.11. A Transatlantic Divergence
(Percent, unless noted otherwise)

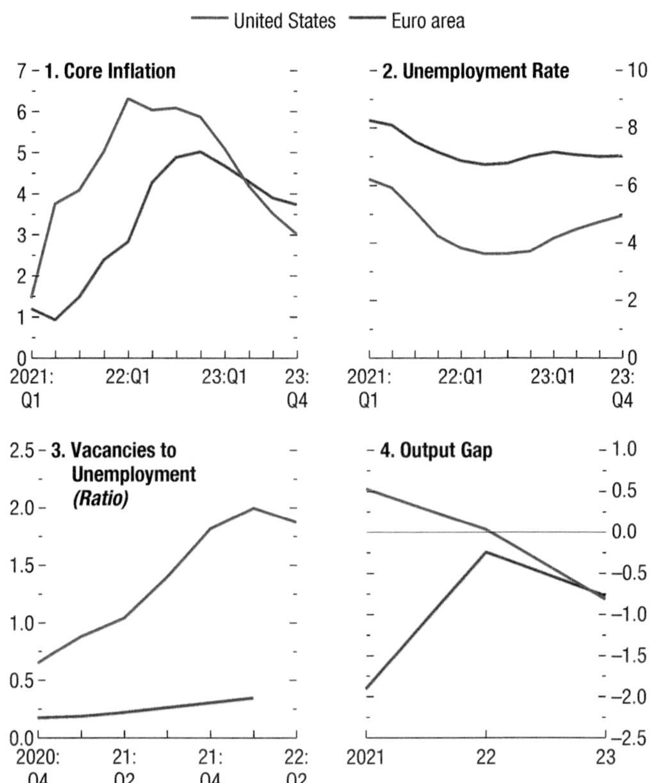

Sources: Haver Analytics; and IMF staff calculations.
Note: Vacancies to unemployment is defined as the ratio of the number of vacancies to the number of unemployed people. For the latter, the age group is 15–64 in the euro area and 16 or older in the United States. Job vacancy data may comprise all sectors or only industry-construction-services depending on data availability at the country level. The euro area vacancy-to-unemployment ratio is computed by summing the country-level data on number of vacancies and unemployed and then computing the ratio.

sooner and has run higher in the US than in the euro area, with tighter labor markets and a higher estimated output gap (Figure 1.11). These differences partly reflect transatlantic differences in the level of direct fiscal stimulus earlier in the pandemic, as well as differences in the impacts of commodity price shocks and changes in private saving (see Figure 2.6). The gap between real and nominal wage growth has also closed more rapidly in the US than in the euro area, which has added further to underlying US inflation momentum. But inflationary pressures are building in the euro area: the war in Ukraine continues to have a very clear impact, with energy and food prices accounting for about two-thirds of the rise in headline inflation and energy price increases passing through into broader inflation measures.

War in Ukraine Causes More Human Suffering and Economic Damage

Russia's war in Ukraine continues to leave a mark on the region and internationally. The war has displaced millions of people and led to substantial loss of human life and damage to physical capital in Ukraine. In addition to financial and technological sanctions aimed at pressuring Russia to end hostilities, the European Union implemented embargoes on imports of coal in August 2022. It also announced a ban on imports of seaborne oil starting at the end of 2022 and a maritime insurance ban. Reduced exports from Russia, most notably of gas, have also affected fossil fuel trade, with the flow of Russian pipeline gas to Europe down to about 20 percent of its level one year ago (Figure 1.12). This has contributed to the steep increase in natural gas prices. The war is having severe economic repercussions in Europe, with higher energy prices, weaker consumer confidence, and slower momentum in manufacturing resulting from persistent supply chain disruptions and rising input costs. Adjoining economies—Baltic and

Figure 1.12. Russian Pipeline Gas Supplies to EU by Route
(Million cubic meters a day)

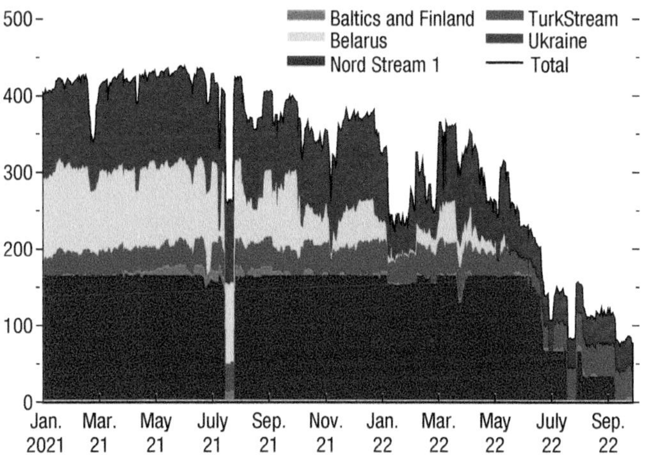

Sources: European Network of Transmission System Operators for Gas; Gas Transmission System Operator of Ukraine; and IMF staff calculations.
Note: Latest data available are for September 18, 2022. Recent data are provisional. Gas flow volumes are measured at EU border crossing points; Belarus excludes flows to Kaliningrad (Russia). EU = European Union.

Figure 1.13. New Confirmed COVID-19 Deaths
(Persons; seven-day moving average)

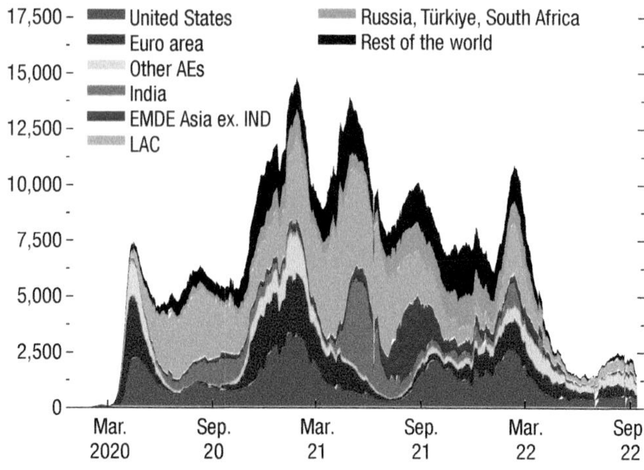

Sources: Our World in Data; and IMF staff calculations.
Note: Data as of September 13, 2022. Economy group and regional classifications are those in the *World Economic Outlook*. "Other AEs" by International Organization for Standardization (ISO) country codes are AUS, CAN, CHE, CZE, DNK, GBR, HKG, ISL, ISR, JPN, KOR, MAC, NOR, NZL, SGP, SMR, SWE, and TWN. AEs = advanced economies; EMDE Asia ex. IND = emerging market and developing economies in Asia excluding India; LAC = Latin American and Caribbean economies.

eastern European states—have felt the largest impact, with their growth slowing sharply in the second and third quarters and their inflation rates soaring.

Russia's economy is estimated to have contracted by 21.8 percent (at a quarterly annualized rate) during the second quarter, although crude oil and nonenergy exports held up. Russian domestic demand is showing some stability, thanks to containment of the effect of sanctions on the domestic financial sector policy support, and a resilient labor market.

The war in Ukraine is also having global consequences for food prices. Despite the recent agreement on Black Sea grain exports, global food prices remain elevated, although they are expected to soften somewhat. This chapter's Special Feature, "Commodity Market Developments and Food Inflation Drivers," points to supply-side factors dominating current food price dynamics, compounded by the export restrictions several countries have implemented. Overall, international inflation has moved higher, propelled by further increases in consumer energy and food prices, as the war has led to a broadening of inflationary pressures. Countries with diets tilted toward foods with the largest price gains, especially wheat and corn; those more dependent on food imports; and those with diets including sizable quantities of foods with large pass-throughs from global to local prices have suffered most. Low-income countries whose citizens were already experiencing acute malnutrition and excess mortality before the war have suffered a particularly severe impact, with especially serious effects in sub-Saharan Africa, as food accounts for about 40 percent of that region's consumption basket, on average, and the pass-through from global to domestic food prices is relatively high at 30 percent (April 2022 *Regional Economic Outlook: Sub-Saharan Africa*).

COVID-19 Continues to Hold Back Economic Progress

As inflation, monetary and fiscal tightening, and the war in Ukraine continue to squeeze global activity, the pandemic (Figure 1.13) is also weighing on the macroeconomic outlook. Pandemic-related forces have been particularly important in China, where a second-quarter contraction contributed to slower global activity. Temporary lockdowns in Shanghai and elsewhere due to COVID-19 outbreaks have weakened local demand, which is reflected in the new-orders component of the purchasing managers' index (Figure 1.1). Other data corroborate this picture of slowing economic activity in China. Manufacturing capacity utilization in the country, for example, slowed to less than 76 percent in the second quarter:

its lowest level in five years, except during the acute phase of the pandemic. Such disruptions in China not only have a domestic effect but also spill over internationally, as lower demand implies fewer exports for foreign suppliers. And capacity constraints in production and logistics delay the unclogging of supply chains, keeping global supply pressures—and hence inflation—elevated.

Resurgent variants of the COVID-19 virus threaten economic recovery elsewhere too. Limited vaccinations make sub-Saharan Africa more prone to ongoing illness and increase the risk of exposures to new variants. African vaccination rates are still a fraction of those of all other regions, at about 26 percent, compared with about 66 percent in other regions. Booster shots have been administered to a mere 2 percent of people in African countries, on average—orders of magnitude lower than the rate on other continents, where booster shots cover between a third and half of their populations. This low vaccination rate has partly contributed to sub-Saharan Africa's real per capita GDP growth lagging behind that of advanced economies in 2022. Pandemic-induced scarring has also slowed human capital buildup as a result of learning losses from lack of schooling and on-the-job skill acquisition (see Barrett and others 2021).

The Forecast: Output Lower Still, but Inflation Peaking

The developments described in the preceding section, with downside risks materializing, mean that projected global growth is declining and, in 2023, now falls between the July WEO *Update* baseline and alternative scenarios. Uncertainties continue to cloud forecasts of global growth and inflation. The baseline forecasts described in the following discussion are predicated on several assumptions that plausibly may fail to hold: that no further sharp reductions in flows of natural gas from Russia to the rest of Europe occur in 2022, beyond the current 80 percent reduction compared with a year ago; that long-term inflation expectations remain stable; and that disinflationary monetary policy tightening does not induce widespread recession (a broad-based contraction in economic activity that usually lasts more than a few months) and disorderly adjustments in global financial markets.

To recognize the uncertainty surrounding the global economy's evolution, this *World Economic Outlook* report presents a baseline forecast in this section and—later on—a fan chart illustrating the distribution of probabilities around the baseline as well as a downside scenario (Box 1.3).

Global Growth: Near-Term Slowdown

A slowdown in global growth is forecast, from 6.0 percent in 2021 to 3.2 percent in 2022 and 2.7 percent in 2023 (Table 1.1). The global slowdown in 2022 is as projected in the July 2022 WEO *Update,* while the forecast for 2023 is lower than projected by 0.2 percentage point (Table 1.1). This prognosis for the global economy is far below average: global economic growth averaged 3.6 percent during 2000–21 (and the same during 1970–2021). For most economies, the outlook is significantly weaker than projected six months ago, in the April 2022 WEO. Forecasts are weaker than expected for 143 economies (accounting for 92 percent of world GDP) for 2023. The forecast for 2023 is the weakest since the 2.5 percent growth rate seen during the global slowdown of 2001—with the exception of those during the global financial and COVID-19 crises.

The world's three largest economies—China, the euro area, and the US—will slow significantly in 2022 and 2023, with downgrades compared with the predictions made in April and, in most cases, July. The negative revisions reflect the materialization of downside risks highlighted in the April 2022 WEO and July 2022 WEO *Update* and discussed at length in the previous section: tightening global financial conditions in most regions, associated with expectations of steeper interest rate hikes by major central banks to fight inflation (October 2022 *Global Financial Stability Report*); a sharper slowdown in China due to extended lockdowns and the worsening property market crisis; and spillover effects from the war in Ukraine with gas supplies from Russia to Europe tightening.

A decline in global GDP or in global GDP per capita—which often happens when there is a global recession—is not currently in the baseline forecast. However, a contraction in real GDP lasting for at least two consecutive quarters (which some economists refer to as a "technical recession") is seen at some point during 2022–23 in about 43 percent of economies with quarterly data forecasts (31 out of 72 economies), amounting to more than one-third of world GDP (Figure 1.14). Moreover, projections for global growth on a fourth-quarter-over-fourth-quarter

Table 1.1. Overview of the *World Economic Outlook* Projections
(Percent change, unless noted otherwise)

		Projections		Difference from July 2022 WEO *Update*[1]		Difference from April 2022 WEO[1]	
	2021	2022	2023	2022	2023	2022	2023
World Output	**6.0**	**3.2**	**2.7**	**0.0**	**–0.2**	**–0.4**	**–0.9**
Advanced Economies	**5.2**	**2.4**	**1.1**	**–0.1**	**–0.3**	**–0.9**	**–1.3**
United States	5.7	1.6	1.0	–0.7	0.0	–2.1	–1.3
Euro Area	5.2	3.1	0.5	0.5	–0.7	0.3	–1.8
Germany	2.6	1.5	–0.3	0.3	–1.1	–0.6	–3.0
France	6.8	2.5	0.7	0.2	–0.3	–0.4	–0.7
Italy	6.7	3.2	–0.2	0.2	–0.9	0.9	–1.9
Spain	5.1	4.3	1.2	0.3	–0.8	–0.5	–2.1
Japan	1.7	1.7	1.6	0.0	–0.1	–0.7	–0.7
United Kingdom[2]	7.4	3.6	0.3	0.4	–0.2	–0.1	–0.9
Canada	4.5	3.3	1.5	–0.1	–0.3	–0.6	–1.3
Other Advanced Economies[3]	5.3	2.8	2.3	–0.1	–0.4	–0.3	–0.7
Emerging Market and Developing Economies	**6.6**	**3.7**	**3.7**	**0.1**	**–0.2**	**–0.1**	**–0.7**
Emerging and Developing Asia	7.2	4.4	4.9	–0.2	–0.1	–1.0	–0.7
China	8.1	3.2	4.4	–0.1	–0.2	–1.2	–0.7
India[4]	8.7	6.8	6.1	–0.6	0.0	–1.4	–0.8
ASEAN-5[5]	3.4	5.3	4.9	0.0	–0.2	0.0	–1.0
Emerging and Developing Europe	6.8	0.0	0.6	1.4	–0.3	2.9	–0.7
Russia	4.7	–3.4	–2.3	2.6	1.2	5.1	0.0
Latin America and the Caribbean	6.9	3.5	1.7	0.5	–0.3	1.0	–0.8
Brazil	4.6	2.8	1.0	1.1	–0.1	2.0	–0.4
Mexico	4.8	2.1	1.2	–0.3	0.0	0.1	–1.3
Middle East and Central Asia	4.5	5.0	3.6	0.2	0.1	0.4	–0.1
Saudi Arabia	3.2	7.6	3.7	0.0	0.0	0.0	0.1
Sub-Saharan Africa	4.7	3.6	3.7	–0.2	–0.3	–0.2	–0.3
Nigeria	3.6	3.2	3.0	–0.2	–0.2	–0.2	–0.1
South Africa	4.9	2.1	1.1	–0.2	–0.3	0.2	–0.3
Memorandum							
World Growth Based on Market Exchange Rates	5.8	2.9	2.1	0.0	–0.3	–0.6	–1.0
European Union	5.4	3.2	0.7	0.4	–0.9	0.3	–1.8
Middle East and North Africa	4.1	5.0	3.6	0.1	0.2	0.0	0.0
Emerging Market and Middle-Income Economies	6.8	3.6	3.6	0.1	–0.2	–0.2	–0.7
Low-Income Developing Countries	4.1	4.8	4.9	–0.2	–0.3	0.2	–0.5
World Trade Volume (goods and services)	**10.1**	**4.3**	**2.5**	**0.2**	**–0.7**	**–0.7**	**–1.9**
Imports							
Advanced Economies	9.5	6.0	2.0	–0.2	–0.8	–0.1	–2.5
Emerging Market and Developing Economies	11.8	2.4	3.0	1.3	–0.3	–1.5	–1.8
Exports							
Advanced Economies	8.7	4.2	2.5	–0.3	–1.0	–0.8	–2.2
Emerging Market and Developing Economies	11.8	3.3	2.9	0.1	–0.4	–0.8	–0.7
Commodity Prices (US dollars)							
Oil[6]	65.9	41.4	–12.9	–9.0	–0.6	–13.3	0.4
Nonfuel (average based on world commodity import weights)	26.3	7.3	–6.2	–2.8	–2.7	–4.1	–3.7
World Consumer Prices[7]	**4.7**	**8.8**	**6.5**	**0.5**	**0.8**	**1.4**	**1.7**
Advanced Economies[8]	3.1	7.2	4.4	0.6	1.1	1.5	1.9
Emerging Market and Developing Economies[7]	5.9	9.9	8.1	0.4	0.8	1.2	1.6

Source: IMF staff estimates.

Note: Real effective exchange rates are assumed to remain constant at the levels prevailing during July 22, 2022–August 19, 2022. Economies are listed on the basis of economic size. The aggregated quarterly data are seasonally adjusted. WEO = *World Economic Outlook*.

[1]Difference based on rounded figures for the current, July 2022 WEO *Update*, and April 2022 WEO forecasts.

[2]See the country-specific note for the United Kingdom in the "Country Notes" section of the Statistical Appendix.

[3]Excludes the Group of Seven (Canada, France, Germany, Italy, Japan, United Kingdom, United States) and euro area countries.

[4]For India, data and forecasts are presented on a fiscal year basis, and GDP from 2011 onward is based on GDP at market prices with fiscal year 2011/12 as a base year.

Table 1.1. Overview of the *World Economic Outlook* Projections *(continued)*
(Percent change, unless noted otherwise)

	Q4 over Q4[9]						
		Projections		Difference from July 2022 WEO *Update*[1]		Difference from April 2022 WEO[1]	
	2021	2022	2023	2022	2023	2022	2023
World Output	**4.5**	**1.7**	**2.7**	**0.0**	**–0.5**	**–0.8**	**–0.8**
Advanced Economies	**4.7**	**0.9**	**1.3**	**–0.4**	**–0.2**	**–1.6**	**–0.7**
United States	5.5	0.0	1.0	–1.0	0.4	–2.8	–0.7
Euro Area	4.6	1.0	1.4	0.3	–0.7	–0.8	–0.9
Germany	1.2	0.6	0.5	0.1	–1.0	–1.8	–2.0
France	5.0	0.4	0.9	0.0	–0.2	–0.5	–0.6
Italy	6.6	0.6	0.5	0.0	–1.1	0.1	–1.7
Spain	5.5	1.3	2.0	0.0	–0.3	–1.0	–2.0
Japan	0.5	2.1	0.9	–0.3	0.3	–1.4	0.1
United Kingdom[2]	6.6	1.0	0.2	0.9	–1.1	–0.1	–1.3
Canada	3.2	2.2	1.3	–0.3	–0.4	–1.3	–0.9
Other Advanced Economies[3]	4.9	1.5	2.3	–0.5	–0.5	–1.0	–0.5
Emerging Market and Developing Economies	**4.3**	**2.5**	**3.9**	**0.4**	**–0.8**	**0.0**	**–1.0**
Emerging and Developing Asia	3.8	4.0	4.2	0.0	–0.5	–0.4	–1.6
China	3.5	4.3	2.6	0.2	–0.6	–0.5	–2.1
India[4]	3.9	3.3	6.8	–0.8	–0.4	0.6	–2.2
ASEAN-5[5]	4.7	3.8	6.0	0.4	–0.1	–1.3	0.7
Emerging and Developing Europe	6.4	–4.0	4.5	3.0	–3.2	2.0	1.2
Russia	4.8	–7.6	1.0	6.3	–3.8	6.5	–2.3
Latin America and the Caribbean	4.0	2.1	2.2	0.3	0.1	0.5	–0.3
Brazil	1.6	2.9	0.7	1.4	–0.8	2.1	–1.2
Mexico	1.2	2.4	1.2	–0.5	0.2	–0.9	–0.7
Middle East and Central Asia	...	...	...	...	...	...	...
Saudi Arabia	6.7	4.5	3.7	–2.4	0.0	–2.4	0.1
Sub-Saharan Africa	...	...	...	...	...	...	...
Nigeria	2.4	2.1	2.3	0.0	0.0	0.0	0.0
South Africa	1.8	2.1	1.0	–0.1	–0.7	–0.2	–0.1
Memorandum							
World Growth Based on Market Exchange Rates	4.5	1.5	2.1	–0.1	–0.4	–1.1	–0.8
European Union	5.0	0.9	2.0	0.0	–0.8	–0.9	–0.7
Middle East and North Africa	...	...	...	...	...	...	...
Emerging Market and Middle-Income Economies	4.3	2.4	3.9	0.4	–0.8	0.0	–1.0
Low-Income Developing Countries	...	...	...	...	...	...	...
Commodity Prices (US dollars)							
Oil[6]	77.0	15.7	–8.3	–12.9	5.1	–12.9	3.3
Nonfuel (average based on world commodity import weights)	16.7	–0.3	–0.3	–6.0	0.3	–9.7	2.2
World Consumer Prices[7]	**5.6**	**9.3**	**4.7**	**1.0**	**0.6**	**2.4**	**0.8**
Advanced Economies[8]	4.9	7.5	3.1	1.2	0.8	2.7	0.9
Emerging Market and Developing Economies[7]	6.2	10.9	6.1	0.9	0.4	2.1	0.8

[5]Indonesia, Malaysia, Philippines, Thailand, Vietnam.

[6]Simple average of prices of UK Brent, Dubai Fateh, and West Texas Intermediate crude oil. The average price of oil in US dollars a barrel was $69.42 in 2021; the assumed price, based on futures markets, is $98.19 in 2022 and $85.52 in 2023.

[7]Excludes Venezuela. See the country-specific note for Venezuela in the "Country Notes" section of the Statistical Appendix.

[8]The inflation rates for 2022 and 2023, respectively, are as follows: 8.3 percent and 5.7 percent for the euro area, 2.0 percent and 1.4 percent for Japan, and 8.1 percent and 3.5 percent for the United States.

[9]For world output, the quarterly estimates and projections account for approximately 90 percent of annual world output at purchasing-power-parity weights. For Emerging Market and Developing Economies, the quarterly estimates and projections account for approximately 85 percent of annual emerging market and developing economies' output at purchasing-power-parity weights.

basis are pointing to a significant weakening, to only 1.7 percent in 2022 and to 2.7 percent in 2023 (Table 1.1). Negative revisions are more pronounced for advanced economies than those for emerging market and developing economies, for which differing exposures to the underlying developments imply a more mixed outlook (Figure 1.15). Overall, the outlook is one of increasing growth divergence between advanced and emerging market and developing economies.

Table 1.2. Overview of the *World Economic Outlook* Projections at Market Exchange Rate Weights
(Percent change)

		Projections		Difference from July 2022 WEO *Update*[1]		Difference from April 2022 WEO[1]	
	2021	2022	2023	2022	2023	2022	2023
World Output	**5.8**	**2.9**	**2.1**	**0.0**	**–0.3**	**–0.6**	**–1.0**
Advanced Economies	**5.2**	**2.3**	**1.1**	**–0.2**	**–0.3**	**–1.0**	**–1.2**
Emerging Market and Developing Economies	**6.7**	**3.6**	**3.6**	**0.1**	**–0.1**	**–0.2**	**–0.6**
Emerging and Developing Asia	7.4	4.0	4.7	–0.1	–0.1	–1.0	–0.7
Emerging and Developing Europe	6.5	0.9	0.2	1.4	0.1	3.0	–0.6
Latin America and the Caribbean	6.7	3.3	1.6	0.5	–0.3	0.9	–0.8
Middle East and Central Asia	4.4	4.7	3.3	0.0	0.1	0.1	–0.1
Sub-Saharan Africa	4.6	3.5	3.6	–0.3	–0.3	–0.3	–0.3
Memorandum							
European Union	5.3	3.1	0.6	0.4	–0.9	0.3	–1.8
Middle East and North Africa	4.2	4.7	3.2	–0.1	0.1	–0.1	0.0
Emerging Market and Middle-Income Economies	6.9	3.5	3.5	0.1	–0.2	–0.2	–0.7
Low-Income Developing Countries	4.1	4.7	4.8	–0.2	–0.3	0.1	–0.5

Source: IMF staff estimates.
Note: The aggregate growth rates are calculated as a weighted average, in which a moving average of nominal GDP in US dollars for the preceding three years is used as the weight. WEO = *World Economic Outlook*.
[1]Difference based on rounded figures for the current, July 2022 WEO *Update*, and April 2022 WEO forecasts.

Figure 1.14. Countries in Contraction as a Share of Global GDP, 2022–23
(Percent)

January 2022 WEO *Update* | April 2022 WEO | July 2022 WEO *Update* | October 2022 WEO

Source: IMF staff calculations.
Note: "Contraction" is defined as consecutive negative quarter-over-quarter growth in 2022 or 2023. The bars show the countries' share in global GDP using purchasing-power-parity-based GDP in 2022 as weights. WEO = *World Economic Outlook*.

Figure 1.15. Global Growth and Inflation Forecasts
(Percent)

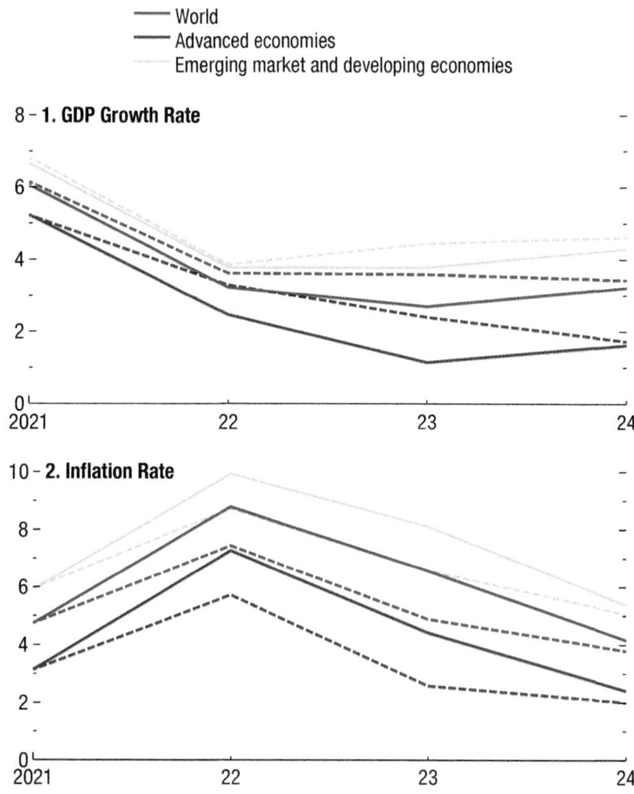

Source: IMF staff calculations.
Note: Solid lines = October 2022 *World Economic Outlook*; dashed lines = April 2022 *World Economic Outlook*.

Growth Forecast for Advanced Economies

For advanced economies, growth is projected to slow from 5.2 percent in 2021 to 2.4 percent in 2022 and 1.1 percent in 2023. With the slowdown gathering strength, growth is revised down compared with the July WEO *Update* (by 0.1 percentage point for 2022 and 0.3 percentage point for 2023). The projected slowdown and the downgrades are concentrated in the US and European economies.

Growth in the *United States* is projected to decline from 5.7 percent in 2021 to 1.6 percent in 2022 and 1.0 percent in 2023, with no growth in 2022 on a fourth-quarter-over-fourth-quarter basis. Growth in 2022 has been revised down by 0.7 percentage point since July, reflecting the unexpected real GDP contraction in the second quarter. Declining real disposable income continues to eat into consumer demand, and higher interest rates are taking an important toll on spending, especially spending on residential investment.

In the *euro area*, the growth slowdown is less pronounced than that in the United States in 2022 but is expected to deepen in 2023. Projected growth is 3.1 percent in 2022 and 0.5 percent in 2023. There is an upward revision of 0.5 percentage point since July for 2022, on account of a stronger-than-projected second-quarter outturn in most euro area economies, and a downward revision of 0.7 percentage point for 2023. This average for the euro area hides significant heterogeneity among individual member countries. In Italy and Spain, a recovery in tourism-related services and industrial production in the first half of 2022 has contributed to projected growth of 3.2 percent and 4.3 percent, respectively, in 2022. However, growth in both countries is set to slow sharply in 2023, with Italy experiencing negative annual growth. Projected growth in 2022 is lower in France, at 2.5 percent, and in Germany, at 1.5 percent, and the slowdown in 2023 is especially sharp for Germany, with negative annual growth. Weak 2023 growth across Europe reflects spillover effects from the war in Ukraine, with especially sharp downward revisions for economies most exposed to the Russian gas supply cuts, and tighter financial conditions, with the European Central Bank having ended net asset purchases and rapidly raising policy rates by 50 basis points in July 2022 and 75 basis points in September 2022. At the same time, a number of factors have contributed to a less rapid near-term slowdown than in the United States, including policy interest rates at still lower levels and, in a number of European economies, NextGenerationEU funds supporting economic activity.

In the *United Kingdom* too, a significant slowdown is projected. Growth is forecast at 3.6 percent in 2022 and 0.3 percent in 2023 as high inflation reduces purchasing power and tighter monetary policy takes a toll on consumer spending and business investment. This forecast was prepared before the announcement (September 23) of the sizable fiscal package and incorporates a less substantial fiscal expansion. The fiscal package is expected to lift growth somewhat above the forecast in the near term, while complicating the fight against inflation.

Growth in *Japan* is expected to be more stable at 1.7 percent in both 2021 and 2022 and 1.6 percent 2023, with a downward revision for 2023 since July of 0.1 percentage point. The revisions reflect mainly external factors, with a negative shift in the terms of trade (ratio of export to import prices) from higher energy import prices as well as lower consumption as price inflation outpaces wage growth.

Growth Forecast for Emerging Market and Developing Economies

Growth in the emerging market and developing economy group is expected to decline to 3.7 percent in 2022 and remain there in 2023, in contrast to the deepening slowdown in advanced economies. The forecast for 2022 is modestly upgraded from the July forecast, reflecting a smaller-than-expected contraction in emerging and developing Europe.

In *emerging and developing Asia*, growth is projected to decline from 7.2 percent in 2021 to 4.4 percent in 2022 before rising to 4.9 percent in 2023, with a 0.2 percentage point and 0.1 percentage point downgrade since July for 2022 and 2023, respectively. The revisions reflect the downgrade for growth in *China*, to 3.2 percent in 2022 (the lowest growth in more than four decades, excluding the initial COVID-19 crisis in 2020). COVID-19 outbreaks and lockdowns in multiple localities, as well as the worsening property market crisis, have held back economic activity in China, although growth is expected to rise to 4.4 percent in 2023. The outlook for *India* is for growth of 6.8 percent in 2022—a 0.6 percentage point downgrade since the July forecast, reflecting a weaker-than-expected outturn in the second quarter and more subdued external demand—and 6.1 percent in 2023, with no change since July. For the Association of Southeast Asian Nations (ASEAN)-5 economies, projected growth in 2023 is revised down to reflect mainly less favorable external conditions, with slower growth in major trading partners such as China, the euro area, and the US; the decline in household purchasing power from higher food and energy prices; and in most cases, more rapid monetary policy tightening to bring inflation back to target.

In *emerging and developing Europe*, growth is projected at 0.0 percent in 2022 and 0.6 percent in 2023, with a 1.4 percentage point upgrade for 2022 and a 0.3 percentage point downgrade for 2023, compared with the July forecast. The economic weakness reflects –3.4 percent and –2.3 percent projected growth in Russia in 2022 and 2023 and a forecast contraction of 35.0 percent in Ukraine in 2022, as a result of the war in Ukraine and international sanctions aimed at pressuring Russia to end hostilities. The contraction in Russia's economy is less severe than earlier projected, reflecting resilience in crude oil exports and in domestic demand with greater fiscal and monetary policy support and a restoration of confidence in the financial system.

Growth in *Latin America and the Caribbean* is forecast at 3.5 percent in 2022 and 1.7 percent in 2023. Growth for 2022 is higher by 0.5 percentage point than projected in July, reflecting stronger-than-expected activity in the first half of 2022 on the back of favorable commodity prices, still-favorable external financing conditions, and the normalization of activities in contact-intensive sectors. However, growth in the region is expected to slow in late 2022 and 2023 as partner country growth weakens, financial conditions tighten, and commodity prices soften.

Growth in the *Middle East and Central Asia* is projected to increase to 5.0 percent in 2022, largely reflecting a favorable outlook for the region's oil exporters and an unexpectedly mild impact of the war in Ukraine on the Caucasus and Central Asia. In 2023 growth in the region is set to moderate to 3.6 percent as oil prices decline and the headwinds from the global slowdown and the war in Ukraine take hold.

In *sub-Saharan Africa*, the growth outlook is slightly weaker than predicted in July, with a decline from 4.7 percent in 2021 to 3.6 percent and 3.7 percent in 2022 and 2023, respectively—downward revisions of 0.2 percentage point and 0.3 percentage point, respectively. This weaker outlook reflects lower trading partner growth, tighter financial and monetary conditions, and a negative shift in the commodity terms of trade.

Figure 1.16. The Shocks of 2022: Persistent Output Losses
(Percentage point deviation from preshock growth forecast)

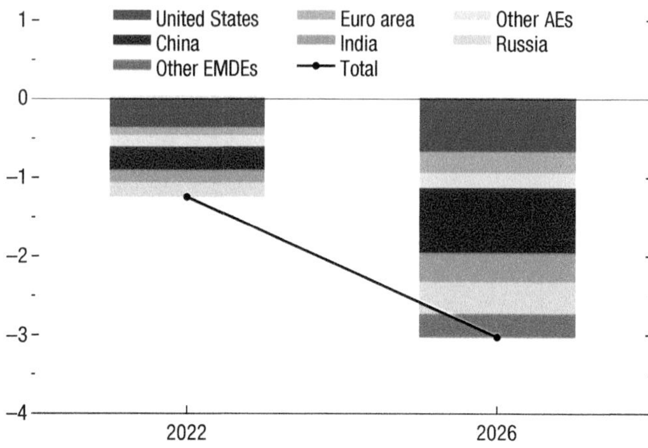

Source: IMF staff estimates.
Note: Figure reports deviations of cumulative growths since 2021 from forecasts in the January 2022 *World Economic Outlook Update*. AEs = advanced economies; EMDEs = emerging market and developing economies.

Medium-Term Scarring

The adverse shocks of 2022 are expected to have long-lasting effects on output. The fall in global real GDP in 2022 compared with forecasts made at the start of 2022 (published in the January WEO *Update*) amounts to 1.3 percent (Figure 1.16). Although windfall gains and gains from reform may protect some countries (for example, Gulf Cooperation Council members), by 2026, the output loss (cumulative growth) compared with those early 2022 forecasts is projected at 3.0 percent: more than double the initial impact. About half of the projected 2022 decline is due to lower growth in China, the euro area, Russia, and the US, with this composition holding fairly steady over the forecast horizon. Long-lasting and widening output losses across economies from the shocks of 2022 reflect several factors, including the combination of the supply-side nature of the initial shocks and macroeconomic policy tightening. For economies directly affected by the war in Ukraine, the damage to activity is likely to last long and affect most industries (Novta and Pugacheva 2021, 2022). The fading of COVID-19 fiscal support packages and anti-inflation monetary policy tightening contrast with the expansive policy support put in place in many economies in 2020. The persistent effects are consistent with economic slowdowns resulting in less investment in capital, training, and research

Figure 1.17. Scarring from the Pandemic
(Percent deviation from pre-pandemic trend)

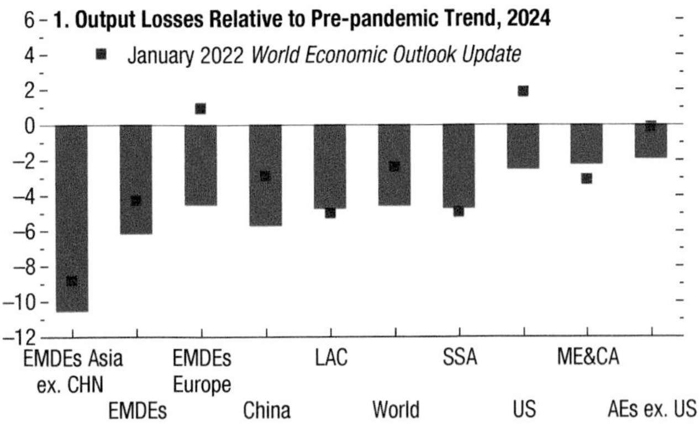

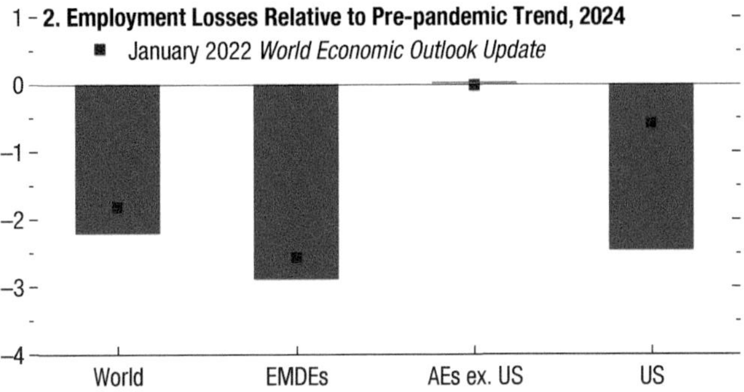

Source: IMF staff calculations.
Note: The figure shows medium-term losses, which are the differences between forecasts of the indicated variable (for 2024) relative to the January 2020 WEO *Update*. The sample of countries in panel 2 comprises those that have comparable employment projections for both times depicted. The emerging market and developing economy (EMDE) employment aggregate excludes China and India owing to changes in employment definitions across vintages. AEs ex. US = advanced economies excluding the United States; EMDEs Asia ex. CHN = EMDEs in Asia excluding China; LAC = Latin American and Caribbean economies; ME&CA = Middle Eastern and Central Asian economies; SSA = sub-Saharan African economies.

and development, implying scarring to economic potential.[1]

The shocks of 2022 are exacerbating the ongoing economic scarring from the pandemic (Figure 1.17), particularly for emerging market and developing economies. At the start of 2022, the pandemic's medium-term impact on global GDP was already projected at about –2.4 percent by 2024 (the difference between the January 2022 WEO *Update* projection and the January 2020 projection, which preceded the pandemic's onset). Emerging market and developing economies bore the projected output and employment losses disproportionately. Advanced economies had on average no projected economic losses, reflecting their ability to implement exceptionally large policy support packages. For the US as of January 2022, real GDP in 2024 was expected to *surpass* pre-pandemic forecasts by 1.8 percent. In contrast, in emerging market and developing economies, with a younger population, greater pandemic disruption to schooling, less policy space, and greater preexisting investment needs, output and employment were expected to remain somewhere below previous trends for years to come (with average losses of 4.3 percent for output and 2.6 percent for employment in 2024). The shocks of 2022 have nearly doubled the projected global output loss for 2024, to 4.6 percent.

Inflation Peaking

The forecast for global headline consumer price index inflation is for a rise from 4.7 percent in 2021 to 8.8 percent in 2022—an upward revision of 0.5 percentage point since July—and a decline to 6.5 percent in 2023 and 4.1 percent in 2024. Forecasts for most economies have been revised up modestly since July but are significantly above forecasts made earlier in 2022. On a four-quarter basis, projected global headline inflation peaks at 9.5 percent in the third quarter of 2022 before declining to 4.7 percent by the fourth quarter of 2023. The disinflation projected for 2023 occurs in almost all economies for which forecasts are available but is most pronounced in advanced economies (Figure 1.18). The faster disinflation for advanced economies—a sharper reduction in 2023 for a given level of inflation in 2022—is consistent with the notion that these economies benefit more than emerging markets from greater credibility of monetary frameworks and that this helps to reduce inflation.

The upward inflation revision is especially large for *advanced economies*, in which inflation is expected to rise from 3.1 percent in 2021 to 7.2 percent in 2022 before declining to 4.4 percent by 2023 (up by 0.6 percentage point and 1.1 percentage point in 2022 and 2023, respectively, compared with the July forecast). Significant increases in headline inflation among such major economies as the US (a 0.4 percentage point upward revision to 8.1 percent) and the euro area (a 1.0 percentage point upward revision to 8.3 percent) are driving the increase for the group. Forecasts for 2024 are relatively unchanged—up by

[1]For a discussion of such hysteresis effects on the supply side of the economy, see, for example, Yellen (2016); Ball (2009, 2014); Blanchard, Cerutti, and Summers (2015); and Adler and others (2017).

Figure 1.18. Inflation Likely to Decline Next Year
(Percent)

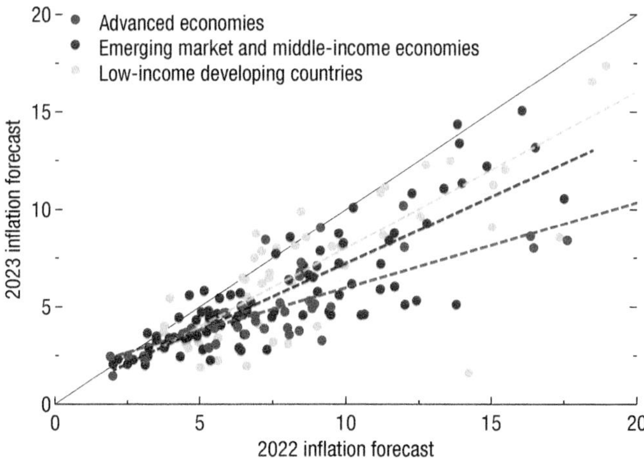

Source: IMF staff calculations.
Note: Figure reports 45-degree line (solid) and lines (dashes) of best fit for each group of economies with matching colors. 16 countries with 2022 inflation higher than 20 percent are not shown. 14 of those countries show 2023 inflation at the same or lower levels than that in 2022.

only 0.1 percentage point—reflecting confidence that inflation will decline as central banks tighten policies and energy prices decline. At the same time, the projected inflation reduction is, as mentioned, proportionately greater for advanced economies than for other country groups.

For *emerging market and developing economies*, inflation is expected to rise from 5.9 percent in 2021 to 9.9 percent in 2022, before declining to 8.1 percent in 2023. Prices in the fourth quarter of 2023 are projected at 6.1 percent higher than in the same quarter of 2022. Revisions for these economies (with annual inflation revised up by 0.4 percentage point and 0.8 percentage point in 2022 and 2023, respectively, compared with the July forecast) display greater variation across economies than those for advanced economies. There is on average a relatively modest upward revision to the inflation forecast for emerging and developing Asia (partly because of a slowdown of activity in China and limited increases in prices of foods that make up a large part of diets) and a modest downward revision for Middle East and Central Asia economies. There are larger revisions to the inflation forecasts for Latin America and the Caribbean (up by 2.2 percentage points for 2023), Emerging and Developing Europe (up by 0.9 percentage point), and Sub-Saharan Africa (up by 2.0 percentage points for 2023).

Global Trade Slowdown, with Wider Balances

Global trade growth is slowing sharply: from 10.1 percent in 2021 to a projected 4.3 percent in 2022 and 2.5 percent in 2023. This is higher growth than in 2019, when rising trade barriers constrained global trade, and during the COVID-19 crisis in 2020, but well below the historical average (4.6 percent for 2000–21 and 5.4 percent for 1970–2021). The slowdown, which is 0.7 percentage point steeper than that projected for 2023 in the July WEO *Update*, mainly reflects the decline in global output growth. Supply chain constraints have been a further drag: the Federal Reserve Bank of New York's Global Supply Chain Pressure Index has declined in recent months—largely because of a decrease in Chinese supply delivery times—but is still above its normal level, indicating continuing disruptions. Nevertheless, supply chains are complex, and pandemic-era disruptions were a product of multiple factors. If other factors continue to improve even as challenges in China remain, supply-side pressures may continue to ease. The dollar's appreciation in 2022—by about 13 percent in nominal effective terms as of September compared with the 2021 average—is likely to have further slowed world trade growth, considering the dollar's dominant role in trade invoicing and the implied pass-through in consumer and producer prices outside the US (Gopinath and others 2020).

Whereas global trade growth is declining, global trade balances have widened. After shrinking during 2011–19, global current account balances—the sum of all economies' current account surpluses and deficits in absolute terms—increased during the COVID-19 crisis and are projected to rise further in 2022 (Figure 1.19). The widening of balances has reflected the pandemic's impact. It has also, in 2022, mirrored the increase in commodity prices associated with the war in Ukraine, which has raised balances for oil net exporters and reduced them for net importers (2022 *External Sector Report*). A widening in global current account balances is not necessarily a negative development, though excessive global imbalances can fuel trade tensions and protectionist measures or increase the risk of disruptive currency and capital flow movements.

Creditor and debtor stock positions are expected to remain elevated in 2022, although they have, on average, moderated slightly from their 2020 peaks, because valuation changes have more than offset the concurrent widening of current account

Figure 1.19. Current Account and International Investment Positions
(Percent of global GDP)

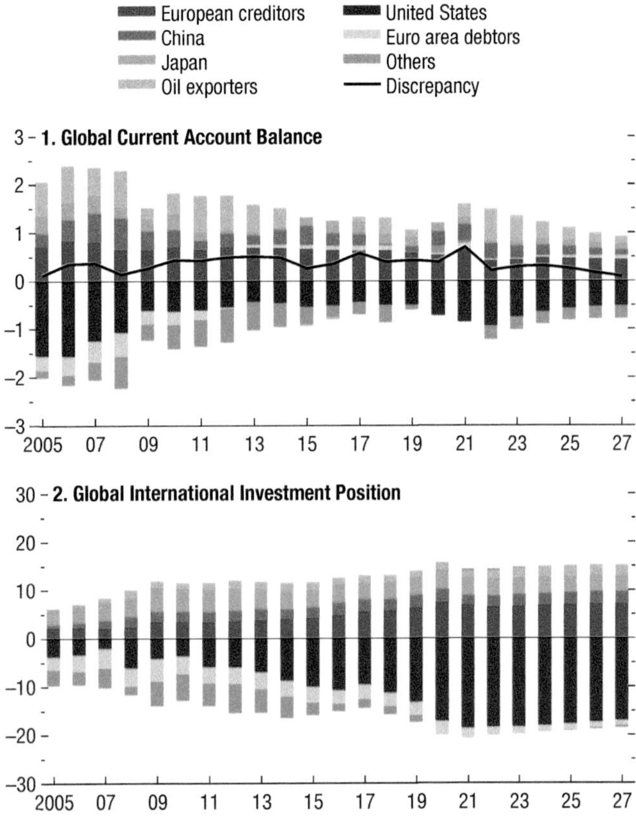

Source: IMF staff calculations.
Note: European creditors = Austria, Belgium, Denmark, Finland, Germany, Luxembourg, The Netherlands, Norway, Sweden, Switzerland; euro area debtors = Cyprus, Greece, Ireland, Italy, Portugal, Slovenia, Spain; oil exporters = Algeria, Azerbaijan, Iran, Kazakhstan, Kuwait, Nigeria, Oman, Qatar, Russia, Saudi Arabia, United Arab Emirates, Venezuela.

Figure 1.20. Corporate Talk of Key Macroeconomic Risks
(Cumulative percent)

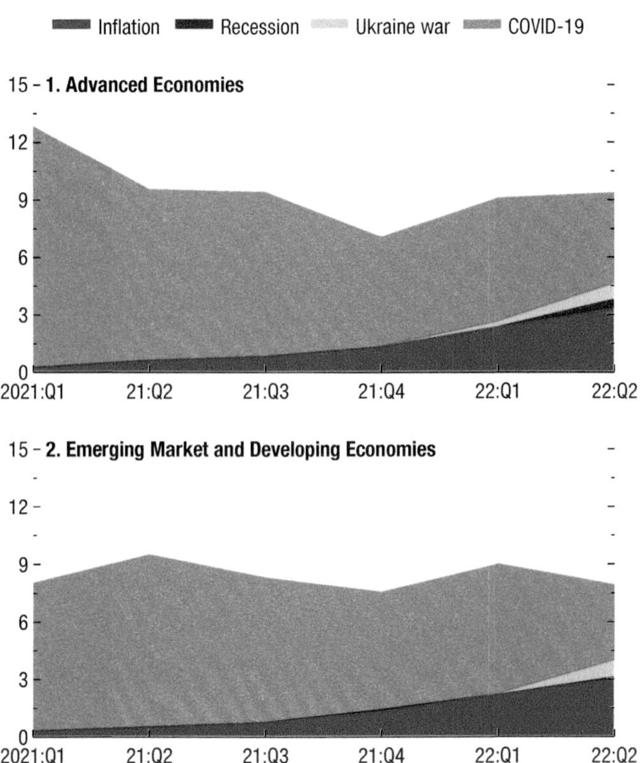

Sources: NL Analytics; and IMF staff calculations.
Note: Each area in the figure shows the number of sentences in companies' earnings calls that mention the respective risk as a percentage of the total number of risk mentions.

balances. The 2022 decline in asset prices in the US—the economy with the world's largest net liability position (external assets minus external liabilities)—could cause valuation losses for foreign holders of US assets. At the same time, however, US dollar appreciation could lead to valuation gains in emerging market and developing economies, which tend to have long positions in foreign currency, while increasing the burden of dollar-denominated public sector debts.

Risks to the Outlook: The Downside Still Dominates

Risks to the outlook continue to be on the downside. Overall, risks are elevated as the world grapples with the impact of Russia's invasion of Ukraine, a slowdown in economic activity as central banks ramp up efforts to quell inflation, and the lingering pandemic. The risks described in this section, if realized, are likely to depress growth further and keep inflation higher for longer. Some of these risks are currently top of mind for the world's largest firms as they navigate a highly uncertain environment. While inflation is increasingly important, firms still see COVID-19 as the dominant risk (Figure 1.20). The continued high numbers of COVID-19 mentions in firms' earnings calls may reflect the pandemic's lingering effect on labor markets and supply chains. Further complicating the outlook, it is not at all straightforward how these risks influence one another. They may well interact to magnify some adverse effects. In what follows, the most prominent risks and uncertainties surrounding the outlook are discussed, followed by a model-based analysis that quantifies the balance of risks to the outlook (Box 1.3).

- *Policy mistakes: under- or overtightening monetary policy*—Major central banks must chart a difficult course. A deteriorating growth outlook with subdued consumer and investor sentiment sits somewhat awkwardly alongside still-tight labor markets. The major economies are also seeing mixed economic readings, such as contradictory signals in output and labor markets in the US and tourism-supported strong growth in Europe during the summer despite the war's impact. While conditioning policy on incoming data, there is a risk that inflation expectations could de-anchor if the fight against inflation loses momentum. So far, consumer inflation expectations seem to remain anchored in major economies (Adrian, Erceg, and Natalucci 2022). It is worth noting, however, that disagreement among households regarding the longer-term outlook for inflation is widening and, in some cases, beginning to shift, with a larger share of households expecting very high inflation (Figure 1.21). The risk of policy mistakes—under- or overtightening—is elevated in these conditions. Not tightening enough may prove a costly mistake: it risks causing inflation to become entrenched, prompting a more hawkish future stance on interest rates at a significant cost to output and employment. On the other hand, overtightening risks sinking many economies into prolonged recession. The outlook already projects a growing number of economies to be in contraction in 2022–23 (Figure 1.14). Uncertainty about the neutral rate of interest and potential transatlantic monetary policy divergence makes navigating this narrow path complicated. Moreover, over- and undertightening do not necessarily have symmetric costs: a policy mistake that leads to spiraling inflation would be the much more detrimental of the two. In addition, uncertainty also clouds the natural level of unemployment: the pandemic significantly changed labor market dynamics in many advanced economies, with low employment compared with pre-pandemic trends coexisting with elevated labor market tightness. Given the uncertain outlook, the coming months are likely to test central banks' mettle in rooting out inflation. In this fight, advanced economy central banks may be able to depend on a larger credibility buffer. While central banks in emerging market economies and lower-income countries have made significant progress in policy strategy and communications in recent years, gaps between these economies and advanced economies persist (Unsal, Papageorgiou, and Garbers 2022). Emerging market economies and lower-income countries may struggle more to defeat inflation. In all cases, however, durably reducing inflation will depend crucially on monetary policymakers' resolve to stay the course and avoid repeating the stop-go cycle of the 1970s.

Figure 1.21. Long-Term Inflation Expectations
(Percent; five years ahead)

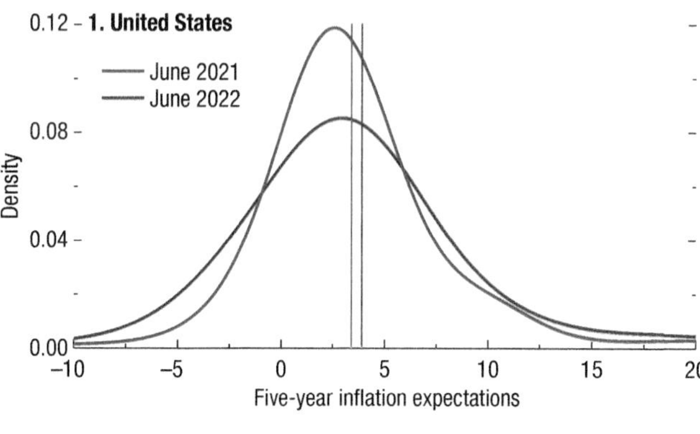

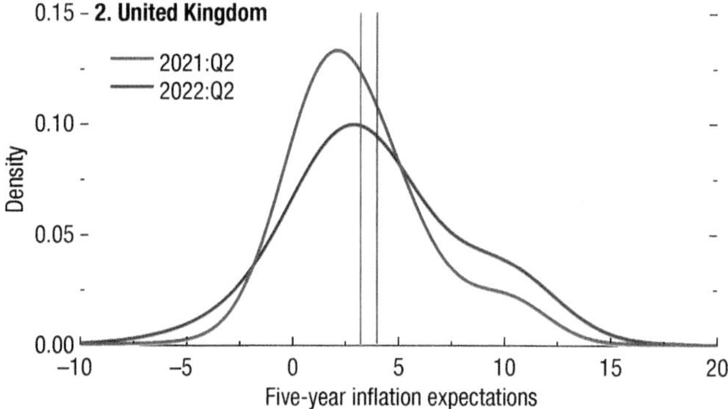

Sources: Bank of England, Inflation Attitudes Survey; University of Michigan, Surveys of Consumers; and IMF staff calculations.
Note: The vertical lines indicate the mean of each distribution.

- *Divergent policy paths and dollar strength*—Divergences in economic policies may continue to contribute to US dollar strength, which could create cross-border tensions. The course of monetary policy tightening in the US and the euro area might continue to diverge if inflation persists for longer and a sharp monetary tightening proves difficult to implement in the euro area in the presence of fragmentation risks. Another dimension of macroeconomic policy divergence is that among China, Japan, the United Kingdom, and the US. In China, output growth has slowed with the COVID-19 outbreaks and troubles in the property sector, and with relatively benign inflation readings, the central bank decided to reduce lending rates in August. Japan's policy rates could continue to remain low, given the low underlying core inflation and weak wage growth. In September, the Japanese authorities intervened to support the yen amid the currency's rapid depreciation and a widening monetary policy divergence with the US. In the United Kingdom, the announcement in September of large debt-financed fiscal loosening, including tax cuts and measures to deal with the high energy prices, was associated with a rise in gilt yields (October 2022 *Global Financial Stability Report*) and a sharp currency depreciation that was later reversed. Overall, policy divergences, and any flight-to-safety effects should geopolitical tensions rise, may cause further US dollar strength. In 2022 the dollar has already appreciated by about 15 percent against the euro, over 10 percent against the renminbi, 25 percent against the yen, and 20 percent against sterling. The associated currency movements may add to cross-border tensions regarding competitiveness; stoke inflation in many economies, given the predominance of dollar pricing in international trade; and lead some countries to tighten policies further to prevent excessive currency depreciation, with negative effects on growth.

- *Inflationary forces persisting for longer*—Inflation is projected to cool in 2023 and 2024, with the forces shaping the outlook pointing to faster disinflation in advanced economies than in emerging market and developing economies (Figure 1.18). However, several factors could delay the moderation of inflation rates. Further shocks to energy and food prices could keep headline inflation higher for longer. Energy prices are and will remain particularly sensitive to the course of the war in Ukraine and the potential flaring up of other geopolitical conflicts. Sustained high energy prices as well as the aforementioned currency depreciation may also pass through to core inflation and so warrant a more hawkish monetary policy response. This would deepen the drag on growth owing to higher costs of borrowing and depressed disposable incomes. And extreme weather events might undermine the global food supply, placing upward pressure on the prices of foods that make up a large part of diets, with dire consequences for the world's poorest countries. Higher-for-longer inflation would also raise the risk of inflation de-anchoring or a wage-price spiral persisting when expectations are more backward-looking. So far, these risks appear contained, partly because of more aggressive monetary tightening (see Chapter 2). Firms enjoying higher markups might choose to absorb the increase in the cost of intermediate goods (Box 1.2), but a prolonged increase in input costs could prompt firms to pass on higher costs to preserve margins. Although the risk of this seems low, firms are increasingly regarding inflation as a prominent risk (Figure 1.20). On the upside, the current surge in inflation is partly related to the stronger-than-anticipated demand recovery from the pandemic shock (Box 1.1). With continued tightness in labor markets, some advanced economies seem to be at the steeper end of the supply curve. This may support rapid disinflation, with lower output and employment costs. Also, a combination of a deteriorating growth outlook and efforts to ramp up crude oil production by the largest producers may soften energy-induced inflationary pressures.
- *Widespread debt distress in vulnerable emerging markets*—The war in Ukraine has helped precipitate a surge in sovereign spreads for some emerging market and developing economies (Figure 1.3). This surge comes amid record debt due to the pandemic. Should inflation remain elevated, further policy tightening in advanced economies may add pressure to borrowing costs for emerging market and developing economies. Some larger emerging market economies are well positioned. But if sovereign spreads increase further, or even just remain at current levels for a prolonged period, debt sustainability may be at risk for many vulnerable emerging market and developing economies, particularly those hit hardest by energy and food price shocks. With a larger import bill, strained fiscal budgets, and limited fiscal space, any loss of access to short-term funding markets will have significant economic and social consequences. The poor are particularly vulnerable, as fiscal policy support is critical to shielding them from the impact of the food inflation shock. A surge in capital outflows might also cause distress in emerging market and developing economies with large external financing needs. A widening debt crisis in these economies would weigh heavily on global growth and could precipitate a global recession. Further US dollar strength can only compound the likelihood of debt distress. The weakening of national currencies in emerging market and developing economies might trigger balance sheet vulnerabilities in economies with large dollar-denominated net liabilities, with immediate risks to financial stability.
- *Halting of gas supplies to Europe*—The war in Ukraine is still sending aftershocks through Europe and global markets. The amount of Russian gas supplied to Europe has fallen to about 20 percent of last

year's level, compared with 40 percent at the time of the July 2022 WEO *Update*. The latest forecasts incorporate the expectation that the volume will decline further, to even lower levels, by mid-2024, in line with major European economies' energy independence goals. Should Russia completely halt gas supplies to Europe in 2022, energy prices would likely increase further over the short term, placing even more pressure on households, and would be expected to cause headline inflation in the euro area to remain elevated for longer. The economic impact of the shock would—as analysis underlying the July 2022 WEO *Update* (Flanagan and others 2022, Lan and others 2022) suggests—vary across the continent with the degree of dependence on Russian gas imports and the ability to address infrastructure bottlenecks to secure alternative gas shipments. The likelihood and magnitude of possible supply shortfalls is smaller today than assessed in July, because higher pipeline and LNG flows and gas demand compression have led to faster-than-expected storage accumulation in the EU in recent months. Countries in central and eastern Europe—particularly the Czech Republic, Hungary, and the Slovak Republic—might face disruptions, given their dependence on Russian gas and the potential difficulty of securing alternative gas supplies. Particularly cold temperatures or insufficient gas demand compression this fall could force energy rationing during the winter in Germany, Europe's largest economy, with drastic effects for industry, weighing heavily on the euro area growth outlook and with potential for negative cross-border spillover effects. Of course, commodity prices might also decline—perhaps if the global downturn is more severe than expected—something that would have an adverse impact on exporting countries.

- *A resurgence of global health scares*—While the latest coronavirus variants are less deadly than earlier ones and show far more manageable hospitalization rates, they are also highly contagious. As such, the COVID-19 pandemic is still taking a heavy toll on the workforce, resulting in prolonged absenteeism, reduced productivity, and falling output. Yet the evolution of more aggressive and lethal coronavirus variants remains a risk for the global economy. Regions where exposure to new variants is highest and those, such as Africa, where vaccination rates are still low are likely to bear a higher burden in any pandemic resurgence (Figure 1.22). Similarly concerning is the risk of new global health scares. For instance, monkeypox currently represents a public health emergency of international concern. While a scenario in which a new pandemic emerges has very low probability, the return to strict lockdowns could reduce demand for contact-intensive services once more. Given squeezed household budgets, there is little likelihood of a partial offset through a rotation toward demand for goods. While this might lessen inflationary pressures, further outbreaks could instead magnify supply chain bottlenecks, which are finally starting to ease. The interplay between these two forces will shape the inflation-output trade-off that central banks now confront. Over the coming years, such risks, if realized, would only deepen the pandemic's human capital scarring and bring productivity down.

Figure 1.22. Africa Least Vaccinated against COVID-19
(Percent, unless noted otherwise)

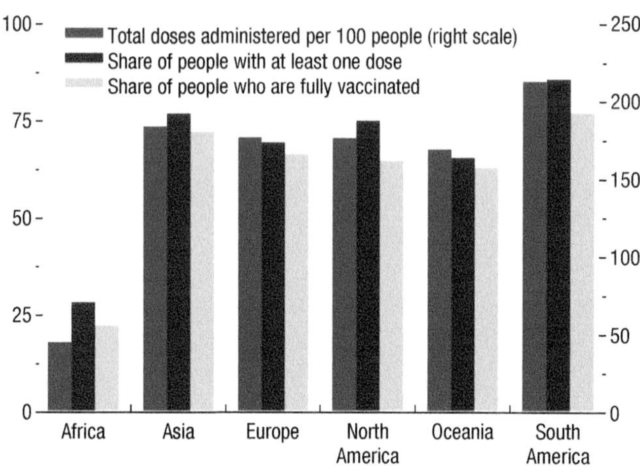

Sources: Our World in Data; and IMF staff calculations.
Note: Latest data available are for September 13, 2022.

- *Worsening of China's real estate woes*—Growth in China has weakened significantly since the start of 2022 and has been subject to downward revision since the April 2022 lockdowns in Shanghai and elsewhere and because of an expected slowdown in global trade (Figure 1.23, panels 1 and 2). Downside risks to China's growth recovery dominate the outlook, with signs of a significant slowdown in the real estate sector, historically an engine of growth for China's economy (Figure 1.23, panel 3). The decline in real estate sales prevents developers from accessing a much-needed source of liquidity to finish ongoing projects, putting pressure on their cash flows and raising the possibility of further debt defaults.

Figure 1.23. Slowdown in China

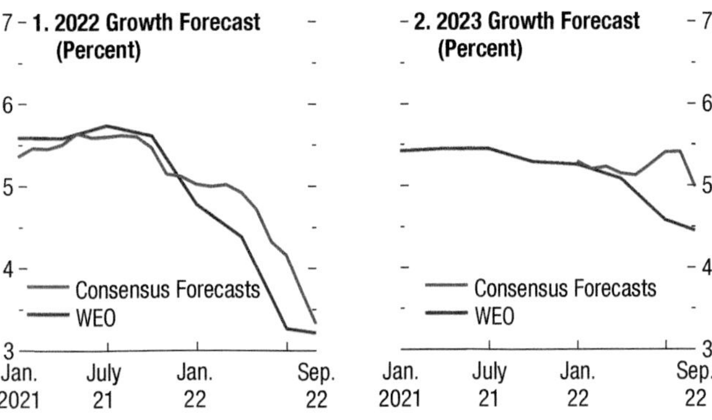

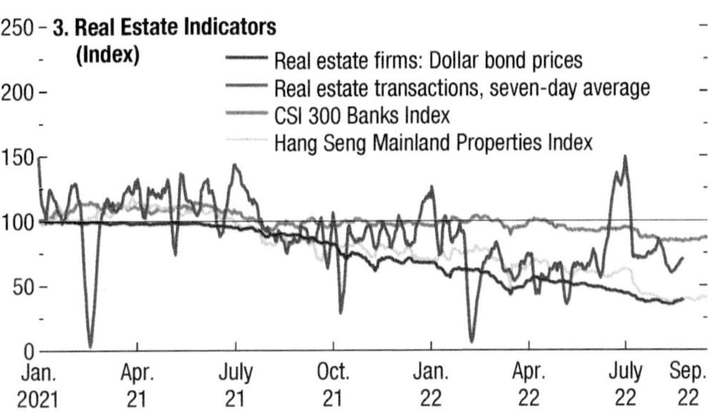

Sources: Bloomberg Finance L.P.; Consensus Economics; Wind Information (HK) Co. Ltd.; and IMF staff calculations.
Note: For panels 1 and 2, Consensus Forecasts are monthly survey basis. For panel 3, all series are indexed to 100 on January 1, 2021, except real estate transactions, which are indexed to average 100 in 2021. WEO = *World Economic Outlook*.

Concerned with the delay in the delivery of residential units, thousands of buyers are calling for a moratorium on mortgage payments that would lead to forbearance and exacerbate the risk of nonperforming loans for banks, as well as the liquidity squeeze developers face. Uncertainty about the property sector could also have an impact on consumption and local government finances. A further intensification of negative feedback loops between housing sales and developer stress risks a larger and more protracted real estate adjustment. This would be a large blow, given that the real estate sector makes up about one-fifth of GDP in China. Furthermore, the potential for banking sector losses may induce broader macro-financial spillovers that would weigh heavily on China's medium-term growth.

- *Fragmentation of the world economy hampering international cooperation*—The Russian invasion of Ukraine fractured relations between Russia and many other countries. New geopolitical tensions—in east Asia and elsewhere—are also becoming more likely. Such tensions risk disrupting trade and eroding the pillars of multilateral cooperation frameworks that took decades to build. While the recent Black Sea grain deal bodes well for increasing the supply of commodities to global markets and is a positive step for international diplomatic efforts, the risks of the world economy fragmenting further are real and could weigh on the outlook, especially over the medium term (the next three to five years). Backtracking on the Black Sea grain deal might lead to a food security crisis, most notably in low-income countries. Further fragmentation in global cooperation would create a significant risk for climate change policy cooperation. Heightened tensions might also see the world fragmenting into different spheres of geopolitical influence, with adverse impacts on global trade and capital flows.
- *Globally consistent risk assessment of the WEO forecast*—Confidence bands for the WEO forecast for annual global growth are obtained using the G20MOD module of the IMF's Flexible System of Global Models. For some regions, the WEO forecast has asymmetric confidence bands, skewed toward lower growth than in the baseline. This skewing reflects the preponderance of negative growth surprises in the past. The resulting risk assessment, displayed in a fan chart, can also be used to calculate the probability of a global economic downturn. The estimated probability of one-year-ahead global growth below 2.0 percent—an outcome that has occurred on only five occasions since 1970 (in 1973, 1981, 1982, 2009, and 2020)—now stands at about 25 percent: more than double the normal probability (Box 1.3). The probability of negative per capita real GDP growth in 2023 is more than 10 percent. Such a weak growth outcome could occur if, as Box 1.3 explains, a plausible combination of shocks were to materialize, including unexpected reductions in global oil supply, a further weakening in China's real estate sector, persistent labor market disruption, and tighter global financial conditions.

Policy Actions: From Inflation to Growth

Although the economic environment is one of the most challenging in many years, difficult times need not last forever. Judicious policy choices can help guide the global economy out of inflation and into an era of sustainable and inclusive growth. Such policies have impacts and interactions in the short, medium, and long term.

Policies with Immediate Impact

Fighting inflation: The priority must be to tackle inflation, normalize central bank balance sheets, and raise real policy rates above their neutral level fast enough and for long enough to keep inflation and inflation expectations under control. Fiscal policy also needs to support monetary policy in softening demand in economies with excess aggregate demand and overheating labor markets. Without price stability, any gains from future growth are at risk of being eaten up by a renewed cost-of-living squeeze. Central banks need to act resolutely while communicating clearly the objectives and the steps to achieve them (October 2022 *Global Financial Stability Report*). Yet taming inflation will come at a cost: unemployment will rise and wages will decline as monetary policy tightens. The appropriate path of anti-inflation policies will be country-specific and depend crucially on the following issues:

- *The timing of the costs and benefits of disinflation:* The costs of monetary contraction tend to come before the benefits. The last major US disinflation began in 1980 and brought an almost immediate recession. But inflation took about three years to fall to manageable levels. More systematic evidence points to similar conclusions. Monetary policy seems to have its peak impact on real variables after about one year, but on inflation after closer to three to four years (Coibion 2012; Cloyne and Hürtgen 2016). This lag between the near-term costs of disinflation policies and their longer-term benefits poses credibility challenges for monetary policymakers, who may expect to receive calls to ease off monetary tightening amid job losses and continued inflation. And if the interest rate consistent with stable inflation (often termed the "natural rate of interest") is higher than previously believed, the costs of disinflation—and the pressures to slow the pace of tightening—will be correspondingly higher. Indeed, some evidence suggests this has already occurred in the US. Although real rates are low, historical relationships between output and inflation are not consistent with the observed increase in inflation alone; instead, it seems possible that the natural rate may have increased slightly, loosening the stance of policy further (Figure 1.24), although there is still a great deal of uncertainty about the natural rate at medium- and long-term horizons. In any case, central banks must stay the course to ensure that inflation durably declines. In this, qualitative forward guidance on objectives and reaction functions will remain valuable. Yielding to pressure to slow the pace of tightening will only undermine credibility, allow inflation expectations to rise, and necessitate more aggressive and painful policy actions later. By reversing course, monetary policymakers will deliver only the pain of tightening, with none of the gain. Moreover, in some economies, slowing the pace of monetary tightening could exacerbate the risks associated with policy divergences. Finally, supply-side efforts can support monetary policy in reducing inflation. Policies to prevent supply shortages will ease pressure on inflation as demand recovers and include upgrading transportation infrastructure, pandemic preparedness, and creating more reliable and resilient supply chains. In turn, long-lasting supply shocks may also necessitate policy responses.
- *International capital flows:* Tighter financial conditions and fear of global recession influence global capital flows, often with negative consequences for emerging market and developing economies. There has been a surge in the US dollar, which in real terms has risen to highs not seen since the early

Figure 1.24. Natural Rate of Interest, United States
(Percent)

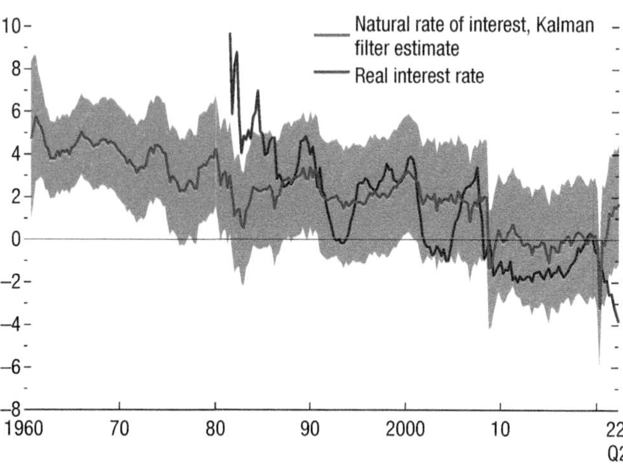

Sources: Federal Reserve Bank of Philadelphia, Survey of Professional Forecasters (SPF); Holston, Laubach, and Williams (2017); and IMF staff calculations.
Note: The Kalman filter estimate is computed from the model of Holston, Laubach, and Williams (2017). Shaded range indicates 95 percent confidence interval. Real interest rates are computed using SPF forecasts of inflation.

Figure 1.25. Broad-Based Dollar Appreciation
(Index, 2010 = 100)

Source: IMF staff calculations.
Note: Figure shows real effective exchange rate of US dollar based on consumer prices.

Figure 1.26. Change in Cyclically Adjusted Primary Balance
(Percentage points)

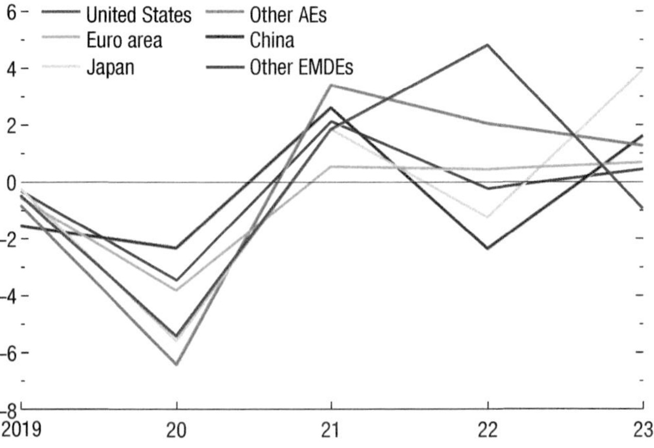

Source: IMF staff calculations.
Note: Each line denotes change in cyclically adjusted primary balance in percent of GDP series from the previous period. "Other AEs" and "Other EMDEs" comprise 11 and 15 economies, respectively. AEs = advanced economies; EMDEs = emerging market and developing economies.

2000s (Figure 1.25). Higher US interest rates and the strong dollar will raise financing costs for emerging market and developing economies, which are already generally facing real rates higher than those in advanced economies. It will also make dollar-invoiced imported goods more expensive, boosting inflation. In this context, the policy response recommended by the IMF's Integrated Policy Framework, both in a prudential manner as well as during the shock, depends on country-specific circumstances. For countries with deep foreign exchange markets and low foreign currency debt, relying on the policy rate and exchange rate flexibility is appropriate. On the other hand, if foreign exchange markets are shallow, the turn in the global financial cycle may be associated with "taper tantrums" as portfolio-constrained investors sell domestic currency assets. In such cases, it would be appropriate to conduct foreign exchange intervention or loosen inflow capital flow management measures (CFMs), instead of moving monetary and fiscal policy away from their appropriate settings. For countries with large foreign currency debts, outflows may generate systemic financial stability risks and a tail risk in growth outcomes. It may be appropriate in certain circumstances for such countries to use preemptive capital flow management or macroprudential measures (measures that are both CFMs and or macroprudential measures) to reduce their foreign exchange mismatches and to diminish the probability and severity of subsequent capital flow reversals. In crisis or near-crisis circumstances, outflow CFMs may be considered. Foreign exchange intervention and inflow CFMs may also be appropriate in emerging market economies in which inflation expectations are at high risk of de-anchoring owing to sharp exchange rate depreciations.

- *Monetary and fiscal policy coordination:* Following a broad loosening of public purse strings during the pandemic, tightening is expected in 2022 and 2023 (Figure 1.26). However, in a number of countries, fiscal policy is expected to loosen, potentially boosting aggregate demand and offsetting monetary policy's disinflationary effect. This is not to say that fiscal policy cannot cushion the disinflationary transition's impact on the vulnerable (more on this topic in the next subsection). Although targeted redistributive policies may be appropriate, deficits should be reduced to help tackle inflation and address debt vulnerabilities. Fiscal consolidation can also send a powerful signal that policymakers are aligned in their fight against inflation. Countries will need to make difficult choices in the composition of spending, given the need to keep a tight fiscal stance. For example, the cost-of-living crisis may put pressure on governments to approve above-inflation public sector pay deals. Without fiscal contraction elsewhere, and with tight supply, unfunded government spending increases or tax cuts will only push inflation up further and make monetary policymakers' jobs harder.

Protecting the vulnerable during the adjustment: As the cost of living continues to rise, policymakers will need to protect the most vulnerable members of society from the impact of higher prices. Poorer households often spend relatively more than others on food, heating, and fuel: categories that have seen particularly steep price increases. Moreover, households cannot easily adjust consumption to minimize spending on these products; everyone must eat and use heating, and transportation (whose price is often determined largely by fuel costs) is often essential to get to work. In countries with well-developed social safety nets, targeted cash transfers to those particularly exposed to higher energy and food prices (such as children and older people) and existing automatic stabilizers (for example, unemployment insurance) are the best ways to limit the impact on those least able to bear it. However, measures to limit the inflationary impact should offset any increase in new spending. In countries lacking well-developed safety nets, governments should look to extend any already active programs. In general, broad price caps or food and energy subsidies should be avoided, as they increase demand while diminishing or removing supply incentives. This can result in rationing and an unbridled underground economy. Moreover, such programs are often expensive and regressive, funneling public cash to those who consume the most rather than to those with the greatest need (see the October 2022 *Fiscal Monitor*).

Warding off pandemic risks: COVID-19 continues to have long-lasting effects on the global economy. Even though many of the new variants are less deadly than early ones, they continue to have considerable economic impact. Although strict lockdowns are increasingly rare, the disease continues to cause economic disruption, as businesses may struggle to adapt to unpredictable absences when workers or their family members fall sick. As the virus persists and continues to evolve, ensuring equitable access to a comprehensive toolkit of vaccines, tests, and treatments worldwide is the best strategy not only to save lives, but also to reduce a key source of uncertainty holding back the global recovery. Regarding vaccinations, the primary focus should be on fully vaccinating the most clinically vulnerable populations. Ongoing investments in research, disease surveillance, and health systems will also be needed to keep a broad set of tools updated as the virus evolves.

The impact of the pandemic is perhaps most keenly felt in China, where intermittent lockdowns in parts of the country have continued to affect economic activity. Temporary disruptions to domestic logistics and supply chains during the largest outbreaks, besides being a drag on private consumption, have hit the country's manufacturers, adding to existing pressures on global supply chains. The recurring outbreaks stress the importance of paving the way for a safe exit from China's zero-COVID strategy, including by adding to the country's successful vaccination campaign, especially for the undervaccinated elderly.

Figure 1.27. Debt in Distress in Emerging Market and Developing Economies
(Percent)

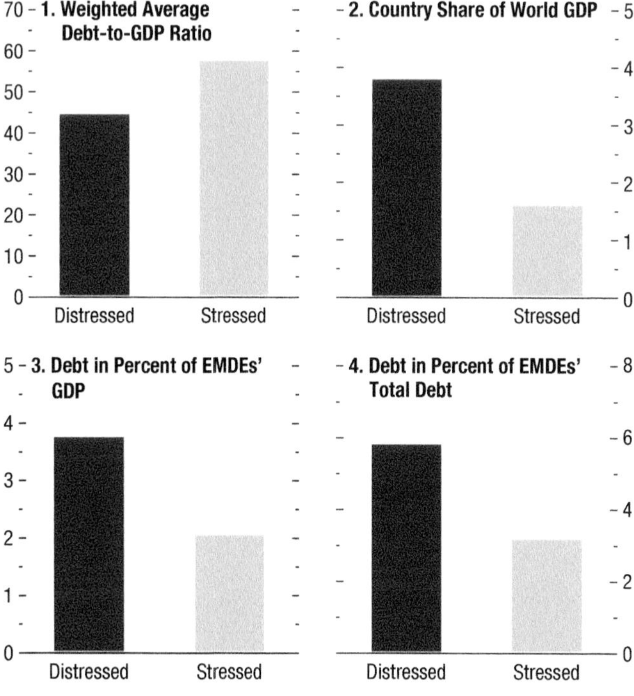

Source: IMF staff calculations.
Note: Groups are classified based on sovereign spread data as of September 9, 2022. Distressed group indicates economies with spreads greater than 1,000 basis points; stressed group indicates economies with spreads of 700–1,000 basis points. EMDEs = emerging market and developing economies.

Policies with Payoffs in the Medium Term

Improved frameworks for debt resolution: Some countries will find their fiscal sectors under considerable pressure, with rising interest rates, a coming global slowdown, and towering pandemic-era debts. Although those most exposed account for only a small share of global output and financial assets (Figure 1.27), spillover effects—most notably contagion, in which a crisis in one country induces investors to run from similar assets elsewhere—can be significant. While the best solution is always an orderly adjustment within a well-founded medium-term fiscal strategy, driven by domestic policy priorities, the likelihood is that more countries will enter debt distress. In such cases, cooperative global policies are essential to stop the spread of crises and can be achieved preferably by setting up appropriate mechanisms or institutions in advance. The IMF, as one such institution, stands ready to support countries with temporary balance-of-payments difficulties in accordance with IMF policies. But other complementary approaches should be developed further. In particular, the common debt resolution framework of the Group of Twenty (G20) can be improved to allow swift and fair resolution in cases of distressed debt, enabling countries to get out of default without extended economic pain. Recent progress in regard to Zambia is welcome, but more is needed. Coverage should be expanded to include a broader set of countries, and creditor committees need to meet and formulate agreements swiftly and transparently. Debt distress in emerging market and developing economies is a growing problem. It is imperative that a well-functioning G20 debt resolution mechanism be put in place as soon as possible.

Preparing for tighter international financial conditions: Tightening monetary policy may also put pressure on financial institutions. The best time to prepare for a tightening of financial conditions is now. As the economy slows, default rates rise and income from new loans decreases. Although higher rates may boost interest income, they are likely to have a negative effect overall on many institutions. As such, macroprudential policy will need to become ever more vigilant, guarding against the failure of systemic institutions, using selected instruments to address pockets of elevated vulnerability (see the October 2022 *Global Financial Stability Report*). In particular, the housing market remains a potential source of macro-financial risk; authorities should assess the systemic effects of a correction in house prices through rigorous stress tests. In China, authorities should enable the restructuring of troubled housebuilders and prepare to tackle the housing market's impact on the financial system more broadly. Tighter international financial conditions may also put pressure on currency exchange rates. Depending on country circumstances and the nature of shocks, policymakers should be ready to step in when flexible exchange rates alone are unable to absorb external shocks. For instance, crises may require policymakers to intervene in foreign exchange markets or introduce capital flow management measures. However, such measures should be strictly temporary, with well-defined goals. And governments with high debt should preemptively reduce reliance on foreign currency borrowing. Prompt and reliable access to reserve currency liquidity—including through IMF precautionary and disbursing arrangements—gives countries breathing room to implement adjustment policies in an orderly manner. Finally, competing pressures in the euro area make a well-designed European Central Bank facility, such as the Transmission Protection Instrument, more of a necessity to support a smooth monetary transmission. This will help policy interest rates better reflect macroeconomic conditions across the euro area. Such an instrument should complement the existing conditional Outright Monetary Transactions instrument and the European Stability Mechanism's lending program. At the same time, it should not distort markets so much that prices no longer reflect fundamental risks.

Structural reforms: Policies that expand supply can boost economic activity while easing inflation, though with somewhat of a lag. In advanced economies, such policies include those that expand the workforce, such as childcare subsidies, earned income tax credits, reformed immigration systems, and better access to COVID-19 vaccinations and treatment. In emerging market and developing economies, better education, business climates, and digital infrastructure can also help.

Policies with Longer-Term Benefits

Climate policies: Climate change continues apace. Extreme temperatures are but one manifestation of the challenges such change presents. Without prompt remedial action, climate change will eventually have catastrophic impacts on health and economic outcomes the world over. Current global targets are not aligned with global temperature goals. Meeting these goals will require emission cuts of at least 25 percent by the end of the decade (Chapter 3). The ongoing energy crisis has also sharpened the energy security benefits countries can derive from transitioning to clean and reliable energy sources to steadily replace their reliance on fossil fuels with renewables and low-carbon energy sources. To accelerate this transition, governments should both set a minimum price for carbon and promote clean alternatives, including subsidies for renewables and investment in enabling infrastructure such as smart grids. In a world of already-high prices, shifting to new energy sources may be politically challenging and apparently risky. But policies to offset the cost of the transition, such as feebates and targeted compensation for those losing out, can help ease the transition. And although the green transition may entail risks, these are minimal compared with the risk of doing nothing. Indeed, new IMF analysis highlighted in Chapter 3 suggests that the cost of the transition to clean electricity need not be inflationary and can be achieved with impacts on GDP that are smaller than the annual variation in normal times. Delay will only cause those costs to rise. The passage of the Inflation Reduction Act in the US, which includes $369 billion for energy security and climate change policies, is welcome. The law aims to reduce US carbon emissions by about 40 percent by 2030, mostly through tax credits and incentives to increase investment in clean energy. Yet the omission of broad-based carbon pricing and sectoral feebates, as well as any elimination of subsidies for fossil fuel and carbon-intensive agriculture, still leaves room for improvement. Likewise, the sizable energy package announced by the UK government, aimed at assisting all families and businesses dealing with high energy prices, has scope for better targeting the vulnerable, which would lower the cost of the package and better preserve incentives to save energy.

Strengthening multilateral cooperation and avoiding fragmentation: The recent spike in global inflation has prompted a corresponding wave of short-term protectionism, most notably in regard to food. And although protectionist policies may be appealing in the short term, there are ultimately no winners. When countries ban exports, they deny themselves the income to buy other goods they might need from abroad. Moreover, export bans in one country often provoke retaliatory bans elsewhere, leaving all parties worse off. A similar principle applies to medical products, which have been subject to trade restrictions at various times during the pandemic. Governments should unwind pre-pandemic trade restrictions and follow through on their commitment to World Trade Organization reform. This includes restoring a fully functioning dispute settlement system and enhancing rules in areas such as agricultural and industrial subsidies. In addition, multilateral cooperation is essential to the advance of technologies to support climate change mitigation and boost green financing. Also, support for low-income countries through concessional funding is needed to catalyze growth-enhancing reform and help them meet their climate targets.

Box 1.1. Dissecting Recent WEO Inflation Forecast Errors

Inflation has repeatedly exceeded World Economic Outlook *(WEO) forecasts during 2021–22 across geographic regions by an abnormally high amount. The forecast errors were generally larger for 2022 than for 2021, but those for core inflation were less prominent for 2022. Larger-than-expected demand recovery in advanced economies and emerging market and developing economies partly explains core inflation forecast errors for 2021, with COVID-19 fiscal stimulus packages likely playing a supporting role in advanced economies.*

Inflation has surprised consistently on the upside since the second quarter of 2021. This has led to successive upward revisions in WEO inflation forecasts (Figure 1.1.1) for both headline and core inflation and for both advanced and emerging market and developing economies. The October 2022 WEO forecast views inflation in advanced economies as peaking later than expected in the January WEO *Update* and April 2022 WEO. Headline inflation in emerging market and developing economies is now expected to peak higher, yet not later, than previously thought.

Inflation forecast errors are larger for 2022 than those for 2021.[1] The increase for 2022 is especially large for economies in Europe (Figure 1.1.2). The errors realized for 2021 and 2022, which average 1.7 percentage points for Europe and 3.2 percentage points globally, compare with a near-zero average for the decade that preceded the COVID-19 crisis. The root-mean-square error is 2.5 times larger for 2021 and 5 times larger for 2022 than it was for 2010–19. The large 2022 inflation surprises for emerging Europe are due to exceptionally high realized inflation in Baltic and other eastern European states as a result of the Russian invasion of Ukraine. Only China and the US saw smaller errors for 2022 than for 2021. China faces an economic slowdown, putting downward pressure on inflation. The US has seen a significant upward revision to the inflation forecast in the January 2022

Figure 1.1.1. Headline Inflation Forecasts
(Percent)

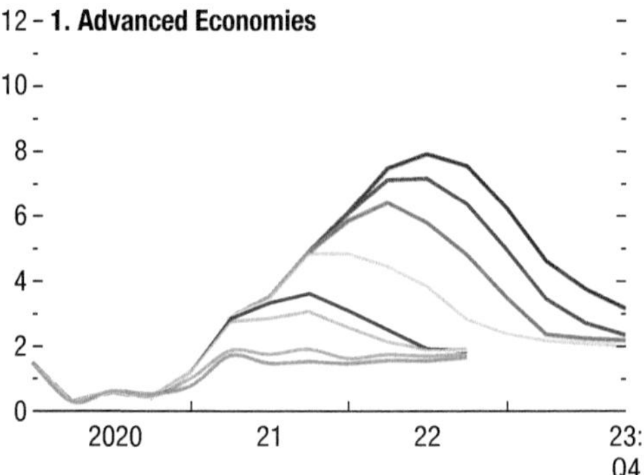

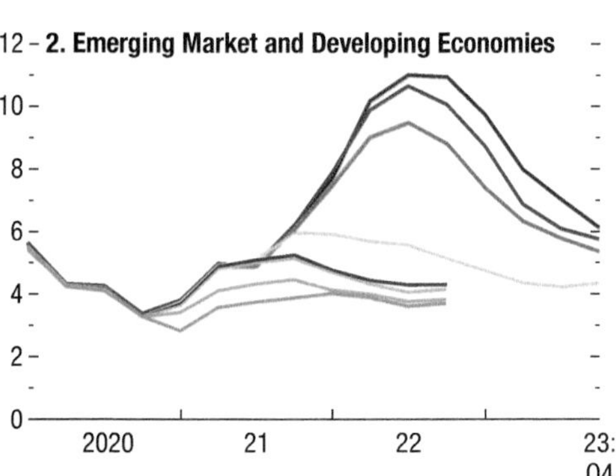

Source: IMF staff calculations.
Note: The lines plot the four-quarter purchasing-power-parity-GDP-weighted inflation forecasts from the January 2021 WEO *Update* to the October 2022 WEO. WEO = *World Economic Outlook.*

WEO *Update*, as early signs of overheating were evident from the elevated core inflation readings since the second quarter of 2021 and from increasingly tight labor markets.[2] Evidence also shows that forecasts of inflation's persistence may have been understated. On average, an additional 1 percentage point inflation surprise for 2021 is associated with an additional

The authors of this box are Christoffer Koch and Diaa Noureldin.

[1]The forecast error in a given year refers to the difference between the actual realization and the forecast issued at the start of the year (January WEO *Update*). Since actual inflation is yet to be realized for 2022, "forecast error" here refers to the forecast revision for 2022 annual inflation made in the October 2022 WEO relative to the January 2022 WEO *Update*. A positive "forecast error" for a particular country for 2022 thus indicates that 2022 inflation is projected (as of October 2022) to be higher than anticipated at the start of 2022.

[2]See Ball, Leigh, and Mishra (forthcoming) for a discussion of labor market tightness and its impact on inflation in the US after the pandemic. See also Duval and others (2022) for evidence for selected advanced economies.

Box 1.1 *(continued)*

Figure 1.1.2. WEO Annual Headline Forecast Errors with Respect to Preceding January WEO *Updates*
(Percentage points)

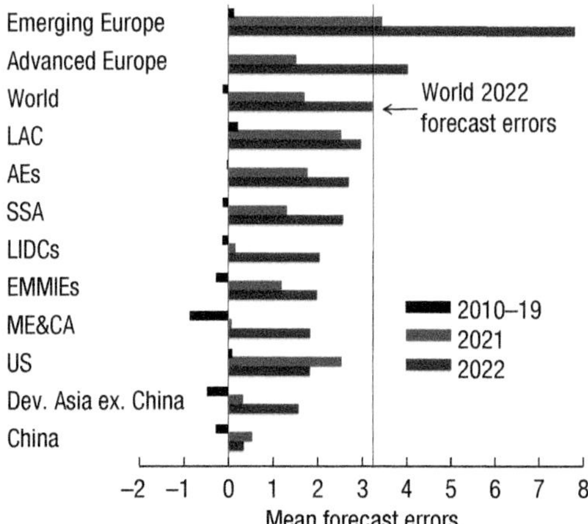

Source: IMF staff calculations.
Note: Mean inflation forecast errors from January 2021 WEO *Update* for 2021 inflation and January 2022 WEO *Update* for 2022 inflation compared with respective mean forecast errors with respect to January WEO *Updates* from 2010–19. Within-group forecast errors are weighted by purchasing power parity. AEs = advanced economies; Dev. Asia ex. China = developing Asia excluding China; EMMIEs = emerging market and middle-income economies; LAC = Latin America and Caribbean economies; LIDCs = low-income developing countries; ME&CA = Middle Eastern and Central Asian economies; SSA = sub-Saharan African economies.

Figure 1.1.3. Core Inflation and Output Forecast Errors
(Percentage points)

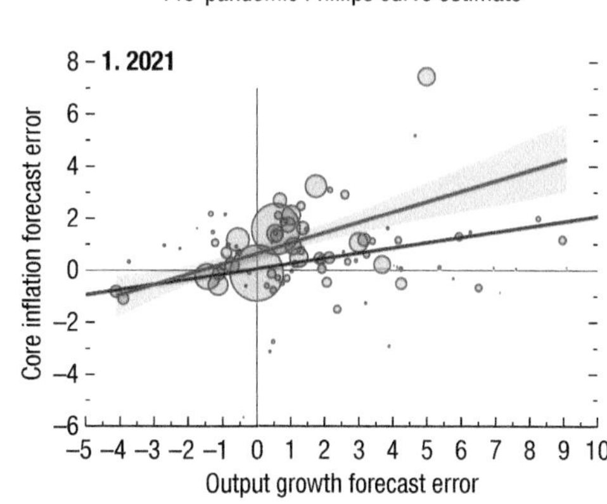

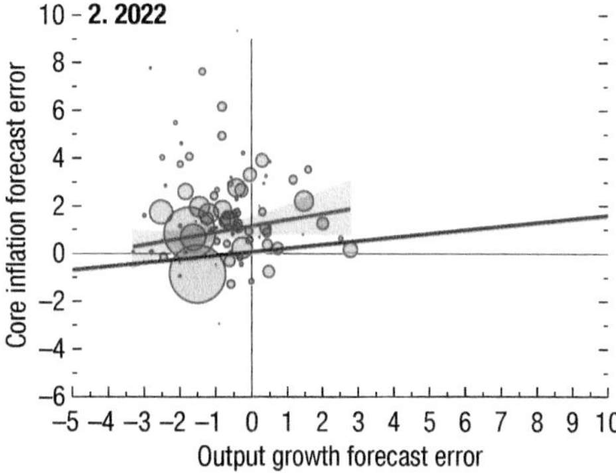

Source: IMF staff calculations.
Note: Outlier observations excluded if the absolute forecast errors exceed 10 percentage points. Russia and Ukraine are excluded in 2022. Regression is PPP-GDP weighted using weights for 2021 in panel 1 and weights for 2022 in panel 2. Bubble size indicates the size of the economy according to the PPP-GDP weights. PPP = purchasing power parity.

subsequent forecast error of 0.22 percentage point for 2022. The relationship is statistically significant (t-statistic = 2.68). Since the forecast error for 2021 was known when the forecasts for 2022 were made, it should not in principle be correlated with subsequent forecast errors.

Core inflation drove inflation forecast errors for 2021, but less so for 2022. Core inflation forecast errors represented the bulk of errors for 2021, at 53.6 percent for advanced economies and 71.9 percent for emerging market and developing economies. In regard to 2022, the core inflation contribution is lower, at 46.5 percent for advanced economies and 47.9 percent for emerging markets. The large contribution of core inflation forecast errors for 2021 likely reflects wide demand-supply imbalances as the strong demand recovery from the COVID-19 shock hit persistent supply disruptions, a topic that is explored later in this box. On the other hand, the inflation errors for 2022 are relatively more concentrated in noncore inflation, suggesting a stronger role for energy and food supply-side shocks, in large part due to the war in Ukraine.

Can the stronger-than-anticipated demand recovery partly explain core inflation forecast errors? A scatterplot of the respective forecast errors shows a positive association between output and core inflation surprises for 2021 (Figure 1.1.3, panel 1). The line of best fit (weighted by purchasing-power-parity GDP) traces out a Phillips curve relationship with a greater slope compared with that of the pre-pandemic

Box 1.1 *(continued)*

Phillips curve estimate.[3] This suggests the global economy may have been at the steeper end of the aggregate supply curve in 2021, as the rapid demand recovery met continually disrupted supply. The July 2021 WEO *Update* and October 2021 WEO documented the strength of the demand recovery. Advanced economies showed a noticeably strong recovery in output (manufacturing and services). Also, supply strain was at its worst in the second half of 2021, as indicated by purchasing managers' index supply delivery times. For 2022 core inflation forecast errors, the line of best fit is flatter and nonsignificantly different from the slope of the pre-pandemic Phillips curve (Figure 1.1.3, panel 2).

The strong association between inflation and output forecast errors for 2021 likely reflects, in part, the COVID-19 fiscal stimulus packages and tight labor markets, particularly in advanced economies. Ambitious fiscal stimulus packages in reaction to the pandemic shock likely boosted demand recovery in 2021. With interest rates at the zero lower bound in most advanced economies, policymakers resorted to fiscal policy to cushion the impact of the pandemic shock and avert long-term scarring. Figure 1.1.4 (panel 1) shows a wide range of magnitudes of fiscal packages announced in 2020, based on the Database of Country Fiscal Measures in Response to the COVID-19 Pandemic (January 2021 *Fiscal Monitor Update*). A number of large economies (for example, Japan, the UK, and the US) committed to spending in excess of 15 percent of GDP in response to the pandemic. The overall scatterplot does not exhibit a strong positive association, confirming that other factors are also at play, yet advanced economies show a strong relationship between inflation forecast errors and fiscal packages. For advanced economies, an additional 10 percent of GDP in fiscal support is associated with a 0.8 percentage point larger-than-expected core inflation rate (t-statistic = 3.38). In real time, forecasters likely underestimated fiscal packages' impact on inflation in those economies. Supply disruptions were not visible merely in the market for goods and in clogged global supply chains: the pandemic and subsequent rapid demand rebound also squeezed domestic labor markets. To highlight the relationship between labor markets and

[3]The pre-pandemic estimate is based on a hybrid Phillips curve specification during 2000–19. See Chapter 2 of the October 2021 WEO for further details.

Figure 1.1.4. Impacts on Core Inflation Forecast Errors
(Percent)

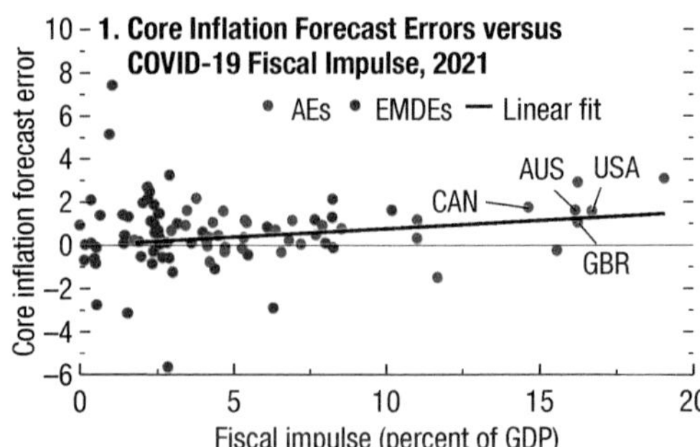

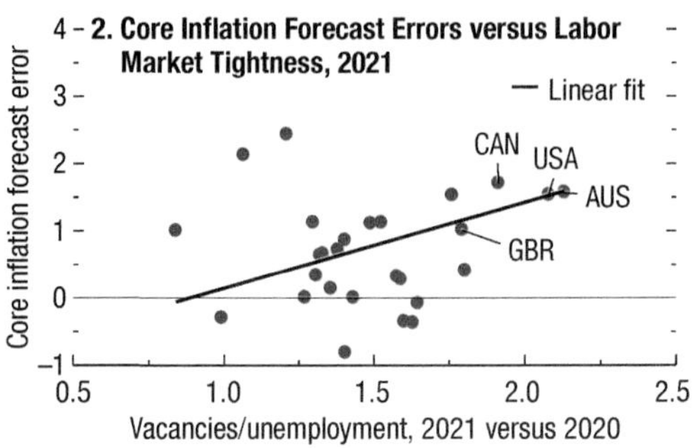

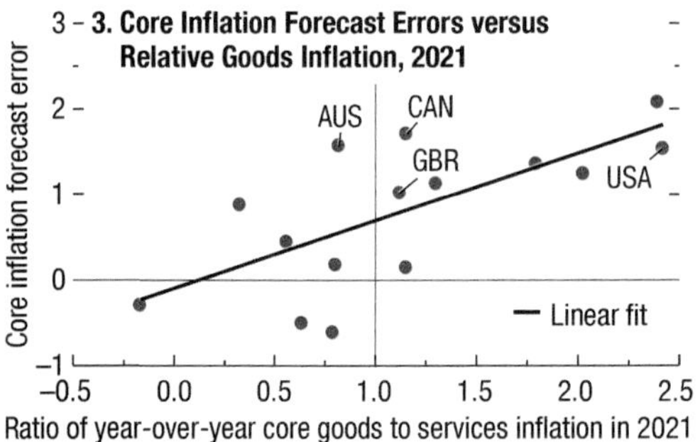

Source: IMF staff calculations.
Note: In panel 1, "fiscal impulse" refers to the announced COVID-19 fiscal support packages in 2020. The solid line is a linear fit of a weighted regression for advanced economies, in which the weights are the 2021 PPP GDP. In panel 2, the linear fit uses 2021 PPP GDP weights. In panel 3, regression is PPP-GDP weighted using weights for 2021. All three panels exclude outlier observations if the absolute forecast errors for core inflation or output growth exceed 10 percentage points. AEs = advanced economies; EMDEs = emerging market and developing economies; PPP = purchasing power parity. Data labels in the figure use International Organization for Standardization (ISO) country codes.

Box 1.1 *(continued)*

core inflation forecast errors, the ratio of vacancies to unemployment in 2021 relative to that in 2020 is computed. This ratio displays a positive relationship with inflation forecast errors (Figure 1.1.4, panel 2). A regression accounts for more than 50 percent of the error variations. Finally, Figure 1.1.4 (panel 3) highlights the role of reshuffling of sectoral demand from services to goods. It plots the ratio of core goods inflation to services inflation in 2021, which was about 2.5 in the US, against core inflation forecast errors in 2021. The positive correlation suggests a role for sectoral demand dislocations in driving unanticipated inflation aberrations. Overall, the patterns in regard to fiscal impulses, labor market tightness, and sectoral shifts are consistent with the notion that fiscal policy supported buoyant demand, when the economy's supply side was still impaired, and so contributed meaningfully to inflation forecast misses.

Box 1.2. Market Power and Inflation during COVID-19

Is corporate market power behind the current wave of inflation? With consumer price growth surging in 2021 and 2022 across numerous advanced economies, this question is at the forefront of policy and academic debates. One potential explanation is that firms take advantage of low competition to shield profits by passing rising input and labor costs on to households through higher prices. This box, however, presents new evidence suggesting that market power has not contributed substantially to inflation at the current conjuncture.

Profits rebounded in 2021 after taking a hit in 2020. Some of the recovery may have resulted from firms' charging higher prices. Decomposing GDP deflator growth into factor income growth shows that the private sector's gross operating surplus, which includes profits, has been an important driver of higher output prices in several advanced economies, alongside rising unit labor costs (Figure 1.2.1). In the US, where the GDP deflator increased 7 percent between 2019 and 2021, roughly 40 percent of this increase can be attributed to rising gross operating surplus, while rising employee compensation accounts for 65 percent. In contrast, production taxes, the decomposition's final component, contributed negatively, reflecting fiscal support during COVID-19. Other advanced economies show similar patterns.

While market power has grown steadily over the past decades in several advanced economies (Díez, Leigh, and Tambunlertchai 2018; April 2019 *World Economic Outlook,* Chapter 2), the recent rise in profits and prices does not necessarily mean that market power has increased further during the pandemic. A variety of other channels could be driving rising profits, such as higher demand or a (temporary) decline in firms' capital expenditures.

To shed light on market power's role in the recent inflationary wave, this box estimates markups for nine advanced economies (Australia, Canada, France, Germany, Italy, Japan, Spain, UK, US) during 2000–21 based on Worldscope data on publicly traded nonfinancial firms.[1] These markups—defined by the price-to-marginal-cost ratio—are common indicators of market power. The analysis follows closely the methodology of De Loecker, Eeckhout, and Unger (2020) and Díez, Leigh, and Tambunlertchai (2018).[2]

Figure 1.2.2 shows that, as discussed in earlier studies (April 2019 *World Economic Outlook*, Chapter 2; Akcigit and others 2021), markups increased steadily across advanced economies in the past decades, suggesting long-term consolidation of firms' market power.[3] However, during the pandemic, markup

Figure 1.2.1. Decomposition of GDP Deflator Growth by Income Components
(Percent)

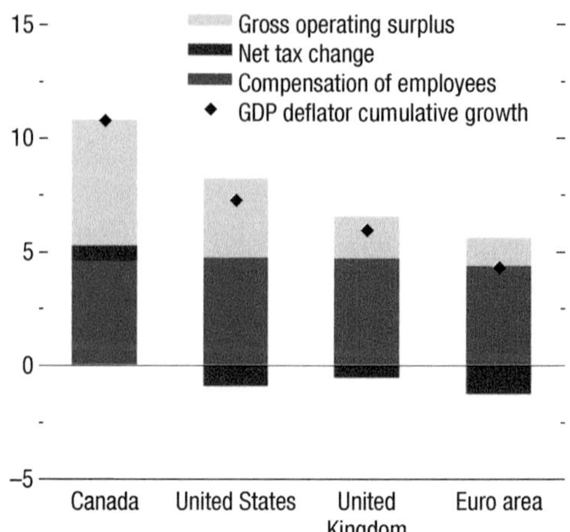

Sources: Haver Analytics; Organisation for Economic Co-operation and Development; and IMF staff calculations.
Note: Black diamonds report the aggregate growth in the GDP deflator from the fourth quarter of 2019 to the fourth quarter of 2021. Each stacked bar computes the contribution of the respective income component by multiplying the component's share of GDP in the fourth quarter of 2019 by the difference between the component's nominal growth rate and the growth rate of aggregate real GDP.

The authors of this box are Federico Díez, Longji Li, Myrto Oikonomou, and Carlo Pizzinelli.

[1]The financial sector is excluded, because markups estimated from a traditional production function may not be the best measure of market power for financial institutions (see Akcigit and others 2021). Konczal and Lusiani (2022) find that 2021 growth in markups in the financial sector was substantially higher than that in other industries. In contrast to those from Worldscope, national accounts data, used in Figure 1.2.1, encompass the entirety of the economy.

[2]A key assumption of this method is that firms face an unconstrained short-term supply of intermediate goods and labor. The assumption of flexible inputs is reasonable even under some labor market rigidities and amid recent supply chain disruptions: the cost-of-goods-sold measure used for the estimation encompasses a diverse basket of labor and intermediate goods, resulting in a flexible composite of inputs.

[3]These results should be interpreted with caution because, while listed firms account for a sizable share of output (especially in the US), evidence shows that privately held firms have different markup dynamics (Díez, Fan, and Villegas-Sánchez 2021).

Box 1.2 *(continued)*

Figure 1.2.2. Sales-Weighted Markups and CPI for Selected Advanced Economies
(Index, 2000 = 100)

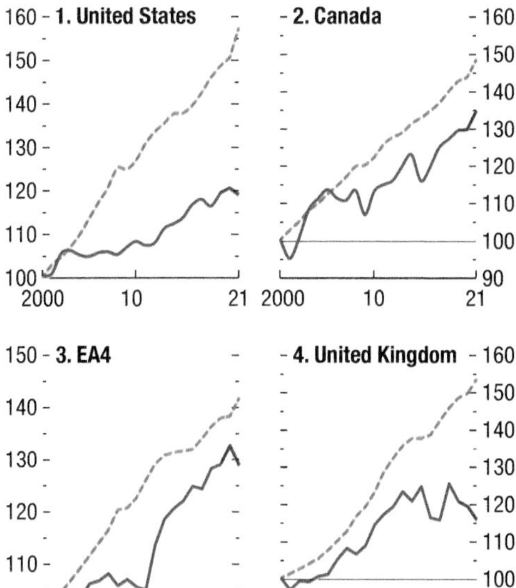

Sources: National statistical offices; Worldscope; and IMF staff calculations.
Note: Markups were computed following Díez, Leigh, and Tambunlertchai (2018). The solid blue lines report the sales-weighted average markup, with the red segment representing the years of the COVID-19 pandemic. To compute the sales-weighted average, raw values of markups and net sales at the firm level are censored below the 5th percentile and above the 95th percentile of the distribution for each country and year. The dashed green lines report the consumer price index (CPI). EA4 = France, Germany, Italy, Spain.

Figure 1.2.3. Coefficient of Production Costs Pass-Through to Prices
(Percent)

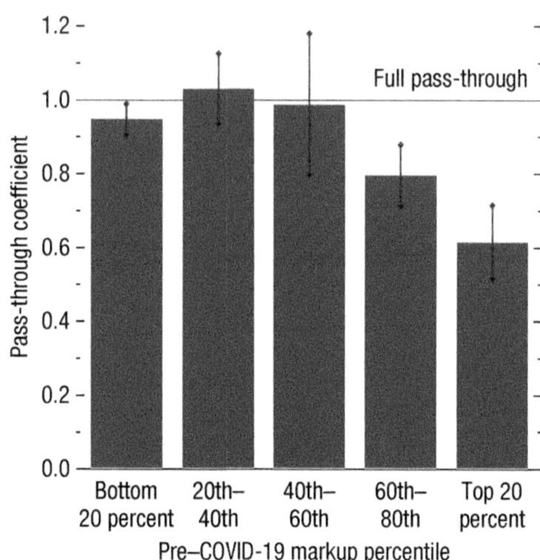

Sources: Worldscope; and IMF staff calculations.
Note: The bars represent the coefficients of pass-through from costs of goods sold (COGS) per employee to firms' markups during 2019–21 for different quintiles of the distribution of pre–COVID-19 markups. The coefficients are computed through a firm-level regression of the percent change in markups on the percent change in COGS per employee, in which the COGS-per-employee variable is interacted with a categorical variable for the quintiles of the distribution of pre-pandemic markups (using the 2016–19 average). This interaction allows the regression coefficient to vary for each quintile of the distribution. The pass-through coefficient is then computed as 1 plus the regression coefficient for the respective quintile.

growth slowed, halted, or even turned slightly negative in some countries. The figure also shows how consumer price inflation, which had grown moderately in the pre-pandemic period, accelerated during 2020–21. While markup and consumer price growth have historically been positively correlated, growing steadily—especially in services—the two have diverged markedly over the past two years.

Despite the slowdown in the growth of markups during COVID-19, the already-high markup levels at the pandemic's onset may have affected the link between rising production costs (due to supply chain disruptions, commodity prices, and labor costs) and consumer prices. On the one hand, thanks to their market power, high-markup firms may have a greater ability to pass higher costs on to consumers through higher prices. On the other hand, high initial markups also imply a greater capacity to absorb cost increases without incurring losses (an issue also potentially related to market power in input markets).

The evidence suggests the latter mechanism was more prominent during the pandemic, as firms with higher pre-pandemic markups absorbed increasing costs to a larger extent than low-markup firms. Figure 1.2.3 reports the estimated pass-through coefficients from a firm-level regression of percent changes

Box 1.2 *(continued)*

in markups on percent changes in variable costs per employee between 2019 and 2021 for US firms. Firms in the top 20 percent of the pre–COVID-19 markup distribution passed 60 percent of their cost increases through to prices, absorbing the remaining 40 percent through markup reductions. In contrast, firms in the bottom 40 percent of the pre–COVID-19 distribution fully passed cost increases on to prices. A similar result also emerges for other advanced economies. Overall, this finding supports the hypothesis that markups are not a major driver of inflationary pressures right now.

Box 1.3. Risk Assessment around the *World Economic Outlook* Baseline Projection

This box provides a quantitative assessment of the risks around the *World Economic Outlook*'s (WEO's) current baseline projection through confidence bands and a downside scenario. Using the approach described in the following section for deriving confidence bands, the risk of global growth next year falling below 2 percent—a low-growth outcome that has occurred only five other times since 1970—is currently estimated to be about 25 percent. The downside scenario illustrates how a plausible combination of shocks, coming from various parts of the world economy and amplified by a large tightening in global financial conditions, could push global growth down to as low as 1 percent.

Confidence Bands

The IMF's G20 model, presented in Andrle and others (2015), is used here to quantify the uncertainty around the baseline projection through confidence bands, drawing on historical data as well as explicit judgment about the likely recurrence of (variations of) historical episodes.[1] The approach should be thought of as complementary to the growth-at-risk framework presented in the *Global Financial Stability Report,* which links the probability distribution of growth projections to financial conditions.

Confidence bands around central projections are a well-known device for conveying forecast uncertainty, and they often reflect both statistical properties of the data and expert judgment. The benefit of using a structural, global model such as the G20 model for this exercise is the ability to analyze many individual countries jointly, consistently, and for multiple macroeconomic variables.

The model is first used to interpret the historical cross-country data on output, inflation for some countries, and oil prices and to estimate the implied economic shocks—to aggregate demand and supply and oil supply. The economic shocks that are estimated this way are correlated across countries and through time, which helps address possible limitations in the propagation mechanisms in the model. Drawing all global and country-specific economic shocks for a given year jointly captures periods in which shocks are synchronized, such as 2020, and periods in which there is greater variation across countries, such as during the recovery from the global financial crisis. The resulting distribution of macroeconomic variables is shaped by the distribution of economic shocks, the properties of the model, and the initial conditions for the projection, including the effective lower bound on monetary policy rates (which is less relevant for the current outlook than it was in previous years).

Underlying the construction of the bands is the idea that, while history does not repeat itself, it rhymes, and so future shocks may partially resemble those in the past. The historical parallels can also be introduced explicitly through expert judgment. If there is a historical episode that shares some features with the current period, then shocks from that episode could be sampled more often when constructing the confidence bands. If no judgment is imposed, then historical shocks are sampled uniformly.

Figure 1.3.1 shows the distribution for global growth that results from this approach, with and without judgment, and under the assumption that the current WEO baseline projection is the mode of the distribution.[2] Each shade of blue represents a 5 percentage point interval, and so the entire band captures 90 percent of the distribution. Panel 1 shows the distribution when shocks are sampled uniformly; panel 2 shows the distribution when shocks from the year 1982 are considered to be 10 times more likely than those from other years. The year 1982 stands out as relevant because it was a time when the world economy was experiencing a slowdown in activity, reflecting contractionary monetary policy in advanced economies to address high inflation, most notably in the US.[3] But there are limits to the historical parallel: while the current inflationary environment is reminiscent of the 1970s or early 1980s, the COVID shock is unprecedented, and policy frameworks today are very different. Nonetheless, drawing on events such as the 1982 episode can help illustrate the balance of risks to the current outlook.

The authors of this box are by Michal Andrle, Jared Bebee, Allan Dizioli, Rafael Portillo, and Aneta Radzikowski.

[1]An early version of the approach is described in Andrle and Hunt (2020).

[2]Shocks to demand and supply and global oil shocks were estimated using the entire WEO sample starting in 1960; shocks to demand were estimated for all G20 countries, whereas shocks to supply were estimated only for the US. Future work will expand the estimation to include supply shocks for all G20 countries, which will allow for a richer assessment of uncertainty around inflation projections.

[3]While there are other episodes in the 1970s and 1980s that share similarities with the current period, 1982 stands out for its impact on global growth

Box 1.3 ***(continued)***

Figure 1.3.1. Distribution of World GDP Growth Forecast
(Percent)

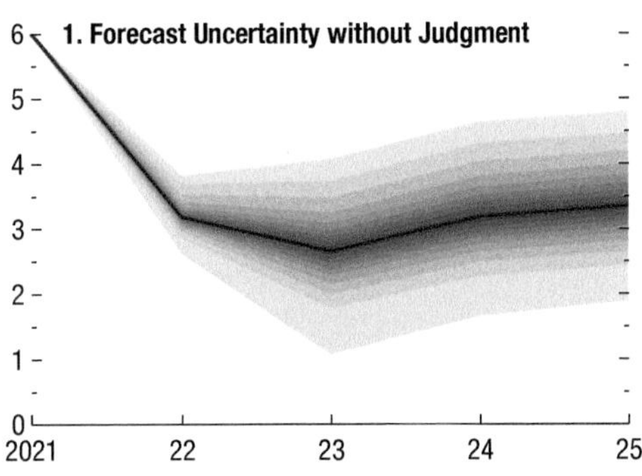

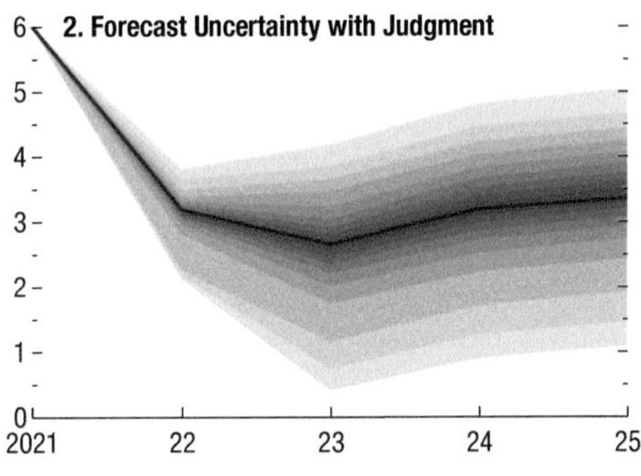

Source: IMF staff calculations.
Note: Each shade of blue represents a 5 percentage point interval. Shocks are sampled uniformly in panel 1, while shocks from 1982 are considered to be 10 times more likely than in other years in panel 2. WEO = *World Economic Outlook.*

Without judgment, very low-growth outcomes are already somewhat likely because global growth is unusually low under the baseline (the mode of the distribution). With the judgment added, however, the distribution skews further down, increasing the probability of historically low outcomes such as 2 percent or even 1 percent global growth.

Downside Scenario

The G20 model is also used to quantify several specific risks to the outlook. The shocks come from various parts of the world economy, underscoring the many sources of uncertainty currently prevailing. Their joint effect would be amplified by a large tightening in global financial conditions. If the downside scenario materializes, the level of global activity will be 1.5 percentage points lower in 2023 and 1.6 percentage points lower in 2024, relative to the current baseline.

The downside scenario consists of the following layers:

- ***Higher oil prices.*** Oil prices are pushed up 30 percent, on average, for 2023 relative to the current baseline because of a combination of (1) ongoing efforts to reduce Russia's oil export revenues and (2) retaliation from Russia in the form of a 25 percent decrease in overall oil exports. Oil prices start to decline in 2024 but stay 15 percent higher than baseline. The shock fades in 2025 as global supply and demand for oil adjust.
- ***China's real estate sector.*** Issues in the real estate sector lead to further decreases in real estate investment over the next two years. The level of total fixed investment falls by as much as 9 percent by 2024, relative to the baseline projection.
- ***Lower potential output from persistent disruptions in labor markets.*** Labor markets show clear signs of overheating, especially in several advanced economies, despite activity remaining below pre-COVID trends. Two labor market developments help account for the disconnect: lower labor force participation and shifts in the Beveridge curve that point to worsened efficiency in matching workers and jobs. In the downside scenario, these two features are more persistent than expected, leading to lower equilibrium employment than in the baseline and higher equilibrium unemployment. Underlying potential output is lower as a result, implying less slack and more inflation and requiring a larger monetary policy response than currently envisaged. The layer differentiates across countries depending on how they fare in the two labor indicators relative to pre-COVID levels: lower labor force participation is more important for some advanced economies and emerging markets, while shifts in the Beveridge curve are more visible in advanced economies such as the US and some European countries (data on vacancies is limited for most emerging markets).

Box 1.3 *(continued)*

- ***Tighter global financial conditions.*** The combination of the first three shocks leads to a large tightening in global financial conditions. Emerging market currencies experience a sizable depreciation with respect to the US dollar: 10 percent in emerging markets outside Asia and 5 percent in Asian emerging markets, including China, on average in 2023. Relatedly, emerging markets (this time excluding China) see an average increase in sovereign premiums of more than 200 basis points in 2023 and an additional increase in corporate premiums of about 80 basis points. Advanced economies experience an increase in corporate premiums of about 100 basis points and are also negatively affected by the large depreciation of emerging market currencies.

The simulations assume monetary policy responds endogenously to movements in inflation. Fiscal policy responds through automatic stabilizers, but no additional fiscal measures are assumed.

Figure 1.3.2 (panels 1 and 2) presents the effects from all four layers on the level of GDP and headline inflation, respectively, for 2023 and 2024. Results are presented as percent deviations from baseline and grouped into three regions (advanced economies, emerging markets excluding China, and China) and the world. Each region-year is shown as a separate bar, with the contribution from each shock shown in stacked form.

As Figure 1.3.2 shows, each of these risks has sizable negative effects on global activity, especially in 2023, with the magnitude of the effects across regions depending on the shock.

- All three regions are affected by higher oil prices, which reduce the level of global GDP by about 0.5 percentage point in 2023, relative to baseline. The effect on the level of global output in 2024 is smaller from this layer as the shock dissipates.
- Issues in China's real estate sector reduce global output by 0.3 percentage point in 2023. The effects amplify over time as China's investment continues to decline relative to baseline in 2024.
- Advanced economies are especially affected by the disruptions in labor markets, through both lower potential and the tightening in monetary policy required to bring down inflation. Emerging markets excluding China are also affected, while the effect on China is smaller and operating through international spillovers. Global output is lower by 0.3 percentage point from this layer in 2023; the effect persists into 2024 and beyond, consistent with the protracted effect on potential output.
- Tighter financial conditions take a large toll on global activity (0.5 percentage point in 2023). The effect amplifies over time as global investment

Figure 1.3.2. Impact of Downside Scenario on GDP and Inflation

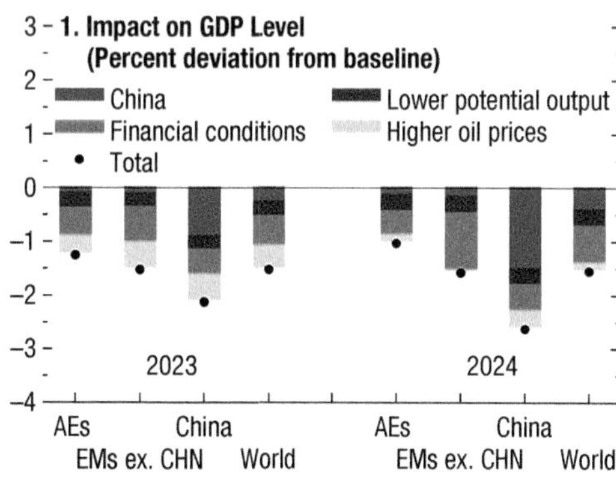

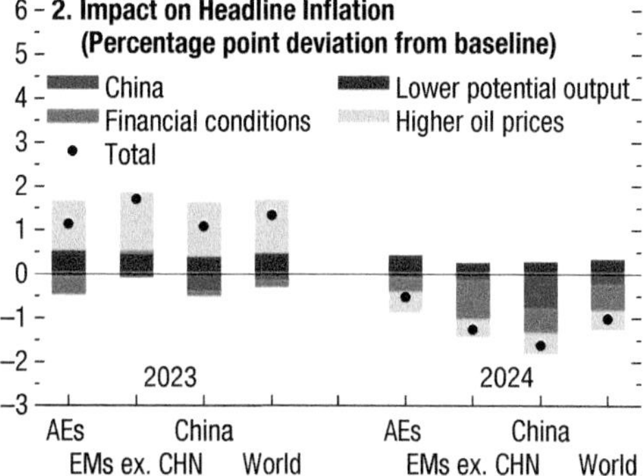

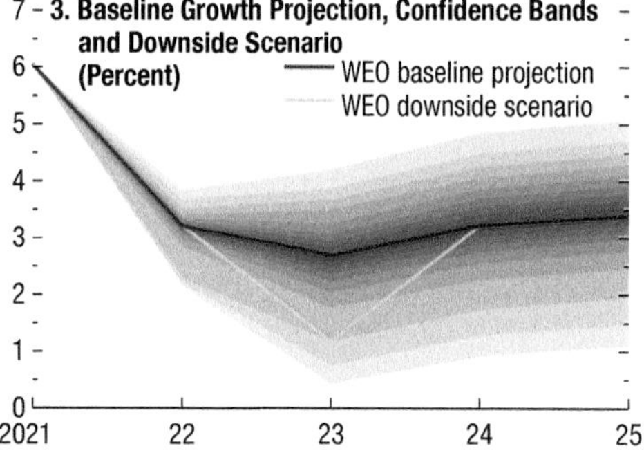

Source: IMF staff calculations.
Note: Each shade of blue in panel 3 represents a 5 percentage point interval. Shocks from 1982 are considered to be 10 times more likely than those in other years. AEs = advanced economies; EMs ex. CHN = emerging markets excluding China; WEO = *World Economic Outlook.*

Box 1.3 *(continued)*

gradually responds to the shock. The impact is most notable in emerging markets, but spillovers to other regions are large.

- The impact from the last three layers continues to build over time, but there is no further deterioration in global activity in 2024 relative to baseline. The decline in oil prices envisaged in the scenario provides some offset, by reducing the impact of the other layers on global purchasing power. As a result, while the level of activity remains well below baseline, there is no impact on global growth in 2024.

While the effects on GDP are uniformly negative, the effects on inflation vary depending on the shock (see Figure 1.3.2, panel 2):

- Higher oil prices contribute 1.1–1.3 percentage points to headline inflation across regions in 2023, before turning disinflationary in 2024.
- The lower potential output layer is also inflationary. The effects are concentrated in advanced economies, as well as emerging markets excluding China, and are also quite persistent.
- Tighter financial conditions and the slowdown in China are instead disinflationary.
- When all the layers are added together, global inflation is about 1.3 percentage points higher than baseline in 2023 and 1 percentage point lower in 2024.

Figure 1.3.2 (panel 3) superposes the resulting global growth in the downside scenario on the confidence bands presented above (with judgment). The downside scenario would imply global growth of 1.1 percent in 2023, which is in the 15th percentile of the distribution.

Special Feature: Commodity Market Developments and Food Inflation Drivers

Commodity prices rose 19.1 percent between February and August 2022. Energy—especially natural gas, up 129.2 percent—led the increase, as Russia cut gas supplies to Europe. Base metal prices declined by 19.3 percent, and precious metal prices fell by 6.0 percent, while those of agricultural commodities fell by 5.4 percent. This special feature analyzes developments in food prices in detail.

Energy Prices Stay Elevated

Crude oil prices, up by 3.5 percent between February and August 2022, surged to $120 a barrel in early March following Russia's invasion of Ukraine (Figure 1.SF.1, panel 1). Prices reflected fears of oil export disruptions at a time of tight supply-demand balances as well as a muted response by the Organization of the Petroleum Exporting Countries and other producers following prior divestments in the fossil fuel sector (see the April 2022 *World Economic Outlook* [WEO]).

Strategic oil reserve releases by members of the International Energy Agency and slower demand amid COVID-19 lockdowns in China caused oil prices to fall below $100 in April. However, announced bans on Russian oil imports and expectations of broader sanctions—including in the area of maritime insurance and trade finance—coupled with outages elsewhere led prices to surge to $120 in early June. Since then, rising interest rates and recession fears have weighed on prices as the International Energy Agency revised global 2022 oil demand growth down from 3.3 million barrels a day (mb/d) to 2.0 mb/d in September. As European and US firms reduced Russian oil purchases, Russian oil was rerouted to China and India at a discount to Brent (Figure 1.SF.1, panel 4). Refined-product prices reached multiyear highs as European refineries adjusted inputs and hit capacity constraints.

Futures markets suggest that oil prices will rise by 41.4 percent in 2022, to average $98.2 a barrel, but will fall in the coming years, to $76.3 in 2025 (Figure 1.SF.1, panel 2). Short- and medium-term risks to the oil futures price outlook are roughly balanced (Figure 1.SF.1, panel 3). Upside risks from additional supply disruptions as a result of sanctions and war as well as higher demand

The contributors of this Special Feature are Christian Bogmans, Andrea Pescatori (Team Lead) and Ervin Prifti, with support from Yousef Nazer and research assistance from Rachel Brasier, Wenchuan Dong, and Tianchu Qi.

Figure 1.SF.1. Commodity Market Developments

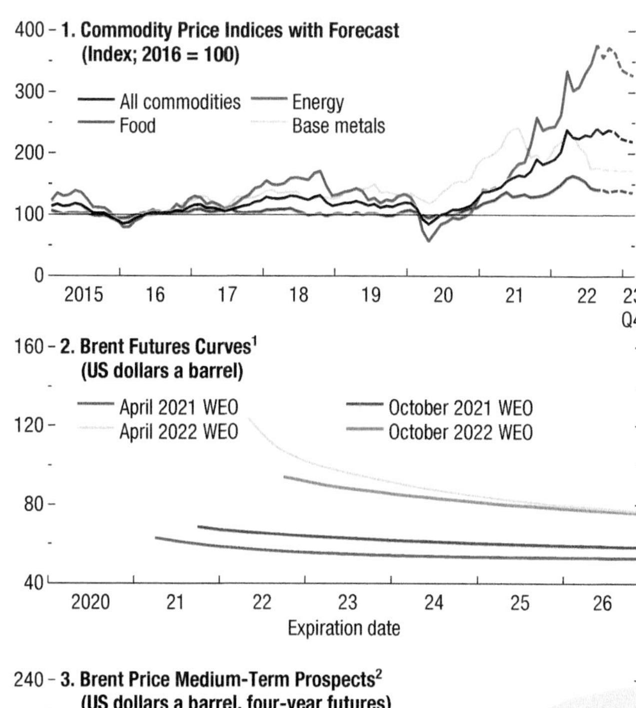

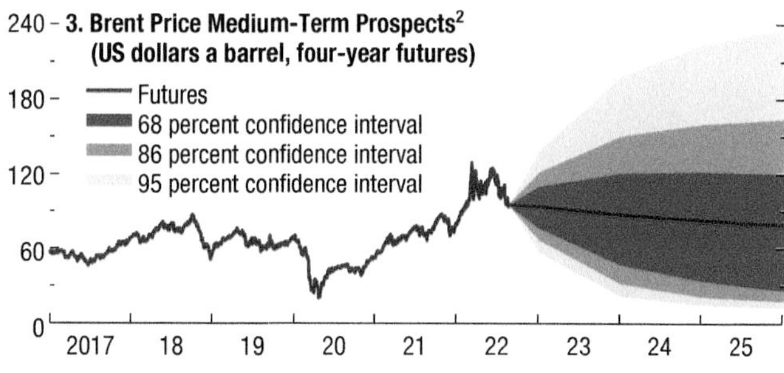

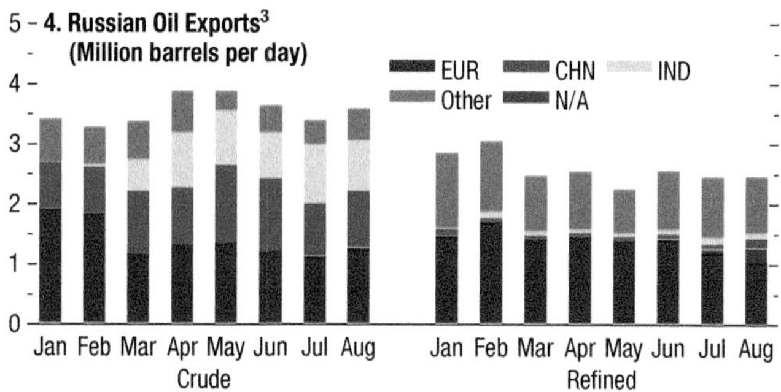

Sources: Bloomberg Finance L.P.; IMF Primary Commodity Price System; Kpler; Refinitiv Datastream; and IMF staff calculation.
Note: "N/A" WEO = *World Economic Outlook.*
[1]WEO futures prices are baseline assumptions for each WEO report and are derived from futures prices. October 2022 WEO prices are based on August 17, 2022, closing.
[2]Derived from prices of futures options on August 17, 2022.
[3]Kpler seaborn export as of September 19, 2022. "N/A" in legend means that oil is exported to unknown destination.

Figure 1.SF.2. Russian Gas Exports and Prices
(Million cubic meters a day; US dollars per million British thermal units)

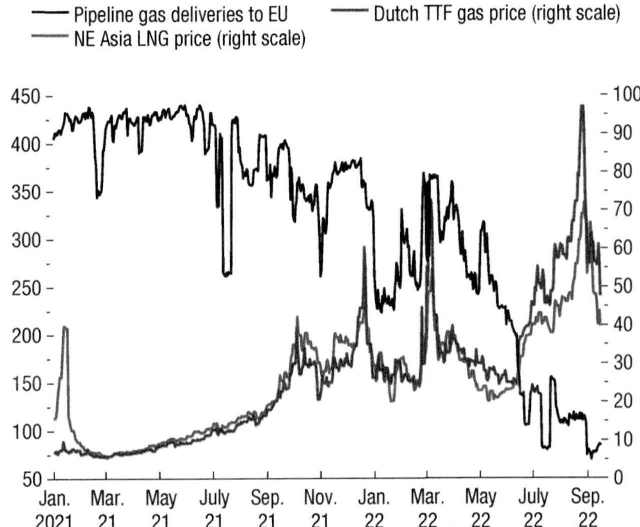

Sources: Argus Media; European Network of Transmission System Operators for Gas; Gas Transmission System Operator of Ukraine; Refinitiv Datastream; and IMF staff calculations.
Note: Last observation is September 16, 2022. EU = European Union; LNG = liquefied natural gas; NE = Northeast; TTF = Title Transfer Facility.

owing to gas-to-oil switching are offsetting downside risks from a slowing global economy, possible additional oil supplies from Iran, and higher-than-expected oil production growth in the US. Sanctions and Russia's potential retaliation have raised uncertainty, and oil price projections may be subject to large revisions.

Supply concerns in Europe have been driving natural gas prices. Russia reduced pipeline gas exports to Europe by about 80 percent in September 2022 relative to the previous year, citing maintenance problems or some countries refusing to pay for gas in rubles. Dutch Title Transfer Facility gas futures rose by 159 percent from February to August 2022, to record highs (Figure 1.SF.2). This has led European countries to increase reliance on global liquefied natural gas supplies (see Albrizio and others 2022) and to discuss a price cap on Russian gas. Prices are expected to stay high until the end of 2023. Coal prices rose 61.4 percent over the reference period and remain historically high, reflecting gas-to-coal switching, an embargo on Russian imports by EU and Group of Seven countries, and production disruptions.

Metal Prices Retreat after Rallying

The base metal price index surged, on account of Russia's invasion of Ukraine, before retreating amid slowing global economic growth to a net 19.3 percent decline from February to August (Figure 1.SF.1, panel 1). The price of aluminum is down by 25.0 percent, that of copper down by 19.6 percent, and that of iron ore down by 21.9 percent. New COVID-19 lockdowns in China, supply chain issues, and monetary policy tightening in the US and elsewhere have depressed both demand for metals and expectations about future demand. The IMF's energy transition metal index covering metals critical for electric vehicles and renewable energy fell 21.0 percent; precious metals fared better, with the IMF index slipping just 6.0 percent.

Base metal prices are expected to fall 5.5 percent, on average, in 2022, compared with a 9.9 percent increase projected in the April WEO, and to decrease by a further 12.0 percent in 2023. Precious metal prices are expected to decline more moderately, by 0.9 percent in 2022 and an additional 0.6 percent in 2023. Risks to this outlook are balanced as investors weigh potential supply reductions by European smelters amid higher energy costs against weakening global demand.

Agricultural Prices Correct from Peak Following Russia's Invasion of Ukraine

Food commodity prices surged after Russia's invasion of Ukraine but corrected to prewar levels in June and July, halting a two-year rally (see following sections). Improved supply conditions and a gradual end to Russia's blockade of Ukrainian grain exports drove the decline, along with macroeconomic factors—including rising interest rates and global recession concerns. Looking ahead, risks of renewed export restrictions (such as Indonesia's April 2022 ban on palm oil exports), droughts in part of China and the US, and pass-through from higher fertilizer prices—which reflect the reduced availability of fertilizers produced in Belarus and Russia—tilt the balance of risks to the upside.

Drivers of Global Food Prices and Transmission to Food Price Inflation

Global food commodity prices entered an expansionary phase in 2020, increasing by 54 percent, from trough to peak, with the prices of foods that make up large parts of diets increasing by 107 percent (Figure 1.SF.3). Although food prices are not new to cyclical fluctuations, this price rally stands out historically (Table 1.SF.1).

Figure 1.SF.3. Selected Commodity Price Indices
(Percent)

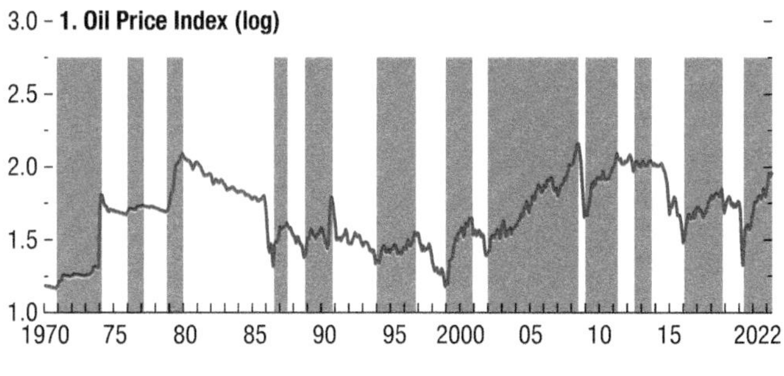

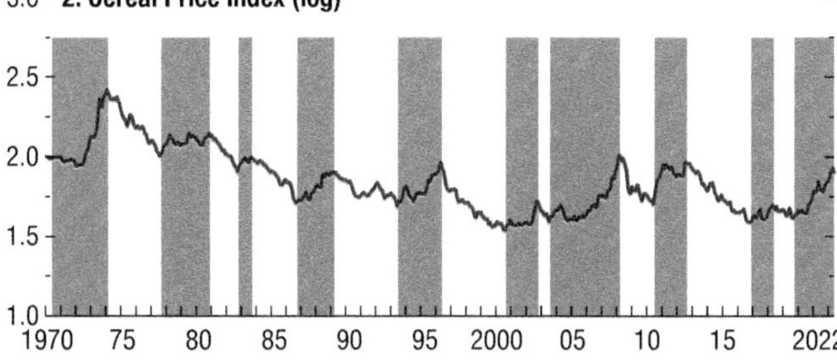

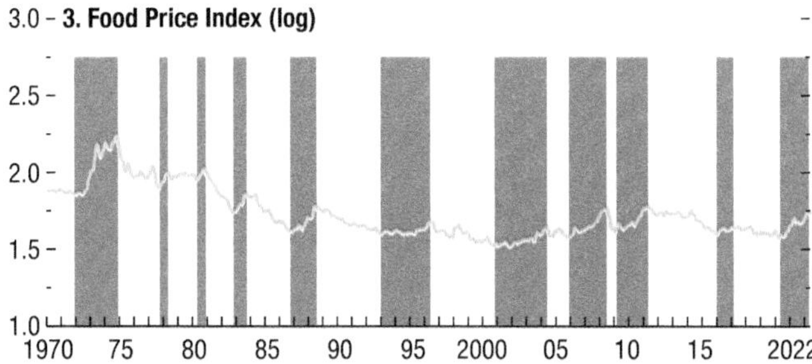

Sources: Haver Analytics; IMF, Consumer Price Index and Primary Commodity Price Series databases; World Bank; and IMF staff calculations.
Note: Shaded areas indicate periods of expansion. All series are deflated by the US consumer price index. Last observation is June 2022.

The price surge has contributed to domestic inflation, making monetary policy more difficult, especially in low-income countries, where food accounts for half of total consumption, and has raised concerns about food security and social unrest (Bellemare 2015; Bogmans, Pescatori, and Prifti 2021; FAO and others, 2021). Moreover, food-importing countries have seen deteriorations in their balance of payments and fiscal balances, which typically occur when social protection increases in response to higher food prices (Ng and Aksoy 2008). The following sections examine trends in cereal prices and their drivers, providing evidence on the pass-through from international food prices to domestic food price inflation. The analysis focuses on cereals (wheat, corn, rice, and a few smaller crops) that are common in diets and hard to substitute; together, these cereals account for two-thirds of global food production.

Table 1.SF.1. Oil, Cereal, and Food Price Boom Phases

		Duration	Amplitude	Sharpness
Oil	Latest	25	322%	12.9%
	Average	29	165%	5.8%
Cereal	Latest	32	107%	3.3%
	Average	32	78%	2.4%
Food	Latest	24	54%	2.3%
	Average	22	45%	2.1%

Sources: Haver Analytics; IMF, Primary Commodity Price System; World Bank; and IMF staff calculations.
Note: Boom phases are identified using the Harding and Pagan (2002) algorithm. Duration is in months. Sharpness is amplitude divided by duration per cycle.

Factors behind Food Price Movements

Food and energy prices have often moved in tandem, magnifying their macroeconomic effects. Food and oil prices have been in the same phase (boom or bust) about 66 percent of the time since 1970; this *concordance* increases to 75 percent for the period since 2004. There are at least three reasons behind the comovement: (1) oil is used *directly* as fuel for farm equipment and transportation, and gas affects farming *indirectly*, being the main input of nitrogen-based fertilizers and pesticides; (2) global economic activity is a common demand factor (even though it is more relevant for energy); and (3) some agricultural products are used as biofuels.

After the introduction of biofuel mandates in the European Union and US in the mid-2000s, the correlation between oil and cereal prices increased strongly (Table 1.SF.2). This was particularly true for corn, which was favored in biofuel policies relative to other cereals. The correlation also rose for vegetable oil. The higher correlation is not confined to commodities used as biofuels, in part because of price spillovers. A more prominent role of common shocks and the increased financialization of commodity markets in the mid-2000s may have also contributed. Finally, the US dollar value and interest rates are also common factors driving food commodity prices (Gilbert 2010; Baffes and Haniotis 2016).

Table 1.SF.2. Oil-Cereal Price Correlation

	1970–2004	2005–June 2022
Cereal	–0.9%	17.4%
Corn	–2.3%	23.1%
Vegetable oil	–4.6%	44.5%

Sources: World Bank; and IMF staff calculations.
Note: Five-year rolling correlations of monthly log differences of oil prices with cereal, corn, and vegetable oil prices. All prices are deflated by the US consumer price index.

Figure 1.SF.4. Response of Cereal Prices to Major Drivers
(Cumulative percent)

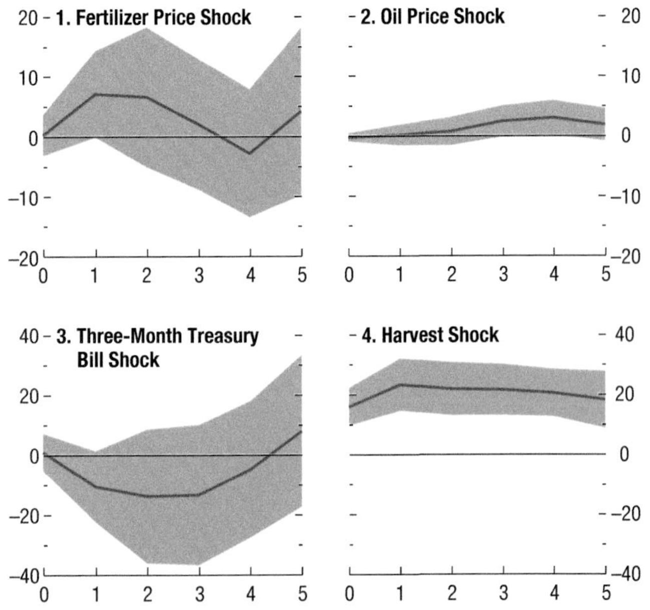

Sources: Haver Analytics; IMF, Consumer Price Index and Primary Commodity Price Series; World Bank; and IMF staff calculations.
Note: Quarters on the *x*-axis. Panels show cumulative impulse response of cereal prices to (panel 1) 10 percent fertilizer price shock; (panel 2) 10 percent oil price shock; (panel 3) 100 basis point shock to three-month Treasury bills; and (panel 4) one-standard-deviation harvest shock. Shaded areas are 90 percent confidence intervals. See Online Annex 1.SF.1 for data descriptions and methodology.

Figure 1.SF.5. Response of Food CPI to International Food Price Shock
(Percent)

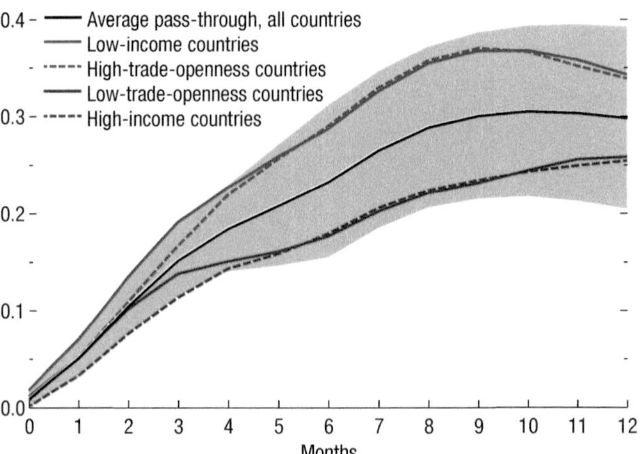

Sources: Haver Analytics; World Bank; and IMF staff calculations.
Note: Response of domestic food consumer price index (CPI) to a 1 percentage point shock to international food prices. Shaded areas are 90 percent confidence bands.

Econometric Analysis

Four drivers of cereal prices are studied here in detail: shocks to fertilizer and oil prices, cereal production, and US interest rates. Control variables include global GDP growth and the US dollar real effective exchange rate (see Online Annex 1.SF.1 for technical details).

Supply shocks dominate fluctuations in cereal prices. A typical (negative) global harvest shock induces a 16 percent rise in prices in the same quarter, with the increase peaking at 23 percent after one quarter (Figure 1.SF.4). Energy prices have a smaller effect especially those related to oil, acting with lags. A negative oil supply shock that raises oil prices by 10 percent leads cereal prices to rise by about 2 percent after three to four quarters (suggesting a modest effect from biofuels, since the cost share of oil in cereal production varies from about 10 to 15 percent). Prices of fertilizers, in contrast, have a delayed but important effect. A 10 percent rise in fertilizer prices (due to a natural gas supply shock) has no immediate effects but leads to a 7 percent rise in cereal prices after one quarter. Though persistent, the effect becomes less precisely estimated at longer horizons. Finally, a 100-basis point US monetary policy shock reduces cereal prices by about 13 percent with a one-quarter lag.

Domestic Food Price Inflation Rising Following Higher Global Food Prices

Taxes, subsidies, price controls, weak market integration, and local distribution costs often limit the transmission of international (producer) food price variations across borders to domestic retail food prices (Figure 1.SF.5). In fact, even though the recent rise in *domestic* food price inflation is broad-based, variation across regions is substantial, with recent inflation levels as low as 5.3 percent in south and east Asia and as high as 12.6 percent in central Asia and Europe.

It is therefore relevant to know the following: (1) What is the timing and the magnitude of the pass-through from international to domestic food prices? and (2) Do certain country characteristics, such as income level and trade openness, make countries more susceptible to such pass-through?

Pass-Through from Global Food Prices to Domestic Food Price Inflation

Panel data and local-projections methods are used here to trace the impact of food commodity prices (instrumented by harvest shocks) on domestic food price inflation. Several control variables are included, such as oil prices (to proxy for road transportation costs), the Baltic Dry Index (to proxy for shipping costs), headline consumer price inflation (to capture monetary factors), and exchange rates (in local currency units per dollar).

After an international food price shock, consumer food price inflation rises linearly and peaks after 10 months, then starts declining but persists at a higher level. In total, food consumer price inflation increases about 0.3 percentage point in response to a 1 percentage point change in international food prices after about 10–12 months (Figure 1.SF.5). The pass-through, which is limited by the cost share of food commodities in food consumer prices, is about 30 percent for the average country.

Some Countries Are More Vulnerable to Global Food Price Shocks

The pass-through is larger for emerging market economies than for advanced economies, in part because food commodities have a higher cost share in the former group. It is also larger for countries that score higher on trade openness, as greater cross-border arbitrage opportunities raise domestic prices' responsiveness to global food price shocks. This greater responsiveness holds for both net food importers and net food exporters and can explain why food exporters are tempted to introduce food export restrictions when commodity prices rise (Laborde Debucquet and Mamun 2022). For a one-standard-deviation rise in GDP per capita, the pass-through declines by 6 percentage points, while it increases by 7 percentage points for a one-standard-deviation rise in trade openness above the global mean (Figure 1.SF.5). High degrees of trade openness can thus explain the relatively high levels of average food price inflation in central Asia compared with those in countries in south and east Asia.

Conclusions and Outlook for Food Prices

International food prices are estimated to have added 5 percentage points to food price inflation for the average country in 2021 and are forecast to add an estimated 6 percentage points in 2022 and 2 percentage points in 2023 (Figure 1.SF.6). A combination of supply-side factors (the 2020–22 La Niña episode and food trade restrictions), cereal-specific demand (China's 2021 restocking), low interest rates, and more recently, the war in Ukraine and the Russian blockade of wheat exports from Ukraine created a perfect storm for global food commodity markets that kept prices on an upward trajectory between April 2020 and May 2022.

The outlook for domestic food price inflation remains uncertain, as global food prices could surprise

Figure 1.SF.6. Conditional Forecast Domestic Food Price Inflation
(Percent)

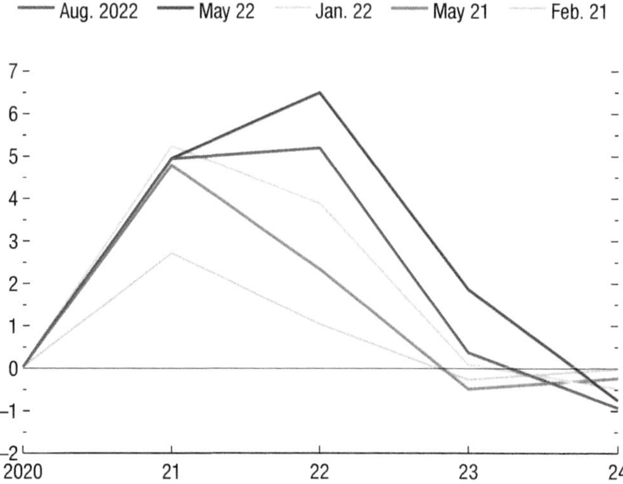

Sources: Bloomberg L.P.; and IMF staff estimates.
Note: Projected domestic food inflation based on recent commodity price forecasts on various dates.

again on the upside, given the high uncertainty about the impact of the war in Ukraine and weather events and the delayed effect of high fertilizer prices. Current estimates already suggest a negative shock for global cereal production equivalent to about a 0.6 standard deviation in cereal growth for 2022 (OECD-FAO, 2022)—contributing to a 23 percent rise in cereal prices this year and outweighing the effects of higher interest rates on food price inflation. Finally, differences in the timing and magnitude of the price pass-through make low-income and high-food-openness countries more susceptible to a resumption of the global food price rally.

Recent events underscore the importance of well-functioning international food markets and of appropriate (domestic) policies to address inevitable price swings, including targeted food aid to vulnerable consumers as well as incentives for the buildup of global food stocks over the medium term. Open food trade raises consumer variety, promotes deeper and more stable markets, and constitutes a hedge against the volatility of domestic production. Policies that promote self-sufficiency weaken the world food trading system and raise environmental costs through land conversion or more intensive farming practices. Especially for small countries (because of within-country spatial correlation of weather patterns), densely populated countries, and countries particularly vulnerable to climate change, international trade will remain indispensable.

Annex Table 1.1.1. European Economies: Real GDP, Consumer Prices, Current Account Balance, and Unemployment
(Annual percent change, unless noted otherwise)

	Real GDP			Consumer Prices[1]			Current Account Balance[2]			Unemployment[3]		
		Projections			Projections			Projections			Projections	
	2021	2022	2023	2021	2022	2023	2021	2022	2023	2021	2022	2023
Europe	**5.9**	**2.1**	**0.6**	**4.9**	**15.3**	**10.9**	**3.0**	**1.6**	**1.7**	. . .	. . .	. . .
Advanced Europe	**5.5**	**3.1**	**0.5**	**2.6**	**8.4**	**6.2**	**3.3**	**1.3**	**1.4**	**6.9**	**6.1**	**6.4**
Euro Area[4,5]	5.2	3.1	0.5	2.6	8.3	5.7	2.5	1.0	1.4	7.7	6.8	7.0
Germany	2.6	1.5	–0.3	3.2	8.5	7.2	7.4	4.2	5.3	3.6	2.9	3.4
France	6.8	2.5	0.7	2.1	5.8	4.6	0.4	–1.3	–1.5	7.9	7.5	7.6
Italy	6.7	3.2	–0.2	1.9	8.7	5.2	2.4	–0.2	0.3	9.5	8.8	9.4
Spain	5.1	4.3	1.2	3.1	8.8	4.9	0.9	–0.2	–0.2	14.8	12.7	12.3
The Netherlands	4.9	4.5	0.8	2.8	12.0	8.0	9.0	7.5	7.7	4.2	3.5	3.9
Belgium	6.2	2.4	0.4	3.2	9.5	4.9	–0.4	–2.2	–0.9	6.3	5.4	5.6
Ireland	13.6	9.0	4.0	2.4	8.4	6.5	14.2	12.2	9.8	6.3	4.7	4.8
Austria	4.6	4.7	1.0	2.8	7.7	5.1	–0.5	–2.6	–2.1	6.2	4.5	4.6
Portugal	4.9	6.2	0.7	0.9	7.9	4.7	–1.2	–1.1	–0.4	6.6	6.1	6.5
Greece	8.3	5.2	1.8	0.6	9.2	3.2	–6.5	–6.7	–6.3	15.0	12.6	12.2
Finland	3.0	2.1	0.5	2.1	6.5	3.5	0.9	–0.8	–0.2	7.6	7.0	7.4
Slovak Republic	3.0	1.8	1.5	2.8	11.9	10.1	–2.0	–3.7	–2.9	6.8	6.2	6.2
Lithuania	5.0	1.8	1.1	4.6	17.6	8.4	1.4	–1.6	–2.1	7.1	7.3	7.0
Slovenia	8.2	5.7	1.7	1.9	8.9	5.1	3.8	–0.1	0.4	4.8	4.3	4.3
Luxembourg	6.9	1.6	1.1	3.5	8.4	3.7	4.8	4.3	4.4	5.7	5.0	5.0
Latvia	4.5	2.5	1.6	3.2	16.5	8.0	–2.9	–3.3	–3.0	7.6	7.4	7.2
Estonia	8.0	1.0	1.8	4.5	21.0	9.5	–1.6	–0.2	0.1	6.2	6.6	6.8
Cyprus	5.6	3.5	2.5	2.2	8.0	3.8	–7.2	–8.5	–7.2	7.5	6.7	6.5
Malta	10.3	6.2	3.3	0.7	5.9	4.6	–4.9	–3.1	–2.2	3.5	3.2	3.3
United Kingdom[6]	7.4	3.6	0.3	2.6	9.1	9.0	–2.6	–4.8	–4.5	4.5	3.8	4.8
Switzerland	4.2	2.2	0.8	0.6	3.1	2.4	9.4	6.2	6.4	3.0	2.2	2.4
Sweden	5.1	2.6	–0.1	2.7	7.2	8.4	5.4	3.8	3.5	8.8	7.6	7.4
Czech Republic	3.5	1.9	1.5	3.8	16.3	8.6	–0.9	–4.3	–2.2	2.8	2.5	2.3
Norway	3.9	3.6	2.6	3.5	4.7	3.8	15.0	19.4	14.5	4.4	3.9	3.8
Denmark	4.9	2.6	0.6	1.9	7.2	3.8	8.8	8.2	7.4	5.1	5.2	5.3
Iceland	4.4	5.1	2.9	4.5	8.4	6.7	–1.6	–2.0	–0.3	6.0	4.0	4.0
Andorra	8.9	6.6	2.0	1.7	5.3	2.8	15.9	16.7	17.3	2.9	2.0	1.8
San Marino	5.4	3.1	0.8	2.1	6.9	4.5	4.0	1.4	0.8	6.1	5.9	5.7
Emerging and Developing Europe[7]	**6.8**	**0.0**	**0.6**	**9.5**	**27.8**	**19.4**	**1.7**	**2.9**	**2.8**	. . .	. . .	. . .
Russia	4.7	–3.4	–2.3	6.7	13.8	5.0	6.9	12.2	11.1	4.8	4.0	4.3
Türkiye	11.4	5.0	3.0	19.6	73.1	51.2	–1.7	–5.7	–3.9	12.0	10.8	10.5
Poland	5.9	3.8	0.5	5.1	13.8	14.3	–0.7	–4.0	–3.3	3.4	2.8	3.2
Romania	5.9	4.8	3.1	5.0	13.3	11.0	–7.0	–8.4	–8.0	5.6	5.5	5.5
Ukraine[6]	3.4	–35.0	. . .	9.4	20.6	. . .	–1.6	. . .	. . .	9.8	. . .	. . .
Hungary	7.1	5.7	1.8	5.1	13.9	13.3	–3.2	–6.7	–3.0	4.1	3.4	3.8
Belarus	2.3	–7.0	0.2	9.5	16.5	13.1	2.7	–1.5	–1.1	3.9	4.5	4.3
Bulgaria[5]	4.2	3.9	3.0	2.8	12.4	5.2	–0.4	–0.9	–1.4	5.3	5.1	4.7
Serbia	7.4	3.5	2.7	4.1	11.5	8.3	–4.4	–8.4	–7.0	10.1	9.9	9.7
Croatia	10.2	5.9	3.5	2.6	9.8	5.5	3.4	2.2	2.0	8.1	6.9	6.6

Source: IMF staff estimates.
Note: Data for some countries are based on fiscal years. Please refer to Table F in the Statistical Appendix for a list of economies with exceptional reporting periods.
[1]Movements in consumer prices are shown as annual averages. Year-end to year-end changes can be found in Tables A6 and A7 in the Statistical Appendix.
[2]Percent of GDP.
[3]Percent. National definitions of unemployment may differ.
[4]Current account position corrected for reporting discrepancies in intra-area transactions.
[5]Based on Eurostat's harmonized index of consumer prices, except in the case of Slovenia.
[6]See country-specific notes for Ukraine and the United Kingdom in the "Country Notes" section of the Statistical Appendix.
[7]Includes Albania, Bosnia and Herzegovina, Kosovo, Moldova, Montenegro, and North Macedonia.

Annex Table 1.1.2. Asian and Pacific Economies: Real GDP, Consumer Prices, Current Account Balance, and Unemployment
(Annual percent change, unless noted otherwise)

	Real GDP			Consumer Prices[1]			Current Account Balance[2]			Unemployment[3]		
		Projections			Projections			Projections			Projections	
	2021	2022	2023	2021	2022	2023	2021	2022	2023	2021	2022	2023
Asia	**6.5**	**4.0**	**4.3**	**2.0**	**4.0**	**3.4**	**2.2**	**1.4**	**1.3**	...	...	...
Advanced Asia	**3.7**	**2.2**	**2.3**	**1.2**	**3.6**	**2.6**	**4.9**	**3.5**	**3.5**	**3.4**	**2.9**	**2.9**
Japan	1.7	1.7	1.6	–0.2	2.0	1.4	2.9	1.4	2.2	2.8	2.6	2.4
Korea	4.1	2.6	2.0	2.5	5.5	3.8	4.9	3.2	3.5	3.7	3.0	3.4
Taiwan Province of China	6.6	3.3	2.8	2.0	3.1	2.2	14.8	14.8	12.7	4.0	3.6	3.6
Australia	4.9	3.8	1.9	2.8	6.5	4.8	3.1	2.1	0.7	5.1	3.6	3.7
Singapore	7.6	3.0	2.3	2.3	5.5	3.0	18.1	12.8	12.5	2.7	2.1	2.1
Hong Kong SAR	6.3	–0.8	3.9	1.6	1.9	2.4	11.3	8.6	5.9	5.2	4.5	4.0
New Zealand	5.6	2.3	1.9	3.9	6.3	3.9	–6.0	–7.7	–6.0	3.8	3.4	3.9
Macao SAR	18.0	–22.4	56.7	0.0	2.5	2.4	13.8	–2.4	22.8	3.0	3.0	2.7
Emerging and Developing Asia	**7.2**	**4.4**	**4.9**	**2.2**	**4.1**	**3.6**	**1.0**	**0.7**	**0.6**	...	...	...
China	8.1	3.2	4.4	0.9	2.2	2.2	1.8	1.8	1.5	4.0	4.2	4.1
India[4]	8.7	6.8	6.1	5.5	6.9	5.1	–1.2	–3.5	–2.9	...	...	...
ASEAN-5	**3.4**	**5.3**	**4.9**	**1.9**	**4.7**	**4.4**	**–0.3**	**0.5**	**0.8**	...	...	...
Indonesia	3.7	5.3	5.0	1.6	4.6	5.5	0.3	2.2	1.1	6.5	5.5	5.3
Thailand	1.5	2.8	3.7	1.2	6.3	2.8	–2.2	–0.5	1.9	1.5	1.0	1.0
Vietnam	2.6	7.0	6.2	1.8	3.8	3.9	–2.0	0.3	1.0	2.7	2.4	2.3
Philippines	5.7	6.5	5.0	3.9	5.3	4.3	–1.8	–4.4	–3.3	7.8	5.7	5.4
Malaysia	3.1	5.4	4.4	2.5	3.2	2.8	3.8	1.6	2.2	4.7	4.5	4.3
Other Emerging and Developing Asia[5]	**3.0**	**3.7**	**4.4**	**5.1**	**12.4**	**11.4**	**–2.9**	**–4.4**	**–3.4**	...	...	...
Memorandum												
Emerging Asia[6]	7.4	4.4	4.9	2.1	3.7	3.3	1.1	0.8	0.7	...	...	...

Source: IMF staff estimates.
Note: Data for some countries are based on fiscal years. Please refer to Table F in the Statistical Appendix for a list of economies with exceptional reporting periods.
[1]Movements in consumer prices are shown as annual averages. Year-end to year-end changes can be found in Tables A6 and A7 in the Statistical Appendix.
[2]Percent of GDP.
[3]Percent. National definitions of unemployment may differ.
[4]See the country-specific note for India in the "Country Notes" section of the Statistical Appendix.
[5]Other Emerging and Developing Asia comprises Bangladesh, Bhutan, Brunei Darussalam, Cambodia, Fiji, Kiribati, Lao P.D.R., Maldives, Marshall Islands, Micronesia, Mongolia, Myanmar, Nauru, Nepal, Palau, Papua New Guinea, Samoa, Solomon Islands, Sri Lanka, Timor-Leste, Tonga, Tuvalu, and Vanuatu.
[6]Emerging Asia comprises the ASEAN-5 economies, China, and India.

Annex Table 1.1.3. Western Hemisphere Economies: Real GDP, Consumer Prices, Current Account Balance, and Unemployment
(Annual percent change, unless noted otherwise)

	Real GDP			Consumer Prices[1]			Current Account Balance[2]			Unemployment[3]		
		Projections			Projections			Projections			Projections	
	2021	2022	2023	2021	2022	2023	2021	2022	2023	2021	2022	2023
North America	**5.5**	**1.8**	**1.0**	**4.7**	**7.9**	**3.8**	**–3.2**	**–3.5**	**–2.8**	**. . .**	**. . .**	**. . .**
United States	5.7	1.6	1.0	4.7	8.1	3.5	–3.7	–3.9	–3.1	5.4	3.7	4.6
Mexico	4.8	2.1	1.2	5.7	8.0	6.3	–0.4	–1.2	–1.2	4.1	3.4	3.7
Canada	4.5	3.3	1.5	3.4	6.9	4.2	0.0	0.5	–0.2	7.4	5.3	5.9
Puerto Rico[4]	2.7	4.8	0.4	2.4	4.4	3.5	. . .	. . .	. . .	7.9	6.0	7.9
South America[5]	**7.3**	**3.6**	**1.6**	**12.1**	**17.4**	**14.3**	**–2.0**	**–1.9**	**–1.5**	**. . .**	**. . .**	**. . .**
Brazil	4.6	2.8	1.0	8.3	9.4	4.7	–1.7	–1.5	–1.6	13.2	9.8	9.5
Argentina	10.4	4.0	2.0	48.4	72.4	76.1	1.4	–0.3	0.6	8.7	6.9	6.9
Colombia	10.7	7.6	2.2	3.5	9.7	7.1	–5.7	–5.1	–4.4	13.8	11.3	11.1
Chile	11.7	2.0	–1.0	4.5	11.6	8.7	–6.7	–6.7	–4.4	8.9	7.9	8.3
Peru	13.6	2.7	2.6	4.0	7.5	4.4	–2.5	–3.0	–2.1	10.9	7.6	7.5
Ecuador	4.2	2.9	2.7	0.1	3.2	2.4	2.9	2.4	2.1	4.2	4.0	3.8
Venezuela	0.5	6.0	6.5	1,588.5	210.0	195.0	–2.1	4.0	6.0	. . .	. . .	. . .
Bolivia	6.1	3.8	3.2	0.7	3.2	3.6	2.0	–1.4	–2.1	7.0	4.5	4.0
Paraguay	4.2	0.2	4.3	4.8	9.5	4.5	0.8	–3.8	–0.1	7.7	7.2	6.4
Uruguay	4.4	5.3	3.6	7.7	9.1	7.8	–1.8	–1.2	–1.9	9.4	7.9	7.9
Central America[6]	**11.0**	**4.7**	**3.6**	**4.5**	**7.4**	**5.4**	**–1.9**	**–3.2**	**–2.5**	**. . .**	**. . .**	**. . .**
Caribbean[7]	**5.1**	**12.4**	**7.3**	**8.4**	**12.3**	**9.6**	**–3.5**	**4.8**	**4.2**	**. . .**	**. . .**	**. . .**
Memorandum												
Latin America and the Caribbean[8]	6.9	3.5	1.7	9.8	14.1	11.4	–1.6	–1.7	–1.4	. . .	. . .	. . .
Eastern Caribbean Currency Union[9]	5.2	7.2	5.4	1.6	5.9	3.6	–16.9	–16.7	–13.2	. . .	. . .	. . .

Source: IMF staff estimates.

Note: Data for some countries are based on fiscal years. Please refer to Table F in the Statistical Appendix for a list of economies with exceptional reporting periods.

[1]Movements in consumer prices are shown as annual averages. Year-end to year-end changes can be found in Tables A6 and A7 in the Statistical Appendix. Aggregates exclude Venezuela.

[2]Percent of GDP.

[3]Percent. National definitions of unemployment may differ.

[4]Puerto Rico is a territory of the United States, but its statistical data are maintained on a separate and independent basis.

[5]See the country-specific notes for Argentina and Venezuela in the "Country Notes" section of the Statistical Appendix.

[6]Central America refers to CAPDR (Central America, Panama, Dominican Republic) and comprises Costa Rica, Dominican Republic, El Salvador, Guatemala, Honduras, Nicaragua, and Panama.

[7]The Caribbean comprises Antigua and Barbuda, Aruba, The Bahamas, Barbados, Belize, Dominica, Grenada, Guyana, Haiti, Jamaica, St. Kitts and Nevis, St. Lucia, St. Vincent and the Grenadines, Suriname, and Trinidad and Tobago.

[8]Latin America and the Caribbean comprises Mexico and economies from the Caribbean, Central America, and South America. See the country-specific notes for Argentina and Venezuela in the "Country Notes" section of the Statistical Appendix.

[9]Eastern Caribbean Currency Union comprises Antigua and Barbuda, Dominica, Grenada, St. Kitts and Nevis, St. Lucia, and St. Vincent and the Grenadines as well as Anguilla and Montserrat, which are not IMF members.

Annex Table 1.1.4. Middle East and Central Asia Economies: Real GDP, Consumer Prices, Current Account Balance, and Unemployment
(Annual percent change, unless noted otherwise)

	Real GDP			Consumer Prices[1]			Current Account Balance[2]			Unemployment[3]		
		Projections			Projections			Projections			Projections	
	2021	2022	2023	2021	2022	2023	2021	2022	2023	2021	2022	2023
Middle East and Central Asia	**4.5**	**5.0**	**3.6**	**12.9**	**13.8**	**13.1**	**2.3**	**6.5**	**5.2**	...	...	...
Oil Exporters[4]	**4.5**	**4.9**	**3.5**	**11.3**	**12.8**	**11.4**	**4.2**	**9.5**	**7.7**	...	...	...
Saudi Arabia	3.2	7.6	3.7	3.1	2.7	2.2	5.3	16.0	12.3	6.7	...	...
Iran	4.7	3.0	2.0	40.1	40.0	40.0	0.7	1.6	1.5	9.2	9.4	9.6
United Arab Emirates	3.8	5.1	4.2	0.2	5.2	3.6	11.4	14.7	12.5	...	...	...
Kazakhstan	4.1	2.5	4.4	8.0	14.0	11.3	–2.9	3.0	1.8	4.9	4.9	4.8
Algeria	3.5	4.7	2.6	7.2	9.7	8.7	–2.8	6.2	0.6	...	...	...
Iraq	7.7	9.3	4.0	6.0	6.5	4.5	7.8	16.3	13.0	...	...	...
Qatar	1.6	3.4	2.4	2.3	4.5	3.3	14.7	21.2	22.1	...	...	...
Kuwait	1.3	8.7	2.6	3.4	4.3	2.4	16.3	29.1	23.0	1.3	...	...
Azerbaijan	5.6	3.7	2.5	6.7	12.2	10.8	15.2	31.7	31.4	6.0	5.9	5.8
Oman	3.0	4.4	4.1	1.5	3.1	1.9	–6.1	6.2	3.6	...	...	...
Turkmenistan	4.6	1.2	2.3	15.0	17.5	10.5	0.6	2.5	2.5	...	...	...
Oil Importers[5,6]	**4.6**	**5.1**	**3.7**	**15.5**	**15.2**	**15.7**	**–3.9**	**–4.8**	**–4.2**	...	...	...
Egypt	3.3	6.6	4.4	4.5	8.5	12.0	–4.4	–3.6	–3.4	7.3	7.3	7.3
Pakistan[7]	5.7	6.0	3.5	8.9	12.1	19.9	–0.8	–4.6	–2.5	6.3	6.2	6.4
Morocco	7.9	0.8	3.1	1.4	6.2	4.1	–2.3	–4.3	–4.1	11.9	11.1	10.7
Uzbekistan	7.4	5.2	4.7	10.8	11.2	10.8	–7.0	–3.3	–4.2	9.5	10.0	9.5
Sudan	0.5	–0.3	2.6	359.1	154.9	76.9	–7.4	–6.4	–7.5	28.3	30.6	30.6
Tunisia	3.3	2.2	1.6	5.7	8.1	8.5	–6.1	–9.1	–8.0	16.2	...	...
Jordan	2.2	2.4	2.7	1.3	3.8	3.0	–8.8	–6.7	–4.8	24.4	...	...
Georgia	10.4	9.0	4.0	9.6	11.6	6.0	–10.1	–7.2	–6.8	20.6	18.7	19.5
Armenia	5.7	7.0	3.5	7.2	8.5	7.0	–3.7	–5.5	–5.1	15.3	15.2	15.1
Tajikistan	9.2	5.5	4.0	9.0	8.3	8.1	8.4	3.8	0.0	...	...	...
Kyrgyz Republic	3.7	3.8	3.2	11.9	13.5	12.4	–8.7	–12.5	–9.6	9.0	9.0	9.0
West Bank and Gaza	7.1	4.0	3.5	1.2	4.9	3.4	–8.2	–10.7	–8.9	26.4	25.7	25.0
Mauritania	2.4	4.0	4.8	3.8	7.1	7.8	–9.4	–11.6	–9.1	...	...	...
Memorandum												
Caucasus and Central Asia	5.6	3.8	4.0	9.2	12.9	10.5	–1.0	4.8	3.8	...	...	...
Middle East, North Africa, Afghanistan, and Pakistan[6]	4.3	5.1	3.6	13.4	13.9	13.4	2.6	6.6	5.3	...	...	...
Middle East and North Africa	4.1	5.0	3.6	14.2	14.2	12.4	2.9	7.4	5.9	...	...	...
Israel[8]	8.6	6.1	3.0	1.5	4.5	3.6	4.2	2.5	3.7	5.0	3.9	3.8
Maghreb[9]	7.8	0.9	4.4	4.7	8.0	6.8	–1.1	1.6	0.2	...	...	...
Mashreq[10]	2.7	5.9	4.2	8.3	11.6	12.1	–5.4	–4.5	–4.2	...	...	...

Source: IMF staff estimates.
Note: Data for some countries are based on fiscal years. Please refer to Table F in the Statistical Appendix for a list of economies with exceptional reporting periods.
[1]Movements in consumer prices are shown as annual averages. Year-end to year-end changes can be found in Tables A6 and A7 in the Statistical Appendix.
[2]Percent of GDP.
[3]Percent. National definitions of unemployment may differ.
[4]Includes Bahrain, Libya, and Yemen.
[5]Includes Djibouti, Lebanon, and Somalia. See the country-specific note for Lebanon in the "Country Notes" section of the Statistical Appendix.
[6]Excludes Afghanistan and Syria because of the uncertain political situation. See the country-specific notes in the "Country Notes" section of the Statistical Appendix.
[7]See the country-specific note for Pakistan in the "Country Notes" section of the Statistical Appendix.
[8]Israel, which is not a member of the economic region, is shown for reasons of geography but is not included in the regional aggregates.
[9]The Maghreb comprises Algeria, Libya, Mauritania, Morocco, and Tunisia.
[10]The Mashreq comprises Egypt, Jordan, Lebanon, and West Bank and Gaza. Syria is excluded because of the uncertain political situation.

Annex Table 1.1.5. Sub-Saharan African Economies: Real GDP, Consumer Prices, Current Account Balance, and Unemployment
(Annual percent change, unless noted otherwise)

	Real GDP			Consumer Prices[1]			Current Account Balance[2]			Unemployment[3]		
		Projections			Projections			Projections			Projections	
	2021	2022	2023	2021	2022	2023	2021	2022	2023	2021	2022	2023
Sub-Saharan Africa	**4.7**	**3.6**	**3.7**	**11.1**	**14.4**	**11.9**	**–1.1**	**–1.7**	**–2.5**	**...**	**...**	**...**
Oil Exporters[4]	**2.9**	**3.2**	**3.0**	**17.0**	**18.2**	**15.5**	**1.0**	**2.3**	**0.5**	**...**	**...**	**...**
Nigeria	3.6	3.2	3.0	17.0	18.9	17.3	–0.4	–0.2	–0.6	...	...	...
Angola	0.8	2.9	3.4	25.8	21.7	11.8	11.2	11.3	5.4	...	...	...
Gabon	1.5	2.7	3.7	1.1	3.5	3.2	–5.7	–1.4	–2.9	...	...	...
Chad	–1.1	3.3	3.4	–0.8	4.9	3.1	–4.5	0.8	–2.4	...	...	...
Equatorial Guinea	–3.2	5.8	–3.1	–0.1	5.1	5.7	–3.4	–1.6	–2.1	...	...	...
Middle-Income Countries[5]	**5.3**	**3.1**	**2.8**	**5.6**	**9.2**	**6.8**	**0.5**	**–1.5**	**–2.5**	**...**	**...**	**...**
South Africa	4.9	2.1	1.1	4.6	6.7	5.1	3.7	1.2	–1.0	34.3	34.6	35.6
Ghana	5.4	3.6	2.8	10.0	27.2	20.9	–3.2	–5.2	–4.4	...	...	...
Côte d'Ivoire	7.0	5.5	6.5	4.2	5.5	4.0	–3.8	–5.2	–5.0	...	...	...
Cameroon	3.6	3.8	4.6	2.3	4.6	2.8	–4.0	–2.3	–2.8	...	...	...
Zambia	4.6	2.9	4.0	22.0	12.5	9.5	7.6	–1.8	–3.7	...	...	...
Senegal	6.1	4.7	8.1	2.2	7.5	3.1	–13.2	–13.0	–9.5	...	...	...
Low-Income Countries[6]	**5.9**	**4.5**	**5.3**	**11.2**	**16.4**	**13.7**	**–5.0**	**–6.4**	**–6.2**	**...**	**...**	**...**
Ethiopia	6.3	3.8	5.3	26.8	33.6	28.6	–3.2	–4.3	–4.4	...	...	...
Kenya	7.5	5.3	5.1	6.1	7.4	6.6	–5.2	–5.9	–5.6	...	...	...
Tanzania	4.9	4.5	5.2	3.7	4.0	5.3	–3.3	–4.4	–3.9	...	...	...
Uganda	6.7	4.4	5.9	2.2	6.4	6.4	–8.3	–8.0	–10.2	...	...	...
Democratic Republic of the Congo	6.2	6.1	6.7	9.0	8.4	9.8	–0.9	0.0	0.0	...	...	...
Burkina Faso	6.9	3.6	4.8	3.9	14.2	1.5	0.2	–3.5	–3.4	...	...	...
Mali	3.1	2.5	5.3	3.8	8.0	3.0	–10.0	–7.9	–7.1	...	...	...

Source: IMF staff estimates.
Note: Data for some countries are based on fiscal years. Please refer to Table F in the Statistical Appendix for a list of economies with exceptional reporting periods.
[1]Movements in consumer prices are shown as annual averages. Year-end to year-end changes can be found in Table A6 and A7 in the Statistical Appendix.
[2]Percent of GDP.
[3]Percent. National definitions of unemployment may differ.
[4]Includes Republic of Congo and South Sudan.
[5]Includes Botswana, Cabo Verde, Eswatini, Lesotho, Mauritius, Namibia, and Seychelles.
[6]Includes Benin, Burundi, Central African Republic, Comoros, Eritrea, The Gambia, Guinea, Guinea-Bissau, Liberia, Madagascar, Malawi, Mozambique, Niger, Rwanda, São Tomé and Príncipe, Sierra Leone, Togo, and Zimbabwe.

Annex Table 1.1.6. Summary of World Real per Capita Output
(Annual percent change; in constant 2017 international dollars at purchasing power parity)

	Average 2004–13	2014	2015	2016	2017	2018	2019	2020	2021	Projections 2022	Projections 2023
World	**2.5**	**2.1**	**2.1**	**1.9**	**2.5**	**2.4**	**1.7**	**–4.1**	**5.4**	**2.4**	**1.6**
Advanced Economies	**1.0**	**1.5**	**1.7**	**1.3**	**2.0**	**1.8**	**1.3**	**–4.9**	**5.1**	**2.2**	**0.9**
United States	0.9	1.6	2.0	0.9	1.6	2.4	1.8	–4.2	5.4	1.4	0.7
Euro Area[1]	0.5	1.2	1.7	1.6	2.4	1.6	1.3	–6.5	5.2	2.9	0.3
Germany	1.4	1.8	0.6	1.4	2.3	0.7	0.8	–3.8	2.6	1.4	–0.4
France	0.6	0.4	0.6	0.7	2.2	1.5	1.5	–8.2	6.5	2.2	0.4
Italy	–0.9	–0.1	0.9	1.5	1.8	1.1	0.7	–8.8	7.4	3.2	–0.1
Spain	–0.4	1.7	3.9	2.9	2.8	1.9	1.3	–11.3	5.0	3.9	0.8
Japan	0.7	0.5	1.7	0.8	1.8	0.8	–0.1	–4.3	1.9	2.0	2.1
United Kingdom[2]	0.5	2.2	1.8	1.4	1.5	1.0	1.1	–9.7	7.0	3.2	–0.1
Canada	0.9	1.8	–0.1	0.0	1.8	1.4	0.4	–6.4	3.9	1.9	0.0
Other Advanced Economies[3]	2.6	2.2	1.5	1.8	2.5	2.1	1.2	–2.3	5.4	2.4	1.8
Emerging Market and Developing Economies	**4.7**	**3.2**	**2.8**	**2.9**	**3.3**	**3.3**	**2.3**	**–3.2**	**5.9**	**2.7**	**2.6**
Emerging and Developing Asia	7.3	5.8	5.9	5.8	5.7	5.6	4.4	–1.5	6.5	3.7	4.3
China	9.7	6.7	6.5	6.2	6.4	6.3	5.6	2.1	8.0	3.2	4.5
India[2]	6.2	6.2	6.8	7.1	5.7	5.4	2.7	–7.5	7.6	5.8	5.1
ASEAN-5[4]	4.0	3.4	3.7	3.9	4.3	4.3	3.7	–4.5	2.5	4.3	3.9
Emerging and Developing Europe	4.1	1.5	0.5	1.6	3.9	3.3	2.3	–1.6	6.8	7.3	0.3
Russia	4.2	–1.1	–2.2	0.0	1.8	2.9	2.2	–2.3	5.2	–3.3	–2.2
Latin America and the Caribbean	2.7	0.1	–0.8	–1.9	0.3	0.2	–1.1	–8.2	6.0	2.6	0.9
Brazil	3.0	–0.4	–4.4	–4.1	0.5	1.0	0.4	–4.6	4.2	2.2	0.4
Mexico	0.8	1.6	2.1	1.5	1.0	1.1	–1.2	–8.9	3.8	1.2	0.3
Middle East and Central Asia	2.3	1.1	0.7	2.0	0.0	0.5	–0.3	–4.7	6.0	3.0	1.8
Saudi Arabia	1.3	2.5	1.7	–0.6	–3.3	0.1	–2.0	–6.3	1.9	5.5	1.6
Sub-Saharan Africa	2.7	2.3	0.5	–1.2	0.2	0.7	0.5	–4.3	2.0	1.0	1.1
Nigeria	4.5	3.5	0.0	–4.2	–1.8	–0.7	–0.4	–4.3	1.1	0.6	0.5
South Africa	1.9	–0.1	–0.2	–0.8	–0.3	0.0	–1.1	–7.7	4.0	0.6	–0.4
Memorandum											
European Union	0.9	1.5	2.1	1.9	2.8	2.0	1.8	–5.8	5.4	3.0	0.5
Middle East and North Africa	1.8	0.7	0.5	2.3	–0.7	0.0	–0.9	–5.1	2.4	3.0	1.8
Emerging Market and Middle-Income Economies	5.0	3.3	3.0	3.2	3.6	3.6	2.5	–3.2	6.1	3.1	2.9
Low-Income Developing Countries	3.6	3.8	2.3	1.5	2.5	2.7	2.6	–1.2	2.5	2.5	2.6

Source: IMF staff estimates.
Note: Data for some countries are based on fiscal years. Please refer to Table F in the Statistical Appendix for a list of economies with exceptional reporting periods.
[1]Data calculated as the sum of data for individual euro area countries.
[2]See the country-specific note for India in the "Country Notes" section of the Statistical Appendix.
[3]Excludes the Group of Seven (Canada, France, Germany, Italy, Japan, United Kingdom, United States) and euro area countries.
[4]ASEAN-5 comprises Indonesia, Malaysia, Philippines, Thailand, and Vietnam.

References

Adler, Gustavo, Romain Duval, Davide Furceri, Sinem Kılıç Çelik, Ksenia Koloskova, and Marcos Poplawski Ribeiro. 2017. "Gone with the Headwinds: Global Productivity." IMF Staff Discussion Note 17/04, International Monetary Fund, Washington, DC.

Adrian, Tobias, Christopher Erceg, and Fabio Natalucci. 2022. "Soaring Inflation Puts Central Banks on a Difficult Journey." *IMF Blog*, August 1, 2022.

Akcigit, Ufuk, Wenjie Chen, Federico J. Díez, Romain Duval, Philipp Engler, Jiayue Fan, Chiara Maggi, and others. 2021. "Rising Corporate Market Power: Emerging Policy Issues." IMF Staff Discussion Note 21/01, International Monetary Fund, Washington, DC.

Albrizio, Silvia, John Bluedorn, Christoffer Koch, Andrea Pescatori, and Martin Stuermer. 2022. "Market Size and Supply Disruptions: Sharing the Pain from a Potential Russian Gas Shut-Off to the European Union." IMF Working Paper 22/143, International Monetary Fund, Washington, DC.

Andrle, Michal, Patrick Blagrave, Pedro Espaillat, Keiko Honjo, Benjamin Hunt, Mika Kortelainen, René Lalonde, and others. 2015. "The Flexible System of Global Models—FSGM." IMF Working Paper 15/64, International Monetary Fund, Washington, DC.

Andrle, Michael, and Benjamin Hunt. 2020. "Model-Based Globally-Consistent Risk Assessment." IMF Working Paper 20/064, International Monetary Fund, Washington, DC.

Baffes, John, and Tassos Haniotis. 2016. "What Explains Agricultural Price Movements?" *Journal of Agricultural Economics* 67 (3): 706–21.

Ball, Laurence, 2009. "Hysteresis in Unemployment: Old and New Evidence." NBER Working Paper 14818, National Bureau of Economic Research, Cambridge, MA.

Ball, Laurence, 2014. "Long-Term Damage from the Great Recession in OECD Countries." NBER Working Paper No. 20185, National Bureau of Economic Research, Cambridge, MA.

Ball, Laurence M., Daniel Leigh, and Prachi Mishra. Forthcoming. "Understanding U.S. Inflation during the COVID-19 Era." IMF Working Paper, International Monetary Fund, Washington, DC.

Barrett, Philip, Sonali Das, Giacomo Magistretti, Evgenia Pugacheva, and Philippe Wingender. 2021. "After-Effects of the COVID-19 Pandemic: Prospects for Medium-Term Economic Damage." IMF Working Paper 21/203, International Monetary Fund, Washington, DC.

Baumeister, Christiane, and Lutz Kilian. 2014. "Do Oil Price Increases Cause Higher Food Prices?" *Economic Policy* 29 (80): 691–747.

Belke, Ansgar, Ingo G. Bordon, and Ulrich Volz. 2013. "Effects of Global Liquidity on Commodity and Food Prices." *World Development* 44: 31–43.

Bellemare, Marc F. 2015. "Rising Food Prices, Food Price Volatility, and Social Unrest." *American Journal of Agricultural Economics* 97 (1): 1–21. https://doi.org/10.1093/ajae/aau038.

Blanchard, Olivier, Eugenio Cerutti, and Lawrence Summers. 2015. "Inflation and Activity—Two Explorations and Their Monetary Policy Implications." NBER Working Paper 21726, National Bureau of Economic Research, Cambridge, MA.

Bogmans, Christian, Andrea Pescatori, and Ervin Prifti. 2021. "Income versus Prices: How Does the Business Cycle Affect Food (In)-Security?" IMF Working Paper 21/238, International Monetary Fund, Washington, DC.

Bukeviciute, Lina, Adriaan Dierx, and Fabienne Ilzkovitz. 2009. "The Functioning of the Food Supply Chain and Its Effect on Food Prices in the European Union." Occasional Papers 47, Office for Infrastructures and Logistics of the European Communities, European Commission, Brussels.

Cloyne, James, and Patrick Hürtgen. 2016. "The Macroeconomic Effects of Monetary Policy: A New Measure for the United Kingdom." *American Economic Journal: Macroeconomics* 8 (4): 75–102.

Coibion, Olivier. 2012. "Are the Effects of Monetary Policy Shocks Big or Small?" *American Economic Journal: Macroeconomics* 4 (2): 1–32.

De Loecker, Jan, Jan Eeckhout, and Gabriel Unger. 2020. "The Rise of Market Power and the Macroeconomic Implications." *Quarterly Journal of Economics* 135 (2): 561–644.

Di Bella, Gabriel, Mark Flanagan, Karim Foda, Svitlana Maslova, Alex Pienkowski, Martin Stuermer, and Frederik Toscani. 2022. "Natural Gas in Europe: The Potential Impact of Disruptions to Supply." IMF Working Paper 22/145, International Monetary Fund, Washington, DC.

Díez, Federico J., Daniel Leigh, and Suchanan Tambunlertchai. 2018. "Global Market Power and Its Macroeconomic Implications." IMF Working Paper 18/137, International Monetary Fund, Washington, DC.

Díez, Federico J., Jiayue Fan, and Carolina Villegas-Sánchez. 2021. "Global Declining Competition?" *Journal of International Economics* 132: 103492.

Dimova, Ralitza. 2015. "The Welfare Impact of Rising Food Prices." *IZA World of Labor* 2015: 135.

Duval, Romain, Yi Ji, Longji Li, Myrto Oikonomou, Carlo Pizzinelli, Ippei Shibata, Alessandra Sozzi, and Marina M. Tavares. 2022. "Labor Market Tightness in Advanced Economies." IMF Staff Discussion Note 2022/01, International Monetary Fund, Washington, DC.

Etienne, Xiaoli L., Scott H. Irwin, and Philip Garcia. 2014. "Bubbles in Food Commodity Markets: Four Decades of Evidence." *Journal of International Money and Finance* 42: 129–55. https://doi.org/10.1016/j.jimonfin.2013.08.008.

Food and Agriculture Organization (FAO), International Fund for Agricultural Development (IFAD), United Nations Children's Fund (UNICEF), World Food Programme (WFP), and World Health Organization (WHO). 2021. "The State of Food Security and Nutrition in the World 2021: Transforming Food Systems for Food Security, Improved Nutrition and Affordable Healthy Diets for All." Rome, FAO.

Ferrucci, Gianluigi, Rebeca Jiménez-Rodríguez, and Luca Onorante. 2012. "Food Price Pass-Through in the Euro Area: Non-Linearities and the Role of the Common Agricultural Policy." *International Journal of Central Banking* 8 (1): 179–217.

Flanagan, Mark, Alfred Kammer, Andrea Pescatori, and Martin Stuermer. "How a Russian Natural Gas Cutoff Could Weigh on Europe's Economies." *IMFBlogs*, July 19, 2022. https://blogs.imf.org/2022/07/19/how-a-russian-natural-gas-cutoff-could-weigh-on-europes-economies.

Furceri, Davide, Prakash Loungani, John Simon, and Susan M. Wachter. 2016. "Global Food Prices and Domestic Inflation: Some Cross-Country Evidence." *Oxford Economic Papers* 68 (3): 665–87. https://doi.org/10.1093/oep/gpw016.

Gilbert, Christopher L. 2010. "How to Understand High Food Prices." *Journal of Agricultural Economics* 61 (2): 398–425. https://doi.org/10.1111/j.1477-9552.2010.00248.x.

Giordani, Paolo E., Nadia Rocha, and Michele Ruta. 2016. "Food Prices and the Multiplier Effect of Trade Policy." *Journal of International Economics* 101: 102–22. https://doi.org/10.1016/j.jinteco.2016.04.001.

Gnutzmann, Hinnerk, and Piotr Spiewanowski. 2016. "Fertilizer Fuels Food Prices: Identification through the Oil-Gas Spread." Unpublished, Leibniz Universität Hannover and Polish Academy of Sciences. http://dx.doi.org/10.2139/ssrn.2808381.

Gopinath, Gita, Emine Boz, Camila Casas, Federico J. Díez, Pierre-Olivier Gourinchas, and Mikkel Plagborg-Møller. 2020. "Dominant Currency Paradigm." *American Economic Review* 110 (3): 677–719.

Harding, Don, and Adrian Pagan. 2002. "Dissecting the Cycle: A Methodological Investigation." *Journal of Monetary Economics* 49 (2): 365–81.

Harris, Donald J. 1970. "Income, Prices, and the Balance of Payments in Underdeveloped Economies: A Short-Run Model." *Oxford Economic Papers* 22 (2): 156–72. https://www.jstor.org/stable/2662255.

Holston, Kathryn, Thomas Laubach, and John C. Williams. 2017 "Measuring the Natural Rate of Interest: International Trends and Determinants." *Journal of International Economics* 108 (Supp. 1): S59–75. https://doi.org/10.1016/j.jinteco.2017.01.004.

Konczal, Mike, and Niko Lusiani. 2022. "Prices, Profits, and Power: An Analysis of 2021 Firm-Level Markups." Brief, Roosevelt Institute, New York. https://rooseveltinstitute.org/publications/prices-profits-and-power.

Laborde Debucquet, David, and Abdullah Mamun. 2022. "Documentation for Food and Fertilizers Export Restriction Tracker: Tracking Export Policy Responses Affecting Global Food Markets during Crisis." Food and Fertilizer Trade Policy Tracker Working Paper 2, International Food Policy Research Institute, Washington, DC.

Ng, Francis, and M. Ataman Aksoy. 2008. "Food Price Increases and Net Food Importing Countries: Lessons from the Recent Past." *Agricultural Economics* 39 (S1): 443–52.

Novta, Natalija, and Evgenia Pugacheva. 2021. "The Macroeconomic Costs of Conflict." *Journal of Macroeconomics* 68: 103286.

Novta, Natalija, and Evgenia Pugacheva. 2022. "Macroeconomic Costs of Conflict: Impact on GDP and Refugee Flows." *VoxEU*, July 29, 2022. https://cepr.org/voxeu/columns/macroeconomic-costs-conflict-impact-gdp-and-refugee-flows.

Osborn, T. J., Jones, P. D., Lister, D. H., Morice, C. P., Simpson, I. R., Winn, J. P., et al. (2021). Land surface air temperature variations across the globe updated to 2019: the CRUTEM5 dataset. *Journal of Geophysical Research: Atmospheres*, 126, e2019JD032352. https://doi.org/10.1029/2019JD032352.

Unsal, D. Filiz, Chris Papageorgiou, and Hendre Garbers. 2022. "Monetary Policy Frameworks: An Index and New Evidence." IMF Working Paper 22/22, International Monetary Fund, Washington, DC.

Yellen, Janet L. 2016. "Macroeconomic Research after the Crisis." Speech delivered at the 60th Annual Federal Reserve Bank of Boston Economic Conference, "The Elusive 'Great' Recovery: Causes and Implications for Future Business Cycle Dynamics." Boston, October 14.

CHAPTER

2 WAGE DYNAMICS POST–COVID-19 AND WAGE-PRICE SPIRAL RISKS

Inflation rose markedly in many economies during 2021, reflecting a mix of supply- and demand-side drivers amid recovery from the COVID-19 shock. Although nominal wage growth has so far generally stayed below inflation, some observers have warned that prices and wages could start feeding off each other, with wage and price inflation continually ratcheting up in a sustained wage-price spiral. This chapter unpacks events of the recent past and sheds light on future prospects using a mix of empirical and model-based analyses. Historical episodes in advanced economies exhibiting wage, price, and labor market dynamics similar to those of the current circumstances—in particular, economies in which real wages (nominal wages deflated by consumer prices) have been flat or falling—did not tend to show a subsequent wage-price spiral. Model-based analysis suggests that different shocks underpinned wage and price developments through 2020–21: production capacity shocks predominantly drove wages, while private saving and pent-up demand figured prominently for prices. Empirical analysis suggests that while labor market conditions remain relevant drivers of wage growth, the importance of inflation expectations has recently increased. A forward-looking analysis points to the critical role of the expectations process in shaping prospects. It demonstrates how front-loaded monetary policy tightening, including through its clear communication, can lower the risk that inflation will become de-anchored from its target. Given that inflationary shocks are originating outside the labor market, falling real wages are helping to slow inflation, and monetary policy is tightening more aggressively, the chances of persistent wage-price spirals emerging appear limited.

The authors of this chapter are Silvia Albrizio, Jorge Alvarez, Alexandre Balduino Sollaci, John Bluedorn (lead), Allan Dizioli, Niels-Jakob Hansen, and Philippe Wingender, with support from Youyou Huang and Evgenia Pugacheva. The chapter benefited from comments by Jason Furman and internal seminar participants and reviewers.

Introduction

With the recovery picking up steam after the acute COVID-19 shock, inflation in 2021 started hitting levels that had not been seen in almost 40 years in many economies.[1] A wide array of factors has underpinned the sharp rises in prices, including pandemic-related supply chain disruptions, commodity price shocks, expansive monetary policy and fiscal support, a surge in pent-up consumer demand, and changes in consumer preferences for goods versus services (Figure 2.1, panels 1 and 3).

At the same time, economic recovery brought a resurgence in demand for labor in many sectors. Labor supply was slow to respond, with some workers hesitant to reengage because of ongoing health concerns and difficulties finding child and family care, among other factors.[2] This demand–supply imbalance led to tighter labor markets and increased wage pressures, with average nominal wages (per worker) rising and the unemployment rate falling beginning in the second half of 2020 across economy groups (Figure 2.1, panels 2 and 5 for advanced economies and panels 4 and 7 for emerging market and developing economies).[3]

Growth in nominal wages mostly brought the average level in 2021 back to the pre-pandemic trend, although there were differences across economies. Importantly, nominal wage growth in 2021 did not

[1]Price inflation is defined with respect to the consumer price index throughout, unless indicated otherwise.

[2]See Bluedorn and others (2021) for a discussion of how the COVID-19 shock generated a "she-cession," reflecting in part the disproportionate impact of these factors on women's employment. See also ILO (2022) for a more recent assessment of the shock's effects on employment and participation and the differentials between men's and women's outcomes.

[3]To achieve the broadest sample coverage possible in the empirical analysis, wages (nominal or real) are defined on a per employed worker basis throughout, unless indicated otherwise. For a smaller sample, the chapter includes some discussion highlighting how hourly wages differ.

Figure 2.1. Recent Wage, Price, and Unemployment Dynamics
(Index, 2019:Q4 = 100, unless noted otherwise)

Consumer price inflation has accelerated markedly since the second quarter of 2020. While the nominal wage largely returned to its pre-pandemic trend, real wages have dipped below their pre-pandemic trend. Unemployment rates have continued to decrease as the economy recovers from the COVID-19 shock.

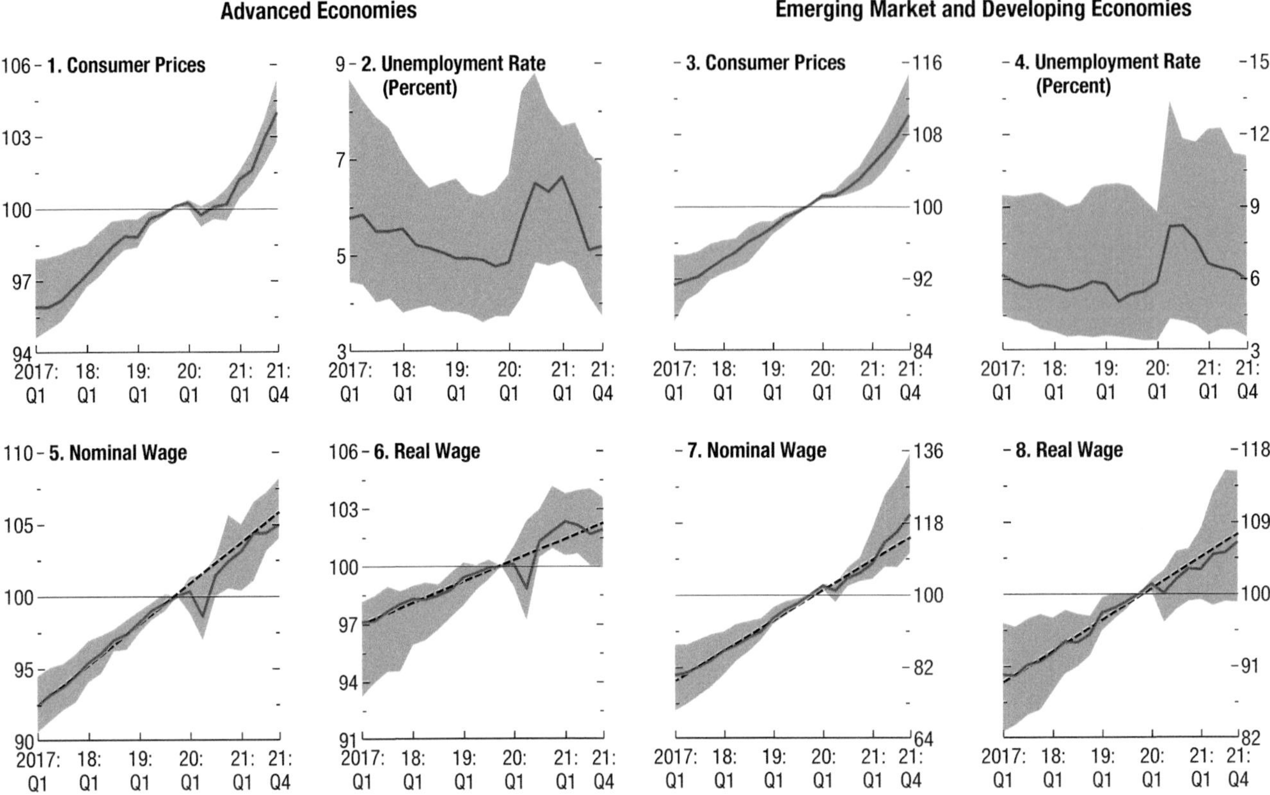

Sources: Haver Analytics; International Labour Organization; Organisation for Economic Co-operation and Development; US Bureau of Economic Analysis; and IMF staff calculations.
Note: Blue lines represent the median across economies; dashed lines indicate the pre–COVID-19 trend; shaded areas represent the interquartile range across economies. Wages (nominal and real) are calculated on a per worker basis. See Online Annex 2.1 for details on the sample coverage.

fully keep up with price inflation.[4] This means that the path of real wages (nominal wages deflated by consumer prices) was fairly flat or falling (Figure 2.1, panels 6 and 8). Against a backdrop of high or even rising price inflation, these nominal and real wage patterns have continued into the first quarter of 2022 for economies for which data are available.

At a sectoral level, nominal wages in both industry and services have tended to converge to their common pre-pandemic trends across economy groups (see Online Annex 2.2 for details on the sectoral perspective). In advanced economies, real wages across sectors largely matched their pre-pandemic trend, before deteriorating in the latter half of 2021 as inflation rose, while in emerging market and developing economies, they have stayed mostly below their pre-pandemic trend. Consistent with the picture of wages by sector, sectoral employment shifts so far have appeared to contribute little to overall wage changes for the average economy—common changes in wages across sectors themselves account for the lion's share of the average overall wage change.

Some observers argue that recent wage and price dynamics could change, so that rising inflation

[4]The distinction between wages per worker and wages per hour became relevant during the pandemic's acute phase, as hours worked were sharply adjusted for many workers (particularly in advanced economies). Annex Figure 2.1.1 shows the dynamics of wages per hour: spiking in the second quarter of 2020 on average across economy groups, but quickly returning to trend. Similarly to the patterns for wages per worker, wages per hour fell short of price inflation by the end of 2021.

expectations and tighter labor markets push workers to persistently demand wage increases to catch up to or exceed recent inflation. Such a "wage-price spiral" is defined here as an episode of several quarters characterized by accelerating wages and prices (that is, in which both wage and price inflation rates rise simultaneously).[5]

This chapter aims to better understand the current circumstances and prospects for wage and price inflation. To this end, crucial questions addressed include the following:

- **How do wage, employment, and price dynamics in the recovery from the COVID-19 shock compare with pre-pandemic dynamics?** Did historical episodes mirroring 2021 patterns in wages, employment, and prices in advanced economies subsequently evolve into wage-price spirals?
- **How well do inflation expectations and labor market conditions explain recent nominal wage growth in advanced and emerging market and developing economies?** What were the deeper, underlying drivers of wages, prices, and employment during 2020–21?
- **Could wage and price pressures in the wake of COVID-19 lead to high and persistent wage and price inflation?** Have wage and price pressures from past inflationary shocks due to increasing global supply pressures lasted long? Historically, has monetary tightening been effective in reducing wage and price pressures? Looking ahead, how could changes in the formation of wage and price expectations affect prospects, and how should policymakers take them into account?

Drawing both on empirical and model-based analyses, the chapter's main findings are as follows:

- *Both wage and price inflation picked up in a broad-based manner through 2021, while real wages have tended to be flat or falling across economies on average.* At a sectoral level, nominal wages in both industry and services tended to converge to their common pre-pandemic trends across economy groups. Consequently, sectoral employment shifts appear to explain little of overall wage changes through the end of 2021.
- *On average, wage-price spirals did not follow historical episodes that were similar to the circumstances currently seen in advanced economies.* Although the COVID-19 shock is unusual and the current conjuncture unlike much recent experience, similar historical episodes of inflation in advanced economies—in which real wages were flat or falling—did not tend to entail a wage-price spiral. In fact, inflation tended to fall in the aftermath while nominal wages gradually caught up.
- *Changes in inflation expectations and labor market slack explain wage dynamics in the second half of 2021 relatively well.* In the immediate aftermath of the COVID-19 shock, wage growth across economies was poorly explained by its earlier empirical relationship with expectations and unemployment. However, by the end of 2021, wage growth was broadly in line with the increases in inflation expectations and labor market tightening observed across economy groups on average.
- *Reflecting the pandemic shock's unusual nature, a complex mix of supply and demand shocks underpinned the 2020–21 behavior of wages and prices.* Analysis using a rich multi-sector, multi-economy structural model points to differences in the shocks underlying historical changes in wages and prices. Over the two years since the pandemic's onset, wages have been driven predominantly by production capacity and labor supply shocks (from social distancing and lockdowns), while prices have been more affected by private saving and the release of pent-up demand. How and when (or if) these deeper shocks unwind will matter for how wage and price inflation develop.
- *When wage and price expectations are more backward-looking, monetary policy actions need to be more front-loaded to minimize the risks of inflation de-anchoring.* Using a newly developed model of expectations and wage and price setting, scenario analysis suggests that the observed decline in real wages has acted as a drag so far, reducing price pressures and thereby helping inhibit development of a wage-price spiral dynamic. However, the more backward-looking (adaptive) expectations are, the greater the chances that inflation could de-anchor to a higher-than-target level. The monetary policy response in this inflationary environment should depend on the nature of wage and price expectations: the more backward-looking they are, the quicker and stronger the tightening needed to avert inflation de-anchoring and prevent large declines in the real wage.

Some important caveats to the analysis presented here should be stated up front. First, the empirical analysis is constrained by the availability of data, both across

[5]See Boissay and others (2022) for a similar definition and discussion on the debate about the possible emergence of wage-price spirals in advanced economies. Further discussion of the concept is in this chapter's section titled "Historical Episodes Similar to Today."

economies and over time. Hence, the exact sample coverage differs across exercises. Second, although the empirical methods used are standard, their findings should be interpreted as associational rather than causal. Third, the empirical analysis and study of historical episodes essentially summarize past patterns in the data, which may not be fully representative of the current circumstances. Moreover, if the COVID-19 shock caused a large structural break in the economy's behavior (such as a sharp shift in expectations formation or wage-setting processes), historical analyses may not be as informative about future prospects. The model-based analysis of expectations provides some insurance against structural breaks, since it allows for the possibility of a limited form of regime shifts in its examination of adaptive learning.

The chapter begins by identifying and examining historical episodes exhibiting wage, price, and employment patterns similar to those in the current circumstances, highlighting how the episodes subsequently developed. The chapter continues by studying how well recent wage dynamics can be explained by changes in inflation expectations and labor market slack and the composition of shocks driving these developments. In the penultimate section, the chapter highlights how inflationary shocks and monetary tightening affect wage (both nominal and real) dynamics. The final section considers how the processes for forming expectations regarding wages and prices may interact with the shock and monetary policy's responses to affect the economy's future path.

Historical Episodes Similar to Today

As explained in the introduction, rising inflation, positive nominal wage growth, declining real wages, and declining unemployment characterized the macroeconomic situation in 2021 in many economies. Although unusual, such conditions are not unprecedented. A sample of advanced economies covering the past 40 years (and for a few the past 60 years) reveals 22 other episodes exhibiting similar conditions.[6]

The current coincidence of rising inflation and nominal wage growth has led to concerns that a wage-price spiral—in which both wages and prices accelerate for a prolonged period—could emerge.[7] This section examines whether wage-price spirals have occurred in similar past episodes.

Similar Past Episodes Do Not Show a Wage-Price Spiral Taking Hold

Similar past episodes were not followed by a wage-price spiral, in which both inflation and nominal wage growth keep rising over a prolonged period (Figure 2.2, panels 1 and 3). Nominal wage growth did tend to increase somewhat after these episodes, but inflation edged down on average. In combination, this led to an increase in real wages (Figure 2.2, panel 4). The unemployment rate generally stabilized after the episodes (Figure 2.2, panel 2).

Although the average subsequent path suggests little cause for alarm, there is heterogeneity across historical episodes. A notable example is the United States in the second quarter of 1979, when inflation was on a sharp upward path immediately following the episode, rising rapidly for four quarters before starting to decline. The unemployment rate also rose more than during the other identified episodes. Underlying these changes was an aggressive monetary tightening that began around the time of the inflation peak: the so-called Volcker disinflation. Nominal wage growth—which had not shown signs of continuing its upward path—was relatively flat during this period, leading to a decline in real wages early on. But as inflation came down, the deterioration in real wages decreased.

A similar policy response is observed in many of the other episodes as well. In fact, monetary policy tightening followed most of the past episodes, which helped to keep inflation contained.[8] Thus, the evidence from similar historical episodes suggests that an appropriate

[6]The 22 episodes are identified within a sample of 30 advanced economies for which data on inflation, wages, prices, and unemployment are available at a quarterly frequency going back to 1960 at the earliest. For most economies in the sample, the quarterly data begin on a regular basis only in the 1980s. The selection criteria are that at least three out of the previous four quarters had (1) rising inflation, (2) positive nominal wage growth, (3) declining real wages, and (4) declining or flat unemployment. If the criteria hold for several quarters within three years, only the first episode in which the criteria held is selected. See Online Annex 2.3 and Alvarez and others (forthcoming) for further details and discussion about these episodes.

[7]The earlier literature on wage-price spirals has considered a wide array of definitions, ranging from a simple feedback between wages (as a cost of production) and prices, to a coincident acceleration of wages and prices, to a situation in which wage inflation persistently exceeds price inflation. As noted in the introduction, this chapter defines a wage-price spiral as an episode of several quarters characterized by accelerating wages and prices (that is, in which wage and price inflation are rising simultaneously).

[8]Out of the 22 episodes illustrated in Figure 2.2, 13 were followed by monetary policy tightening (Annex Table 2.3.2).

Figure 2.2. Changes in Wages, Prices, and Unemployment after Similar Past Episodes

(Percentage point differences relative to first quarter in which criteria are fulfilled)

After past episodes with similar macroeconomic conditions to today's, consumer price inflation typically declined, while nominal and real wage growth increased.

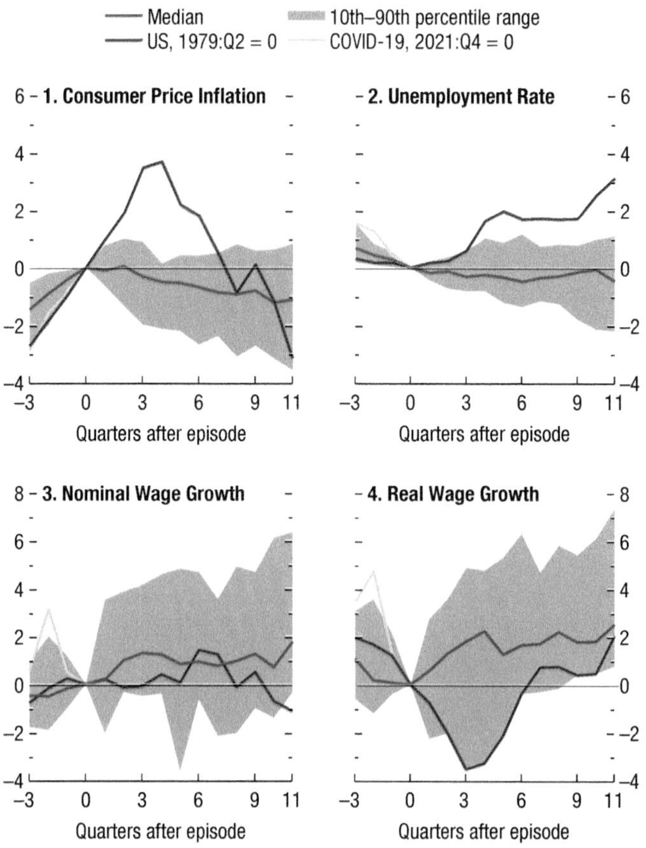

Sources: International Labour Organization; Organisation for Economic Co-operation and Development; US Bureau of Economic Analysis; and IMF staff calculations.

Note: The figure shows developments following episodes in which at least three of the preceding four quarters have (1) accelerating prices/rising price inflation, (2) positive nominal wage growth, (3) falling or constant real wages, and (4) a declining or flat unemployment rate. Twenty-two such episodes are identified within a sample of 30 advanced economies, the earliest going back to 1960. The COVID-19 episode represents an average of economies in the sample for the period starting in 2021:Q4. See Online Annex 2.3 for details.

monetary policy response can contain the risks of a subsequent wage-price spiral in the current circumstances to very low levels.

Wage-Price Spiral Episodes Did Not Typically Last Long

Turning to past episodes of wage-price spirals (regardless of the behavior of real wages or unemployment), further sustained wage-price acceleration did not typically follow the initial dynamics.[9] Following such episodes, inflation and nominal wage growth on average tended to stabilize in the subsequent quarters, leaving real wage growth broadly unchanged (Figure 2.3, blue lines). At the same time, the unemployment rate tended to edge down slightly.

However, in some rare examples, more extreme outcomes followed such episodes. For example, during the US episode starting in the third quarter of 1973, price inflation surged for five additional quarters—spurred by the first Organization of the Petroleum Exporting Countries oil embargo of the 1970s—before starting to come down in 1975 (Figure 2.3, red lines). On the other hand, nominal wage growth did not increase, leading real wage growth to decline. Another relevant example is that from Belgium during 1973, in which both nominal wage growth and price inflation surged markedly before coming down (see Online Annex 2.3). In that case, wage growth was high and exceeded price inflation for a while, partly owing to the wide prevalence of wage indexation.[10]

Farther back in time, another notable example occurred in 1946–48 in the United States, just after World War II concluded. Over those years, price controls due to the war were lifted and pent-up demand was released. As the economy shifted from wartime, price inflation and nominal wage growth picked up during 1946, both reaching about 20 percent year over year by the first quarter of 1947.[11] Thereafter, though, inflation and wage growth started to come down gradually while remaining at high levels for about a year. Toward the latter half of 1948 and into early 1949, inflation came down sharply, as supply chains had readjusted and pent-up

[9]A wage-price spiral episode is identified if, for at least three of the preceding four quarters, (1) wages were accelerating (wage growth was rising) and (2) prices were accelerating (price inflation was rising). Note that these are less restrictive criteria than those used to identify historical episodes similar to today's circumstances.

[10]See also Battistini and others (2022) and Baba and Lee (2022) for further discussion and analysis of the historical effects of oil price and energy shocks on price inflation and wages and the effects' relationship to an economy's structural characteristics.

[11]Wages are proxied by average hourly earnings in manufacturing, as an economy-wide wage measure is not available that far back in time.

Figure 2.3. Changes in Wages, Prices, and Unemployment after Past Episodes with Accelerating Prices and Wages
(Percentage point differences relative to first quarter in which criteria are fulfilled)

A period of stable wage growth and inflation typically followed past episodes with accelerating wages and prices.

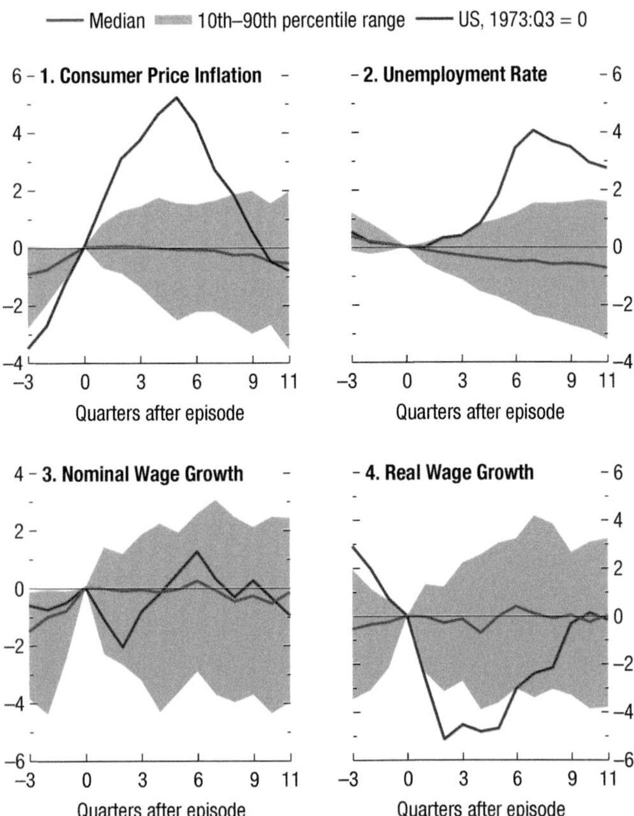

Sources: International Labour Organization; Organisation for Economic Co-operation and Development; US Bureau of Economic Analysis; and IMF staff calculations.
Note: The figure shows the developments following episodes in which at least three of the preceding four quarters have (1) accelerating prices/rising price inflation and (2) accelerating nominal wages/rising nominal wage growth. Seventy-nine such episodes are identified within a sample of 30 advanced economies, the earliest going back to 1960. The bands indicate the 10th–90th percentile of the outcomes in the identified episodes. See Online Annex 2.3 for details.

demand became exhausted (with a mild recession in 1949).[12]

Overall, the historical evidence suggests that episodes characterized by about a year of accelerating prices and wages have not generally lasted, with nominal wage growth and price inflation tending to stabilize on average. It is important to remark that this means that inflation and wage growth remained elevated for several quarters on average after these past episodes.[13]

Wage Drivers during the COVID-19 Shock and Recovery

This section studies wage, price, and employment drivers in the context of the pandemic and subsequent recovery. It first examines recent wage dynamics empirically through the lens of the wage Phillips curve, which relates wage growth to inflation expectations and labor market slack. The section then attempts to further unpack wage and price changes over the past two years, using a rich structural model to identify the complex mix of underlying supply and demand shocks driving wages and prices.

An Empirical Decomposition of Recent Dynamics Using the Wage Phillips Curve

Although the COVID-19 shock and recovery bear many unusual features, a recurring question is whether previous economic relationships can still explain recent dynamics. For wages, this means examining whether empirical estimates using the workhorse wage Phillips curve—relating wage growth to measures of inflation expectations, labor market slack, and productivity growth—do well at capturing the variation in wage developments.[14] The chapter first employs this framework to study the pre–COVID-19 wage-setting process. It then uses

[12]See Online Annex 2.3 for further details on this case. Rouse, Zhang, and Tedeschi (2021) also describe this and other past inflationary episodes in the United States with some features similar to those in today's recovery from the pandemic. Caplan (1956) provides a close-in-time and in-depth discussion of the situation in the late 1940s.

[13]The relevance of this finding hinges critically on the sample coverage. As in Figure 2.2, quarterly time coverage for the critical variables starts only in the 1980s or later for most economies. For robustness, the exercise was thus repeated using a narrower wage concept (hourly earnings for the manufacturing sector only) allowing for time coverage back to the early 1970s for more economies. This did not overturn the broad results shown in Figure 2.3, although a few additional extreme outcomes were identified. See Online Annex 2.3 for additional information.

[14]The specification used is based on Chapter 2 of the October 2017 *World Economic Outlook*, inspired by Galí's (2011) work micro-founding the wage Phillips curve as the outcome of a wage-setting process. The baseline specification using the unemployment rate and its change as measures of labor market slack permits wider coverage of advanced and emerging market economies in the sample. Given recent inflation dynamics, the relationship between wage growth and inflation expectations is a key focus of this chapter's study. Online Annex 2.4 includes details on the baseline specification.

the framework to decompose wage growth changes since the pandemic across economy groups, to see how well it performs.

Wage Growth Tends to Rise with Inflation Expectations and Fall with Labor Market Slack

Consistent with earlier empirical and theoretical literature, the analysis suggests that rises in inflation expectations[15] and productivity growth are associated with increases in nominal wage growth, while increases in labor market slack (captured by the unemployment rate and its change) are correlated with a slowdown in wage growth (Figure 2.4, panel 1). These relationships are statistically significant in both the advanced and emerging market economy groups.

The positive relationship with inflation expectations—a focus of the conjuncture—is consistent with a forward-looking wage-setting process in which workers demand higher wages as prices are expected to rise.[16] These nominal wage pressures add to those stemming from increases in the real returns on labor—as captured by productivity growth—and survive even if lagged inflation is controlled for. Wage growth appears to be highly sensitive to inflation expectations in advanced economies: a 1 percentage point increase in inflation expectations is associated with a close to 1 percentage point increase in wage growth (compared with 0.6 percentage point in emerging market economies). This relationship, however, weakened in the period after the global financial crisis, when inflation was remarkably low and stable.[17]

The negative relationship with unemployment is consistent with high (or widening) slack in the labor market, which reduces wage pressures as workers struggle to find jobs and accept lower wages. This last correlation is robust to using other measures of labor market slack, such as unemployment gaps, which allow for time-varying natural unemployment

[15]This section focuses on one-year-ahead inflation expectations. See Online Annex 2.1 for details on the measure used.

[16]Additional robustness checks, including lagged inflation as a regressor, are shown in Online Annex 2.4.

[17]See Online Annex 2.4 for a discussion of how coefficients have declined in advanced economies. Part of this observed flattening in the wage Phillips curve may reflect improvements in monetary policy credibility, as discussed by Hazell and others (2022) for the price Phillips curve.

Figure 2.4. A Look at Nominal Wage Growth through the Lens of the Wage Phillips Curve
(Percentage points)

Wage dynamics during COVID-19 did not follow the wage Phillips curve relationship closely, but more recent nominal wage growth is consistent with rising inflation expectations and labor market tightening.

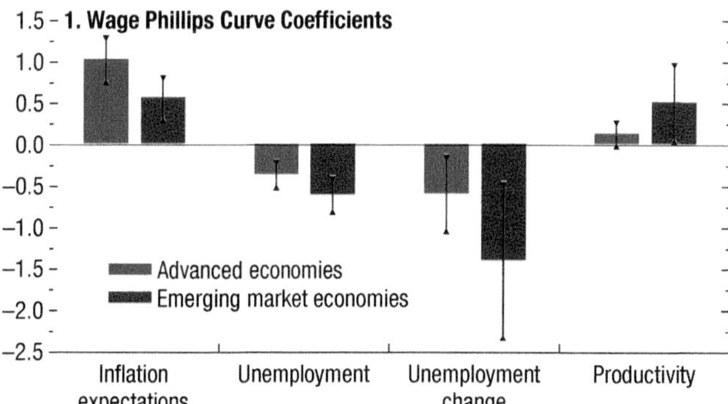

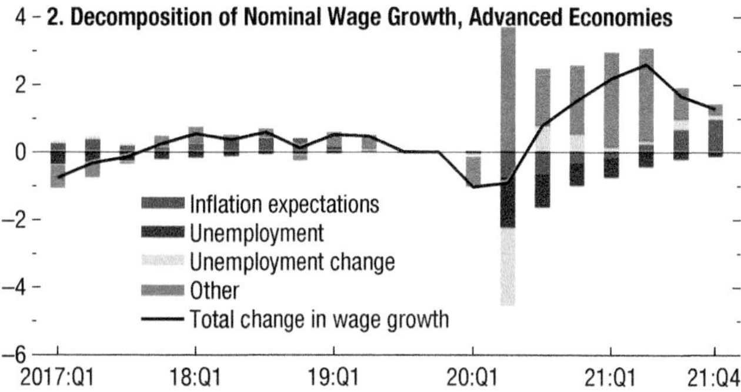

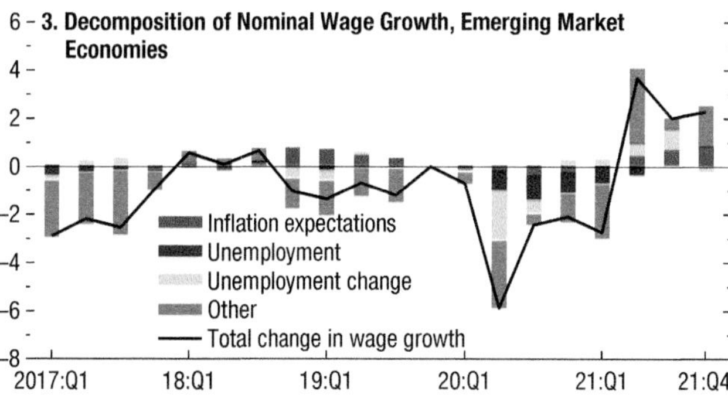

Source: IMF staff calculations.
Note: Panel 1 reports the estimated effects (coefficients) from 1 percentage point rises in the indicated variables from a wage Phillips curve regression. The sample covering 2000:Q1–19:Q4 consists of 31 advanced and 15 emerging market economies. Whiskers indicate 90 percent confidence intervals. See Online Annex 2.1 for further details on the sample and estimation. For panels 2 and 3, bars show contributions of each component relative to the contributions observed in 2019:Q4. Contributions are calculated using pooled wage Phillips curve coefficients for the indicated economy group. Line depicts average overall nominal wage growth per worker observed relative to 2019:Q4. Only economies with continuously available data from 2017:Q1–21:Q4 are used for the contributions and aggregated using GDP purchasing-power-parity weights. "Other" category contains the contributions of productivity growth, the residual, and time fixed effects.

rates and unemployment-to-vacancy ratios.[18] Point estimates suggest that emerging market wages can be more sensitive than those in advanced economies to changes in labor market and productivity conditions, although variation in past experiences is substantial.

Part of the heterogeneity in experiences could be due to differences across economies and over time in structural factors that may affect wage-setting processes. In economies with more stringent employment protections, wage growth appears to be on average more sensitive to changes in labor market slack (unemployment) and inflation expectations (Figure 2.5, panel 1). This would be consistent with labor prices (wages) adjusting faster to changing conditions when restrictions on labor quantities (firing or hiring of workers) are present. In economies in which firms exhibit greater market power in product markets—as proxied by the average price markup—wages appear slightly more responsive to unemployment changes (Figure 2.5, panel 2). Such a finding is consistent with evidence from the literature showing that higher-markup firms are more likely to use their margins to absorb cost changes and preserve their market shares.[19]

Relatedly, using long cross-sectional time series for Europe that help identify the effects of within-economy structural changes, Baba and Lee (2022) find that the pass-through of inflation shocks (captured by oil price changes) to wages can increase when union density and the degree of centralized

Figure 2.5. The Role of Structural Characteristics in Wage Dynamics
(Percentage points)

Regulatory and structural features can shape how unemployment and inflation expectations affect nominal wages.

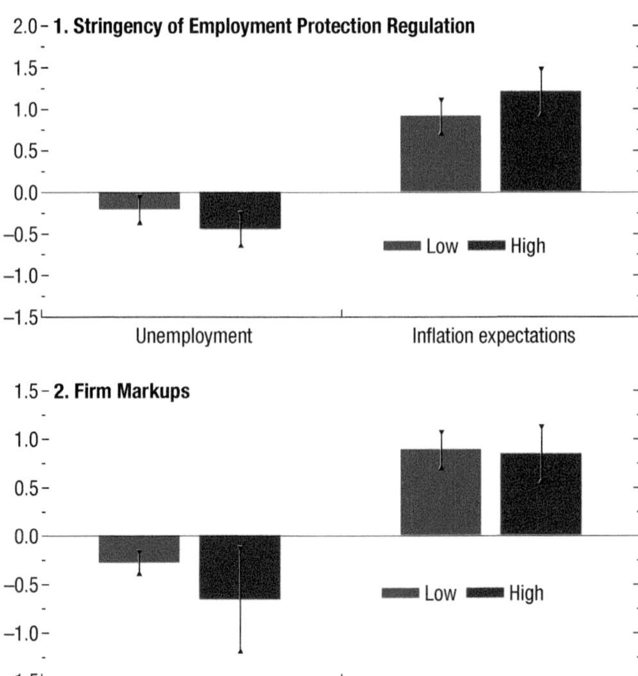

Source: IMF staff calculations.
Note: The figure shows average marginal effects of unemployment and inflation expectations on nominal wage growth, conditional on the level of the structural characteristic. High (low) refers to the average value of each structural indicator, given that it is above (below) the cross-economy median. "Stringency of employment protection regulation" refers to a composite indicator on the stringency of regulations related to individual dismissal of workers on regular contracts. The indicator of "firm markups" (a measure of firms' market power in output markets) is the sales-weighted average of sectoral markups. See Online Annex 2.4 for details.

bargaining are high.[20] Although disentangling specific structural factors that cause differences in wage setting is empirically challenging, these results and others from the literature suggest that regulatory, institutional, and structural features affect wages' responsiveness to changes in inflation expectations and slack.

[18]There has recently been much discussion about how alternative slack measures—such as unemployment rate gaps (unemployment rate minus natural rate of unemployment) and the ratio of the number of unemployed people to the number of job vacancies in an economy—could perform better. In robustness checks for the larger sample, using the unemployment gap does not make any marked differences in the relationships discussed. To study the unemployment-to-vacancy ratio, a further robustness check using the US (for which data are available on a sufficiently long basis) was also conducted, with broadly similar results, although the unemployment-to-vacancy ratio performed better in explaining recent wage growth. This is similar to the evidence from Ball, Leigh, and Mishra (forthcoming), who find that the price Phillips curve using the unemployment-to-vacancy ratio explains inflation since the COVID-19 shock better in the US than alternative measures, without sacrificing its explanatory power before the pandemic. See Online Annex 2.4 for further details.

[19]See Box 2.1 for some discussion of this mechanism and Box 1.2 for a discussion of the relationship between market power and inflation.

[20]Battistini and others (2022) also analyze the effects of energy shocks, comparing the second-round effects in the 1970s with those from today using model simulations calibrated to the relevant economic features. They find only limited second-round effects in the present circumstances, unlike what was observed in the 1970s. This difference likely reflects changes in economic structure, particularly in labor market bargaining and wage-setting processes. See also Boissay and others (2022) for additional discussion.

Wage Changes Were Highly Unusual in the Acute Pandemic Phase but Recently Appear Broadly in Line with Developments in Inflation Expectations and Slack

How wages respond to changing conditions in labor markets and inflation also depends on the sources of shocks and their mechanics. The COVID-19 shock's unprecedented nature and asymmetric sectoral effects meant that, overall, average wages did not move in line with the relationships predicted by the wage Phillips curve. A decomposition of average wage growth in advanced and emerging market economies using the wage Phillips curve unveils several notable features (Figure 2.4, panels 2 and 3).

First, both the acute shock and the recovery were unique, exhibiting abrupt swings that deviated from those explained by inflation expectations and unemployment changes according to the estimated wage Phillips curve.[21] Only part of these deviations was due to movements in hours worked, as employers and employees adjusted along the intensive margin of employment.[22] Importantly, the deviations were quantitatively and qualitatively different from those observed in the years preceding the pandemic and during the global financial crisis.[23] They also differed across economies. At the beginning of the pandemic, the drop in wage growth was less prominent than predicted by inflation and unemployment movements in advanced economies (particularly in the US), while the opposite was true in emerging markets.[24]

Second, in both advanced and emerging market economies, the recovery of wage growth since the crisis peak has been largely in line with the observed drops in unemployment and increase in inflation expectations. In fact, by the end of 2021, wage growth in advanced economies did not seem to be abnormally above that predicted by falling unemployment and rising inflation expectations alone, with a shrinking contribution of the residual and other components in both advanced and emerging market economies. On average, the rise in inflation expectations appears to account for more of the very latest movements in wage growth.[25] Chapter 1 provides evidence on how the average and distribution of inflation expectations have evolved in 2022 for selected economies.

Relative Contributions of Supply and Demand Shocks to Wages and Prices

The large, unexplained movements in wage growth observed during the COVID-19 shock and recovery likely reflect the shock's unprecedented and complex nature, as well as the large policy responses. To help unpack the breakdown of the wage Phillips curve during the pandemic's acute phase, this subsection deploys a rich multi-economy, multisector general equilibrium model featuring nominal rigidities and credit constraints. Based on recent work by Baqaee and Farhi (2022a, 2022b) and Gourinchas and others (2021), the model facilitates the study of how different demand and supply shocks propagate and contribute to wage, price, and employment changes.

In total, seven types of shocks are considered, all of which have been cited as being important for understanding the COVID-19 shock and its effects. On the supply side, the model includes three types of shocks:

- *Production capacity (or labor supply) shocks*, arising from lockdowns and social distancing, which had a particularly large impact on labor supply: These shocks are calibrated according to changes in the number of hours worked by sector over time.
- *International trade cost shocks*, as measured by the shipping costs by product for US imports: Freight and insurance costs showed marked increases starting in 2020.
- *Commodity price changes for energy and food:* Energy and food prices went up by 85 percent and 20 percent year over year, respectively, in 2021.

[21]The large increase in temporary layoffs observed in some economies, which were particularly concentrated among lower-paid workers, could partly explain these wage growth swings (Duval and others 2022). This reason is also cited for some of the strange behavior of the price Phillips curve in the United States (Ball and others 2021).

[22]See Online Annex 2.4 for a decomposition including hours worked using a more limited sample of economies.

[23]See Online Annex 2.4 for a similar decomposition over the period spanning the global financial crisis.

[24]Worker composition shifts during this period, particularly in the US, where greater employment losses among low-wage workers pushed average wages upward at the start of the pandemic, could partly explain the differences.

[25]The prominence of tighter labor markets for higher wage growth in the latest period appears greater when unemployment-to-vacancy indicators—particularly for the case of the United States—are considered, as these indicators point to tighter labor markets than before the pandemic. Alternative labor market slack measures co-moved closely during the pandemic, but the degree of tightening relative to the fourth quarter of 2019 varies for some economies (including the US) depending on the measure used. See Online Annex 2.4 for details.

The analysis also incorporates four types of demand shocks:

- *Changes in private saving behavior:* These shocks are calibrated by adjusting households' discount rate to track saving rates over time.
- *Consumption composition changes:* The pandemic led to a large reallocation of consumption away from services toward goods, driven by both availability and preferences. Consumer taste shocks are derived using changes in expenditure shares for different types of goods and services over time.
- *Fiscal policy support,* which was substantial in many advanced economies in 2020: This shock is derived from changes in government consumption and changes in spending on unemployment insurance.
- *Monetary policy support,* which was also extensive: This shock is obtained by calibrating the domestic interest rate to that observed for central bank policy rates.

A historical decomposition of key economic variables—including wages and prices—for the United States, euro area, and Mexico (an emerging market economy) are presented for 2020 and 2021 (Figure 2.6).[26]

Wage Changes since 2019 Have Been More Related to Supply-Side Shocks from the Pandemic, While Demand-Side Shocks Have Contributed More to Price Changes

Although all shocks contribute to the variation in an economy, two main contributors emerge from the results. First, reductions in production capacity (dark red bars in Figure 2.6) were the predominant contributors to nominal wage changes during 2020 and 2021. Second, changes in households' saving behavior (dark blue bars) were one of the most important drivers of price changes over the same years. These findings suggest that the future paths for these variables could depend heavily on whether and how these shocks unwind, as well as on whether new shocks arise.

[26]The impacts of individual shocks do not necessarily add up to the total impact in combination because of interactions in general equilibrium. It is also important to note that the total model-based impacts by variable are broadly aligned, but not exactly equal to actual outturns. The economies studied were selected based on a combination of their economic size, availability of data required for the model calibration (which is a constraint for many emerging market and developing economies), and diversity of policy support responses.

Figure 2.6. Drivers of Changes in Wages, Prices, and Employment during the COVID-19 Pandemic and Recovery

(Cumulative percent change, relative to pre–COVID-19 trend)

Reductions in production capacity and changes in households' saving behavior were the predominant contributors to wage and price changes during the pandemic.

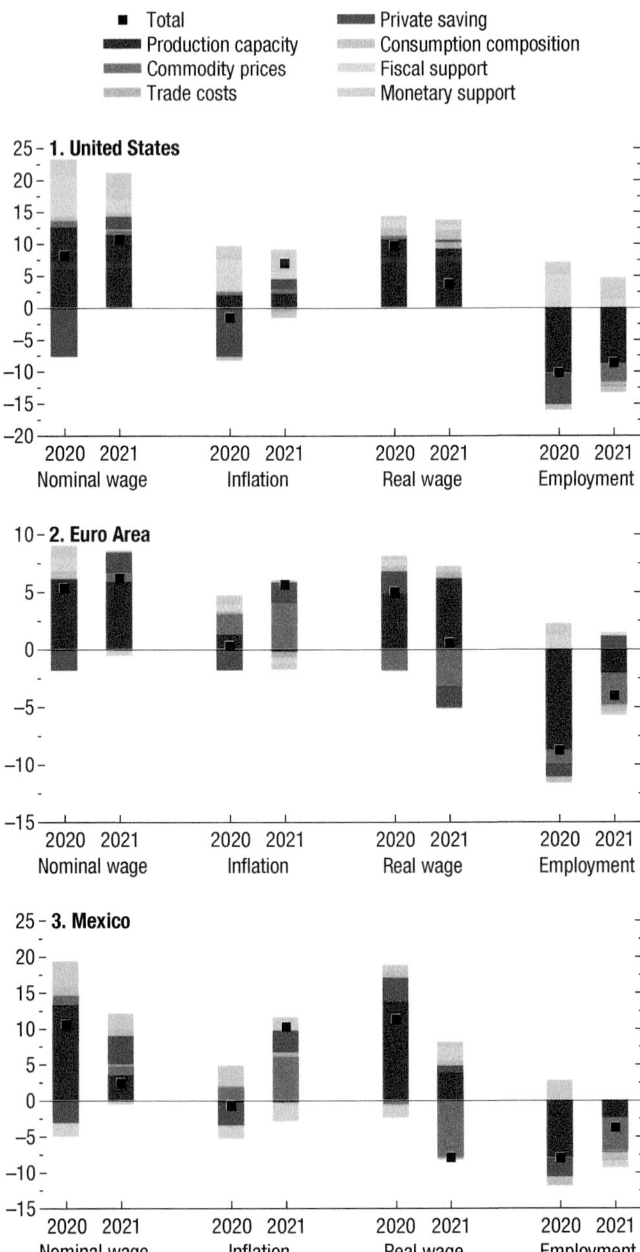

Source: IMF staff calculations.
Note: Nominal and real wages are defined on a per hour basis for the results exhibited in this figure. Estimated impacts are calculated using a multi-sector, multi-economy general equilibrium model based on Baqaee and Farhi (2020). See Online Annex 2.5 for further details. The impacts of individual shocks do not necessarily add up to the total impact in combination as a result of interactions in general equilibrium. Total impacts are model-based and broadly aligned with outturns.

In 2020, the main determinant of wages and employment across all three economies was the drop in production capacity that took place early in the pandemic (dark red bars). Lockdowns and the rise in social distancing due to the pandemic translated into decreases in production capacity and a lower labor supply. These decreases led to a decline in employment and an increase in hourly wages.

The second key driver in 2020, particularly for prices, was the rise in private saving (dark blue bars)—a contractionary force for aggregate demand—due to the myriad uncertainties surrounding the pandemic and its consequences. This negative demand shock had the usual disinflationary impact on nominal wages and consumer prices, particularly in the United States. Finally, the expansive fiscal and monetary policy responses in the United States and the euro area limited early damages to employment from the pandemic and helped support nominal wages.[27] In contrast, fiscal policy support in Mexico shrank in 2020, pulling wages and prices down to some extent (yellow bars). Monetary policy expansion in Mexico was effective at sustaining employment, along with pushing nominal wages and prices up (light green bars). For all three economies, the combination of a sharp increase in nominal wages and muted price responses led to strong increases in real wages.

In 2021, the main driver overall was the rebound in aggregate demand running ahead of production capacity—a supply-demand imbalance. The positive impact on consumer prices as private savings began to be drawn down—a reversal of the negative impact of higher savings in 2020—shows this most clearly. Production capacity recovered somewhat last year, especially in the euro area and Mexico, but the recovery was not enough to fully boost employment as the cumulative impact was still negative. Continued monetary accommodation in the United States also pushed wages and prices up further. For the euro area and Mexico, the inflationary effects of monetary support were reduced. Fiscal policy support across economies decreased in 2021 compared with 2020, relieving some of the earlier upward pressure on prices.[28] The mix of nominal wage and price changes led real wages to decline across the board last year, especially in Mexico.

The other major contributor to wages and prices in 2021 was the steep rise in commodity prices (dark green bars). The euro area and Mexico felt the impacts of those energy and food shocks on economy-wide prices more strongly than the United States, but commodity price rises were a drag on employment across the board. Commodity prices have risen even further in 2022 (particularly with the shock of the Russian invasion of Ukraine) and are pushing inflation up even more. Wage and price prospects will depend in part on how long these and other shocks persist.

Inflation De-anchoring: Expectations and Policy Responses

Beyond the potential for more persistent and additional inflationary demand and supply shocks, the risks for inflation de-anchoring or the emergence of a wage-price spiral will also depend on how businesses and workers form their expectations for wages and prices. This section delves into this issue. It first studies empirically the dynamic responses of wages, prices, and expectations about them to an inflationary shock (driven by global supply pressures) and monetary policy tightening.

Building on the insights from the empirical exercise, the section then demonstrates how the dynamic effects of inflationary shocks and the effectiveness of monetary policy responses depend critically on how wage and price expectations are formed. Taking account of current monetary policy plans, it considers a couple of forward-looking scenarios under different assumptions about the formation of wage and price expectations. The findings suggest that more backward-looking expectations will require stronger monetary policy responses to reduce the risks of de-anchoring, but they also indicate that the risks of a wage-price spiral are low.

[27]Note that there are important aspects of the design and composition of fiscal support policies that the model abstracts away from. See Chapter 3 of the April 2021 *World Economic Outlook* and the October 2022 *Fiscal Monitor* for a discussion on how the appropriate mix of job retention support and other measures may make fiscal policy support more effective.

[28]Fiscal support likely had further, indirect inflationary effects through its effects on private saving and labor supply as a result of income transfers, but these channels are difficult to quantify precisely in the Baqaee and Farhi (2020) model used here. See Online Annex 2.5 for further details. See Ramey (2016) for a summary of the considerable empirical literature on the dynamic effects of fiscal support.

Inflationary Shocks and Monetary Tightening

The empirical analysis estimates the dynamic effects of inflationary shocks and monetary tightening on wages and prices using local projections. Inflationary shocks are proxied by the Federal Reserve Bank of New York's Global Supply Chain Pressure Index, which captures the state of international supply chain pressures and disruptions (which are highly relevant to the current circumstances).[29] The index can be regarded as reflecting supply-side variation, since the manufacturing data and transportation costs used in its construction have been purged of demand factors. Finally, to account for differences in economies' exposures to global supply chain developments, the index is interacted with trade openness by economy.[30]

For a one-standard-deviation increase in global supply chain pressures, the inflation response outstrips that of nominal wage growth (Figure 2.7, panels 1 and 6). Both realized and short-term expected inflation increase persistently, taking three years (beyond the horizon shown) before reverting to their long-term means. In parallel, nominal wage growth increases slightly in the very near term and then deteriorates as the shock's depressive effects on activity take hold. Together, these dynamics engender a fall in real wage growth (Figure 2.7, panel 5). Most important, there are no signs that such inflationary shocks kick off a wage-price spiral.[31]

In contrast, monetary tightening brings inflation down, with similar depressive effects on nominal wage growth. To estimate the effects of monetary policy tightening, the analysis uses the series of identified European Central Bank monetary shocks from Jarociński and Karadi (2020).[32] The impact of a one-standard-deviation monetary tightening on realized and expected inflation is shorter lived than the effect of an inflationary supply chain shock (Figure 2.7, panels 3 and 4). At the same time, nominal and real wage growth decline, further helping mitigate any inflationary pressures (Figure 2.7, panels 7 and 8). In the background, the unemployment rate rises alongside increases in the long-term rates on government debt.[33]

This empirical evidence suggests that supply-chain-related inflationary shocks tend to have temporary effects on inflation and wage growth and do not give rise to a wage-price spiral. However, supply chain pressures do appear to have a more prolonged effect on expected inflation than monetary tightening. The differences in dynamic effects may suggest that monetary policymakers should respond aggressively to such shocks, particularly in contexts like the current conjuncture, in which inflation is high and rising and wage growth is sensitive to inflation expectations (as shown earlier).

If inflation expectations become less anchored to the monetary policy target rate, the effects on wages and prices could change and increase the risks of a persistent wage-price spiral emerging. When inflation expectations are more anchored, they are comparatively less sensitive to an inflationary shock from higher global supply chain pressures, implicitly decreasing the risk of future de-anchoring (Figure 2.8, red line compared with blue line).[34]

[29]The estimation sample excludes the United States and includes a set of small open advanced economies in the euro area to help avoid the reverse causality and simultaneity concerns that would arise with the inclusion of large economies, which could have sizable direct effects on the global economy (given the inflationary shock considered). Moreover, recent evidence suggests that changes in the index have had a meaningful impact on inflation in euro area producer prices and consumer goods prices (Akinci and others 2022). The sample comprises 16 economies: Austria, Belgium, Estonia, Finland, France, Germany, Greece, Ireland, Italy, Latvia, Lithuania, The Netherlands, Portugal, the Slovak Republic, Slovenia, and Spain. To avoid confusion with the large number of shocks occurring with the COVID-19 pandemic, the estimation sample ends in the fourth quarter of 2019. See Benigno and others (2022a, 2022b) for details on the construction of the index.

[30]Trade openness is defined here as the sum of an economy's imports and exports as a share of GDP. To address concerns about simultaneity, the estimation uses the lagged value of the supply chain pressure index. See Online Annex 2.6 for further details on the empirical specification and set of controls included.

[31]Behind the scenes, the long-term interest rate on government bonds and the unemployment rate increase in response to such a shock. These increases could reflect the effects of endogenous monetary tightening in response to the adverse supply shock. See Online Annex 2.6 for further details on the dynamic responses of the long-term interest rate and the unemployment rate, along with a more detailed discussion of the specification and robustness.

[32]See Online Annex 2.6 for a detailed description of the analysis. Note that the effect of monetary policy shocks could be seen as lower-bound estimates since the effective lower bound may reduce the variation in some of the overnight indexed swap rates used in the construction of the shock.

[33]See Online Annex 2.6 for further details.

[34]The Global Supply Chain Pressure Index is interacted with a dummy equal to one if the lagged economy's strength of inflation anchoring, proxied by the Bems and others' (2021) index, is above the cross-economy and cross-time median of the indicator. See Online Annex 2.6 for details on the construction of the indicator. This result is also in line with that of Carrière-Swallow and others (2022), who find that increases in the Baltic Dry Index lead to larger inflationary effects among economies with weaker monetary policy frameworks. To better anchor expectations, the recent literature has emphasized the role played by central banks' communication strategies and guidance, in addition to more traditional policy actions, such as interest rate changes (Coibion, Gorodnichenko, and Weber 2022).

Figure 2.7. Cumulative Effects of Supply Chain Pressures and Monetary Tightening on Wages and Prices
(Percentage points; dynamic response)

Increases in supply chain pressures tend to raise inflation and depress wage growth, with more persistent effects on inflation expectations. Monetary tightening is effective at bringing both inflation and inflation expectations down, but the actions required to offset inflationary shocks from supply chain pressures could be large.

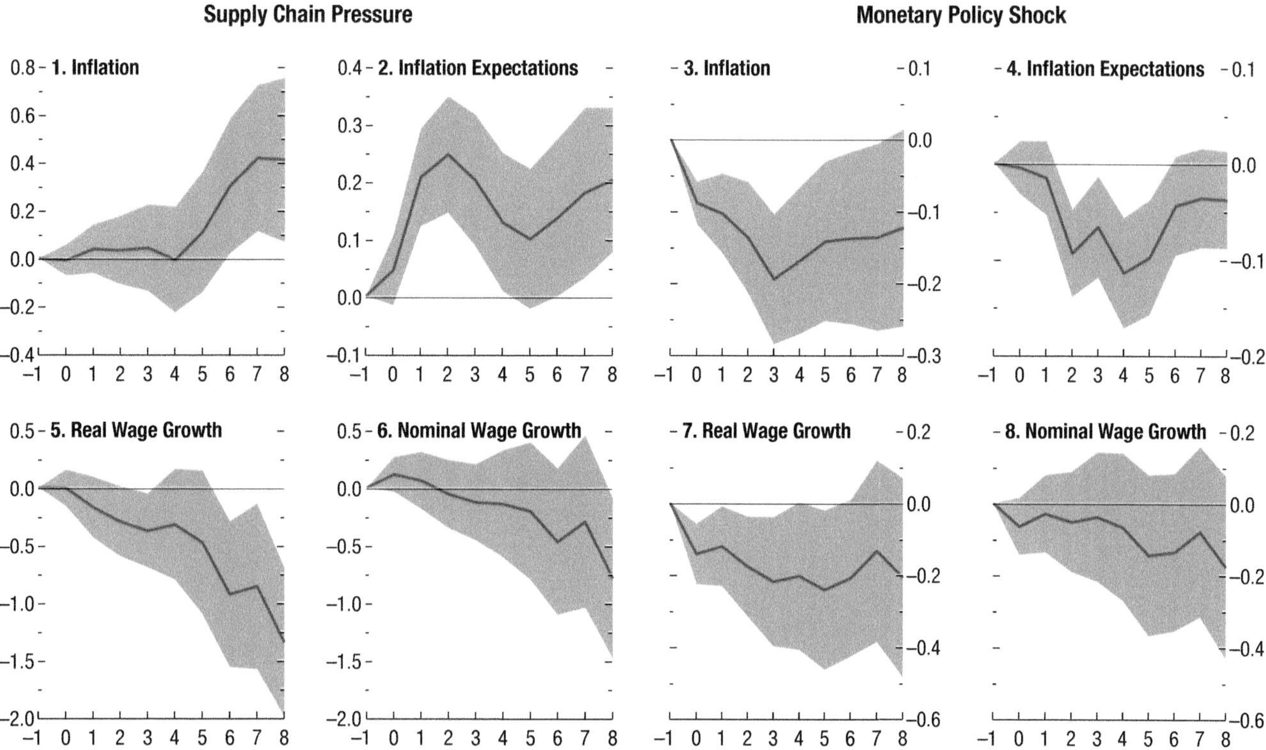

Sources: Federal Reserve Bank of New York; Haver Analytics; Jarociński and Karadi (2020); Organisation for Economic Co-operation and Development; and IMF staff calculations.
Note: Lines show the estimated impulse responses of the indicated variable to the indicated shock, with the shaded area representing the 90 percent confidence interval. The horizontal axes show time in quarters, where $t = 0$ is the initial impact quarter of the shock. The estimation sample includes euro area economies during 1999:Q4–2019:Q4. Panels 1, 2, 5, and 6 are the responses to a supply chain pressure shock, defined as a one-standard-deviation increase in the Federal Reserve Bank of New York's Global Supply Chain Pressure Index. To account for economies' different degrees of exposure, the index is weighted by an economy's trade openness. Panels 3, 4, 7, and 8 are the responses to a one-standard-deviation monetary policy shock, as identified in Jarociński and Karadi (2020). "Inflation expectations" are 12-month-ahead expected inflation. See Online Annex 2.1 for details on the sample and Online Annex 2.6 for further details on the estimation.

The Role of Expectations and Monetary Policy Responses in Wage and Price Inflation

Central banks often discuss the importance of monitoring price expectations to assess the proper stance of monetary policy, aiming to ensure that expectations do not drift away from central bank targets. As the world economy recovers from a global pandemic and inflation reaches levels not seen in decades in many economies, there are concerns about a break from recent-past trends, with expectations changing sharply. This subsection zooms in on how differences in the expectations formation process can affect an economy's dynamics, with particular focus on the behavior of nominal wages and prices.

The analysis estimates a small, standard dynamic stochastic equilibrium model conditional on different expectation formation processes, thereby isolating their role in shaping the economy's response to shocks and policy actions. The model incorporates price and wage Phillips curves (which relate price and wage inflation, respectively, to expectations, the gap between real wages and productivity, and slack in the economy), an investment-savings curve (relating output to the nominal interest rate and inflation expectations), and a monetary policy reaction function.[35]

[35]See Online Annex 2.7 for more details about the model and its structure. See also Alvarez and Dizioli (forthcoming).

Figure 2.8. Cumulative Effects of Supply Chain Pressures on Inflation Expectations
(Percentage points; dynamic response)

More anchored inflation expectations respond less to supply chain pressures.

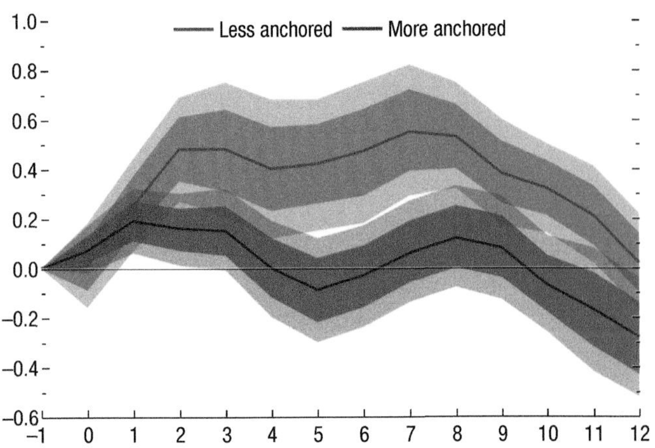

Sources: Bems and others (2021); Federal Reserve Bank of New York; Haver Analytics; Organisation for Economic Co-operation and Development; and IMF staff calculations.
Note: Lines show the estimated impulse responses of inflation expectations (12 months ahead) to a one-standard-deviation rise in the Federal Reserve Bank of New York's Global Supply Chain Pressure Index (weighted by an economy's trade openness), conditional on the strength of inflation anchoring (defined by Bems and others [2021] over a five-year-ahead horizon). The red (blue) line is the response for economies with inflation anchoring above (below) the cross-economy median. Lighter-shaded areas represent the 90 percent confidence interval; darker-shaded areas are the 68 percent confidence intervals. The horizontal axis shows time in quarters, where $t = 0$ is the initial impact quarter of the shock. The estimation sample includes euro area economies during 1999:Q4–2019:Q4. See Online Annex 2.1 for details on the sample and Online Annex 2.6 for further details on the estimation.

With acknowledgment of the uncertainties surrounding expectations at the current juncture, three kinds of expectations formation processes are considered:

1. *Rational expectations:* Standard in much economic modeling because of the tractability of rational expectations, businesses and households understand the economy's complete structure, including the distribution of potential shocks. This means that businesses and households make accurate forecasts on average about future outcomes so that their expectations about the future are correct in the absence of further shocks.
2. *Fully adaptive expectations:* At the other extreme, businesses and households have fully adaptive expectations, which means they look at the value of a variable only in the recent past and assume that it will stay at that value in the future. Therefore, they project future variables to be exactly equal to their latest realization.
3. *Adaptive learning:* Partway between rational expectations and fully adaptive expectations, adaptive learning assumes that businesses and households form expectations using small statistical models for key variables such as wages and prices. They update these expectations regularly as new data become available, learning from their mistakes and adjusting their expectations process.[36]

How Wage and Price Expectations Form Matters More the Farther Away Inflation and Inflation Expectations Are from Target

Estimating the model for the United States, a scenario in which there are no new shocks to inflation and interest rates are exogenously set according to the Federal Reserve's dot plot as of June 2022, a soft landing appears feasible if expectations for wages and prices are rational (Figure 2.9, dashed lines).[37] In this case, the current inflationary shock is assumed to dissipate smoothly over the subsequent 12 quarters, allowing the output gap to converge smoothly to zero and core inflation to come down to the Federal Reserve's target of 2 percent.

In contrast, if wage and price expectations are fully adaptive, there is a fast near-term acceleration in wage and price inflation because businesses and households expect them to be identical to their most recent realizations, which have been higher than usual (Figure 2.9, red lines). Moreover, the economy is still facing large cost-push shocks that exacerbate price pressures and mostly offset the near-term disinflationary effects of falling real wages (since wage growth does not keep up fully with price inflation). As shocks dissipate and the real wage gap becomes even more negative, price inflation quickly declines after five quarters. However, although inflation comes down and there are no further future shocks assumed, price inflation remains 1.5 percentage points over target even 12 quarters later. To bring inflation down more quickly under this type of expectations formation, monetary policy would need to tighten much more sharply than is currently anticipated.

[36]See Online Annex 2.7 for further discussion of the alternative expectations formation processes, including the specific functional forms assumed for the adaptive learning process.

[37]The findings do not change in a meaningful way if monetary policy instead follows the estimated monetary policy reaction function, pointing to a high degree of consistency between the reaction function and announced policy. See Online Annex 2.7.

Figure 2.9. Near-Term Scenarios with Set Interest Rate Path under Different Expectations
(Percent)

With cost-push shocks originating outside the labor market, real wage dynamics help to stabilize inflation even when wage and price expectations are backward-looking (adaptive). If policy actions are not sufficiently responsive, inflation and inflation expectations can de-anchor from target the more adaptive the expectations.

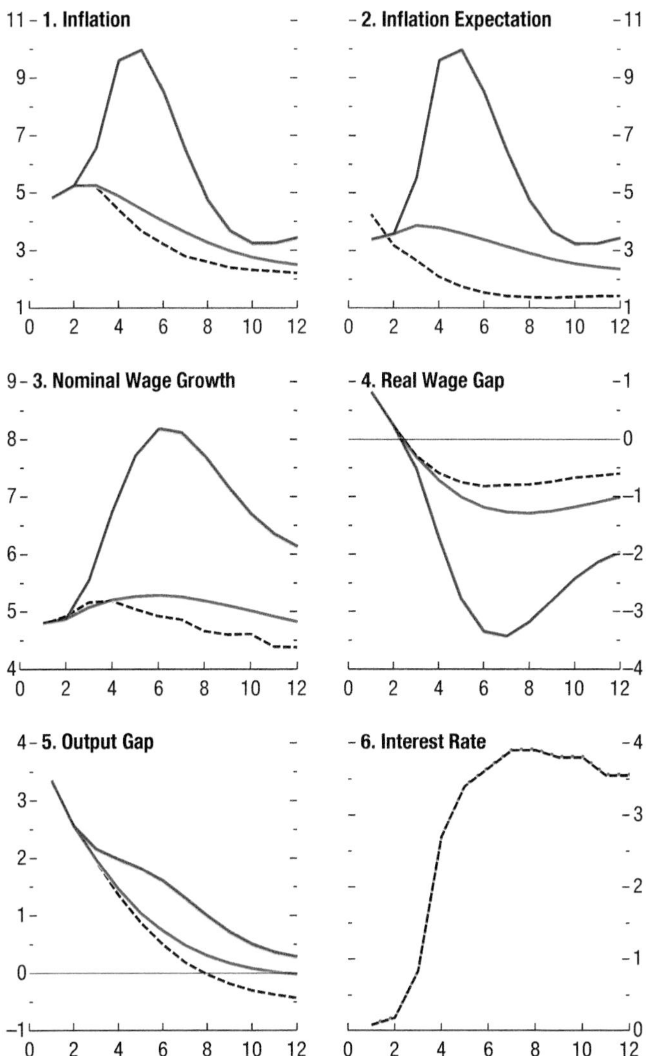

Source: IMF staff calculations.
Note: The responses illustrate scenarios calibrated to the United States, assuming that the inflationary shocks as of early 2022 dissipate as estimated based on previous experience. Inflation is core inflation. The horizontal axes show time in quarters since 2021:Q4. See Online Annex 2.7 for further details on the structure and estimation of the underlying small dynamic stochastic general equilibrium model.

Under adaptive learning, which is the most realistic of the three expectations processes since the process is estimated to fit recent data on wage and price dynamics, the paths of inflation, wage growth, and the output gap lie between those for rational and fully adaptive expectations (Figure 2.9, blue lines). There is somewhat greater inertia than with rational expectations, but nowhere near the level seen in the fully adaptive case.[38] Even so, while the output gap mostly closes, inflation is still about half a percentage point above target after 12 quarters.

The results from simulations of the model estimated for the case of Brazil—an emerging market economy—exhibit broad patterns across the three expectations processes that are similar to those for the United States (see Online Annex 2.7). However, they show an even greater sensitivity to inflationary shocks and higher risks of de-anchoring in general. The greater sensitivity could entail a stronger reaction from the central bank to anchor expectations.

In all cases, the dynamics of real wages are critical to the evolution of wage and price inflation since they can affect price pressures. For simplicity, wages are the only determinant of marginal costs in the model employed here. Because of this, the model can also illustrate the likelihood of a wage-price spiral dynamic taking hold. This modeling choice not only allows the assessment of the likelihood of wage-price spirals in the simulated scenarios but also shows that wages can be an important anchor to inflation when cost-push shocks hit an economy. When inflationary cost-push shocks occur, the negative real wage gap characterizing the current circumstances helps anchor inflation, even in the case of fully adaptive expectations.[39] When the real costs of labor fall, they help bring inflation down. Moreover, the larger the increase in inflation, the more negative the real wage gap becomes and the more powerful this anchoring mechanism is. Using a different methodology and focusing on the United States, Box 2.1 empirically examines the feedback from wages

[38]The model is estimated over a period in which the monetary policy framework had high credibility, and hence the adaptive learning process begins centered on the inflation target, similar to the anchoring that occurs with rational expectations. Consequently, a very large shift in how expectations are formed would be needed to push the adaptive learning scenario to approximate the fully adaptive case. The greater economic inertia seen in the adaptive learning case is a function of the greater inertia in expectations.

[39]A negative real wage gap means that the real wage (the ratio of the wage to the price level) has not kept up with labor productivity.

Figure 2.10. Optimal Policy Scenario under Adaptive Learning Expectations
(Percent)

Front-loading monetary policy tightening is optimal to lessen the buildup of inflation expectations, helping to achieve target more quickly and smoothly.

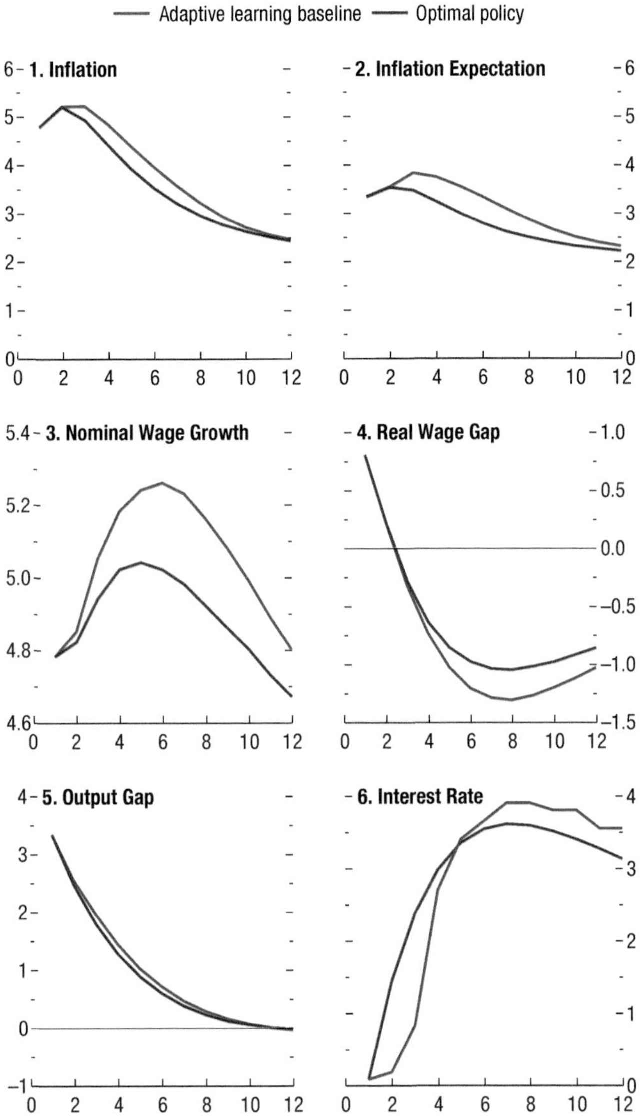

Source: IMF staff calculations.
Note: The responses illustrate scenarios calibrated to the United States, assuming that the inflationary shocks as of early 2022 dissipate as estimated based on previous experience. Inflation is core inflation. The horizontal axes show time in quarters since 2021:Q4. Optimal policy is determined using an objective function that equally weights output and inflation deviations from potential and target, respectively, with some weight given also to policy rate smoothing. See Online Annex 2.7 for further details on the structure and estimation of the underlying small dynamic stochastic general equilibrium model.

to prices by sector and finds only limited pass-through from wage-cost shocks to prices.

As alluded to earlier, more backward-looking expectations will typically require a faster and stronger monetary tightening in response to an inflationary shock. But how much faster? For the case of the United States, with a positive output gap and persistent cost-push shocks, if expectations are formed through adaptive learning, a central bank that minimizes a standard welfare function would choose to initially tighten policy more and start easing earlier than the path implied by the Federal Reserve's dot plot as of June 2022 (Figure 2.10).[40] Even so, it would take several quarters for inflation to come down, although the inflation gains would accumulate over time. Monetary policy affects inflation dynamics through three channels: (1) higher interest rates lower the output gap and real wages through the wage and price Phillips curves; (2) as expectations are partially adaptive, lower inflation realizations contribute to lower expected inflation; and (3) through recognizing mistakes in their forecasts, businesses and households learn over time and place less importance on past outcomes when it comes to their expectations.

Conclusions

Many economies have seen sharp rises in price inflation since 2021 as adverse supply shocks buffet the global economy and labor markets appear tight in the wake of the acute COVID-19 shock. These inflation rises have raised concerns among some observers that prices and wages could start feeding off each other and accelerate, leading to a wage-price spiral dynamic. Using a mix of empirical and model-based analyses, this chapter has examined recent developments, trying to shed light on the prospects for wages and the chances that a wage-price spiral could emerge.

Although wage and price inflation picked up in a broad-based manner through 2021, real wages tended to be flat or falling across economies on average. This is an important aspect of the current conjuncture, since falling real wages can be disinflationary by lowering

[40]The determination of an optimal monetary policy response depends on the following assumptions: (1) the central bank minimizes a welfare function that equally weighs output and inflation deviations (a quadratic loss function) and (2) the central bank knows the expectations formation process and has full information on future cost-push shocks. See Online Annex 2.7 for more details on the exercise.

firms' real costs. An analysis of historical episodes with features similar to today's suggests that these episodes did not tend to be followed by a wage-price spiral. In fact, inflation tended to fall gradually afterward on average, and nominal wages gradually caught up over several quarters. However, in some cases, inflation remained elevated for a while.

Wage dynamics during 2020 and into early 2021 are poorly explained by inflation expectations and labor market slack, likely reflecting the highly unusual constellation of shocks arising with the COVID-19 pandemic. Model-based analysis of 2020–21 wages and prices suggests disparate underlying shocks: wages were driven predominantly by production capacity and labor supply shocks, while private saving was important for price changes. That said, in the second half of 2021, wage growth appears to be relatively well explained by inflation expectations and labor market slack on average, potentially pointing to a gradual shift toward more normal economic dynamics. Of course, this shift is highly contingent on whether the earlier shocks continue unwinding and whether new shocks arise.

Finally, the analysis suggests a critical role for the expectations formation process in shaping wage and price prospects. When wage and price expectations are more backward-looking, monetary policy actions need to be more front-loaded to minimize the risks of inflation de-anchoring. As monetary policy tightens more aggressively and the decline in real wages helps reduce price pressures, according to the scenario analysis, the risk of a persistent wage-price spiral emerging in the current episode is contained on average, assuming no more persistent inflationary shocks or structural changes in wage- and price-setting processes (such as sharply higher pass-through from prices to wages or vice versa).

Box 2.1. Pass-Through from Wages to Prices: Estimates from the United States

The empirical literature offers limited evidence on the pass-through of wages to consumer prices. At the macroeconomic level, the link between labor cost and price inflation has weakened over the past three decades.[1] Meanwhile, analysis at a more disaggregated level has not reached much of a consensus on the pass-through of labor costs to retail prices.[2]

Using a novel estimation approach, this box finds that the recent pickup in nominal wage growth has added only modestly to consumer price inflation, mostly through its effects on prices of certain services. The analysis studies the pass-through of labor costs to consumer prices (as measured by the personal consumption expenditure, or PCE, price index) by looking at disaggregated sectoral data. The main empirical challenge is that consumer prices, which reflect the final product of multiple production processes, cannot be readily matched to the costs of labor inputs, which are recorded at the industry level. To overcome this measurement problem, input-output matrices are used to construct the cumulative costs of labor inputs (traced through the supply chain of intermediate goods and services) for 73 subcomponents of the PCE index. Using the local projection method in Heise, Karahan, and Şahin (2020), with sectoral productivity growth and time and industry fixed effects controlled for, the impulse response of prices to wage changes shows a pass-through of about 10 percent to services after five quarters, but no measurable pass-through to goods prices (Figure 2.1.1). The lack of pass-through in goods compared with that in services could be due to firms absorbing more labor cost changes, on the back of higher market power and import penetration. The estimated pass-through appears materially unchanged from the mid-2000s up to the pandemic.

There is some tentative evidence that the pass-through from wages to service prices is stronger during periods or in sectors in which labor costs increased more quickly. Pre-2020 data suggest that contemporaneous pass-through in the services sector picks up to 20 percent (and is statistically significant at the 99 percent confidence level) when wage growth is at or above the 75th percentile (that is, 3.9 percent), while pass-through is about zero in periods with lower wage growth. In addition, the cross section from the sectoral data suggests that the point estimate of the pass-through from wages to service prices has been increasing since the first quarter of 2021 but is not statistically significant.

Figure 2.1.1. Pass-Through from Wages to Prices
(Percent)

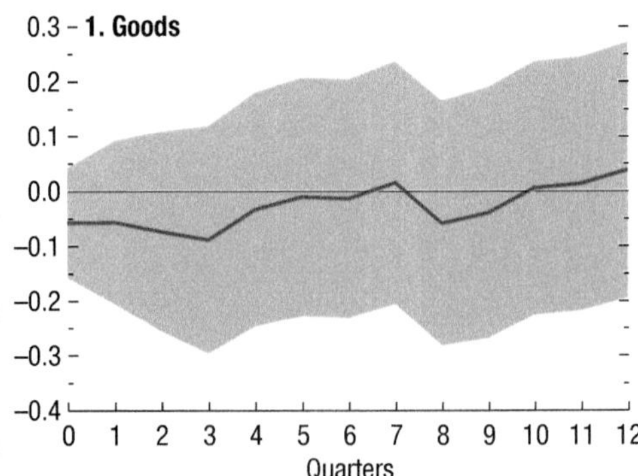

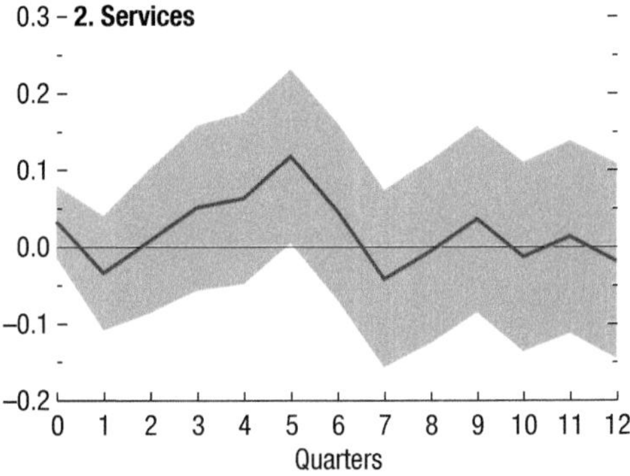

Sources: US Bureau of Economic Analysis; US Bureau of Labor Statistics; and IMF staff calculations.
Note: Lines show the dynamic pass-through from a 1 percentage point change in current wage growth (at $t = 0$, measured by the four-quarter change in wages) to inflation (measured by the four-quarter change in the indicated sectoral prices). Shaded areas show the 90 percent confidence interval.

The authors of this box are Moya Chin and Li Lin.

[1]See Bobeica, Ciccarelli, and Vansteenkiste (2021) for evidence on this.

[2]For further background on the debate, see Rissman (1995) and Heise, Karahan, and Şahin (2021), among others.

References

Akinci, Ozge, Gianluca Benigno, Ruth Cesar Heymann, Julian di Giovanni, Jan J. J. Groen, Lawrence Lin, and Adam I. Noble. 2022. "The Global Supply Side of Inflationary Pressures." *Liberty Street Economics* (blog), January 28, 2022.

Alvarez, Jorge, John Bluedorn, Niels-Jakob Hansen, Youyou Huang, Evgenia Pugacheva, and Alexandre Sollaci. Forthcoming. "Wage-Price Spirals: What Is the Historical Evidence?" IMF Working Paper, International Monetary Fund, Washington, DC.

Alvarez, Jorge, and Allan Dizioli. Forthcoming. "How Costly Will Reining in Inflation Be? It Depends on How Rational We Are." IMF Working Paper, International Monetary Fund, Washington, DC.

Baba, Chikako, and Jaewoo Lee. 2022. "Second-Round Effects of Oil Price Shocks—Implications for Europe's Inflation Outlook." IMF Working Paper 22/173, International Monetary Fund, Washington, DC.

Ball, Laurence M., Daniel Leigh, and Prachi Mishra. Forthcoming. "Understanding U.S. Inflation during the COVID-19 Era." IMF Working Paper, International Monetary Fund, Washington, DC.

Ball, Laurence M., Daniel Leigh, Prachi Mishra, and Antonio Spilimbergo. 2021. "Measuring U.S. Core Inflation: The Stress Test of COVID-19." NBER Working Paper 29609, National Bureau of Economic Research, Cambridge, MA.

Baqaee, David, and Emmanuel Farhi. 2022. "Networks, Barriers, and Trade." NBER Working Paper 26108, National Bureau of Economic Research, Cambridge, MA.

Baqaee, David, and Emmanuel Farhi. 2020. "Supply and Demand in Disaggregated Keynesian Economies with an Application to the COVID-19 Crisis." *American Economic Review* 112 (5): 1397–436.

Battistini, Niccolò, Helen Grapow, Elke Hahn, and Michel Soudan. 2022. "Wage Share Dynamics and Second-Round Effects on Inflation after Energy Price Surges in the 1970s and Today." *ECB Economic Bulletin* 5.

Bems, Rudolfs, Francesca Caselli, Francesco Grigoli, and Bertrand Gruss. 2021. "Expectations' Anchoring and Inflation Persistence." *Journal of International Economics* 132: 103516.

Benigno, Gianluca, Julian di Giovanni, Jan J. J. Groen, and Adam I. Noble. 2022a. "The GSCPI: A New Barometer of Global Supply Chain Pressures." *Liberty Street Economics* (blog), January 4, 2022.

Benigno, Gianluca, Julian di Giovanni, Jan J. J. Groen, and Adam I. Noble. 2022b. "Global Supply Chain Pressure Index: March 2022 Update." *Liberty Street Economics* (blog), March 3, 2022.

Bluedorn, John, Francesca Caselli, Niels-Jakob Hansen, Ippei Shibata, and Marina M. Tavares. 2021. "Gender and Employment in the COVID-19 Recession: Evidence on 'She-cessions.'" IMF Working Paper 21/95, International Monetary Fund, Washington, DC.

Bobeica, Elena, Matteo Ciccarelli, and Isabel Vansteenkiste. 2021. "The Changing Link between Labor Cost and Price Inflation in the United States." Working Paper Series 2583, European Central Bank, Frankfurt, Germany.

Boissay, Frederic, Fiorella De Fiore, Deniz Igan, Albert Pierres-Tejada, and Daniel Rees. 2022. "Are Major Advanced Economies on the Verge of a Wage-Price Spiral?" BIS Bulletin 53, Bank for International Settlements, Basel.

Caplan, Benjamin. 1956. "A Case Study: The 1948–1949 Recession." In *Policies to Combat Depression*, edited by Universities-National Bureau Committee for Economic Research, 27–58. Cambridge, MA: National Bureau of Economic Research.

Carrière-Swallow, Yan, Pragyan Deb, Davide Furceri, Daniel Jiménez, and Jonathan D. Ostry. 2022. "Shipping Costs and Inflation." IMF Working Paper 22/61, International Monetary Fund, Washington, DC.

Coibion, Olivier, Yuriy Gorodnichenko, and Michael Weber. 2022. "Monetary Policy Communications and Their Effects on Household Inflation Expectations." *Journal of Political Economy* 130 (6): 1537–84.

Duval, Romain, Yi Ji, Longji Li, Myrto Oikonomou, Carlo Pizzinelli, Ippei Shibata, Alessandra Sozzi, and Marina M. Tavares. 2022. "Labor Market Tightness in Advanced Economies." IMF Staff Discussion Note 2022/001, International Monetary Fund, Washington, DC.

Galí, Jordi. 2011. "The Return of the Wage Phillips Curve." *Journal of the European Economic Association* 9 (3): 436–61.

Gourinchas, Pierre-Olivier, Şebnem Kalemli-Özcan, Veronika Penciakova, and Nick Sander. 2021. "Fiscal Policy in the Age of COVID: Does It 'Get in All of the Cracks?'" NBER Working Paper 29293, National Bureau of Economic Research, Cambridge, MA.

Hazell, Jonathon, Juan Herreño, Emi Nakamura, and Jón Steinsson. 2022. "The Slope of the Phillips Curve: Evidence from U.S. States." *The Quarterly Journal of Economics*, 137 (3): 1299–344.

Heise, Sebastian, Fatih Karahan, and Ayşegül Şahin. 2020. "The Missing Inflation Puzzle: The Role of the Wage-Price Pass-Through." *Journal of Money, Credit and Banking* 54 (Suppl. 1): 7–51.

International Labour Organization (ILO). 2022. *World Employment and Social Outlook: Trends 2022*. Geneva, Switzerland: ILO Publications.

Jarociński, Marek, and Peter Karadi. 2020. "Deconstructing Monetary Policy Surprises—The Role of Information Shocks." *American Economic Journal: Macroeconomics* 12 (2): 1–43.

Ramey, Valerie A. 2016. "Macroeconomic Shocks and Their Propagation." In *Handbook of Macroeconomics*, vol. 2A, edited by John B. Taylor and Harald Uhlig, 71–162. Amsterdam: Elsevier.

Rissman, Ellen R. 1995. "Sectoral Wage Growth and Inflation." *Economic Perspectives* 19 (4): 16–28.

Rouse, Cecilia, Jeffery Zhang, and Ernie Tedeschi. 2021. "Historical Parallels to Today's Inflationary Episode." Blog post, United States White House, July 6, 2021.

CHAPTER 3

NEAR-TERM MACROECONOMIC IMPACT OF DECARBONIZATION POLICIES

Decades of procrastination have transformed what could have been a smooth transition to a more carbon-neutral society into what will likely be a more challenging one. By the end of the decade, the global economy needs to emit 25 percent less greenhouse gases than in 2022 to have a fighting chance to reach the goals set in Paris in 2015 and avert catastrophic climate disruptions. Because the energy transition needed to accomplish this has to be rapid, it is bound to involve some costs in the next few years. While there is little consensus on the expected near-term macroeconomic consequences of climate change policies, this chapter's central message is that if the right measures are implemented immediately and phased in gradually over the next eight years, the costs will remain manageable and are dwarfed by the innumerable long-term costs of inaction. Different assumptions regarding the speed at which electricity generation can transition toward low-carbon technologies put these costs somewhere between 0.15 and 0.25 percentage point of GDP growth and an additional 0.1 to 0.4 percentage point of inflation a year with respect to the baseline, if budget-neutral policies are assumed. To avoid amplifying these costs, it is important that both climate and monetary policies be credible. Stop-and-go policies and further procrastinating on the grounds that "now is not the time" will only exacerbate the toll.

Introduction

The scientific consensus recently summarized by the Intergovernmental Panel on Climate Change (IPCC 2022) suggests that to limit catastrophic climate disruptions, large-scale policy changes need to take place rapidly. Decades of procrastination have transformed what could have been a slow transition to a carbon-neutral society into what will now have to be a more abrupt one. To have a fighting chance to reach the 2015 Paris Agreement's goal of limiting global warming (relative to the preindustrial age) to well below 2°C, and preferably 1.5°C, and to achieve net carbon neutrality by 2050 requires immediate and ambitious action. By 2030, global emissions have to be reduced by at least 25 percent compared with today's emissions, which would require a combination of a sustained and large increase in greenhouse gas (GHG) emission taxes, regulations on emissions, and large investment in low-carbon technologies.[1] Advanced economies cannot accomplish the needed reduction alone; large emitters in emerging markets also have to step up the pace of their emission reduction activities (Parry, Black, and Roaf 2021).

Concerns about the energy transition's real economic costs have been a key determinant of decades-long procrastination on the policy front; while costs are often perceived as clear and present, benefits are seen as distant and uncertain, despite overwhelming evidence that any short-term costs will be dwarfed by the long-term benefits (with respect to output, financial stability, health) of arresting climate change (October 2020 *World Economic Outlook*; IPCC 2022). And hesitation in implementing the necessary climate mitigation policies seems to have even grown recently against a backdrop of rising commodity prices fueling inflation (Morawiecki 2022) and worries about energy security (see Chapter 1). In some circles, concerns have been raised that fighting climate change could cause a global inflation shock (Morison 2021), exacerbating the output-inflation trade-offs central banks currently face and increasing risks to medium-term price stability (Schnabel 2022). But are these concerns warranted?

The authors of this chapter are Mehdi Benatiya Andaloussi, Benjamin Carton (co-lead), Christopher Evans, Florence Jaumotte, Dirk Muir, Jean-Marc Natal (co-lead), Augustus J. Panton, and Simon Voigts, with support from Carlos Morales, Cynthia Nyakeri, and Yiyuan Qi. They thank Jean Pisani-Ferry for helpful comments on an earlier draft.

[1]See Black and others (2022) and Chateau, Jaumotte, and Schwerhoff (2022a) for an analysis of the equivalence between regulation on emissions and carbon taxes. Note that while incentives for investment in green technology and renewables are an important part of any climate package, they are best supplemented by carbon taxes or equivalent regulations that will help decrease demand for fossil fuels and achieve a faster transition.

There is little consensus on the expected near-term macroeconomic consequences of climate change mitigation policies, such as GHG taxes. At the most fundamental level, imposing GHG taxes amounts to putting a price on a resource—the right to pollute—that used to be free. Internalizing this negative externality increases the cost of fossil fuels—an adverse supply shock—which on the surface bears many similarities to a standard oil price shock (Pisani-Ferry 2021). But the economics of climate policy and fossil fuel price shocks have important differences. First and foremost, GHG taxes lead to lower (net-of-tax) prices for fossil fuel producers, an important deterrent to investment in this kind of energy source. Second, while fossil fuel price shocks entail a transfer of revenues to fossil fuel exporters, GHG taxes generate fiscal revenues that can be allocated in many different ways to partly alleviate their negative effect on consumption and production and to compensate low-income households, which an increase in energy prices affects the most. Depending on how these revenues are used, they can have vastly different effects on the economy. Third, while fossil fuel price shocks are usually temporary and sudden adverse supply shocks, GHG taxes are meant to be permanent and assumed to be implemented gradually (October 2020 *World Economic Outlook*, Chapter 3). Forward-looking firms and households will understand that future output and income will be durably lower than previously expected and will want to scale down investment and consumption; the balance of supply and demand effects and the net effect on output will depend greatly on other policies governments undertake. Fourth, fossil fuel price surges that do not alter relative prices according to the fuel's carbon content (those that do not increase coal prices more than gasoline prices, for example) do not provide incentives for emission reduction to the same extent as a carbon tax, in particular when the surges are expected to be temporary. Also, considerable uncertainty surrounds the pace at which electricity generation could transition to low-carbon technologies. And as this chapter shows, this has important implications for the energy transition's macroeconomic costs.

This chapter employs the IMF's novel Global Macroeconomic Model for the Energy Transition (GMMET) to inform the current policy debate. It voluntarily abstracts from issues related to long-term costs and benefits of climate policies—largely covered elsewhere[2]—and focuses on *near-term* macroeconomic costs borne by agents whose horizon is limited. The focus is also on budget-neutral climate policies exclusively.[3] This strategy makes it possible to clearly disentangle the individual impacts of climate and fiscal policies on GDP and inflation. Moreover, in the current context of high public debt, high inflation, and rising interest rates, a strong case can be made to avoid further debt-financed demand stimulation (Chapter 1).

This chapter aims to illustrate the effect of feasible climate policies that balance the need to limit output losses against the inflationary effects of higher taxes, while ensuring low-income households do not bear a disproportionate share of any costs the transition entails.[4]

Given that the resulting output-inflation trade-offs could vary a great deal depending on the design and credibility of those policies, and in particular their interaction with fiscal and monetary policy and the pace at which electricity production can be decarbonized, this chapter puts a great deal of emphasis on robustness. By shedding light on the range of possible outcomes the required transition implies over the next eight years, it will help policymakers quantify alternative options and better tailor policies to their individual situations.

[2]See Acemoglu and others (2012) and the October 2020 *World Economic Outlook*, Chapter 3, for a comprehensive discussion.

[3]The assumption of budget neutrality is in contrast to that in Chapter 3 of the October 2020 *World Economic Outlook*, which studies the effect of deficit-financed public investment on green infrastructure investment. In the context of depressed economic activity related to the COVID-19 pandemic, a fiscal stimulus was the right policy; the proposed policy mix—carbon tax and public investment—led to fiscal deficit and temporarily boosted GDP (October 2020 *World Economic Outlook*, Figure 3.6). However, in the current context of high inflation and rising interest rates, fiscal policy should avoid undermining monetary policy's efforts to tame inflation and further build up public debt.

[4]Complementing the analysis in the October 2020 WEO—where the impact of direct public investment in low-carbon technology and infrastructure was analyzed—this chapter looks at the impact of cost-effective subsidies for investment in renewables. This modeling choice makes it possible to target sectors that already have low-emission technologies, that is, renewables-based, nuclear, and hydroelectric production and electric transportation. To some extent, the difference between public investment and subsidies is a semantic issue, as these sectors are fully or partly in public hands in many countries.

More specifically, this chapter tackles the following questions:

- *Energy transition and macroeconomic costs*: How fast could countries transition toward renewable sources of energy? What would be the costs, if any, to households and firms?
- *Credibility and design of climate policies*: How do alternative policy packages fare in terms of their effects on employment, investment, consumption and output growth, inflation, and income distribution? What does a lack of policy credibility imply?
- *Challenges for monetary policy*: How great is the output-inflation trade-off arising from higher GHG taxes? How great is it likely to be if central banks lose credibility or never had it in the first place?
- *Macroeconomic cost of procrastination*: Is delaying GHG emission reduction policies a preferable option in light of the current inflation environment? Can starting later and doing it faster achieve the same emission reductions? How great would the costs be in terms of output lost and inflation?

Answers to these questions can be summarized as follows:

- *The energy transition will entail some costs, but they should remain manageable if countries do not delay.* The speed at which countries are assumed to be able to wean themselves off fossil fuels for electricity generation plays a key role in explaining the near-term macroeconomic costs associated with the energy transition. The more difficult it is to produce clean electricity, the more costly it will be to transition, as higher GHG taxes (or tighter regulations) will be needed to trigger the necessary drop in the use of carbon-intensive goods and services in the rest of the economy. Costs will also be variable across regions, with the block (in the model employed in this chapter) representing the rest of the world (dominated by fossil fuel exporters and carbon-intensive economies) seeing the largest transition costs (see Online Annex 3.3 for an analysis of costs when alternative policies are envisioned for these countries). To reflect the uncertainty surrounding the energy transition, this chapter considers two alternative calibrations for the elasticity of substitution between renewables and fossil fuels in electricity generation. In the most pessimistic case, a sharper increase in GHG taxes (about twice as large as in the benchmark case) will be necessary to reach the same decarbonization goal. While still manageable, the energy transition's macroeconomic costs—measured in terms of lost output and higher inflation—are expected to be about twice as large and will crucially depend on policy design. Cognizant of this uncertainty, this chapter estimates global growth could be lower by 0.15 to 0.25 percentage point annually and inflation could be 0.1 to 0.4 percentage point higher. For China, Europe, and the United States, GDP growth costs are expected to be lower and in a range between 0.05 and 0.20 percentage point annually.
- *Policy design has a major influence on climate policy's final impact on output, inflation, and income distribution.* All policy packages are assumed to be financed by GHG taxation only. Using the receipts of GHG taxes to cut *labor income taxes* reduces distortions and leads to relatively higher labor supply; higher wages net of tax; and higher consumption, investment, and output. Recycling part of the GHG tax receipts into *subsidies for investment in low-carbon technologies* (renewables, nuclear and hydroelectric, electric vehicles) facilitates the transition. The same decarbonization level can be achieved with lower GHG taxes thanks to investment in carbon-neutral technology. The impact on inflation is accordingly smaller, which reduces the potential trade-offs for monetary policy. *Transferring* tax revenues to low-income households helps increase the acceptance of climate policies but comes at a cost in terms of output growth.
- *Climate policies have a limited impact on output and inflation and thus do not present a significant challenge for central banks.* Gradual and credible implementation gives agents motive and time to transition toward a low-emission economy. Induced mild inflationary pressures require some monetary policy adjustments to ensure expectations remain anchored, but at minimal GDP costs. There may even be some room to ease in the near term to facilitate the transition. In this respect, climate policies contrast greatly with supply shocks, in which the sudden increase in the energy price creates an immediate challenge for monetary authorities. Less credible climate policies require sharper adjustments down the road and generate more inflationary pressures and more challenges for monetary authorities. Larger costs materialize only with eroded monetary policy credibility, as inflationary pressures call for more policy response.
- *Further delay would only amplify any costs associated with the energy transition.* Concerns about inflation

and energy security have prompted some to suggest that decarbonization should wait until current inflationary pressures have been overcome. But this would only amplify transition costs. This chapter's analysis shows that further delay would require GHG taxes to be raised by even more and faster than in the gradual scenario, with much larger costs (the resulting inflationary impulse is about three times stronger, and preventing it would require sacrificing roughly 1 percent of GDP over the course of four years).

This chapter starts with a general survey, stressing the urgency of cutting GHG emissions by 2030 at least to an extent that is compatible with limiting warming at the end of the century to well below 2°C. It then introduces the analytical apparatus by illustrating the impact on growth and inflation of increasing GHG taxes gradually. The next section discusses the importance of credibility and complementarity between climate and monetary policy for a successful transition. The last section quantifies the macroeconomic costs of further delay and stresses that now is the time to act.

Figure 3.1. Historical and Projected Global Emissions
(Gigatons a year)

Total projected emissions in 2030 are greater than emissions compatible with the 2°C goal.

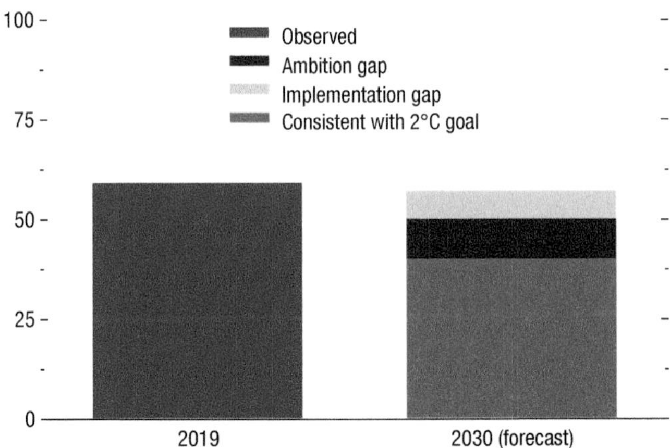

Source: Intergovernmental Panel on Climate Change.
Note: The overhang of projected emissions in 2030 over the amount compatible with 2°C warming consists of the ambition gap (the amount by which pledged emissions exceed the 2°C-compatible amount) and the implementation gap (emissions pledged to be avoided but forecast to arise under current policies).

Decarbonizing the Economy: Now Is the Time to Become Credible

Lay of the Land

The Paris Agreement enshrined the goal of 193 countries to limit global warming by the end of the century to well below 2°C and preferably to below 1.5°C. So far, countries have collectively failed to honor their pledges, and the relentless rise in emissions following the agreement has made achieving the 1.5°C target extremely difficult. Temperatures are set to rise further, and the adverse consequences are understood to be nonlinear; every increment of warming raises the risk of crossing "tipping points" that would push the global climate system into abrupt and irreversible changes (Lenton and others 2019).[5]

Limiting global warming to below 2°C requires that emissions decline by 25 percent relative to current levels by 2030, which would mean an unprecedented acceleration in mitigation efforts, but one that is crucial to limit the extent of damage to the Earth's climate system. Unfortunately, such a regime change in climate policy remains elusive in almost all countries (UNEP and UNEP-CCC 2021; IPCC 2022; Black and others 2021). The IPCC projects that under policies currently in place, emissions in 2030 will be more than 42 percent higher than those required to reach the Paris Agreement target (Figure 3.1). Not only are existing policy pledges insufficiently ambitious (the "ambition gap" in the figure), but they are also projected to be missed under current policies (the "implementation gap"). While pledges are more ambitious among advanced economies than among countries in other economic groups, climate goals can be achieved only through a global effort (October 2020 *World Economic Outlook*, Chapter 3).

Enhancing Credibility of Climate Policy for More Effectiveness

Lack of ambition and failing implementation characterize the history of climate policy, which allows parallels to be drawn with other areas of public policy. For example, Kydland and Prescott (1977) demonstrate how central bankers concerned about inflation as well as short-term unemployment form time-inconsistent monetary policies that lead to higher inflation with no

[5]Some tipping points amplify global warming itself; for example, GHGs released by thawing permafrost or the vanishing of ice sheets, which help reflect solar heat.

gains in employment. Similarly, governments announce carbon-reducing policies but have incentives to renege on them to try to maximize output or employment or safeguard particular interests (Brulle 2018) during their terms.

With investment and research and development decisions based on long planning horizons, it is key that (to affect behaviors) new climate policy measures and commitments to future carbon-reducing policies (for example, increments in GHG taxes, regulations, and subsidies) be perceived as credible and irreversible (see "Credible Policies: Key for a Successful Transition"). As is the case for monetary policy, the credibility—and thereby effectiveness—of climate policy will be enhanced if (1) there is a clearly defined *rules-based commitment* rather than pure discretion on how future decarbonization targets will be achieved, (2) instruments and analysis of policies to reach such targets are *transparent*, and (3) the targets are implemented *independently*, insulated from the political process (Nemet and others 2017). Ideally, the third criterion would involve an institutional arrangement akin to central banks' mandates to pursue price stability as their primary goal, along with operational independence, granted by law. However, this is still a high bar, even in countries with the most advanced climate mitigation policies (such as Denmark and Sweden). To overcome the absence of institutional independence, some countries have taken explicit account of political economy constraints when designing climate policies. For instance, because the impact of GHG taxes tends to fall disproportionately on the poor in many countries, it is important to carve out some transfers for the poor from GHG tax revenues to amplify support for GHG tax policy; widespread acceptance greatly increases credibility. Pragmatic policy design may then have to sacrifice some efficiency (usually achieved by cutting distortionary taxes) for equity and allow some amount of redistribution (Box 3.2).

Climate Policies to Keep Paris within Reach

Conceptual Framework

Past experiences with GHG mitigation policies throw only a partial light on such policies' near-term macroeconomic impacts. Most empirical studies point to negligible near-term effects of mitigation policies on output and inflation (Metcalf and Stock 2020; Konradt and Weder di Mauro 2021). But the policies analyzed in these studies are much smaller in scale and scope than the policies that will be required to achieve a path consistent with reaching the Paris Agreement's goals, which limits the studies' empirical information content for the questions at hand.

The literature has long recognized this tension, and numerous large-scale general equilibrium global models have been used to analyze the impact of GHG mitigation policies on emissions and economic activity in the long term. However, very few have been designed to simultaneously incorporate enough granularity in key sectors (energy generation, transportation), model-consistent expectations, nonlinearities that reflect increasing marginal cost to the decarbonization process, and the nominal and real rigidities required to analyze the near-term consequences of large policy changes for inflation and output (see Box 3.1 for a review of the empirical literature and an indirect validation of the GMMET's quantitative properties based on a battery of large-scale models' simulations of the effect of a gradual rise in carbon tax in the United States).

This chapter relies on the new GMMET, which shares a set of key features with the IMF's workhorse Global Integrated Monetary and Fiscal (GIMF) model. Like the GIMF model, the GMMET is a multicountry, microfounded, nonlinear dynamic general equilibrium model used to simulate the transition between an initial condition and a final steady state. Households and firms are forward-looking and choose consumption, labor supply, asset holdings, and investment optimally, considering their preferences and expected lifetimes. Nominal and real frictions as well as the explicit modeling of expectations allow the analysis of cyclical fluctuations and governments' related stabilization policies. The GMMET is configured for four regions: China, the euro area, the United States, and a block representing the rest of the world.

The purpose of the GMMET is to analyze the short- and medium-term macroeconomic impact of curbing GHG emissions. Such an analysis requires a detailed description of GHG-emission-generating activities and their interaction with the rest of the economy. These activities include fossil fuel mining and trade, electricity generation using various technologies (capturing the intermittence of renewable sources, discussed in more detail in Box 3.3), transportation with electric vehicles and conventional cars (with network externalities between electric vehicles and charging stations accounted for), and energy use in the production of goods and for residential heating, as well as activities that emit non-fossil-fuel GHGs, such as agriculture. Online Annex 3.1 and Carton and others (2022) outline these activities, which are novel relative to the GIMF model.

Under the Hood: Analytical Simulations Using the GMMET

To set the stage, this section focuses on *analytical* simulations that allow the effect of key elasticities to be disentangled and different plans for recycling GHG tax revenues to be contrasted. In all exercises in this section, GHG taxes are increased gradually and globally over the next eight years, such that every region decreases its GHG emissions by about 25 percent. Each region chooses a different level for its GHG price, as each has different degrees of emission intensity in electricity generation and in its productive industries. For example, Chinese steel manufacturing relies heavily on coal, the euro area already has a large share of renewables technology for its electricity generation, and the United States has the highest level of consumer use of electricity and of fossil fuel usage for heating and transportation.[6]

A key caveat of this chapter's simulation exercises is that they implicitly compare policy scenarios against a no-catastrophe, no-action baseline that is environmentally not feasible. Forgoing mitigation action until 2030 implies irreversible jeopardization of the future of the climate system whose long-term costs are expected to be very large, even if difficult to quantify (October 2020 *World Economic Outlook*, Chapter 3; Keen and others 2021). The exercises on delayed mitigation policy presented in the following subsections address this point by comparing mitigation action today with its true alternative: rushed delayed action.

Energy Transition: How Quickly Can It Be Achieved?

The pace at which an economy can transition out of fossil fuels hinges heavily on the pace at which electricity generation can wean itself off such fuels, and, in particular, off coal. Two elasticities are key for this process in the GMMET: the elasticity of substitution of fossil fuels—especially coal—for renewables in electricity generation and the elasticity of substitution of electricity for other fossil fuels in the production of goods and services. Considerable uncertainty surrounds the value of the first elasticity. On the one hand, structural, technological, and geopolitical impediments (such as insufficient backup power and grid integration for intermittent renewables, slow technological progress in regard to electricity storage, bottlenecks in the supply of metals for renewables and the electricity grid, trade restrictions, and supply chain issues) may prevent a rapid transition to renewables-based electricity generation. On the other hand, rapid technological progress has led to massive improvements in efficiency and drops in prices of renewable energy, and the outlook for storage capacity technology is favorable (October 2020 *World Economic Outlook*, Chapter 3).[7]

Under the *benchmark* calibration, the share of renewables in electricity generation increases by 20 percentage points by 2030. This increase is broadly in line with the experiences of Germany and California but is faster than what larger countries or regions have achieved so far.[8] An *alternative* calibration assumes the pace at which electricity generation can be decarbonized to be roughly half as fast under the same policies, reflecting the experience of China and the United States over the past decade (the European Union is in between, with an increase in the share of renewables by about 15 percentage points). In this calibration, industry and consumers have to shoulder a larger part of the required decarbonization, and a sharper increase in GHG taxes (as much as twice as large) will be necessary to reach the goal of a 25 percent drop in emission by 2030.

Under the *alternative* calibration, elasticities of substitution related to the use of fossil fuels are lower (reduced to one-fourth in electricity generation, halved in the manufacturing sector; see Annex Table 3.1.2). Figure 3.2 contrasts the outcome of the two calibrations and displays the range of possible macroeconomic effects of the energy transition in two different cases. The first case assumes that tax revenues are fully rebated to households in the form of a lump-sum

[6]To understand details on the differences in model calibration that have an impact on results in the four regions, please see "Calibrating the Energy Sectors" in Online Annex 3.1 and "Decarbonization in Different Regions: A Primer" in Online Annex 3.3.

[7]See Online Annex 3.1 for a more complete description of the energy generation sector in the GMMET, as well as key elasticities driving the pace of energy transition and its importance for investment in high- and low-carbon-intensity capital.

[8]The improvements in renewables technologies and the decline in prices since Germany and California deployed such technologies suggest a higher speed of decarbonization could be envisioned today in certain countries.

Figure 3.2. Macroeconomic Impact in 2030 of a GHG Tax under Different Calibrations of Elasticities
(Deviation from baseline)

Lower elasticities require higher GHG prices to achieve the same reduction in emissions by 2030 and magnify the macroeconomic impacts.

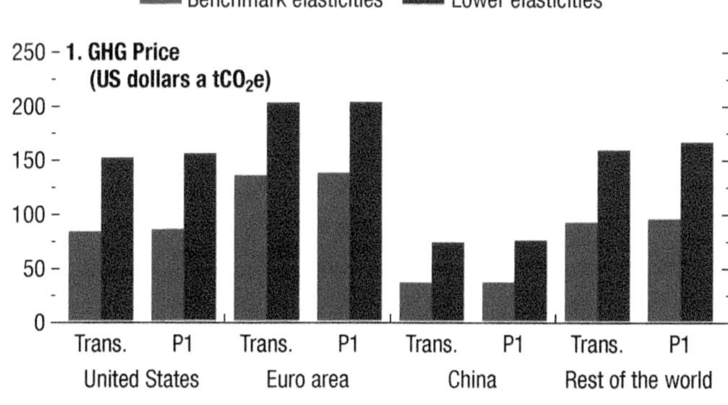

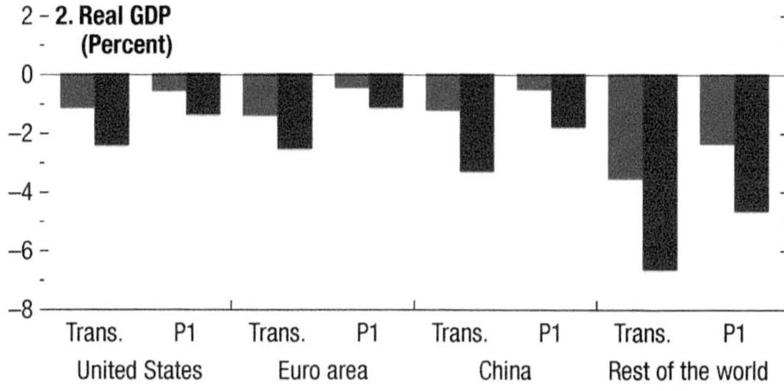

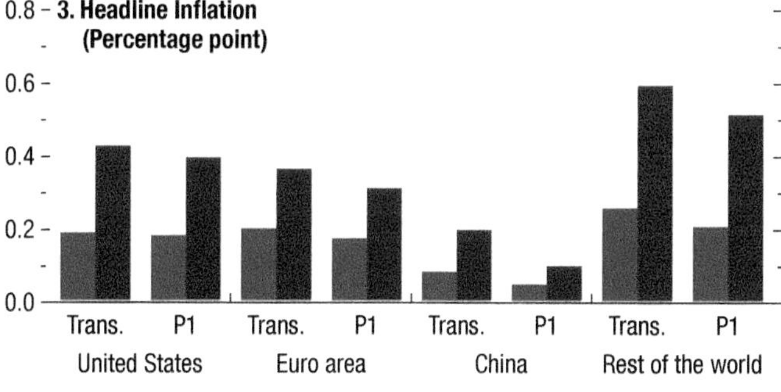

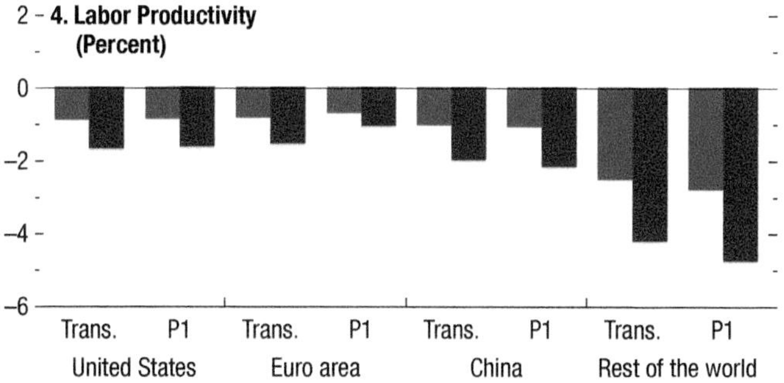

Sources: Global Macroeconomic Model for the Energy Transition; and IMF staff estimates.
Note: P1 = Policy Package 1: two-thirds labor tax cuts and one-third transfers to households; GHG = greenhouse gas; tCO_2e = metric ton of carbon dioxide equivalent; Trans. = recycling GHG tax revenue as transfers to households.

transfer (labeled "Trans." in the figure). This isolates the effect of climate policy from fiscal policy, since fiscal policy using lump-sum transfers is nondistortionary and budget-neutral. The second case is described later in this section and assumes that tax receipts are partly recycled through a labor income tax cut (Policy Package 1, labeled "P1" in the figure). Under the alternative calibration, Policy Package 1 reduces GDP by 1–2 percent in China, the euro area, and the US by 2030.[9] These costs are roughly twice as large as those under the benchmark calibration but remain manageable; the two calibrations span a range of 0.15–0.25 percentage point of annual growth.[10] They are dwarfed by the immense risks to lives and livelihoods across the world (IPCC 2022) and very large long-term output costs associated with a business-as-usual policy potentially leading to catastrophic climate disruptions (see Chapter 3 of the October 2020 *World Economic Outlook* for estimates of averted damage).

Alternative Options to Recycle GHG Tax Revenues

A higher GHG tax, because it increases the price of energy, has been compared to an oil price shock (Pisani-Ferry 2021). But the apparent similarity can be misleading. GHG tax revenues can be redistributed domestically to alleviate some of the burden of the new tax for producers, consumers, or both.[11] Moreover, oil price shocks are often sudden, unexpected, and temporary, whereas in the simulations here, GHG taxes rise gradually from 2022 onward. A better frame of reference is the literature on productivity shocks (see, for example, Galí 2015). In this chapter's simulations, a GHG tax leads to a permanent decline in future productivity. Forward-looking agents will anticipate a drop in future profits and income due to higher expected future energy prices and will cut investment and

[9]For illustration, 1.5 percent of US GDP is about $320 billion and corresponds to the climate portion of that country's recently passed Inflation Reduction Act; the costs would be spread over eight years, or $40 billion a year.

[10]The rest-of-the-world region aggregates different economies, and drawing conclusions in regard to individual countries is not possible. The region encompasses the bulk of fossil fuel producers and is characterized by high energy intensity—in particular, high oil intensity. On net, the GDP impact is dominated by fossil fuel producers that are particularly affected during the transition as demand for fossil fuel and investment drops (see Chapter 3 of the October 2020 *World Economic Outlook* and "Decarbonization in Different Regions: A Primer" in Online Annex 3.3 for further discussions).

[11]In a supply-and-demand analogy, an oil price shock represents a shift of the supply curve, while a GHG tax is a shift along the supply curve.

consumption accordingly.[12] In the short to medium term, while the tax is still low, lower aggregate demand dominates the increase in energy costs, and a central bank focused on stabilizing core inflation will want to accommodate the shock (see Online Annex 3.3 and Chapter 2 of the *2022 External Sector Report* for a discussion of the impact on the real interest rate).[13]

GHG taxes generate fiscal revenues that can be used to (1) help accelerate the transition, through incentives, subsidies, and public investment; (2) cushion the taxes' effect on firms' output and household income; or (3) compensate low-income households through targeted transfers. These options are part of fiscal policy, and countries will choose among them in line with their preferences and political economy considerations.[14] The following illustrates the implications of these choices for macroeconomic outcomes. Figure 3.3 contrasts three different strategies by which GHG tax revenues are recycled in the economy, by (1) reducing distortionary labor income taxes,[15] (2) subsidizing production by sector to offset the effect of the tax and provide incentives for the transition to less-carbon-intensive energy (akin to a "feebate"), or (3) simply rebating the tax's proceeds to households.

The tax has a very similar impact on inflation across the different strategies, reflecting the central bank's assumed credibility, that is, that it would respond to inflation to keep firms' and households' inflation expectations anchored. Increasing the GHG tax increases the relative price of fossil fuels and, given that other prices in the economy do not move quickly, also increases the overall price level. Absent indexation schemes,

Figure 3.3. Macroeconomic Impact of Different Recycling Options in the United States
(Percent deviation from baseline, unless noted otherwise)

Different revenue-recycling options shape the impacts of a given greenhouse gas price path on the US economy.

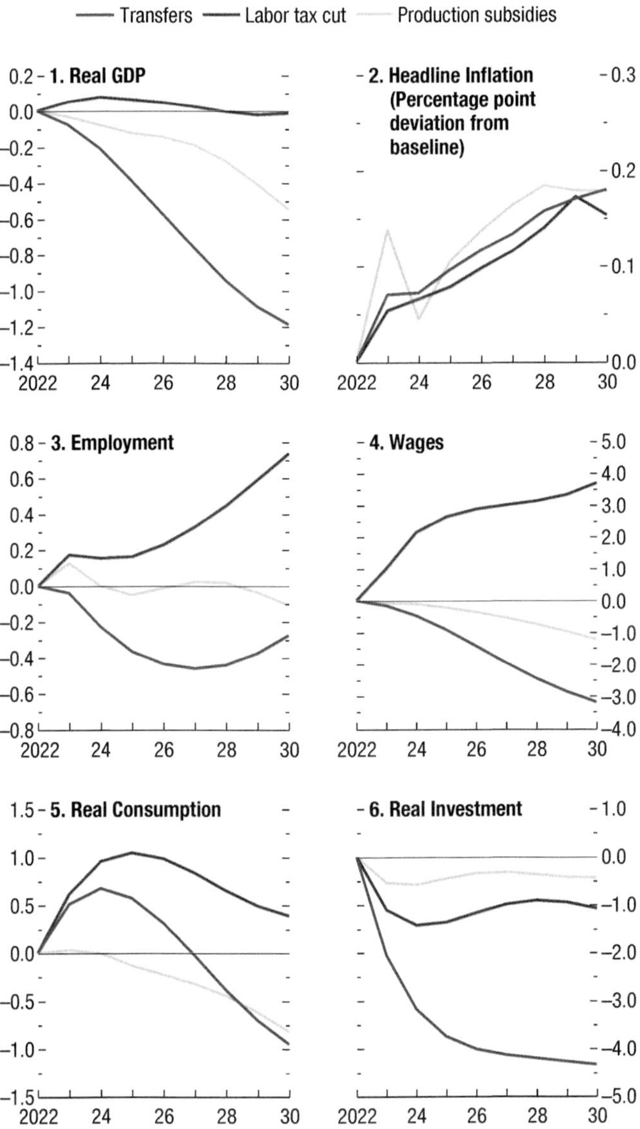

Sources: Global Macroeconomic Model for the Energy Transition; and IMF staff estimates.
Note: Results based on benchmark elasticities.

the impact is limited to the tax's first-round effect on energy prices. However, the impacts on the labor market, output, and output's use differ substantially across the three recycling strategies. While both lump-sum transfers and labor tax cuts boost consumption by transferring more income to households, only labor tax cuts, by reducing a disincentive to work, have a positive

[12]Investment in carbon-intensive capital will drop as firms adjust to the soon-to-become-obsolete capital stock. Investment in renewables and associated capital increases but not enough to offset the drop in carbon-intensive capital (see Online Annex 3.2). The price of energy in general increases. If lump-sum transfers are large, consumption increases in the short term, but the effect is short-lived. In the medium to long term, consumption declines as well owing to the tax's impact on households' permanent income.

[13]Note that the material that follows makes no attempt to derive "optimal (in the sense of welfare-maximizing) policy." The goal is to illustrate and guide, not to be normative, as the preferred policy is left to countries' authorities, given their individual situations and preferences. For discussions of optimal policy in response to an oil price shock, please refer to Blanchard and Galí (2007); Castillo, Montoro, and Tuesta (2007); Nakov and Pescatori (2010); and Natal (2012).

[14]Recycling tax revenues through lump-sum transfers is budget-neutral and nondistortionary, which averts any mixing up of the effects of climate and fiscal policy.

[15]The labor supply elasticity is 0.15, in the middle of the range of available estimates.

impact on both employment and output. Transfers compensate low-income households for higher energy prices and thereby mitigate the regressive effects of the GHG tax. Production subsidies have a beneficial effect on investment but at the expense of consumption, as they preclude transfers or tax cuts to households.

Feasible and Balanced Climate Policy Packages to Keep Paris within Reach

This subsection looks at feasible climate policy packages designed to align emissions by 2030 with the Paris Agreement while striking a balance among maximizing employment, output growth, investment in renewables, and compensating low-income households. The three policy packages examined have different objectives, but all attempt a compromise in which energy transition is realized at relatively low cost in terms of output and inflation. All packages allow for some income redistribution through transfers but combine different policy instruments and tax-recycling strategies (see Table 3.1). Policy Package 1, by using two-thirds of GHG tax revenues to cut labor income taxes, focuses on the need to engineer the required decarbonization without overly penalizing consumption. Relatively higher GHG taxes are required to provide incentives for reallocation toward less-carbon-intensive production processes, and investment declines more than in the other packages. Policy Package 3 focuses on supporting firms during the transition. The transition is then relatively smooth in terms of investment, which drops much less than in Policy Package 1. Because tax receipts are entirely rebated to firms, households bear the brunt of the tax-induced slowdown, and the consumption-to-investment ratio declines. Policy Package 2 can be seen as a combination of Policy Packages 1 and 3, as it complements measures to support households during the transition with subsidies to low-emission sectors (renewables, nuclear and hydro power plants, and purchase of electric vehicles). Subsidies support investment more than in Policy Package 1. Using the revenues for subsidies comes at the expense of consumption, as it reduces the allocations to tax cuts and transfers. Moreover, because Policy Package 2 offers incentives for investment, the required emission reduction can occur with lower GHG taxes and therefore less inflation (see Online Annex 3.3 for more details, including the external dimension). This scenario illustrates that a strategy relying on large subsidies for low-emission technologies poses little risk of inflation.

Differences across countries and regions reflect mainly different starting values in terms of energy use, proportion of fossil fuels in the consumption basket, and GHG tax increases required to reach the 25 percent decarbonization goal (Figure 3.4). Projections for inflation in China are a case in point. Because households' direct energy consumption accounts for a lower share of the consumer price index (CPI) in China, the GHG tax increase does not affect the CPI as much there as in the other regions in the simulation. As a result, the demand-contracting effect of the tax dominates and pushes the core part of the price index down. The impact on growth is much larger in the rest of the world—a residual category dominated by fossil fuel exporters and oil-intensive economies—reflecting the rapid energy transition assumed in the chapter's homogeneous reduction of emissions by 25 percent. To reflect the Paris Agreement's principle that responsibility for decarbonization efforts must be simultaneous but can be differentiated, Online Annex 3.3 analyzes the global impact on emissions, output, and inflation when the rest of the world

Table 3.1. Three Policy Packages Reducing Emissions by 25 Percent in 2030

Package 1	Package 2	Package 3
Gradual GHG price increase from 2023 to 2030	Gradual GHG price increase from 2023 to 2026	Gradual GHG price increase from 2023 to 2030
Two-thirds of revenue used to reduce labor taxes	One-third of revenue used to reduce labor taxes	GHG revenue rebated at the sectoral level (electricity generation, manufacturing, services)
One-third of revenue transferred to households	One-third of revenue transferred to households	GHG revenue from households' activities (residential energy and individual transportation) transferred back to households
	One-third of revenue used to subsidize low-emission sectors: • Renewables investment • Nuclear and hydro power plants • Electric-vehicle purchase	Regulation of share of electric vehicles

Source: IMF staff compilation.
Note: GHG = greenhouse gas.

Figure 3.4. Macroeconomic Impact of the Three Policy Packages in Regions in the Simulation

Green subsidies (Package 2) reduce the need for greenhouse gas price increases and result in lower inflation for the same policy rule. Production subsidies (Package 3) boost investment and GDP with little impact on inflation.

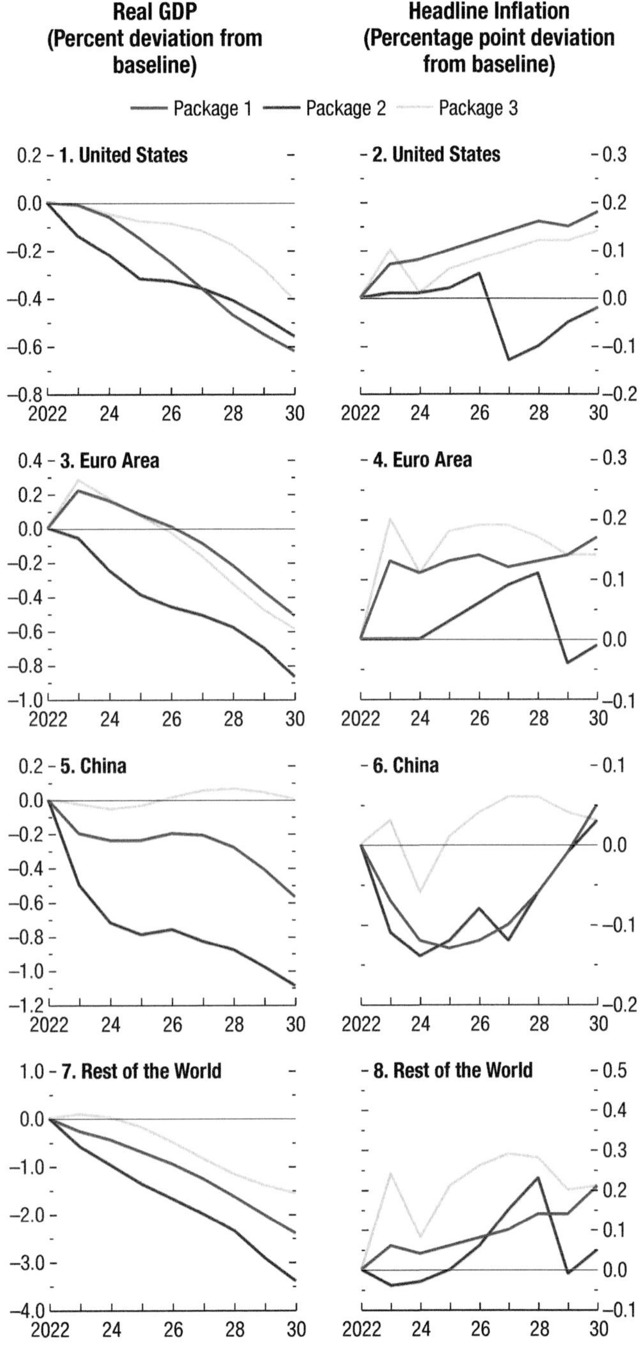

Sources: Global Macroeconomic Model for the Energy Transition; and IMF staff estimates.
Note: Results based on benchmark elasticities. Policy Package 1: one-third transfers to households, two-thirds labor tax cuts; Policy Package 2: one-third transfers to households, one-third labor tax cuts, one-third green subsidies; Policy Package 3: production subsidies and transportation regulation. See Table 3.1 for a full description of the three policy packages.

does not introduce any new policy.[16] In such a case, the rest of the world's investment declines only in extraction industries, and the GDP impact is muted (see Annex Figure 3.3.3).

All simulations discussed so far have assumed perfectly credible monetary and climate policies. The next section analyzes the implications of climate policy for the macroeconomy when announced policies are less than perfectly credible.

Credible Policies: Key for a Successful Transition

Credibility of Climate Policy

So far, the scenarios presented have assumed governments' climate policies to be fully credible: the private sector (both firms and households) takes current and future policies, including the path of the GHG price, into account to adjust its decisions. Policy Package 2, in which credible green subsidies provide powerful incentives to unleash private green investment and allow the required emission reduction with lower GHG taxes than in Policy Package 1, clearly shows the importance of credible policy. This subsection illustrates the importance of credible climate policy by relaxing the assumption of full credibility under Policy Package 1, with its gradually increasing GHG tax path. Climate policy is assumed to be believed only gradually over time (partial credibility): more specifically, each increment of the GHG tax is expected to remain in place, but future increments of the GHG price path come as a surprise, thereby having no impact on households' and firms' current decisions.

For given GHG price paths, partial credibility slows down the emission reduction process relative to the full-credibility case (the cumulative emission reduction by 2030, expressed as a share of 2022 emissions, is about 20 percent lower under partial credibility than under full credibility; see Figure 3.5), as investment in emission-intensive capital does not decline as rapidly. The key reason lies in the adjustment of investment in

[16]See Mirzoev and others (2020) for a discussion of carbon transition risks in Gulf Cooperation Council countries. For these countries, accelerating the diversification of their economies is key. Policies that seek to strengthen the non-oil sector through better business regulation, greater credit availability, reforms to the labor market, and increased sources of non-oil revenue for the government should be prioritized. In cases in which the transition involves a large drop in aggregate demand, fiscal stimulus can be envisioned, provided fiscal space is comfortable enough (see Chapter 3 of the October 2020 *World Economic Outlook* for further analysis).

Figure 3.5. Impact in 2030 of Fully and Partially Credible Mitigation Policies

Less credible policies either miss the GHG reduction target when meeting GHG price paths, owing to insufficient shifts in the capital structure, or require higher GHG prices to meet the GHG reduction targets at a higher macroeconomic cost.

Fully credible
Partially credible—same GHG price paths
Partially credible—same GHG reduction targets

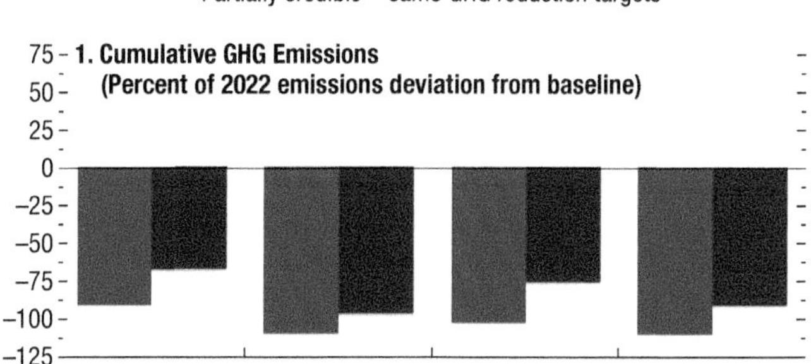

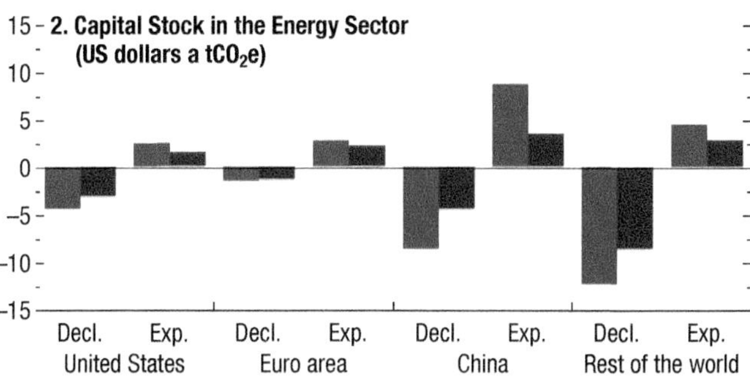

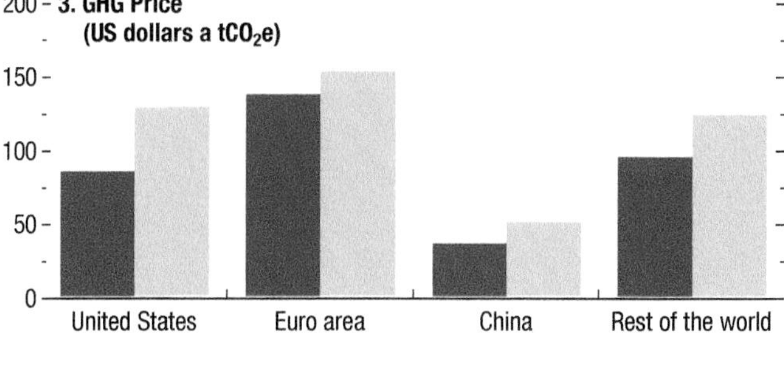

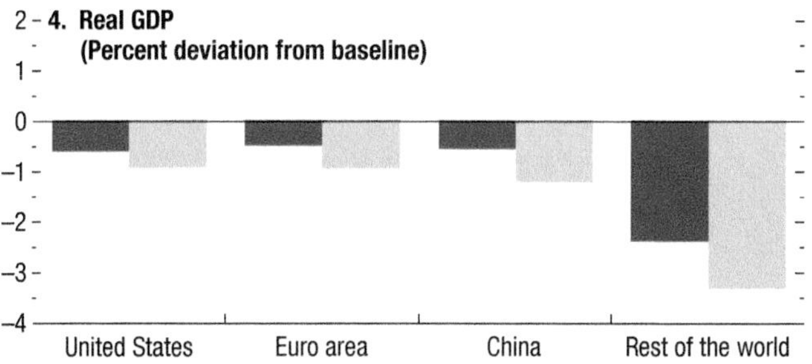

Sources: Global Macroeconomic Model for the Energy Transition; and IMF staff estimates.
Note: Results based on Policy Package 1 with benchmark elasticities.
Decl. = declining energy sector: fossil fuel extractions and coal power plants; Exp. = expanding sectors: renewables, nuclear, hydro and fossil gas generation, electricity grid. See Table 3.1 for a full description of the three policy packages. GHG = greenhouse gas; tCO_2e = metric ton of carbon dioxide equivalent.

the electricity sector. When climate policy is fully credible, the anticipation of further GHG price increases—which will undermine future profitability—accelerates the shift of capital away from emission-intensive investments, such as coal power plants, toward low-emission alternatives.

Partially credible policy requires higher GHG taxes to reach the same decarbonization goal, leading to larger GDP losses by the end of the decade (in the United States, the euro area, and China, GDP declines by 1.0, 1.0, and 1.2 percent, respectively, rather than 0.6, 0.5, and 0.6 percent).

Credibility of Monetary Policy

The current high-inflation environment has raised concerns that climate policy could create large output-inflation trade-offs, complicate the job of central banks, and potentially stoke wage-price spirals. This subsection shows that as long as central banks retain their inflation-fighting credentials, any trade-offs implied by the sort of climate policy studied in this chapter are bound to be small. As a matter of fact, climate policy, if implemented gradually, should be easier for central banks to handle than supply shocks in which the energy price increases suddenly and creates an immediate challenge for monetary authorities. If central banks lose credibility, however, trade-offs will be amplified, underscoring the importance of monetary policy credibility. Climate policy is no exception in this respect. If monetary policy is not credible, any cost-push shock is bound to entail larger trade-offs (Woodford 2003; Galí 2015). When monetary policy credibility prevents the de-anchoring of inflation expectations, a gradually implemented climate policy package will not give rise to a material output-inflation trade-off (see Figure 3.6 for results in regard to Policy Package 1). A comparison of the impact of a higher GHG tax on output and inflation under two different monetary policy rules reveals no major differences between targeting core inflation (that is, excluding energy items) and a modified version in which the targeting includes the change in GHG price (core plus GHG price). Targeting core inflation will give rise to slightly higher headline inflation because of the tax's direct impact on noncore CPI components, while targeting the modified version of core inflation (core plus GHG price) will have a larger cost in terms of lost output (necessary to bring about the required decline in marginal costs and core inflation to offset the tax's

Figure 3.6. Macroeconomic Impact of Different Monetary Policy Targets in the United States

(Percentage point deviation from baseline, unless noted otherwise)

Including the impact of the GHG price on the consumer price index has limited macroeconomic implications as long as monetary policy credibility prevents any de-anchoring of inflation expectations.

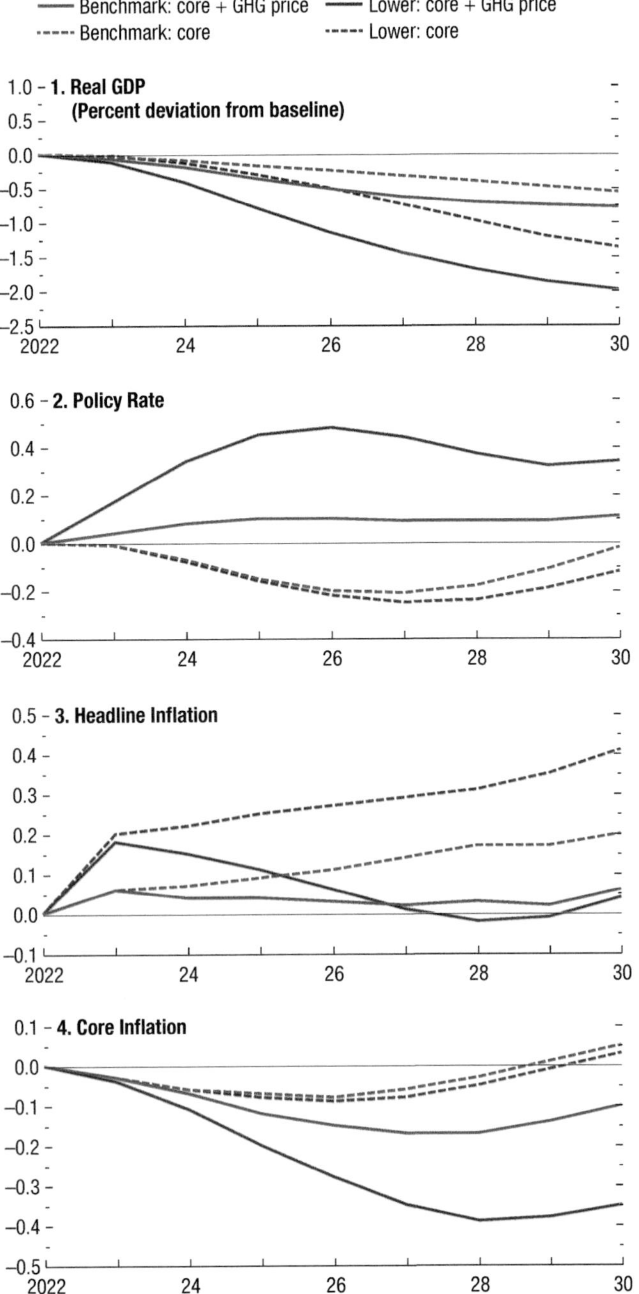

Sources: Global Macroeconomic Model for the Energy Transition; and IMF staff estimates.

Note: Results based on Policy Package 1 with benchmark and lower elasticities described in Annex Table 3.1.1. See Table 3.1 for a full description of the three policy packages. GHG = greenhouse gas.

impact on noncore prices) but will drive headline inflation back to target. The difference in magnitudes remains quite small. In essence, core plus GHG price targeting keeps headline inflation close to target in the absence of shocks to other noncore components.

Of course, a great deal depends on how easily electricity generation can transition out of fossil fuels toward renewables. Larger frictions than assumed in the benchmark calibration would imply that to reach decarbonization goals, governments would have to increase GHG taxes substantially more and faster (than in the benchmark elasticity case), with implications for growth and inflation. Figure 3.6 illustrates the differences. For example, under the alternative (lower-elasticity) calibration and core plus GHG price targeting, by 2030 GDP would be about 1¼ percent lower than under the benchmark calibration.

In today's high-inflation environment, if monetary policy were to lose credibility, wages could start indexing to past inflation levels. As a result, the inflation process would become more inertial, which would result in inflation depending more on past inflation rather than being anchored to the inflation target. In such an environment, introducing climate policies, such as Policy Package 1, could potentially lead to second-round effects and larger output-inflation trade-offs. Figure 3.7 shows that in such a case, stabilizing the modified version of core inflation (core plus GHG price) would have a significantly higher cost in terms of output, while stabilizing output could trigger a wage-price spiral as the central bank stimulates the economy enough to keep labor demand and real wages in check, pushing up nominal wages and prices in a feedback loop.

Inflation expectations have remained broadly anchored in a majority of countries and, in particular, in the large emitters that are the chapter's focus (see Chapters 1 and 2). In countries where central banks might be less credible, alternative policy packages that have a much smaller impact on prices (for example, Policy Package 2) could be favored in case concerns about the anchoring of inflation expectations are warranted.[17]

While this exercise is meant to be mainly illustrative, highlighting the unpleasant trade-offs that could

[17]In such a case, policies that entail a smaller pass-through to headline inflation may be favored, such as combining a GHG price with subsidies for low-emission technologies in electricity or transportation.

Figure 3.7. Macroeconomic Impact of Different Monetary Policy Targets under Wage Indexation

Wage indexation worsens the output-inflation trade-off.

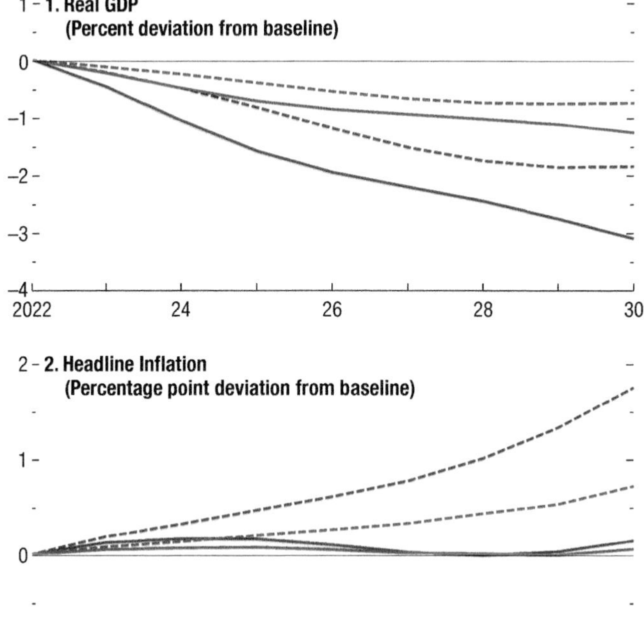

Sources: Global Macroeconomic Model for the Energy Transition; and IMF staff estimates.
Note: Results based on Policy Package 1. See Table 3.1 for a full description of the three policy packages. Panels depict alternative wage and price Phillips curves. Benchmark and lower elasticities described in Annex Table 3.1.1. GHG = greenhouse gas.

result from a lack of central bank credibility could raise the question of whether it is reasonable to wait—as some have proposed—until inflation is tamed before implementing the required climate policies. The next section shows that waiting would only complicate the transition.

Transition Costs under Further Delays

As noted earlier in this chapter, gradually phased-in climate policy packages that are rolled out without delay would have only very limited consequences in regard to inflation, provided central banks remain credible. A prominent concern at the current juncture, however, is that climate mitigation policies could de-anchor inflation expectations by raising the specter of future GHG-price-driven inflationary pressures in an already-high-inflation environment. This section asks whether delaying the necessary climate action by a few years, until inflation is brought under control, could be an option.

To assess this policy option, Policy Package 1 starting in 2023 is compared with a delayed mitigation policy package that starts in 2027 but is still compatible with the Paris Agreement's objective in that it achieves the same reduction in cumulative emissions in the long term. The results are reported only for the United States; Online Annex 3.4 presents other regions' results. The delayed package has the same composition as Policy Package 1 but is phased in more rapidly and has a higher GHG tax for some years, since a steeper decline in emissions is required to offset the unmitigated accumulation of emissions from 2023 to 2026. Both packages assume credible monetary policy.

The higher speed at which the transition must take place if it is delayed significantly worsens the output-inflation trade-off (Figure 3.8). First, larger annual increments in the GHG tax directly generate larger increases in headline inflation. Second, a shorter transition period leads to a rapid fall in the utilization of capital for the production of fossil fuels, at a large cost to firms and their profitability. This is in addition to the decline in investment by all firms to allow them to shift out of any emission-intensive capital. If monetary policy targets output (to decline at the same pace as in the gradual scenario), headline inflation increases by much more than in Policy Package 1 (dashed red line); if it targets the modified version of core (core plus GHG price), output drops much faster (solid red line).

Therefore, if the concern is that higher GHG taxes may end up threatening central banks' credibility, leading to larger output-inflation trade-offs, delaying climate policy does not appear to be a reasonable option. A *risk management approach* to monetary policy might instead suggest starting to implement the necessary GHG taxes right away and leaning against their impact on headline inflation. Doing so (solid blue line in Figure 3.6) would minimize the risk that higher headline inflation will weaken the central bank's credibility and lead to widespread wage indexation and higher inflation inertia.

Comparing this policy approach with the alternative of delaying climate policy implementation to after 2026 highlights the much larger costs, in both

Figure 3.8. Gradual and Delayed GHG Mitigation Policies in the United States

Delaying mitigation policies considerably worsens the output-inflation trade-off.

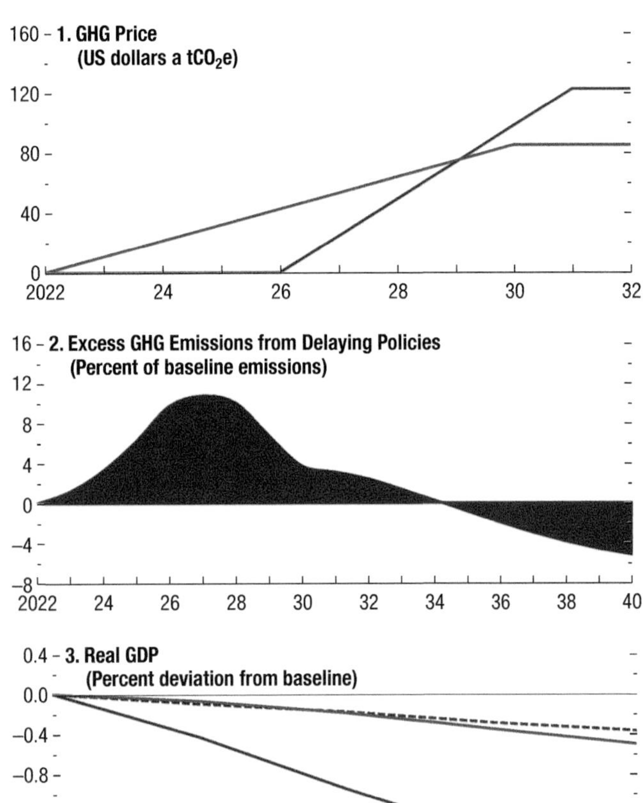

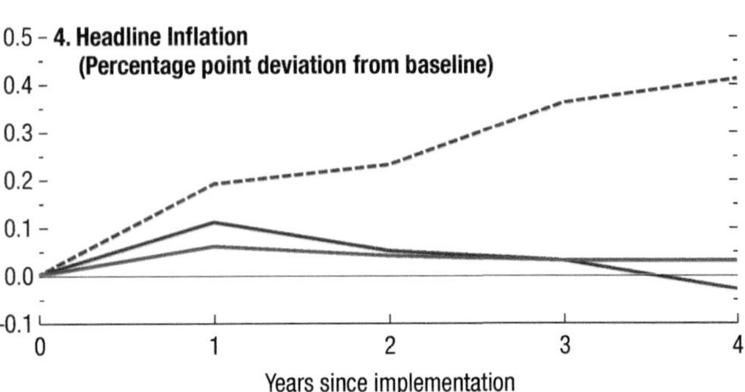

Sources: Global Macroeconomic Model for the Energy Transition; and IMF staff estimates.
Note: Results based on Policy Package 1 with benchmark elasticities. Monetary policy targets Core + GHG price under "Gradual" and "Delayed"; Under "Delayed (GDP target)," monetary policy targets the same GDP as in "Gradual." GHG = greenhouse gas; tCO_2e = metric ton of carbon dioxide equivalent.

inflation and output, of the latter option. Further procrastinating requires an even more rushed transition in which inflation can be contained only at significant cost to real GDP.

Conclusions and Policy Implications

Decades of procrastination on climate policy have made it all the more urgent to act now. To keep the Paris Agreement's goal within reach, GHG emissions must decline by 25 percent, with respect to current levels, by 2030. Achieving such a result would require unprecedented global effort and would represent a serious acceleration with respect to the past decade. Rising concerns about energy independence offer the opportunity to bolster the transition in the energy sector.

How costly such efforts could be depends a great deal on how quickly electricity generation can be decarbonized. The more difficult it is to transition to clean electricity, the larger the GHG tax increase will have to be to provide incentives for larger efforts in other sectors—and the larger the macroeconomic costs in terms of growth and inflation. Different calibrations of elasticities of substitution away from fossil fuels suggest global GDP could be between 0.9 and 2.0 percent below baseline by 2030, which would amount to a slowdown of 0.15 to 0.25 percentage point in yearly growth. Inflation could increase to reach 0.1 to 0.4 percentage point above baseline. Considerable variation across regions is to be expected, with the largest effects concentrated among fossil fuel exporters.

While not trivial, these costs are manageable and dwarfed by the innumerable long-term benefits (in regard to output, financial stability, health) of arresting climate change (October 2020 *World Economic Outlook*; IPCC 2022) that have been thoroughly documented by climate science. However, the route to Paris could become more onerous if a series of conditions are not met. First, the required climate policies need to be implemented immediately. Further delaying implementation will amplify the output-inflation trade-offs that central banks may face. An immediate start will allow a gradual process whereby GHG taxes can be increased in small and predictable increments, driving private expectations and behaviors and limiting inflationary pressures. Second, it is important that new climate policy be credible. Credible climate policies offer incentives for investment and research and development in carbon-neutral technology and help accelerate the shift in consumption patterns toward low-carbon alternatives. International experience shows that rebating tax revenues to low-income households (which are bound to suffer the most from the new carbon pricing) helps bolster acceptance and reinforces such policies' credibility. Third, monetary policy credibility complements climate policy credibility and is essential to keep output-inflation trade-offs low. Doubts about central banks' price stabilization credentials could lead to more widespread wage indexation and higher inflation inertia, which would further amplify output-inflation trade-offs and the cost of future stabilization. Concerns about current high inflation offer no justification for delaying necessary actions.

It is not too late to avert the most catastrophic climate damages, but ensuring that temperature increases remain well below 2°C at a reasonable cost will require immediate, credible, transparent, and ambitious action. Because GHGs know no borders, the effort to accomplish this goal needs to be global. The rise in geopolitical tensions related to the Russian invasion of Ukraine and the recent deterioration in China–US relationships have put global cooperation on climate goals at risk. If different international standards arose, carbon border adjustment taxes could help prevent excess leakage and accelerate the convergence of tax and regulations to the highest global standard. International coordination in GHG taxation could also allow faster decarbonization, as low-hanging fruit could be plucked in many countries that have not yet started decarbonization. Productive areas of cooperation might include bridging data gaps, improving reporting standards, and increasing access to climate finance in emerging market and developing economies (October 2022 *Global Financial Stability Report*, Chapter 2; Ferreira and others 2021).

Box 3.1. Near-Term Implications of Carbon Pricing: A Review of the Literature

Most empirical studies find that carbon-pricing programs implemented so far, even though quite modest, have led to significant reductions in emissions. Over the past two decades, a number of countries have rolled out carbon-pricing programs, with carbon tax rates and coverage of various magnitudes (Figure 3.1.1). Empirical analyses find that despite low carbon prices, emission-trading markets and carbon taxes have led to sizable reductions in emissions. For instance, the European Union (EU) Emissions Trading System (ETS)[1] has been found to have reduced EU-wide emissions by 3.8 percent between 2008 and 2016, although the market covered only 50 percent of EU carbon emissions and the price remained below €20 a ton up to 2018 (Bayer and Aklin 2020). ETS-regulated manufacturing plants have been found to have reduced emissions by close to 15–20 percent in France (Wagner and others 2014) and Germany (Petrick and Wagner 2014). An emission market introduced in the northeastern US states and targeting emissions from the power sector has also been determined to have contributed more than half of emission reductions achieved in the sector[2] in the late 2000s and early 2010s (Murray and Maniloff 2015), despite a low price averaging \$2–\$3 a ton during the time period.

Figure 3.1.1. Carbon Pricing in 2022 for Selected Economies

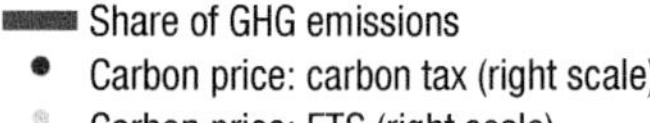

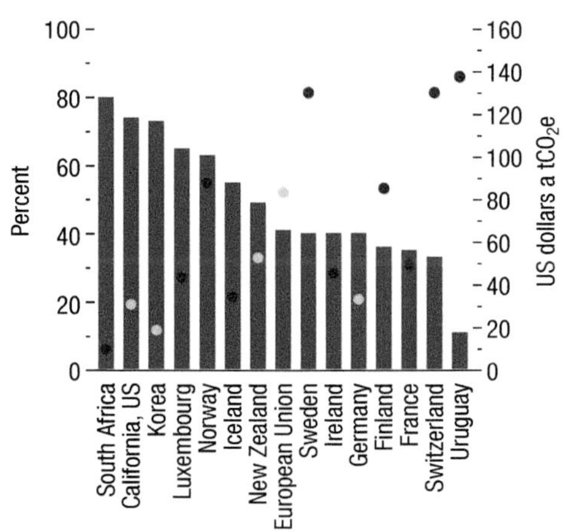

Sources: International Carbon Action Partnership; World Bank (2022); and IMF staff calculations.
Note: ETS = Emissions Trading System; GHG = greenhouse gas; tCO_2e = metric ton of carbon dioxide equivalent.

Carbon pricing's macroeconomic impact remains indiscernible, however, even though effects are more tangible at the sectoral level. Recent macro empirical studies have assessed the impact of carbon taxes on GDP using cross-country panel regressions and have found no evidence that carbon taxes have led to reductions in activity. Metcalf and Stock (2020) and Konradt and Weder di Mauro (2022) focus on the economic response to carbon tax changes in EU countries, controlling for previous tax changes or GDP growth, and point to negligible near-term effects of mitigation policies on output and inflation. One of the reasons could be related to the fact that these countries were able to achieve emission reductions through investment in abatement technologies, the switching of production and demand to cleaner technologies, and energy efficiency gains.

The effect of carbon pricing on activity seems easier to identify using microeconomic data. Several studies have found that the EU ETS has led firms to reduce the carbon intensity of their production through improvements in energy efficiency. An energy tax implemented in the UK resulted in energy use reductions of 23 percent in targeted manufacturing plants, leading them to cut emissions without cutting production or employment or reducing productivity (Martin, de Preux, and Wagner 2014). On the other end, carbon pricing has been shown to affect sectors differently, depending on their carbon intensity. For example, sectoral data analysis reveals that the carbon taxation implemented in British Columbia, Canada, led to a fall in employment in carbon-intensive and trade-intensive sectors (Yamazaki 2017). Studies also show that the 1970 US Clean Air Act[3] had a negative impact

The authors of this box are Mehdi Benatiya Andaloussi and Augustus J. Panton.

[1]The ETS is the EU's flagship climate policy, establishing in 2005 a carbon market across Europe, with more than 11,400 plants in 31 countries regulated at present.

[2]In states involved in the emission market, power sector emissions dropped by close to 25 percent between 2000 and 2011.

[3]The Clean Air Act regulates the emission of local air pollutants in the United States.

Box 3.1 *(continued)*

Table 3.1.1. Cross-Model Comparison of Changes in GDP
(Percent deviation from baseline)

	2030		
Model	Lump-Sum Rebates	Labor Income Tax Cuts	Capital Income Tax Cuts
E3	−0.8	−0.7	−0.6
DIEM	−0.4	−0.2	0.8
IGEM	−0.8	0.2	0.5
NewERA	−0.5	−0.4	0.2
RTI-ADAGE	−0.8	−0.6	0.9
ReEDS-USREP	−0.3	−0.1	0.0
Model average	−0.6	−0.3	0.3

Source: Goulder and Hafstead (2018).
Note: DIEM = Dynamic Integrated Evaluation Model; E3 = Goulder-Hafstead Environment-Energy-Economy; IGEM = Intertemporal General Equilibrium Model; NewERA = National Economic Research Associates economic consulting model; RTI-ADAGE = Applied Dynamic Analysis of the Global Economy; ReEDS-USREP = Region Energy Deployment System model–US Regional Energy Policy model.

on employment in pollution-intensive industries over the medium term: Employment in polluting sectors fell by 15 percent in the 10 years following an increase in the stringency of the regulation rolled out in the 1990s (Walker 2011).

There are limitations to how much can be inferred from past experiences to project future macroeconomic impacts of carbon pricing. First, the available empirical evidence refers to policies that were much smaller in scale and scope than those that will be required to achieve a path consistent with reaching the Paris Agreement's goals. Second, the impact of carbon pricing on output and inflation will vary depending on the way climate policies are designed and the other policies that accompany them. The multiplicity of channels through which climate policies have an impact implies that disentangling their effects (for example, on output and inflation) is empirically challenging. The literature has long recognized this tension, and numerous large-scale general equilibrium global models have been used to analyze the impact of greenhouse gas mitigation policies on emissions and economic activity. The modeling literature suggests that climate policies comparable to those needed to achieve the Paris Agreement targets have moderate adverse effects on output. It is important to note that these output costs pale in comparison with the macroeconomic risk associated with the catastrophic climate damages these policies aim to avert. Models with low elasticities of substitution between carbon-intensive and green-energy-generating technologies (NGFS 2022) and high capital adjustment costs (McKibbin and Wilcoxen 2013), limited public subsidization of the development of green technologies (Acemoglu and others 2012), and difficulty in scaling up green energy supply (IEA 2021) typically show higher output costs. The design of climate policies also matters. For instance, recycling carbon tax revenues as lump-sum transfers to households helps support consumption (Williams and others 2015; Goulder and others 2019), while using the revenues to reduce distortionary taxes, including labor income taxes, enhances growth and investment more (Chiroleu-Assouline and Fodha 2014; Caron and others 2018; McFarland and others 2018; Böhringer and others 2021).

Goulder and Hafstead (2018) compare the output costs for the US from an economy-wide carbon tax starting at $25 a ton in 2020 (and increasing by 5 percent annually until 2050) in six leading models under three common recycling plans (see Table 3.1.1). This would imply a carbon price reaching close to $38 a ton in 2030 or about half of the $75 a ton tax analyzed in this chapter across advanced economies.[4] Under a lump-sum recycling scheme, model averaging would suggest a cost of 1.2 percent of GDP by 2030 in the US, similar in scale to results from the Global Macroeconomic Model for the Energy Transition (GMMET) in advanced economies. Under a labor income tax cut, model averaging would imply a 0.6 percent loss in GDP by 2030, while the GMMET suggests essentially no loss in output over this horizon, thanks to an increase in labor supply.

[4]With a linear approximation assumed, results in Table 3.1.1 could be multiplied by 2 to reflect the impact of a carbon tax that is twice as high as in the experiment conducted in the study.

Box 3.1 *(continued)*

The use of comprehensive policy packages and coordinated approaches to drive the green transition can help reduce short-term output costs. Complementing carbon taxes with green public investments can boost aggregate demand in the short term and reduce energy supply bottlenecks (October 2020 *World Economic Outlook*, Chapter 3; Pahle and others 2022). Internationally coordinated policy action, for instance, through an international carbon price floor arrangement in which emission reduction obligations are equitably differentiated by countries' level of development, would address concerns about carbon leakage and competitiveness impacts on energy-intensive and trade-exposed industries that would arise from unilateral or uncoordinated action (Parry, Black, and Roaf 2021; Chateau, Jaumotte, and Schwerhoff 2022b). Finally, how central banks respond to the climate-policy-related supply shock can affect the magnitude of the output and inflation effects (McKibbin and others 2020).

Box 3.2. Political Economy of Carbon Pricing: Experiences from South Africa, Sweden, and Uruguay

This box examines the political economy of the introduction of carbon pricing in very different countries: one advanced economy and two emerging market economies. The long-standing experience of Sweden shows that with a judicious policy design that includes *gradualism*, strong *distributional incentives*, and a *rules-based and transparent framework*, a credible mitigation strategy involving carbon pricing is possible (Nemet and others 2017). More recently, South Africa, a highly fossil-fuel-dependent economy, and Uruguay embarked on decarbonization using similar strategies. It is worth emphasizing that—for all economies—climate mitigation policies can be effective only if they are deemed credible. Sudden departures from previously announced policies—analogous to Australia's carbon tax reversal in 2014—undermine policy credibility. Also, gradual and distribution-friendly policies are more likely to overcome political resistance (France's Yellow Vests movement is a counterexample).

Sweden became, in 1991, one of the first countries in the world to introduce a carbon tax (Andersson 2019; Jonsson, Ydstedt, and Asen 2020). While environmental taxes were already part of the Swedish tax system prior to the carbon tax, strengthening political buy-in for the carbon tax required a *gradual* implementation and the use of *distributional incentives*, notably exemptions. Sweden's carbon tax rate started at a low level and increased to $130 a ton (as of 2022, and covering 40 percent of total emissions), giving society time to adapt and thereby minimizing the overall economic impact (Figure 3.2.1). The inclusion of exemptions—motivated by concerns about carbon leakage and international competitiveness—also strengthened political support for the tax by making the carbon tax regime more *robust to resistance from different sectoral interests*. For example, in its early phase, the carbon tax regime had two tiers, with some carbon-intensive and trade-exposed industries fully exempt (for example, steel), while others faced a tax rate as low as 25 percent of the general carbon tax rate (for example, mining, agriculture) (Figure 3.2.1). Most exemptions were finally removed in 2019. While the carbon tax revenues were not directly earmarked in Sweden's budget, a reduction in labor income taxes was implemented alongside the imposition of the carbon tax, in effect recycling carbon tax revenues to help improve efficiency.

The author of this box is Augustus J. Panton.

Figure 3.2.1. Carbon Price in Sweden
(US dollars a tCO_2e)

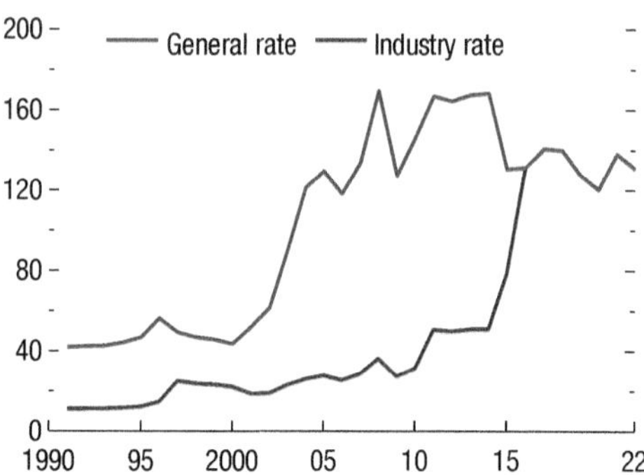

Source: World Bank (2022).
Note: tCO_2e = metric ton of carbon dioxide equivalent.

Over the years, Sweden has strengthened the credibility of its climate policy by defining a clear climate mitigation target that is *rules-based and transparent*, as articulated in the 2018 Climate Act of the Riksdag (Swedish parliament). Transitional rules-based targets (for example, 63 percent emission reduction by 2030 relative to 1990 levels) and a predefined provision for national review of progress every four years—entrusted to an independent body of scientific experts, the *Swedish Climate Policy Council*—support the national goal of reaching net-zero emissions by 2045.

South Africa, one of the world's most fossil-fuel-dependent economies, became the first African country in 2019 to implement a formal carbon-pricing regime, with a carbon tax rate starting at $9.20 a ton of carbon dioxide and covering 80 percent of total emissions (Figure 3.2.2; World Bank 2022). The tax was largely premised on positioning the South African economy to be competitive and compliant with potential climate-related trade restrictions (for example, border carbon adjustment) (South African National Treasury 2013). The national Integrated Resource Plan, focused on decarbonizing the electricity sector, and the Green Transport Strategy complement the carbon tax, thus creating a *robust strategy* and *mix of policy instruments* to drive the green transition. Given the South African economy's high fossil fuel dependence, the need for strong political incentives to galvanize support cannot be overemphasized. As in the Swedish two-tier carbon tax regime, the transitional phase (2020–25) is characterized by *strong distributional*

Box 3.2 *(continued)*

incentives aimed at gradually transitioning people and firms to a low-carbon economy. During this phase, carbon-tax-free allowances range from 60 to 95 percent of firms' emissions, with a further 10 percent for trade-exposed firms. Other transitional incentives, such as an electricity price neutrality commitment (that is, offsets to make electricity prices carbon-tax-neutral), have been put in place to get buy-in from energy-intensive sectors (for example, steel). Also, while the tax is integrated within a carbon budget framework (that is, caps on emissions over a given period), the enforcement of carbon budgets is expected only after the transition period. While distributional incentives, including tax-free emission allowances, are critical for broadening political support in the early stages of carbon pricing, their eventual removal must be well telegraphed to anchor expectations. In this context, the extension of the transitional phase of South Africa's carbon tax to 2025 (instead of the end of 2022, as initially announced) risks weakening credibility, locking in fossil fuel investments while undermining green private investments. Furthermore, the exemption of Eskom, the state-owned power company and South Africa's largest emitter, from the carbon tax strongly weakens the carbon tax regime's effectiveness. It is also worth noting that the full implementation of South Africa's climate mitigation agenda is conditional on the country's receiving external climate finance support, including the 2021 United Nations Climate Change Conference (COP26) commitment by the European Union, France, Germany, the United Kingdom, and the United States to finance South Africa's transition away from coal. Such conditionality creates uncertainty regarding the future direction of policy, weakening credibility. The establishment in 2020 of the *Presidential Climate Commission* is a step in the right direction for strengthening credibility. Further insulating the commission from political influence would help increase *transparency* and *trust* in the green transition.

Uruguay embarked on a carbon-pricing journey earlier this year by converting its gasoline excise tax regime into a formal carbon tax, with the 2022 tax rate set at $137 a ton of carbon dioxide. Despite the lower coverage in terms of total greenhouse gas emissions, the tax covers about half of carbon dioxide emissions (Figure 3.2.2). While not resorting to exemptions—reflecting the low share of carbon emissions in total greenhouse gas emissions—Uruguay is earmarking a portion of the carbon tax revenues to be spent on a different set of *incentives*, including subsidies for purchases of electric vehicles

Figure 3.2.2. Carbon Price and Emissions Coverage, 2022

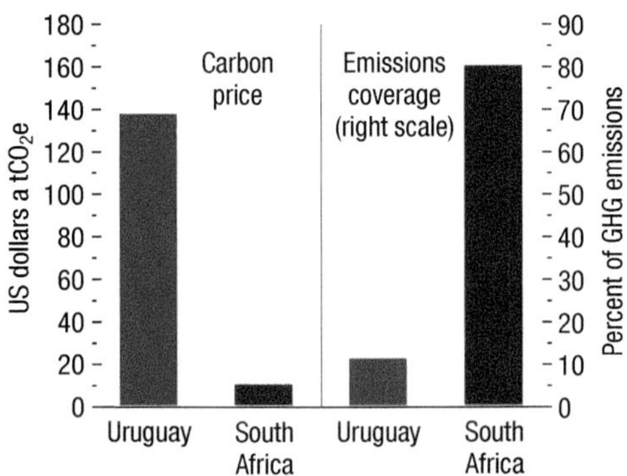

Source: World Bank (2022).
Note: GHG = greenhouse gas; tCO_2e = metric ton of carbon dioxide equivalent.

and investment in green public transport.[1] Whether these incentives are enough to broaden support for further stringency in the carbon tax—currently applied only to gasoline—remains to be seen.

Uruguay passed into law a carbon tax bill in November of last year, but challenges to the credibility of further advances in this direction remain. The lack of a rules-based mitigation path, specifically indicating how and the conditions under which the country's sectoral emission intensity targets would be adjusted, could create uncertainty for long-term private investment decisions. Uruguay's climate mitigation agenda would not be fully implemented without external climate finance support, adding to uncertainty. Finally, while the country's carbon tax framework is still in its infancy, delegating the periodic evaluation of climate policy and progress to an independent body would enhance transparency and trust.[2] Such transparency would be crucial not just locally but also internationally, given the Uruguayan government's plan for issuing sustainability-linked sovereign bonds tied to its climate mitigation agenda.

In sum, while a one-size-fits-all climate mitigation strategy does not exist, the experiences of these countries suggest that starting at a gradual pace, using targeted incentives and redistribution arrangements, can help establish a credible mitigation program and ease resistance to the use of carbon taxes for green transition.

[1]See the IMF Article IV Consultation for Uruguay (IMF 2021).
[2]Uruguay's new Sovereign Sustainability-Linked Bond Framework, launched on September 20, 2022, would help in that direction.

Box 3.3. Decarbonizing the Power Sector while Managing Renewables' Intermittence

Intermittent renewables, such as solar and wind, will be a key component of power sector decarbonization. Their penetration has already increased steadily over the past two decades, surpassing 20 percent in some countries, amid a favorable policy environment and rapidly falling capital costs. To bring emissions in line with the 2°C goal, simulations discussed in this chapter suggest that intermittent-renewables penetration will need to grow further and reach between 34 and 47 percent of power generation by 2030.

Intermittence presents challenges to electricity price variability and power system stability. Since storing electricity at grid scale remains very expensive, power systems need to be balanced at every point in time, with generation continuously matching fluctuating electricity demand. Power plants are turned on to satisfy demand, and priority is given to those with the lowest cost of production. Because renewables' cost of production is close to zero, as their fuel is free (for example, wind, sun), they will always be prioritized to supply electricity. Where electricity markets follow marginal pricing,[1] electricity prices will be pushed down—as costlier units are forced to turn off—and can even reach zero in the hours renewables produce enough electricity to satisfy demand and become the marginal unit.[2] Conversely, when renewables do not produce enough to satisfy demand, electricity prices can jump sharply, particularly if the sources for the marginal units that need to be turned on to satisfy demand have a high cost of production. As the availability of wind and solar varies within a day and across days and seasons, intermittence can lead to price volatility.

Several measures, including enhanced electricity grid interconnections and low-cost backup technologies, have dampened intermittence's impact on price variability so far. In Europe, price volatility from intermittence has remained limited. Before the pandemic, monthly price variability was similar in countries with high and low penetration of intermittent renewables (Figure 3.3.1). To increase the penetration of intermittent renewables while avoiding sharp swings in electricity prices, countries have adopted a multipronged approach, including by ensuring greater interconnection of electricity grids, which allows surplus production from renewables to satisfy demand in neighboring countries (for example, Denmark), or by using low-cost backup technologies—such as hydro (for example, Norway) or gas power plants (for example, Spain). Indeed, low gas prices allowed backup gas power plants to run at low cost when production from renewables dropped, limiting price variability. Between 2015 and 2019, electricity prices remained low and varied little day to day, getting closer to zero when renewables accounted for larger shares of electricity generation, but staying low even on days with low renewables penetration, as the cost of backup gas units remained low (blue circles in Figure 3.3.2).

This stability contrasts with the high volatility that has come from disruption in gas supplies during Russia's recent invasion of Ukraine. Electricity prices have risen sharply on wholesale markets amid recent gas price spikes, including in countries that rely more

Figure 3.3.1. Monthly Wholesale Electricity Prices in Selected European Economies
(Euros a megawatt-hour)

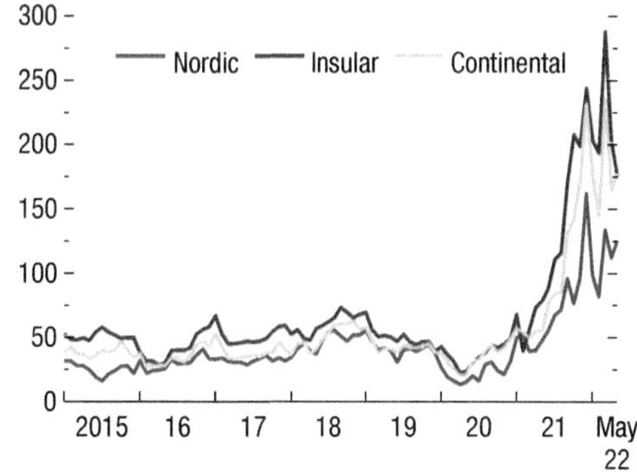

Sources: European Network of Transmission System Operators for Electricity; and IMF staff calculations.
Note: Country grouping reflects the degree of grid interconnectedness. "Insular" countries (Ireland, Portugal, Spain) have limited interconnections with continental Europe and have high gas dependence (32 percent of generation in 2019) and high renewables penetration (29 percent). "Continental" countries are well interconnected, with high penetration of renewables (23 percent) and high dependence on gas (16 percent). "Nordic" countries (Denmark, Finland, Norway, Sweden) constitute a well-interconnected group and use hydro as a backup for renewables (12 percent of production), with low gas dependence (2.6 percent).

The author of this box is Mehdi Benatiya Andaloussi.

[1]In such markets, wholesale electricity prices are set equal to the operational cost of the costliest unit among those selected to satisfy demand at any point in time.

[2]An emerging body of literature documents that wind and solar generation push wholesale electricity prices down, having done so, for instance, in Australia (Csereklyei, Qu, and Ancev 2019), California (Bushnell and Novan 2018), and Europe (Halttunen and others 2020).

Box 3.3 *(continued)*

Figure 3.3.2. Daily Electricity Prices in Selected European Countries as a Function of Share of Renewables in Power Production

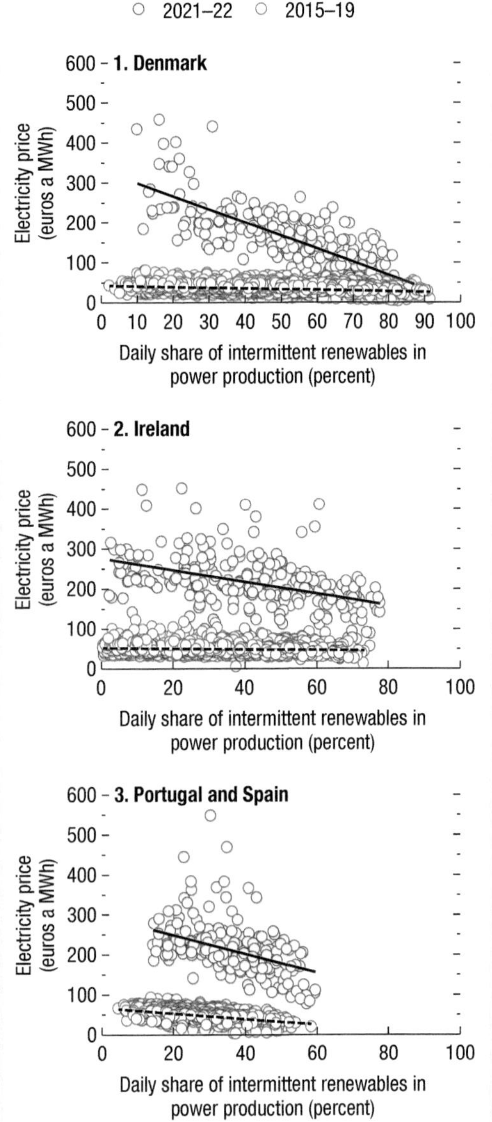

Sources: European Network of Transmission System Operators for Electricity; and IMF staff calculations.
Note: The solid and dashed lines represent the linear fit. MWh = megawatt-hour.

heavily on intermittent renewables, such as Denmark, Ireland, Portugal, and Spain. But where renewables are backed up by hydro (for example, Norway and Sweden), price volatility has increased only partly in response to the gas price spike (see Figure 3.3.1).[3] Furthermore, price volatility has increased sharply in countries that have high penetrations of renewables and use gas as a backup. At the end of 2021 and in 2022, as gas prices have surged, the cost of production of electricity from gas units has climbed, leading to high electricity prices when gas units have become marginal on days with low generation from renewables, while prices have pointed downward on days with high penetration from renewables (red circles in Figure 3.3.2). That has been true even where gas represents only a small share of generation, as in Denmark—where it accounts for less than 10 percent of production, whereas wind represented close to 60 percent of power production in 2021—since prices are set for the whole market by the marginal unit. Gas power plants were envisioned as becoming the choice of backup that would allow greater penetration of renewables. Yet, this choice risks exposing electricity prices to price swings in gas markets.

Looking ahead, decarbonizing the power sector will require a system-wide approach. As many sectors turn to electricity, electricity prices will become ever more central to price setting in vast swaths of the economy. Ensuring affordable and reliable electricity is thus crucial. Sector-level regulations and investment will be needed to accommodate higher intermittent-renewables penetration. These could include regulations to ensure adequate investment in backup capacity (for example, capacity markets), demand management to align peak demand with peak supply from renewables (for example, time-of-day pricing), public investment in grid interconnections, and support for research and development on storage (including from electric vehicles) and low-cost dispatchable backup technologies (for example, hydrogen, modular nuclear power plants) (see, for instance, ACER 2022; Green 2021; and Cleary, Fischer, and Palmer 2021). Further investment will also be needed to limit price volatility in gas markets (for example, liquid natural gas terminals). Finally, using a diversified mix of decarbonized power sources (for example, renewables, hydropower, and nuclear energy) will enhance power sector resilience.

[3]Pass-through to retail electricity prices has been more limited so far as a result of regulations (Ari and others, 2022).

References

Acemoglu, Daron, Philippe Aghion, Leonardo Bursztyn, and David Hémous. 2012. "The Environment and Directed Technical Change." *American Economic Review* 102 (1): 131–66.

Agency for the Cooperation of Energy Regulators (ACER). 2022. *Final Assessment of the EU Wholesale Electricity Market Design*. Ljublana, Slovenia.

Andersson, Julius J. 2019. "Carbon Taxes and CO_2 Emissions: Sweden as a Case Study." *American Economic Journal: Economic Policy* 11 (4): 1–30. https://www.aeaweb.org/articles?id=10.1257/pol.20170144.

Ari, Anil, Nicolas Arregui, Simon Black, Oya Celasun, Dora Iakova, Aiko Mineshima, Victor Mylonas, and others. 2022. "Surging Energy Prices in Europe in the Aftermath of the War: How to Support the Vulnerable and Speed Up the Transition away from Fossil Fuels." IMF Working Paper 22/152, International Monetary Fund, Washington, DC.

Bayer, Patrick, and Michael Aklin. 2020. "The European Union Emissions Trading System Reduced CO_2 Emissions Despite Low Prices." *Proceedings of the National Academy of Sciences of the United States of America* 117 (16): 8804–12. https://www.pnas.org/doi/10.1073/pnas.1918128117.

Black, Simon, Danielle Minnett, Ian Parry, James Roaf, and Karlygash Zhunussova. 2022. "The Carbon Price Equivalence of Climate Mitigation Policies." Unpublished, International Monetary Fund, Washington, DC.

Black, Simon, Ian Parry, James Roaf, and Karlygash Zhunussova. 2021. "Not Yet on Track to Net Zero: The Urgent Need for Greater Ambition and Policy Action to Achieve Paris Temperature Goals." IMF Staff Climate Note 2021/005, International Monetary Fund, Washington, DC.

Blanchard, Olivier, and Jordi Galí. 2007. "The Macroeconomic Effects of Oil Shocks: Why Are the 2000s So Different from the 1970s?" NBER Working Paper 13368, National Bureau of Economic Research, Cambridge, MA.

Böhringer, Christoph, Sonja Peterson, Thomas Rutherford, Jan Schneider, and Malte Winkler. 2021. "Climate Policies after Paris: Pledge, Trade and Recycle; Insights from the 36th Energy Modeling Forum Study (EMF36)." *Energy Economics* 103: 105471. https://doi.org/10.1016/j.eneco.2021.105471.

Brulle, Robert J. 2018. "The Climate Lobby: A Sectoral Analysis of Lobbying Spending on Climate Change in the USA, 2000 to 2016." *Climatic Change* 149 (3): 289–303.

Bushnell, James, and Kevin Novan. 2018. "Setting with the Sun: The Impacts of Renewable Energy on Wholesale Power Markets." NBER Working Paper 24980, National Bureau of Economic Research, Cambridge, MA.

Caron, Justin, Stuart M. Cohen, Maxwell Brown, and John M. Reilly. 2018. "Exploring the Impacts of a National U.S. CO_2 Tax and Revenue Recycling Options with a Coupled Electricity-Economy Model." *Climate Change Economics* 9 (1): 1840015. https://doi.org/10.1142/S2010007818400158.

Carton, Benjamin, Christopher Evans, Dirk Muir, and Simon Voigts. 2022. "Getting to Know GMMET: The Theoretical Structure and Simulation Properties of the Global Macroeconomic Model for the Energy Transition." Unpublished, International Monetary Fund, Washington, DC.

Castillo, Paul, Carlos Montoro, and Vicente Tuesta. 2007. "Inflation Premium and Oil Price Volatility." CEP Discussion Paper 782, Centre for Economic Performance, London School of Economics and Political Science, London, UK.

Chateau, Jean, Florence Jaumotte, and Gregor Schwerhoff. 2022a. "Climate Policy Options: A Comparison of Economic Performance." Unpublished, International Monetary Fund, Washington, DC.

Chateau, Jean, Florence Jaumotte, and Gregor Schwerhoff. 2022b. "Economic and Environmental Benefits from International Cooperation on Climate Policies." IMF Departmental Paper 2022/007, International Monetary Fund, Washington, DC.

Chiroleu-Assouline, Mireille, and Mouez Fodha. 2014. "From Regressive Pollution Taxes to Progressive Environmental Tax Reforms." *European Economic Review* 69: 126–42.

Cleary, Kathryne, Carolyn Fischer, and Karen Palmer. 2021. "Tools and Policies to Promote Decarbonization of the Electricity Sector." In *Handbook on Electricity Markets*, edited by Jean-Michel Glachant, Paul L. Joskow, and Michael G. Pollitt, 383–407. Cheltenham, UK: Elgar. https://econpapers.repec.org/bookchap/elgeechap/18895_5f14.htm.

Csereklyei, Zsuzsanna, Songze Qu, and Tihomir Ancev. 2019. "The Effect of Wind and Solar Power Generation on Wholesale Electricity Prices in Australia." *Energy Policy* 131: 358–69. https://doi.org/10.1016/j.enpol.2019.04.007.

Ferreira, Caio, David Lukáš Rozumek, Ranjit Singh, and Felix Suntheim. 2021. "Strengthening the Climate Information Architecture." IMF Staff Climate Note 2021/003, International Monetary Fund, Washington, DC.

Galí, Jordi. 2015. *Monetary Policy, Inflation, and the Business Cycle: An Introduction to the New Keynesian Framework and Its Applications.* 2nd ed. Princeton, NJ: Princeton University Press.

Goulder, Lawrence H., and Marc A. C. Hafstead. 2018. *Confronting the Climate Challenge: U.S. Policy Options.* New York: Columbia University Press.

Goulder, Lawrence H., Marc A. C. Hafstead, GyuRim Kim, and Xianling Long. 2019. "Impacts of a Carbon Tax across US Household Income Groups: What Are the Equity-Efficiency Trade-Offs?" *Journal of Public Economics* 175: 44–64. https://doi.org/10.1016/j.jpubeco.2019.04.002.

Green, Richard. 2021. "Shifting Supply as Well as Demand: The New Economics of Electricity with High Renewables." In *Handbook on Electricity Markets*, edited by Jean-Michel Glachant, Paul L. Joskow, and Michael G. Pollitt, 408–27. Cheltenham, UK: Elgar. https://econpapers.repec.org/bookchap/elgeechap/18895_5f15.htm.

Halttunen, Krista, Iain Staffell, Raphael Slade, Richard Green, Yves-Marie Saint-Drenan, and Malte Jansen. 2020. "Global Assessment of the Merit-Order Effect and Revenue Cannibalisation for Variable Renewable Energy." Preprint, posted December 2, 2020. https://ssrn.com/abstract=3741232.

Intergovernmental Panel on Climate Change (IPCC). 2022. *Climate Change 2022: Impacts, Adaptation and Vulnerability: Contribution of Working Group II to the Sixth Assessment Report of the Intergovernmental Panel on Climate Change*, edited by Hans-O. Pörtner, Debra C. Roberts, Melinda Tignor, Elvira S. Poloczanska, Katja Mintenbeck, Andrés Alegría, Marlies Craig, and others. Geneva, Switzerland.

International Energy Agency (IEA). 2021. *World Energy Outlook 2021*. Paris, France. https://iea.blob.core.windows.net/assets/4ed140c1-c3f3-4fd9-acae-789a4e14a23c/WorldEnergyOutlook2021.pdf.

International Monetary Fund (IMF). 2021. "Uruguay: Staff Report for the 2021 Article IV Consultation." International Monetary Fund, Washington, DC. https://www.imf.org/en/Publications/CR/Issues/2022/01/25/Uruguay-2021-Article-IV-Consultation-Press-Release-Staff-Report-and-Statement-by-the-512205.

Jonsson, Samuel, Anders Ydstedt, and Elke Asen. 2020. "Looking Back on 30 Years of Carbon Taxes in Sweden." Fiscal Fact 727, Tax Foundation, Washington, DC. https://taxfoundation.org/sweden-carbon-tax-revenue-greenhouse-gas-emissions.

Keen, Stephen, Timothy M. Lenton, Antoine Godin, Devrim Yilmaz, Matheus Grasselli, and Timothy J. Garrett. 2021. "Economists' Erroneous Estimates of Damages from Climate Change." arXiv preprint arXiv:2108.07847.

Konradt, Maximillian, and Beatrice Weder di Mauro. 2021. "Carbon Taxation and Greenflation: Evidence from Europe and Canada." CEPR Discussion Paper 16396, Centre for Economic Policy Research, London.

Kydland, Finn E., and Edward C. Prescott. 1977. "Rules Rather Than Discretion: The Inconsistency of Optimal Plans." *The Journal of Political Economy* 85 (3): 473–92.

Lenton, Timothy M., Johan Rockström, Owen Gaffney, Stefan Rahmstorf, Katherine Richardson, Will Steffen, and Hans Joachim Schellnhuber. 2019. "Climate Tipping Points—Too Risky to Bet Against." *Nature* 575 (7784): 592–95.

Martin, Ralf, Laure B. de Preux, and Ulrich J. Wagner. 2014. "The Impact of a Carbon Tax on Manufacturing: Evidence from Microdata." *Journal of Public Economics* 117: 1–14. https://www.sciencedirect.com/science/article/pii/S0047272714001078.

Maximilian Konradt and Beatrice Weder di Mauro. 2022. "Carbon Taxation and Greenflation: Evidence from Europe and Canada." CEPR Discussion Paper No. DP16396. Centre for Economic Policy Research, London.

McFarland, James R., Allen A. Fawcett, Adele C. Morris, John M. Reilly, and Peter J. Wilcoxen. 2018. "Overview of the EMF 32 Study on US Carbon Tax Scenarios." *Climate Change Economics* 9 (1): 1840002. https://doi.org/10.1142/S201000781840002X.

McKibbin, Warwick J., Adele C. Morris, Peter J. Wilcoxen, and Augustus J. Panton. 2020. "Climate Change and Monetary Policy: Issues for Policy Design and Modelling." *Oxford Review of Economic Policy* 36 (3): 579–603. https://doi.org/10.1093/oxrep/graa040.

McKibbin, Warwick J., and Peter J. Wilcoxen. 2013. "A Global Approach to Energy and the Environment: The G-Cubed Model." In *Handbook of Computable General Equilibrium Modeling*, Vol. 1A, edited by Peter B. Dixon and Dale W. Jorgenson, 995–1068. North Holland, Netherlands: Elsevier.

Metcalf, Gilbert E., and James H. Stock. 2020. "The Macroeconomic Impact of Europe's Carbon Taxes." NBER Working Paper 27488, National Bureau of Economic Research, Cambridge, MA.

Mirzoev, Tokhir N., Ling Zhu, Yang Yang, Andrea Pescatori, and Akito Matsumoto. 2020. "The Future of Oil and Fiscal Sustainability in the GCC Region." IMF Departmental Paper 20/01, International Monetary Fund, Washington, DC.

Morawiecki, Mateusz. 2022. "Polish PM: The Green Transition Cannot Come at the Cost of European Security." *Financial Times*, July 4. https://www.ft.com/content/3d592adc-b0b0-4098-8616-9d615c9fcde5.

Morison, Rachel. 2021. "The Climate-Change Fight Is Adding to the Global Inflation Scare." Bloomberg, June 18. https://www.bloomberg.com/news/articles/2021-06-18/the-climate-change-fight-is-adding-to-the-global-inflation-scare#xj4y7vzkg.

Murray, Brian C., and Peter T. Maniloff. 2015. "Why Have Greenhouse Emissions in RGGI States Declined? An Econometric Attribution to Economic, Energy Market, and Policy Factors." *Energy Economics* 51: 581–89.

Nakov, Anton, and Andrea Pescatori. 2010. "Monetary Policy Trade-Offs with a Dominant Oil Producer." *Journal of Money, Credit and Banking* 42 (1): 1–32.

Natal, Jean-Marc. 2012. "Monetary Policy Response to Oil Price Shocks." *Journal of Money, Credit and Banking* 44 (1): 53–101.

Nemet, Gregory F., Michael Jakob, Jan Christoph Steckel, and Ottmar Edenhofer. 2017. "Addressing Policy Credibility Problems for Low-Carbon Investment." *Global Environmental Change* 42: 47–57.

Network for Greening the Financial System (NGFS). 2022. "Running the NGFS Scenarios in G-Cubed: A Tale of Two Modelling Frameworks." NGFS Occasional Paper, Banque de France, Paris, France. https://www.ngfs.net/sites/default/files/medias/documents/running_the_ngfs_scenarios_in_g-cubed_a_tale_of_two_modelling_frameworks.pdf.

Pahle, Michael, Oliver Tietjen, Sebastian Osorio, Florian Egli, Bjarne Steffen, Tobias Schmidt, and Ottmar Edenhofer. 2022. "Safeguarding the Energy Transition against Political Backlash to Carbon Markets." *Nature Energy* 7 (3): 290–96. https://doi.org/10.1038/s41560-022-00984-0.

Parry, Ian, Simon Black, and James Roaf. 2021. "Proposal for an International Carbon Price Floor among Large Emitters." IMF Staff Climate Note 2021/001, International Monetary Fund, Washington, DC. https://www.imf.org/-/media/Files/Publications/Staff-Climate-Notes/2021/English/CLNEA2021001.ashx.

Petrick, Sebastian, and Ulrich J. Wagner. 2014. "The Impact of Carbon Trading on Industry: Evidence from German Manufacturing Firms." Kiel Working Paper 1912, Kiel Institute for the World Economy, Kiel, Germany. https://papers.ssrn.com/sol3/papers.cfm?abstract_id=2389800.

Pisani-Ferry, Jean. 2021. "Climate Policy Is Macroeconomic Policy, and the Implications Will Be Significant." Policy Brief 21-20, Peterson Institute for International Economics, Washington, DC.

Schnabel, Isabel. 2022. "A New Age of Energy Inflation: Climateflation, Fossilflation and Greenflation." Speech delivered at "Monetary Policy and Climate Change" panel, 22nd "The ECB and Its Watchers" Conference, Frankfurt am Main, March 17. https://www.ecb.europa.eu/press/key/date/2022/html/ecb.sp220317_2~dbb3582f0a.en.html.

South African National Treasury. 2013. "Reducing Greenhouse Gas Emissions and Facilitating the Transition to a Green Economy." Carbon Tax Policy Paper, Pretoria. http://www.treasury.gov.za/public%20comments/Carbon%20Tax%20Policy%20Paper%202013.pdf.

United Nations Environment Programme (UNEP) and UNEP Copenhagen Climate Centre (UNEP-CCC). 2021. *Emissions Gap Report 2021: The Heat Is On; A World of Climate Promises Not Yet Delivered.* Nairobi, Kenya.

Wagner, Ulrich, Mirabelle Muûls, Ralf Martin, and Jonathan Colmer. 2014. "The Causal Effects of the European Union Emissions Trading Scheme: Evidence from French Manufacturing Plants." Paper presented at the IZA Institute of Labor Economics workshop "Labor Market Effects of Environmental Policies," Bonn, Germany, September 4–5. https://conference.iza.org/conference_files/EnvEmpl2014/martin_r7617.pdf.

Walker, W. Reed. 2011. "Environmental Regulation and Labor Reallocation: Evidence from the Clean Air Act." *American Economic Review* 101 (3): 442–47.

Williams III, Roberton C., Hal Gordon, Dallas Burtraw, Jared C. Carbone, and Richard D. Morgenstern. 2015. "The Initial Incidence of a Carbon Tax across Income Groups." *National Tax Journal* 68 (1): 195–213. https://doi.org/10.17310/ntj.2015.1.09.

Woodford, Michael. 2003. *Interest and Prices: Foundations of a Theory of Monetary Policy.* Princeton, NJ: Princeton University Press.

World Bank. 2022. "Carbon Pricing Dashboard." Washington DC. https://carbonpricingdashboard.worldbank.org/map_data.

Yamazaki, Akio. 2017. "Jobs and Climate Policy: Evidence from British Columbia's *Revenue-Neutral* Carbon Tax." *Journal of Environmental Economics and Management* 83: 197–216.

STATISTICAL APPENDIX

The Statistical Appendix presents historical data as well as projections. It comprises eight sections: Assumptions, What's New, Data and Conventions, Country Notes, Classification of Countries, General Features and Composition of Groups in the *World Economic Outlook* Classification, Key Data Documentation, and Statistical Tables.

The first section summarizes the assumptions underlying the estimates and projections for 2022–23. The second section briefly describes the changes to the database and statistical tables since the April 2022 *World Economic Outlook* (WEO). The third section offers a general description of the data and the conventions used for calculating country group composites. The fourth section presents key information for selected countries. The fifth section summarizes the classification of countries in the various groups presented in the WEO, and the sixth section explains that classification in further detail. The seventh section provides information on methods and reporting standards for the member countries' national account and government finance indicators included in the report.

The last, and main, section comprises the statistical tables. (Statistical Appendix A is included here; Statistical Appendix B is available online at www.imf.org/en/Publications/WEO).

Data in these tables have been compiled on the basis of information available through September 26, 2022. The figures for 2022–23 are shown with the same degree of precision as the historical figures solely for convenience; because they are projections, the same degree of accuracy is not to be inferred.

Assumptions

Real effective *exchange rates* for the advanced economies are assumed to remain constant at their average levels measured during July 22, 2022–August 19, 2022. For 2022 and 2023 these assumptions imply average US dollar–special drawing right conversion rates of 1.346 and 1.330, US dollar–euro conversion rates[1] of 1.057 and 1.025, and yen–US dollar conversion rates of 128.4 and 129.3, respectively.

It is assumed that the *price of oil* will average $98.19 a barrel in 2022 and $85.52 a barrel in 2023.

National authorities' established *policies* are assumed to be maintained. Box A1 describes the more specific policy assumptions underlying the projections for selected economies.

With regard to *interest rates*, it is assumed that the *three-month government bond yield* for the United States will average 1.8 percent in 2022 and 4.0 percent in 2023, that for the euro area will average –0.2 percent in 2022 and 0.8 percent in 2023, and that for Japan will average –0.1 percent in 2022 and 0.0 percent in 2023. Further it is assumed that the *10-year government bond yield* for the United States will average 3.2 percent in 2022 and 4.4 percent in 2023, that for the euro area will average 0.9 percent in 2022 and 1.3 percent in 2023, and that for Japan will average 0.2 percent in 2022 and 0.3 percent in 2023.

What's New

- For Algeria, starting with the October 2022 WEO, total government expenditure and net lending/borrowing include net lending by the government, which mostly reflects support to the pension system and other public sector entities.
- Ecuador's fiscal sector projections, which were previously omitted because of ongoing program review discussions, are now included.
- Tunisia's forecast data, which were previously omitted because of ongoing technical discussions pending potential program negotiations, are now included.

[1] In regard to the introduction of the euro, on December 31, 1998, the Council of the European Union decided that, effective January 1, 1999, the irrevocably fixed conversion rates between the euro and currencies of the member countries adopting the euro are as described in Box 5.4 of the October 1998 WEO. See that box as well for details on how the conversion rates were established. For the most recent table of fixed conversion rates, see the Statistical Appendix of the October 2020 WEO.

- Turkey is now referred to as Türkiye.
- For Sri Lanka, certain projections for 2023–27 are excluded from publication owing to ongoing discussions on sovereign debt restructuring, following the recently reached staff-level agreement on an IMF-supported program.
- For Venezuela, following methodological upgrades, historical data have been revised from 2012 onward. Nominal variables that were omitted from publication in the April 2022 WEO are now included.

Data and Conventions

Data and projections for 196 economies form the statistical basis of the WEO database. The data are maintained jointly by the IMF's Research Department and regional departments, with the latter regularly updating country projections based on consistent global assumptions.

Although national statistical agencies are the ultimate providers of historical data and definitions, international organizations are also involved in statistical issues, with the objective of harmonizing methodologies for the compilation of national statistics, including analytical frameworks, concepts, definitions, classifications, and valuation procedures used in the production of economic statistics. The WEO database reflects information from both national source agencies and international organizations.

Most countries' macroeconomic data as presented in the WEO conform broadly to the 2008 version of the *System of National Accounts* (SNA 2008). The IMF's sector statistical standards—the sixth edition of the *Balance of Payments and International Investment Position Manual* (BPM6), the *Monetary and Financial Statistics Manual and Compilation Guide,* and the *Government Finance Statistics Manual 2014* (GFSM 2014)—have been aligned with the SNA 2008. These standards reflect the IMF's special interest in countries' external positions, financial sector stability, and public sector fiscal positions. The process of adapting country data to the new standards begins in earnest when the manuals are released. However, full concordance with the manuals is ultimately dependent on the provision by national statistical compilers of revised country data; hence, the WEO estimates are only partly adapted to these manuals. Nonetheless, for many countries, conversion to the updated standards will have only a small impact on major balances and aggregates. Many other countries have partly adopted the latest standards and will continue implementation over a number of years.[2]

The fiscal gross and net debt data reported in the WEO are drawn from official data sources and IMF staff estimates. While attempts are made to align gross and net debt data with the definitions in the GFSM 2014, as a result of data limitations or specific country circumstances, these data can sometimes deviate from the formal definitions. Although every effort is made to ensure the WEO data are relevant and internationally comparable, differences in both sectoral and instrument coverage mean that the data are not universally comparable. As more information becomes available, changes in either data sources or instrument coverage can give rise to data revisions, sometimes substantial ones. For clarification on the deviations in sectoral or instrument coverage, please refer to the metadata for the online WEO database.

Composite data for country groups in the WEO are either sums or weighted averages of data for individual countries. Unless noted otherwise, multiyear averages of growth rates are expressed as compound annual rates of change.[3] Arithmetically weighted averages are used for all data for the emerging market and developing economies group—except data on inflation and money growth, for which geometric averages are used. The following conventions apply:

Country group composites for exchange rates, interest rates, and growth rates of monetary aggregates are weighted by GDP converted to US dollars at market exchange rates (averaged over the preceding three years) as a share of group GDP.

Composites for other data relating to the domestic economy, whether growth rates or ratios, are weighted by GDP valued at purchasing power parity as a share of total world or group GDP.[4] For the aggregation of

[2] Many countries are implementing the SNA 2008 or the European System of National and Regional Accounts 2010, and a few countries use versions of the SNA older than that from 1993. A similar adoption pattern is expected for the BPM6 and GFSM 2014. Please refer to Table G, which lists the statistical standards to which each country adheres.

[3] Averages for real GDP, inflation, GDP per capita, and commodity prices are calculated based on the compound annual rate of change, except in the case of the unemployment rate, which is based on the simple arithmetic average.

[4] See Box 1.1 of the October 2020 WEO for a summary of the revised purchasing-power-parity-based weights as well as "Revised Purchasing Power Parity Weights" in the July 2014 WEO *Update*, Appendix 1.1 of the April 2008 WEO, Box A2 of the April 2004 WEO, Box A1 of the May 2000 WEO, and Annex IV of the May 1993 WEO. See also Anne-Marie Gulde and Marianne Schulze-Ghattas, "Purchasing Power Parity Based Weights for the *World Economic Outlook*," in *Staff Studies for the World Economic Outlook* (Washington, DC: International Monetary Fund, December 1993), 106–23.

world and advanced economies (and subgroups) inflation, annual rates are simple percentage changes from the previous years; for the aggregation of emerging market and developing economies (and subgroups) inflation, annual rates are based on logarithmic differences.

Composites for real GDP per capita in *purchasing-power-parity* terms are sums of individual country data after conversion to the international dollar in the years indicated.

Unless noted otherwise, composites for all sectors for the euro area are corrected for reporting discrepancies in intra-area transactions. Unadjusted annual GDP data are used for the euro area and for the majority of individual countries, except for Cyprus, Ireland, Portugal, and Spain, which report calendar-adjusted data. For data prior to 1999, data aggregations apply 1995 European currency unit exchange rates.

Composites for fiscal data are sums of individual country data after conversion to US dollars at the average market exchange rates in the years indicated.

Composite unemployment rates and employment growth are weighted by labor force as a share of group labor force.

Composites relating to external sector statistics are sums of individual country data after conversion to US dollars at the average market exchange rates in the years indicated for balance of payments data and at end-of-year market exchange rates for debt denominated in currencies other than US dollars.

Composites of changes in foreign trade volumes and prices, however, are arithmetic averages of percent changes for individual countries weighted by the US dollar value of exports or imports as a share of total world or group exports or imports (in the preceding year).

Unless noted otherwise, group composites are computed if 90 percent or more of the share of group weights is represented.

Data refer to calendar years, except in the case of a few countries that use fiscal years; Table F lists the economies with exceptional reporting periods for national accounts and government finance data.

For some countries, the figures for 2021 and earlier are based on estimates rather than actual outturns; Table G lists the latest actual outturns for the indicators in the national accounts, prices, government finance, and balance of payments for each country.

Country Notes

For *Afghanistan*, data and projections for 2021–27 are omitted because of an unusually high degree of uncertainty given that the IMF has paused its engagement with the country owing to a lack of clarity within the international community regarding the recognition of a government in Afghanistan.

For *Albania*, projections were prepared prior to the 2022 Article IV mission that ended on October 10th and thereby do not reflect updates during the mission.

For *Algeria*, starting with the October 2022 WEO, total government expenditure and net lending/borrowing include net lending by the government, which mostly reflects support to the pension system and other public sector entities.

For *Argentina*, the official national consumer price index (CPI) starts in December 2016. For earlier periods, CPI data for Argentina reflect the Greater Buenos Aires Area CPI (prior to December 2013), the national CPI (IPCNu, December 2013 to October 2015), the City of Buenos Aires CPI (November 2015 to April 2016), and the Greater Buenos Aires Area CPI (May 2016 to December 2016). Given limited comparability of these series on account of differences in geographical coverage, weights, sampling, and methodology, the WEO does not report average CPI inflation for 2014–16 and end-of-period inflation for 2015–16. Also, Argentina discontinued the publication of labor market data starting in the fourth quarter of 2015, and new series became available starting in the second quarter of 2016.

Data and forecasts for *Bangladesh* are presented on a fiscal year basis. However, country group aggregates that include Bangladesh use calendar year estimates of real GDP and purchasing-power-parity GDP.

For *Costa Rica*, the central government definition has been expanded as of January 1, 2021, to include 51 public entities as per Law 9524. Data back to 2019 are adjusted for comparability.

The fiscal series for the *Dominican Republic* have the following coverage: public debt, debt service, and the cyclically adjusted/structural balances are for the consolidated public sector (which includes the central government, the rest of the nonfinancial public sector, and the central bank); the remaining fiscal series are for the central government.

For *Ecuador*, the authorities are undertaking revisions of the historical fiscal data with technical support from the IMF.

For *Honduras*, projections were prepared prior to the 2022 Article IV mission that ended on October 5th and thereby do not reflect updates.

India's real GDP growth rates are calculated as per national accounts: for 1998–2001 with base year 2004/05 and, thereafter, with base year 2011/12.

For *Lebanon*, data and projections for 2021–27 are omitted owing to an unusually high degree of uncertainty.

Against the backdrop of a civil war and weak capacity, the reliability of *Libya*'s data, especially those regarding national accounts and medium-term projections, is low.

The 2022 projections for *Pakistan* are based on information available as of the end of August and do not include the impact of the recent floods.

Sierra Leone redenominated its currency on July 1, 2022; however, local currency data are expressed in the old leone for the October 2022 WEO.

For *Sri Lanka*, certain projections for 2023–27 are excluded from publication owing to ongoing discussions on sovereign debt restructuring, following the recently reached staff-level agreement on an IMF-supported program.

Data for *Syria* are excluded from 2011 onward because of the uncertain political situation.

For *Turkmenistan*, real GDP data are IMF staff estimates compiled in line with international methodologies (SNA), using official estimates and sources as well as United Nations and World Bank databases. Estimates of and projections for the fiscal balance exclude receipts from domestic bond issuances as well as privatization operations, in line with GFSM 2014. The authorities' official estimates for fiscal accounts, which are compiled using domestic statistical methodologies, include bond issuance and privatization proceeds as part of government revenues.

For *Ukraine,* all projections for 2022–27 except those for real GDP and consumer prices are omitted owing to an unusually high degree of uncertainty. Real GDP and consumer prices are projected through 2022. Revised national accounts data are available beginning in 2000 and exclude Crimea and Sevastopol from 2010 onward.

The projections for the *United Kingdom* are based on information available as of September 12, 2022, and do not fully incorporate the fiscal announcement on September 23, 2022.

In December 2020 the *Uruguay* authorities began reporting the national accounts data according to SNA 2008, with the base year 2016. The new series begin in 2016. Data prior to 2016 reflect the IMF staff's best effort to preserve previously reported data and avoid structural breaks.

Since October 2018 *Uruguay*'s public pension system has been receiving transfers in the context of a new law that compensates persons affected by the creation of the mixed pension system. These funds are recorded as revenues, consistent with the IMF's methodology. Therefore, data and projections for 2018–22 are affected by these transfers, which amounted to 1.2 percent of GDP in 2018, 1.1 percent of GDP in 2019, 0.6 percent of GDP in 2020, and 0.3 percent of GDP in 2021 and are projected to be 0.1 percent of GDP in 2022 and 0 percent thereafter. See IMF Country Report 19/64 for further details.[5] The disclaimer about the public pension system applies only to the revenues and net lending/borrowing series.

The coverage of the fiscal data for *Uruguay* was changed from consolidated public sector to nonfinancial public sector with the October 2019 WEO. In Uruguay, nonfinancial public sector coverage includes central government, local government, social security funds, nonfinancial public corporations, and Banco de Seguros del Estado. Historical data were also revised accordingly. Under this narrower fiscal perimeter—which excludes the central bank—assets and liabilities held by the nonfinancial public sector for which the counterpart is the central bank are not netted out in debt figures. In this context, capitalization bonds issued in the past by the government to the central bank are now part of the nonfinancial public sector debt. Gross and net debt estimates for 2008–11 are preliminary.

Projecting the economic outlook in *Venezuela*, including assessing past and current economic developments used as the basis for the projections, is rendered difficult by the lack of discussions with the authorities (the last Article IV consultation took place in 2004), incomplete metadata of limited reported statistics, and difficulties in reconciling reported indicators with economic developments. The fiscal accounts include the budgetary central government; social security; FOGADE (insurance deposit institution); and a reduced set of public enterprises, including Petróleos de Venezuela, S.A. (PDVSA). Following some methodological upgrades to achieve a more robust nominal GDP, historical data and indicators expressed as percentage of GDP have been revised from 2012 onward. For most indicators, data for 2018–22 are IMF staff estimates. The effects of

[5] *Uruguay: Staff Report for the 2018 Article IV Consultation,* Country Report 19/64 (Washington, DC: International Monetary Fund, February 2019).

hyperinflation and the paucity of reported data mean that IMF staff's projected macroeconomic indicators need to be interpreted with caution. Wide uncertainty surrounds these projections. Venezuela's consumer prices are excluded from all WEO group composites.

In 2019 *Zimbabwe* authorities introduced the Real Time Gross Settlement dollar, later renamed the Zimbabwe dollar, and are in the process of redenominating their national accounts statistics. Current data are subject to revision. The Zimbabwe dollar previously ceased circulating in 2009, and during 2009–19, Zimbabwe operated under a multicurrency regime with the US dollar as the unit of account.

Classification of Countries

Summary of the Country Classification

The country classification in the WEO divides the world into two major groups: advanced economies and emerging market and developing economies.[6] This classification is not based on strict criteria, economic or otherwise, and it has evolved over time. The objective is to facilitate analysis by providing a reasonably meaningful method of organizing data. Table A provides an overview of the country classification, showing the number of countries in each group by region and summarizing some key indicators of their relative size (GDP valued at purchasing power parity, total exports of goods and services, and population).

Some countries remain outside the country classification and therefore are not included in the analysis. Cuba and the Democratic People's Republic of Korea are examples of countries that are not IMF members, and the IMF therefore does not monitor their economies.

General Features and Composition of Groups in the *World Economic Outlook* Classification

Advanced Economies

Table B lists the 40 advanced economies. The seven largest in terms of GDP based on market exchange rates—the United States, Japan, Germany, France, Italy, the United Kingdom, and Canada—constitute the subgroup of major advanced economies often referred to as the Group of Seven. The members of the euro area are also distinguished as a subgroup. Composite data shown in the tables for the euro area cover the current members for all years, even though the membership has increased over time.

Table C lists the member countries of the European Union, not all of which are classified as advanced economies in the WEO.

Emerging Market and Developing Economies

The group of emerging market and developing economies (156) includes all those that are not classified as advanced economies.

The regional breakdowns of emerging market and developing economies are emerging and developing Asia; emerging and developing Europe (sometimes also referred to as "central and eastern Europe"); Latin America and the Caribbean; Middle East and Central Asia (which comprises the regional subgroups Caucasus and Central Asia; and Middle East, North Africa, Afghanistan, and Pakistan); and sub-Saharan Africa.

Emerging market and developing economies are also classified according to *analytical criteria* that reflect the composition of export earnings and a distinction between net creditor and net debtor economies. Tables D and E show the detailed composition of emerging market and developing economies in the regional and analytical groups.

The analytical criterion *source of export earnings* distinguishes between the categories *fuel* (Standard International Trade Classification 3) and *nonfuel* and then focuses on *nonfuel primary products* (Standard International Trade Classifications 0, 1, 2, 4, and 68). Economies are categorized into one of these groups if their main source of export earnings exceeded 50 percent of total exports on average between 2017 and 2021.

The financial and income criteria focus on *net creditor economies, net debtor economies, heavily indebted poor countries* (HIPCs), *low-income developing countries* (LIDCs), and *emerging market and middle-income economies.* Economies are categorized as net debtors when their latest net international investment position, where available, was less than zero or their current account balance accumulations from 1972 (or earliest available data) to 2021 were negative. Net debtor economies are further differentiated on the basis of *experience with debt servicing.*[7]

[6] As used here, the terms "country" and "economy" do not always refer to a territorial entity that is a state as understood by international law and practice. Some territorial entities included here are not states, although their statistical data are maintained on a separate and independent basis.

[7] During 2017–21, 37 economies incurred external payments arrears or entered into official or commercial bank debt-rescheduling agreements. This group is referred to as *economies with arrears and/or rescheduling during 2017–21.*

The HIPC group comprises the countries that are or have been considered by the IMF and the World Bank for participation in their debt initiative known as the HIPC Initiative, which aims to reduce the external debt burdens of all the eligible HIPCs to a "sustainable" level in a reasonably short period of time.[8] Many of these countries have already benefited from debt relief and have graduated from the initiative.

The LIDCs are countries that have per capita income levels below a certain threshold (set at $2,700 in 2016 as measured by the World Bank's Atlas method), structural features consistent with limited development and structural transformation, and external financial linkages insufficiently close for them to be widely seen as emerging market economies.

The emerging market and middle-income economies group comprises emerging market and developing economies that are not classified as LIDCs.

[8] See David Andrews, Anthony R. Boote, Syed S. Rizavi, and Sukwinder Singh, "Debt Relief for Low-Income Countries: The Enhanced HIPC Initiative," IMF Pamphlet Series 51 (Washington, DC: International Monetary Fund, November 1999).

Table A. Classification by *World Economic Outlook* Groups and Their Shares in Aggregate GDP, Exports of Goods and Services, and Population, 2021[1]
(Percent of total for group or world)

		GDP		Exports of Goods and Services		Population	
	Number of Economies	Advanced Economies	World	Advanced Economies	World	Advanced Economies	World
Advanced Economies	**40**	**100.0**	**42.0**	**100.0**	**61.4**	**100.0**	**14.0**
United States		37.4	15.7	15.0	9.2	30.8	4.3
Euro Area	19	28.5	12.0	42.3	26.0	31.6	4.4
Germany		7.9	3.3	11.8	7.2	7.7	1.1
France		5.5	2.3	5.4	3.3	6.1	0.9
Italy		4.4	1.9	4.0	2.5	5.5	0.8
Spain		3.2	1.4	2.9	1.8	4.4	0.6
Japan		9.1	3.8	5.4	3.3	11.7	1.6
United Kingdom		5.5	2.3	5.0	3.1	6.3	0.9
Canada		3.3	1.4	3.6	2.2	3.5	0.5
Other Advanced Economies	17	16.2	6.8	28.7	17.6	16.1	2.3
Memorandum							
Major Advanced Economies	7	73.2	30.7	50.2	30.8	71.6	10.0
		Emerging and Developing Economies	World	Emerging and Developing Economies	World	Emerging and Developing Economies	World
Emerging Market and Developing Economies	**156**	**100.0**	**58.0**	**100.0**	**38.6**	**100.0**	**86.0**
Emerging and Developing Asia	30	55.9	32.5	52.2	20.2	56.0	48.1
China		32.0	18.6	33.1	12.8	21.3	18.4
India		12.0	7.0	6.4	2.5	21.1	18.1
ASEAN-5[2]	5	9.4	5.5	11.4	4.4	8.8	7.6
Emerging and Developing Europe	16	13.4	7.8	16.7	6.5	5.7	4.9
Russia		5.3	3.1	5.1	2.0	2.2	1.9
Latin America and the Caribbean	33	12.6	7.3	12.8	4.9	9.7	8.3
Brazil		4.0	2.3	3.0	1.1	3.2	2.8
Mexico		3.1	1.8	4.9	1.9	1.9	1.7
Middle East and Central Asia	32	12.8	7.4	14.1	5.5	12.4	10.7
Saudi Arabia		2.1	1.2	2.7	1.0	0.5	0.5
Sub-Saharan Africa	45	5.4	3.1	4.1	1.6	16.2	14.0
Nigeria		1.4	0.8	0.5	0.2	3.2	2.7
South Africa		1.0	0.6	1.2	0.5	0.9	0.8
Analytical Groups[3]							
By Source of Export Earnings							
Fuel	26	10.1	5.9	13.7	5.3	9.6	8.2
Nonfuel	128	89.8	52.1	86.2	33.3	90.3	77.7
Of Which, Primary Products	37	5.6	3.3	5.6	2.1	9.4	8.0
By External Financing Source							
Net Debtor Economies	122	49.9	28.9	42.8	16.6	67.9	58.4
Net Debtor Countries by Debt-Servicing Experience							
Countries with Arrears and/or Rescheduling during 2017–21	37	4.8	2.8	3.1	1.2	11.7	10.1
Other Groups[3]							
Emerging Market and Middle-Income Economies	96	91.7	53.2	93.1	36.0	76.8	66.1
Low-Income Developing Countries	59	8.3	4.8	6.9	2.7	23.2	19.9
Heavily Indebted Poor Countries	39	2.8	1.6	2.0	0.8	11.8	10.2

[1]The GDP shares are based on the purchasing-power-parity valuation of economies' GDP. The number of economies comprising each group reflects those for which data are included in the group aggregates.

[2]Indonesia, Malaysia, Philippines, Thailand, and Vietnam.

[3]Syria and West Bank and Gaza are omitted from the source of export earnings, and Syria is omitted from the net external position group composites because of insufficient data.

Table B. Advanced Economies by Subgroup

Major Currency Areas		
United States		
Euro Area		
Japan		
Euro Area		
Austria	Greece	The Netherlands
Belgium	Ireland	Portugal
Cyprus	Italy	Slovak Republic
Estonia	Latvia	Slovenia
Finland	Lithuania	Spain
France	Luxembourg	
Germany	Malta	
Major Advanced Economies		
Canada	Italy	United States
France	Japan	
Germany	United Kingdom	
Other Advanced Economies		
Andorra	Israel	San Marino
Australia	Korea	Singapore
Czech Republic	Macao SAR[2]	Sweden
Denmark	New Zealand	Switzerland
Hong Kong SAR[1]	Norway	Taiwan Province of China
Iceland	Puerto Rico	

[1]On July 1, 1997, Hong Kong was returned to the People's Republic of China and became a Special Administrative Region of China.

[2]On December 20, 1999, Macao was returned to the People's Republic of China and became a Special Administrative Region of China.

Table C. European Union

Austria	France	Malta
Belgium	Germany	The Netherlands
Bulgaria	Greece	Poland
Croatia	Hungary	Portugal
Cyprus	Ireland	Romania
Czech Republic	Italy	Slovak Republic
Denmark	Latvia	Slovenia
Estonia	Lithuania	Spain
Finland	Luxembourg	Sweden

Table D. Emerging Market and Developing Economies by Region and Main Source of Export Earnings[1]

	Fuel	Nonfuel Primary Products
Emerging and Developing Asia		
	Brunei Darussalam	Kiribati
	Timor-Leste	Marshall Islands
		Papua New Guinea
		Solomon Islands
		Tuvalu
Latin America and the Caribbean		
	Ecuador	Argentina
	Trinidad and Tobago	Bolivia
	Venezuela	Chile
		Guyana
		Paraguay
		Peru
		Suriname
		Uruguay
Middle East and Central Asia		
	Algeria	Afghanistan
	Azerbaijan	Mauritania
	Bahrain	Somalia
	Iran	Sudan
	Iraq	Tajikistan
	Kazakhstan	Uzbekistan
	Kuwait	
	Libya	
	Oman	
	Qatar	
	Saudi Arabia	
	Turkmenistan	
	United Arab Emirates	
	Yemen	
Sub-Saharan Africa		
	Angola	Benin
	Chad	Botswana
	Republic of Congo	Burkina Faso
	Equatorial Guinea	Burundi
	Gabon	Central African Republic
	Nigeria	Democratic Republic of the Congo
	South Sudan	Côte d'Ivoire
		Eritrea
		Ghana
		Guinea
		Guinea-Bissau
		Liberia
		Malawi
		Mali
		Sierra Leone
		South Africa
		Zambia
		Zimbabwe

[1]Emerging and Developing Europe is omitted because no economies in the group have fuel or nonfuel primary products as the main source of export earnings.

Table E. Emerging Market and Developing Economies by Region, Net External Position, Heavily Indebted Poor Countries, and per Capita Income Classification

	Net External Position[1]	Heavily Indebted Poor Countries[2]	Per Capita Income Classification[3]
Emerging and Developing Asia			
Bangladesh	*		*
Bhutan	*		*
Brunei Darussalam	•		•
Cambodia	*		*
China	•		•
Fiji	*		•
India	*		•
Indonesia	*		•
Kiribati	•		*
Lao P.D.R.	*		*
Malaysia	•		•
Maldives	*		•
Marshall Islands	*		•
Micronesia	•		•
Mongolia	*		•
Myanmar	*		*
Nauru	*		•
Nepal	•		*
Palau	*		•
Papua New Guinea	*		*
Philippines	*		•
Samoa	*		•
Solomon Islands	*		*
Sri Lanka	*		•
Thailand	•		•
Timor-Leste	•		*
Tonga	*		•
Tuvalu	•		•
Vanuatu	*		•
Vietnam	*		*
Emerging and Developing Europe			
Albania	*		•
Belarus	*		•
Bosnia and Herzegovina	*		•
Bulgaria	*		•
Croatia	*		•
Hungary	*		•
Kosovo	*		•
Moldova	*		*
Montenegro	*		•
North Macedonia	*		•
Poland	*		•
Romania	*		•
Russia	•		•
Serbia	*		•
Türkiye	*		•
Ukraine	*		•
Latin America and the Caribbean			
Antigua and Barbuda	*		•
Argentina	•		•
Aruba	*		•
The Bahamas	*		•
Barbados	*		•
Belize	*		•
Bolivia	*	•	•
Brazil	*		•
Chile	*		•
Colombia	*		•
Costa Rica	*		•
Dominica	*		•
Dominican Republic	*		•
Ecuador	*		•
El Salvador	*		•
Grenada	*		•
Guatemala	*		•
Guyana	*	•	•
Haiti	*	•	*
Honduras	*	•	*
Jamaica	*		•
Mexico	*		•
Nicaragua	*	•	*
Panama	*		•
Paraguay	*		•
Peru	*		•
St. Kitts and Nevis	*		•
St. Lucia	*		•
St. Vincent and the Grenadines	*		•
Suriname	*		•
Trinidad and Tobago	•		•
Uruguay	*		•
Venezuela	•		•

Table E. Emerging Market and Developing Economies by Region, Net External Position, Heavily Indebted Poor Countries, and per Capita Income Classification *(continued)*

	Net External Position[1]	Heavily Indebted Poor Countries[2]	Per Capita Income Classification[3]
Middle East and Central Asia			
Afghanistan	•	•	*
Algeria	•		•
Armenia	*		•
Azerbaijan	•		•
Bahrain	•		•
Djibouti	*		*
Egypt	*		•
Georgia	*		•
Iran	•		•
Iraq	•		•
Jordan	*		•
Kazakhstan	*		•
Kuwait	•		•
Kyrgyz Republic	*		*
Lebanon	*		•
Libya	•		•
Mauritania	*	•	*
Morocco	*		•
Oman	*		•
Pakistan	*		•
Qatar	•		•
Saudi Arabia	•		•
Somalia	*	*	*
Sudan	*	*	*
Syria[4]	. . .		. . .
Tajikistan	*		*
Tunisia	*		•
Turkmenistan	•		•
United Arab Emirates	•		•
Uzbekistan	•		*
West Bank and Gaza	*		•
Yemen	*		*
Sub-Saharan Africa			
Angola	*		•
Benin	*	•	*
Botswana	•		•
Burkina Faso	*	•	*
Burundi	*	•	*
Cabo Verde	*		•
Cameroon	*	•	*
Central African Republic	*	•	*
Chad	*	•	*
Comoros	*	•	*
Democratic Republic of the Congo	*	•	*
Republic of Congo	*	•	*
Côte d'Ivoire	*	•	*
Equatorial Guinea	•		•
Eritrea	•	*	*
Eswatini	•		•
Ethiopia	*	•	*
Gabon	•		•
The Gambia	*	•	*
Ghana	*	•	*
Guinea	*	•	*
Guinea-Bissau	*	•	*
Kenya	*		*
Lesotho	*		*
Liberia	*	•	*
Madagascar	*	•	*
Malawi	*	•	*
Mali	*	•	*
Mauritius	•		•
Mozambique	*	•	*
Namibia	*		•
Niger	*	•	*
Nigeria	*		*
Rwanda	*	•	*
São Tomé and Príncipe	*	•	*
Senegal	*	•	*
Seychelles	*		•
Sierra Leone	*	•	*
South Africa	•		•
South Sudan	*		*
Tanzania	*	•	*
Togo	*	•	*
Uganda	*	•	*
Zambia	*	•	*
Zimbabwe	*		*

[1]Dot (star) indicates that the country is a net creditor (net debtor).
[2]Dot instead of star indicates that the country has reached the completion point, which allows it to receive the full debt relief committed to at the decision point.
[3]Dot (star) indicates that the country is classified as an emerging market and middle-income economy (low-income developing country).
[4]Syria is omitted from the net external position group and per capita income classification group composites for lack of a fully developed database.

Table F. Economies with Exceptional Reporting Periods[1]

	National Accounts	Government Finance
The Bahamas		Jul/Jun
Bangladesh	Jul/Jun	Jul/Jun
Barbados		Apr/Mar
Bhutan	Jul/Jun	Jul/Jun
Botswana		Apr/Mar
Dominica		Jul/Jun
Egypt	Jul/Jun	Jul/Jun
Eswatini		Apr/Mar
Ethiopia	Jul/Jun	Jul/Jun
Fiji		Aug/Jul
Haiti	Oct/Sep	Oct/Sep
Hong Kong SAR		Apr/Mar
India	Apr/Mar	Apr/Mar
Iran	Apr/Mar	Apr/Mar
Jamaica		Apr/Mar
Lesotho	Apr/Mar	Apr/Mar
Marshall Islands	Oct/Sep	Oct/Sep
Mauritius		Jul/Jun
Micronesia	Oct/Sep	Oct/Sep
Myanmar	Oct/Sep	Oct/Sep
Nauru	Jul/Jun	Jul/Jun
Nepal	Aug/Jul	Aug/Jul
Pakistan	Jul/Jun	Jul/Jun
Palau	Oct/Sep	Oct/Sep
Puerto Rico	Jul/Jun	Jul/Jun
St. Lucia		Apr/Mar
Samoa	Jul/Jun	Jul/Jun
Singapore		Apr/Mar
Thailand		Oct/Sep
Tonga	Jul/Jun	Jul/Jun
Trinidad and Tobago		Oct/Sep

[1]Unless noted otherwise, all data refer to calendar years.

Table G. Key Data Documentation

		National Accounts					Prices (CPI)	
Country	Currency	Historical Data Source[1]	Latest Actual Annual Data	Base Year[2]	System of National Accounts	Use of Chain-Weighted Methodology[3]	Historical Data Source[1]	Latest Actual Annual Data
Afghanistan	Afghan afghani	NSO	2020	2016	SNA 2008		NSO	2020
Albania	Albanian lek	IMF staff	2020	1996	ESA 2010	From 1996	NSO	2020
Algeria	Algerian dinar	NSO	2021	2001	SNA 1993	From 2005	NSO	2021
Andorra	Euro	NSO	2021	2010	. . .		NSO	2021
Angola	Angolan kwanza	NSO and MEP	2021	2002	ESA 1995		NSO	2021
Antigua and Barbuda	Eastern Caribbean dollar	CB	2020	2006[6]	SNA 1993		NSO	2021
Argentina	Argentine peso	NSO	2020	2004	SNA 2008		NSO	2021
Armenia	Armenian dram	NSO	2021	2005	SNA 2008		NSO	2021
Aruba	Aruban florin	NSO	2021	2013	SNA 1993	From 2000	NSO	2021
Australia	Australian dollar	NSO	2021	2020	SNA 2008	From 1980	NSO	2021
Austria	Euro	NSO	2021	2015	ESA 2010	From 1995	NSO	2021
Azerbaijan	Azerbaijan manat	NSO	2021	2005	SNA 1993	From 1994	NSO	2021
The Bahamas	Bahamian dollar	NSO	2021	2012	SNA 1993		NSO	2021
Bahrain	Bahrain dinar	NSO and IMF staff	2020	2010	SNA 2008		NSO	2021
Bangladesh	Bangladesh taka	NSO	2021/22	2015/16	SNA 2008		NSO	2021/22
Barbados	Barbados dollar	NSO and CB	2020	2010	SNA 2008		NSO	2021
Belarus	Belarusian ruble	NSO	2020	2018	SNA 2008	From 2005	NSO	2021
Belgium	Euro	CB	2021	2015	ESA 2010	From 1995	CB	2021
Belize	Belize dollar	NSO	2020	2014	SNA 2008		NSO	2021
Benin	CFA franc	NSO	2021	2015	SNA 2008		NSO	2021
Bhutan	Bhutanese ngultrum	NSO	2020/21	1999/2000[6]	SNA 2008		NSO	2020/21
Bolivia	Bolivian boliviano	NSO	2021	1990	SNA 2008		NSO	2021
Bosnia and Herzegovina	Bosnian convertible marka	NSO	2021	2015	ESA 2010	From 2000	NSO	2021
Botswana	Botswana pula	NSO	2021	2016	SNA 2008		NSO	2021
Brazil	Brazilian real	NSO	2021	1995	SNA 2008		NSO	2021
Brunei Darussalam	Brunei dollar	MoF	2021	2010	SNA 2008		MoF	2020
Bulgaria	Bulgarian lev	NSO	2021	2015	ESA 2010	From 1996	NSO	2021
Burkina Faso	CFA franc	NSO and MEP	2020	2015	SNA 2008		NSO	2021
Burundi	Burundi franc	NSO and IMF staff	2019	2005	SNA 1993		NSO	2021
Cabo Verde	Cabo Verdean escudo	NSO	2020	2007	SNA 2008	From 2011	NSO	2020
Cambodia	Cambodian riel	NSO	2020	2000	SNA 1993		NSO	2020
Cameroon	CFA franc	NSO	2021	2016	SNA 2008	From 2016	NSO	2021
Canada	Canadian dollar	NSO	2021	2012	SNA 2008	From 1980	MoF and NSO	2021
Central African Republic	CFA franc	NSO	2020	2005	SNA 1993		NSO	2021
Chad	CFA franc	CB	2017	2005	SNA 1993		NSO	2021
Chile	Chilean peso	CB	2021	2018[6]	SNA 2008	From 2003	NSO	2021
China	Chinese yuan	NSO	2021	2015	SNA 2008		NSO	2021
Colombia	Colombian peso	NSO	2021	2015	SNA 2008	From 2005	NSO	2021
Comoros	Comorian franc	MoF	2019	2007	SNA 1993	From 2007	NSO	2021
Democratic Republic of the Congo	Congolese franc	NSO	2020	2005	SNA 1993		CB	2020
Republic of Congo	CFA franc	NSO	2019	2005	SNA 1993		NSO	2021
Costa Rica	Costa Rican colón	CB	2021	2017	SNA 2008		CB	2021

Table G. Key Data Documentation *(continued)*

	Government Finance					Balance of Payments		
Country	Historical Data Source[1]	Latest Actual Annual Data	Statistics Manual in Use at Source	Subsectors Coverage[4]	Accounting Practice[5]	Historical Data Source[1]	Latest Actual Annual Data	Statistics Manual in Use at Source
Afghanistan	MoF	2020	2001	CG	C	NSO, MoF, and CB	2020	BPM 6
Albania	IMF staff	2020	1986	CG,LG,SS,MPC, NFPC	. . .	CB	2020	BPM 6
Algeria	MoF	2021	1986	CG	C	CB	2021	BPM 6
Andorra	NSO and MoF	2021	. . .	CG,LG,SS	C	NSO	2020	BPM 6
Angola	MoF	2021	2001	CG,LG	. . .	CB	2021	BPM 6
Antigua and Barbuda	MoF	2020	2001	CG	Mixed	CB	2020	BPM 6
Argentina	MEP	2021	1986	CG,SG,SS	C	NSO	2020	BPM 6
Armenia	MoF	2021	2001	CG	C	CB	2021	BPM 6
Aruba	MoF	2021	2001	CG	Mixed	CB	2021	BPM 6
Australia	MoF	2021	2014	CG,SG,LG,TG	A	NSO	2021	BPM 6
Austria	NSO	2020	2014	CG,SG,LG,SS	A	CB	2020	BPM 6
Azerbaijan	MoF	2021	2001	CG	C	CB	2021	BPM 6
The Bahamas	MoF	2020/21	2014	CG	C	CB	2021	BPM 6
Bahrain	MoF	2020	2001	CG	C	CB	2021	BPM 6
Bangladesh	MoF	2020/21	. . .	CG	C	CB	2021/22	BPM 6
Barbados	MoF	2021/22	2001	BCG	C	CB	2021	BPM 6
Belarus	MoF	2020	2001	CG,LG,SS	C	CB	2020	BPM 6
Belgium	CB	2021	ESA 2010	CG,SG,LG,SS	A	CB	2021	BPM 6
Belize	MoF	2021	1986	CG,MPC	Mixed	CB	2021	BPM 6
Benin	MoF	2021	1986	CG	C	CB	2021	BPM 6
Bhutan	MoF	2020/21	1986	CG	C	CB	2020/21	BPM 6
Bolivia	MoF	2021	2001	CG,LG,SS,NMPC, NFPC	C	CB	2021	BPM 6
Bosnia and Herzegovina	MoF	2021	2014	CG,SG,LG,SS	Mixed	CB	2021	BPM 6
Botswana	MoF	2021/22	1986	CG	C	CB	2021	BPM 6
Brazil	MoF	2021	2001	CG,SG,LG,SS,NFPC	C	CB	2021	BPM 6
Brunei Darussalam	MoF	2021	1986	CG,BCG	C	NSO and MEP	2020	BPM 6
Bulgaria	MoF	2021	2001	CG,LG,SS	C	CB	2021	BPM 6
Burkina Faso	MoF	2021	2001	CG	CB	CB	2021	BPM 6
Burundi	MoF	2020	2001	CG	Mixed	CB	2020	BPM 6
Cabo Verde	MoF	2020	2001	CG	A	NSO	2020	BPM 6
Cambodia	MoF	2020	2001	CG,LG	Mixed	CB	2021	BPM 5
Cameroon	MoF	2021	2001	CG,NFPC,NMPC	Mixed	MoF	2021	BPM 5
Canada	MoF and NSO	2021	2001	CG,SG,LG,SS,other	A	NSO	2021	BPM 6
Central African Republic	MoF	2021	2001	CG	C	CB	2020	BPM 5
Chad	MoF	2021	1986	CG,NFPC	C	CB	2013	BPM 5
Chile	MoF	2021	2001	CG,LG	A	CB	2021	BPM 6
China	MoF	2020	. . .	CG,LG,SS	C	GAD	2021	BPM 6
Colombia	MoF	2021	2001	CG,SG,LG,SS	. . .	CB and NSO	2021	BPM 6
Comoros	MoF	2020	1986	CG	Mixed	CB and IMF staff	2019	BPM 5
Democratic Republic of the Congo	MoF	2020	2001	CG,LG	A	CB	2020	BPM 6
Republic of Congo	MoF	2021	2001	CG	A	CB	2019	BPM 6
Costa Rica	MoF and CB	2021	1986	CG	C	CB	2021	BPM 6

Table G. Key Data Documentation *(continued)*

		National Accounts					Prices (CPI)	
Country	Currency	Historical Data Source[1]	Latest Actual Annual Data	Base Year[2]	System of National Accounts	Use of Chain-Weighted Methodology[3]	Historical Data Source[1]	Latest Actual Annual Data
Côte d'Ivoire	CFA franc	NSO	2019	2015	SNA 2008		NSO	2021
Croatia	Croatian kuna	NSO	2021	2015	ESA 2010		NSO	2021
Cyprus	Euro	NSO	2021	2010	ESA 2010	From 1995	NSO	2021
Czech Republic	Czech koruna	NSO	2021	2015	ESA 2010	From 1995	NSO	2021
Denmark	Danish krone	NSO	2021	2010	ESA 2010	From 1980	NSO	2021
Djibouti	Djibouti franc	NSO	2020	2013	SNA 2008		NSO	2021
Dominica	Eastern Caribbean dollar	NSO	2020	2006	SNA 1993		NSO	2021
Dominican Republic	Dominican peso	CB	2021	2007	SNA 2008	From 2007	CB	2021
Ecuador	US dollar	CB	2021	2007	SNA 2008		NSO and CB	2021
Egypt	Egyptian pound	MEP	2020/21	2016/17	SNA 2008		NSO	2021/22
El Salvador	US dollar	CB	2021	2014	SNA 2008		NSO	2021
Equatorial Guinea	CFA franc	MEP and CB	2021	2006	SNA 1993		MEP	2021
Eritrea	Eritrean nakfa	IMF staff	2019	2011	SNA 1993		NSO	2018
Estonia	Euro	NSO	2021	2015	ESA 2010	From 2010	NSO	2021
Eswatini	Swazi lilangeni	NSO	2020	2011	SNA 2008		NSO	2021
Ethiopia	Ethiopian birr	NSO	2020/21	2015/16	SNA 2008		NSO	2021
Fiji	Fijian dollar	NSO	2021	2014	SNA 2008		NSO	2021
Finland	Euro	NSO	2021	2015	ESA 2010	From 1980	NSO	2021
France	Euro	NSO	2021	2014	ESA 2010	From 1980	NSO	2021
Gabon	CFA franc	MoF	2021	2001	SNA 1993		NSO	2021
The Gambia	Gambian dalasi	NSO	2020	2013	SNA 2008		NSO	2021
Georgia	Georgian lari	NSO	2021	2015	SNA 2008	From 1996	NSO	2021
Germany	Euro	NSO	2021	2015	ESA 2010	From 1991	NSO	2021
Ghana	Ghanaian cedi	NSO	2021	2013	SNA 2008		NSO	2021
Greece	Euro	NSO	2021	2015	ESA 2010	From 1995	NSO	2021
Grenada	Eastern Caribbean dollar	NSO	2021	2006	SNA 1993		NSO	2021
Guatemala	Guatemalan quetzal	CB	2021	2013	SNA 2008	From 2001	NSO	2021
Guinea	Guinean franc	NSO	2020	2010	SNA 1993		NSO	2021
Guinea-Bissau	CFA franc	NSO	2018	2015	SNA 2008		NSO	2020
Guyana	Guyanese dollar	NSO	2021	2012[6]	SNA 1993		NSO	2021
Haiti	Haitian gourde	NSO	2020/21	2011/12	SNA 2008		NSO	2020/21
Honduras	Honduran lempira	CB	2021	2000	SNA 1993		CB	2021
Hong Kong SAR	Hong Kong dollar	NSO	2021	2020	SNA 2008	From 1980	NSO	2021
Hungary	Hungarian forint	NSO	2021	2015	ESA 2010	From 1995	IEO	2021
Iceland	Icelandic króna	NSO	2020	2015	ESA 2010	From 1990	NSO	2020
India	Indian rupee	NSO	2021/22	2011/12	SNA 2008		NSO	2021/22
Indonesia	Indonesian rupiah	NSO	2021	2010	SNA 2008		NSO	2021
Iran	Iranian rial	CB	2021/22	2016/17	SNA 2008		CB	2021/22
Iraq	Iraqi dinar	NSO	2021	2007	. . .		NSO	2021
Ireland	Euro	NSO	2021	2020	ESA 2010	From 1995	NSO	2021
Israel	Israeli new shekel	NSO	2021	2015	SNA 2008	From 1995	NSO	2021
Italy	Euro	NSO	2021	2015	ESA 2010	From 1980	NSO	2021
Jamaica	Jamaican dollar	NSO	2020	2007	SNA 1993		NSO	2020

Table G. Key Data Documentation *(continued)*

	Government Finance					Balance of Payments		
Country	Historical Data Source[1]	Latest Actual Annual Data	Statistics Manual in Use at Source	Subsectors Coverage[4]	Accounting Practice[5]	Historical Data Source[1]	Latest Actual Annual Data	Statistics Manual in Use at Source
Côte d'Ivoire	MoF	2020	1986	CG	A	CB	2020	BPM 6
Croatia	MoF	2021	2014	CG,LG	A	CB	2021	BPM 6
Cyprus	NSO	2021	ESA 2010	CG,LG,SS	A	CB	2021	BPM 6
Czech Republic	MoF	2021	2014	CG,LG,SS	A	NSO	2021	BPM 6
Denmark	NSO	2021	2014	CG,LG,SS	A	NSO	2021	BPM 6
Djibouti	MoF	2021	2001	CG	A	CB	2021	BPM 5
Dominica	MoF	2020/21	1986	CG	C	CB	2020	BPM 6
Dominican Republic	MoF	2021	2014	CG,LG,SS,NMPC	A	CB	2021	BPM 6
Ecuador	CB and MoF	2021	1986	CG,SG,LG,SS,NFPC	Mixed	CB	2021	BPM 6
Egypt	MoF	2020/21	2001	CG,LG,SS,MPC	C	CB	2020/21	BPM 5
El Salvador	MoF and CB	2021	1986	CG,LG,SS,NFPC	C	CB	2021	BPM 6
Equatorial Guinea	MoF and MEP	2021	1986	CG	C	CB	2017	BPM 5
Eritrea	MoF	2020	2001	CG	C	CB	2018	BPM 5
Estonia	MoF	2021	1986/2001	CG,LG,SS	C	CB	2021	BPM 6
Eswatini	MoF	2020/21	2001	CG	A	CB	2021	BPM 6
Ethiopia	MoF	2020/21	1986	CG,SG,LG,NFPC	C	CB	2020/21	BPM 5
Fiji	MoF	2020/21	1986	CG	C	CB	2021	BPM 6
Finland	MoF	2021	2014	CG,LG,SS	A	NSO	2021	BPM 6
France	NSO	2021	2014	CG,LG,SS	A	CB	2021	BPM 6
Gabon	IMF staff	2021	2001	CG	A	CB	2019	BPM 5
The Gambia	MoF	2020	1986	CG	C	CB and IMF staff	2020	BPM 6
Georgia	MoF	2021	2001	CG,LG	C	CB	2021	BPM 6
Germany	NSO	2021	ESA 2010	CG,SG,LG,SS	A	CB	2021	BPM 6
Ghana	MoF	2021	2001	CG	C	CB	2021	BPM 5
Greece	NSO	2021	ESA 2010	CG,LG,SS	A	CB	2021	BPM 6
Grenada	MoF	2020	2014	CG	CB	CB	2020	BPM 6
Guatemala	MoF	2021	2001	CG	C	CB	2020	BPM 6
Guinea	MoF	2021	1986	CG	C	CB and MEP	2021	BPM 6
Guinea-Bissau	MoF	2020	2001	CG	A	CB	2020	BPM 6
Guyana	MoF	2021	1986	CG,SS,NFPC	C	CB	2021	BPM 6
Haiti	MoF	2020/21	1986	CG	C	CB	2020/21	BPM 5
Honduras	MoF	2021	2014	CG,LG,SS,other	Mixed	CB	2021	BPM 5
Hong Kong SAR	MoF	2020/21	2001	CG	C	NSO	2021	BPM 6
Hungary	MEP and NSO	2021	ESA 2010	CG,LG,SS,NMPC	A	CB	2021	BPM 6
Iceland	NSO	2020	2001	CG,LG,SS	A	CB	2020	BPM 6
India	MoF and IMF staff	2019/20	1986	CG,SG	C	CB	2021/22	BPM 6
Indonesia	MoF	2021	2001	CG,LG	C	CB	2021	BPM 6
Iran	MoF	2020/21	2001	CG	C	CB	2021/22	BPM 5
Iraq	MoF	2021	2001	CG	C	CB	2021	BPM 6
Ireland	MoF and NSO	2021	2001	CG,LG,SS	A	NSO	2021	BPM 6
Israel	MoF and NSO	2020	2014	CG,LG,SS	. . .	NSO	2021	BPM 6
Italy	NSO	2021	2001	CG,LG,SS	A	NSO	2021	BPM 6
Jamaica	MoF	2021/22	1986	CG	C	CB	2021	BPM 6

Table G. Key Data Documentation *(continued)*

		National Accounts					Prices (CPI)	
Country	Currency	Historical Data Source[1]	Latest Actual Annual Data	Base Year[2]	System of National Accounts	Use of Chain-Weighted Methodology[3]	Historical Data Source[1]	Latest Actual Annual Data
Japan	Japanese yen	GAD	2021	2015	SNA 2008	From 1980	GAD	2021
Jordan	Jordanian dinar	NSO	2020	2016	SNA 2008		NSO	2020
Kazakhstan	Kazakhstani tenge	NSO	2021	2005	SNA 1993	From 1994	CB	2021
Kenya	Kenyan shilling	NSO	2021	2016	SNA 2008		NSO	2021
Kiribati	Australian dollar	NSO	2020	2006	SNA 2008		IMF staff	2020
Korea	South Korean won	CB	2021	2015	SNA 2008	From 1980	NSO	2021
Kosovo	Euro	NSO	2021	2016	ESA 2010		NSO	2021
Kuwait	Kuwaiti dinar	MEP and NSO	2020	2010	SNA 1993		NSO and MEP	2021
Kyrgyz Republic	Kyrgyz som	NSO	2021	2005	SNA 1993	From 2010	NSO	2021
Lao P.D.R.	Lao kip	NSO	2020	2012	SNA 1993		NSO	2021
Latvia	Euro	NSO	2021	2015	ESA 2010	From 1995	NSO	2021
Lebanon	Lebanese pound	NSO	2020	2010	SNA 2008	From 2010	NSO	2021
Lesotho	Lesotho loti	NSO	2020/21	2012/13	SNA 2008		NSO	2021
Liberia	US dollar	IMF staff	2016	2018	SNA 1993		CB	2021
Libya	Libyan dinar	MEP	2021	2013	SNA 1993		NSO	2021
Lithuania	Euro	NSO	2021	2015	ESA 2010	From 2005	NSO	2021
Luxembourg	Euro	NSO	2020	2015	ESA 2010	From 1995	NSO	2020
Macao SAR	Macanese pataca	NSO	2021	2020	SNA 2008	From 2001	NSO	2021
Madagascar	Malagasy ariary	NSO	2018	2007	SNA 1993		NSO	2021
Malawi	Malawian kwacha	NSO	2020	2017	SNA 2008		NSO	2021
Malaysia	Malaysian ringgit	NSO	2021	2015	SNA 2008		NSO	2021
Maldives	Maldivian rufiyaa	MoF and NSO	2020	2014	SNA 2008		CB	2021
Mali	CFA franc	NSO	2020	1999	SNA 1993		NSO	2021
Malta	Euro	NSO	2021	2015	ESA 2010	From 2000	NSO	2021
Marshall Islands	US dollar	NSO	2020/21	2014/15	SNA 2008		NSO	2020/21
Mauritania	New Mauritanian ouguiya	NSO	2021	2014	SNA 2008	From 2014	NSO	2021
Mauritius	Mauritian rupee	NSO	2021	2006	SNA 2008	From 1999	NSO	2021
Mexico	Mexican peso	NSO	2021	2013	SNA 2008		NSO	2021
Micronesia	US dollar	NSO	2017/18	2003/04	SNA 2008		NSO	2019/20
Moldova	Moldovan leu	NSO	2021	1995	SNA 2008		NSO	2021
Mongolia	Mongolian tögrög	NSO	2021	2015	SNA 2008		NSO	2021
Montenegro	Euro	NSO	2021	2006	ESA 2010		NSO	2020
Morocco	Moroccan dirham	NSO	2021	2014	SNA 2008	From 2007	NSO	2021
Mozambique	Mozambican metical	NSO	2021	2014	SNA 2008		NSO	2021
Myanmar	Myanmar kyat	MEP	2019/20	2015/16	. . .		NSO	2020/21
Namibia	Namibian dollar	NSO	2021	2015	SNA 1993		NSO	2021
Nauru	Australian dollar	IMF staff	2018/19	2006/07	SNA 2008		NSO and IMF staff	2019/20
Nepal	Nepalese rupee	NSO	2019/20	2000/01	SNA 1993		CB	2020/21
The Netherlands	Euro	NSO	2021	2015	ESA 2010	From 1980	NSO	2021
New Zealand	New Zealand dollar	NSO	2021	2009[6]	SNA 2008	From 1987	NSO and IMF staff	2021
Nicaragua	Nicaraguan córdoba	CB	2021	2006	SNA 2008	From 1994	CB	2020
Niger	CFA franc	NSO	2020	2015	SNA 2008		NSO	2020
Nigeria	Nigerian naira	NSO	2020	2010	SNA 2008		NSO	2020
North Macedonia	Macedonian denar	NSO	2021	2005	ESA 2010		NSO	2021
Norway	Norwegian krone	NSO	2021	2019	ESA 2010	From 1980	NSO	2021

Table G. Key Data Documentation *(continued)*

	Government Finance					Balance of Payments		
Country	Historical Data Source[1]	Latest Actual Annual Data	Statistics Manual in Use at Source	Subsectors Coverage[4]	Accounting Practice[5]	Historical Data Source[1]	Latest Actual Annual Data	Statistics Manual in Use at Source
Japan	GAD	2020	2014	CG,LG,SS	A	MoF	2021	BPM 6
Jordan	MoF	2020	2001	CG,NFPC	C	CB	2020	BPM 6
Kazakhstan	NSO	2021	2001	CG,LG	C	CB	2021	BPM 6
Kenya	MoF	2021	2001	CG	C	CB	2021	BPM 6
Kiribati	MoF	2020	1986	CG	C	NSO and IMF staff	2020	BPM 6
Korea	MoF	2021	2001	CG,SS	C	CB	2021	BPM 6
Kosovo	MoF	2021	. . .	CG,LG	C	CB	2021	BPM 6
Kuwait	MoF	2020	2014	CG,SS	Mixed	CB	2020	BPM 6
Kyrgyz Republic	MoF	2021	. . .	CG,LG,SS	C	CB	2021	BPM 6
Lao P.D.R.	MoF	2020	2001	CG	C	CB	2020	BPM 6
Latvia	MoF	2021	ESA 2010	CG,LG,SS	C	CB	2021	BPM 6
Lebanon	MoF	2020	2001	CG	C	CB and IMF staff	2021	BPM 5
Lesotho	MoF	2021/22	2001	CG,LG	C	CB	2021/22	BPM 6
Liberia	MoF	2020	2001	CG	A	CB	2020	BPM 5
Libya	CB	2021	1986	CG,SG,LG	C	CB	2020	BPM 5
Lithuania	MoF	2021	2014	CG,LG,SS	A	CB	2021	BPM 6
Luxembourg	MoF	2020	2001	CG,LG,SS	A	NSO	2020	BPM 6
Macao SAR	MoF	2020	2014	CG,SS	C	NSO	2020	BPM 6
Madagascar	MoF	2021	1986	CG	CB	CB	2021	BPM 6
Malawi	MoF	2021	2014	CG	C	NSO and GAD	2020	BPM 6
Malaysia	MoF	2021	2001	CG,SG,LG	C	NSO	2021	BPM 6
Maldives	MoF	2020	1986	CG	C	CB	2020	BPM 6
Mali	MoF	2021	2001	CG	Mixed	CB	2021	BPM 6
Malta	NSO	2021	2001	CG,SS	A	NSO	2021	BPM 6
Marshall Islands	MoF	2020/21	2001	CG,LG,SS	A	NSO	2020/21	BPM 6
Mauritania	MoF	2021	1986	CG	C	CB	2021	BPM 6
Mauritius	MoF	2020/21	2001	CG,LG,NFPC	C	CB	2021	BPM 6
Mexico	MoF	2021	2014	CG,SS,NMPC,NFPC	C	CB	2021	BPM 6
Micronesia	MoF	2017/18	2001	CG,SG	. . .	NSO	2017/18	BPM 6
Moldova	MoF	2021	1986	CG,LG	C	CB	2021	BPM 6
Mongolia	MoF	2021	2001	CG,SG,LG,SS	C	CB	2021	BPM 6
Montenegro	MoF	2020	1986	CG,LG,SS	C	CB	2020	BPM 6
Morocco	MEP	2021	2001	CG	A	GAD	2021	BPM 6
Mozambique	MoF	2021	2001	CG,SG	Mixed	CB	2021	BPM 6
Myanmar	MoF	2019/20	2014	CG,NFPC	C	IMF staff	2020/21	BPM 6
Namibia	MoF	2021	2001	CG	C	CB	2021	BPM 6
Nauru	MoF	2020/21	2001	CG	Mixed	IMF staff	2019/20	BPM 6
Nepal	MoF	2019/20	2001	CG	C	CB	2020/21	BPM 5
The Netherlands	MoF	2021	2001	CG,LG,SS	A	CB	2021	BPM 6
New Zealand	NSO	2020	2014	CG,LG	A	NSO	2021	BPM 6
Nicaragua	MoF	2020	1986	CG,LG,SS	C	IMF staff	2020	BPM 6
Niger	MoF	2021	1986	CG	A	CB	2020	BPM 6
Nigeria	MoF	2020	2001	CG,SG,LG	C	CB	2020	BPM 6
North Macedonia	MoF	2021	1986	CG,SG,SS	C	CB	2021	BPM 6
Norway	NSO and MoF	2021	2014	CG,LG,SS	A	NSO	2021	BPM 6

Table G. Key Data Documentation *(continued)*

		National Accounts					Prices (CPI)	
Country	Currency	Historical Data Source[1]	Latest Actual Annual Data	Base Year[2]	System of National Accounts	Use of Chain-Weighted Methodology[3]	Historical Data Source[1]	Latest Actual Annual Data
Oman	Omani rial	NSO	2021	2018	SNA 2008		NSO	2021
Pakistan	Pakistan rupee	NSO	2020/21	2015/16[6]	SNA 2008		NSO	2020/21
Palau	US dollar	MoF	2020/21	2018/19	SNA 1993		MoF	2020/21
Panama	US dollar	NSO	2021	2007	SNA 1993	From 2007	NSO	2021
Papua New Guinea	Papua New Guinea kina	NSO and MoF	2019	2013	SNA 2008		NSO	2021
Paraguay	Paraguayan guaraní	CB	2020	2014	SNA 2008		CB	2021
Peru	Peruvian sol	CB	2021	2007	SNA 2008		CB	2021
Philippines	Philippine peso	NSO	2021	2018	SNA 2008		NSO	2021
Poland	Polish złoty	NSO	2021	2015	ESA 2010	From 2015	NSO	2021
Portugal	Euro	NSO	2021	2016	ESA 2010	From 1980	NSO	2021
Puerto Rico	US dollar	NSO	2019/20	1954	. . .		NSO	2021
Qatar	Qatari riyal	NSO and MEP	2020	2018	SNA 1993		NSO and MEP	2020
Romania	Romanian leu	NSO	2021	2015	ESA 2010	From 2000	NSO	2021
Russia	Russian ruble	NSO	2021	2016	SNA 2008	From 1995	NSO	2021
Rwanda	Rwandan franc	NSO	2021	2017	SNA 2008		NSO	2021
Samoa	Samoan tālā	NSO	2020/21	2012/13	SNA 2008		NSO	2021/22
San Marino	Euro	NSO	2020	2007	ESA 2010		NSO	2021
São Tomé and Príncipe	São Tomé and Príncipe dobra	NSO	2020	2008	SNA 1993		NSO	2020
Saudi Arabia	Saudi riyal	NSO	2021	2010	SNA 2008		NSO	2021
Senegal	CFA franc	NSO	2021	2014	SNA 2008		NSO	2021
Serbia	Serbian dinar	NSO	2021	2015	ESA 2010	From 2010	NSO	2021
Seychelles	Seychelles rupee	NSO	2021	2014	SNA 1993		NSO	2021
Sierra Leone	Sierra Leonean leone	NSO	2021	2006	SNA 2008	From 2010	NSO	2021
Singapore	Singapore dollar	NSO	2021	2015	SNA 2008	From 2015	NSO	2021
Slovak Republic	Euro	NSO	2021	2015	ESA 2010	From 1997	NSO	2021
Slovenia	Euro	NSO	2021	2010	ESA 2010	From 2000	NSO	2021
Solomon Islands	Solomon Islands dollar	CB	2020	2012	SNA 1993		NSO	2021
Somalia	US dollar	NSO	2021	2017	SNA 2008		NSO	2021
South Africa	South African rand	NSO	2021	2015	SNA 2008		NSO	2021
South Sudan	South Sudanese pound	NSO and IMF staff	2018	2010	SNA 1993		NSO	2021
Spain	Euro	NSO	2021	2015	ESA 2010	From 1995	NSO	2021
Sri Lanka	Sri Lankan rupee	NSO	2021	2015	SNA 2008		NSO	2021
St. Kitts and Nevis	Eastern Caribbean dollar	NSO	2020	2006	SNA 1993		NSO	2021
St. Lucia	Eastern Caribbean dollar	NSO	2021	2018	SNA 2008		NSO	2021
St. Vincent and the Grenadines	Eastern Caribbean dollar	NSO	2020	2018	SNA 1993		NSO	2021
Sudan	Sudanese pound	NSO	2019	1982	. . .		NSO	2021
Suriname	Surinamese dollar	NSO	2020	2015	SNA 2008		NSO	2021

Table G. Key Data Documentation *(continued)*

	Government Finance					Balance of Payments		
Country	Historical Data Source[1]	Latest Actual Annual Data	Statistics Manual in Use at Source	Subsectors Coverage[4]	Accounting Practice[5]	Historical Data Source[1]	Latest Actual Annual Data	Statistics Manual in Use at Source
Oman	MoF	2021	2001	CG	C	CB	2021	BPM 5
Pakistan	MoF	2020/21	1986	CG,SG,LG	C	CB	2020/21	BPM 6
Palau	MoF	2020/21	2001	CG	. . .	MoF	2020/21	BPM 6
Panama	MoF	2021	2014	CG,SG,LG,SS,NFPC	C	NSO	2021	BPM 6
Papua New Guinea	MoF	2020	1986	CG	C	CB	2021	BPM 5
Paraguay	MoF	2021	2001	CG,SG,LG,SS,MPC	C	CB	2020	BPM 6
Peru	CB and MoF	2021	2001	CG,SG,LG,SS	Mixed	CB	2021	BPM 5
Philippines	MoF	2021	2001	CG,LG,SS	C	CB	2021	BPM 6
Poland	MoF and NSO	2021	ESA 2010	CG,LG,SS	A	CB	2021	BPM 6
Portugal	NSO	2021	2001	CG,LG,SS	A	CB	2021	BPM 6
Puerto Rico	MEP	2019/20	2001	. . .	A	. . .	. . .	. . .
Qatar	MoF	2021	1986	CG,other	C	CB and IMF staff	2021	BPM 5
Romania	MoF	2021	2001	CG,LG,SS	C	CB	2021	BPM 6
Russia	MoF	2021	2014	CG,SG,SS	Mixed	CB	2021	BPM 6
Rwanda	MoF	2021	2014	CG	Mixed	CB	2021	BPM 6
Samoa	MoF	2020/21	2001	CG	A	CB	2021/22	BPM 6
San Marino	MoF	2020	. . .	CG	. . .	Other	2020	BPM 6
São Tomé and Príncipe	MoF and Customs	2020	2001	CG	C	CB	2020	BPM 6
Saudi Arabia	MoF	2021	2014	CG	C	CB	2021	BPM 6
Senegal	MoF	2021	2001	CG	C	CB and IMF staff	2020	BPM 6
Serbia	MoF	2021	1986/2001	CG,SG,LG,SS,other	C	CB	2021	BPM 6
Seychelles	MoF	2021	2001	CG,SS	C	CB	2021	BPM 6
Sierra Leone	MoF	2021	1986	CG	C	CB	2020	BPM 6
Singapore	MoF and NSO	2021/22	2014	CG	C	NSO	2021	BPM 6
Slovak Republic	NSO	2021	2001	CG,LG,SS	A	CB	2021	BPM 6
Slovenia	MoF	2021	2001	CG,LG,SS	A	CB	2021	BPM 6
Solomon Islands	MoF	2020	1986	CG	C	CB	2021	BPM 6
Somalia	MoF	2021	2001	CG	C	CB	2021	BPM 5
South Africa	MoF	2021	2001	CG,SG,SS,other	C	CB	2021	BPM 6
South Sudan	MoF and MEP	2019	. . .	CG	C	MoF, NSO, MEP, and IMF staff	2018	BPM 6
Spain	MoF and NSO	2020	ESA 2010	CG,SG,LG,SS	A	CB	2021	BPM 6
Sri Lanka	MoF	2021	1986	CG	C	CB	2021	BPM 6
St. Kitts and Nevis	MoF	2020	1986	CG,SG	C	CB	2020	BPM 6
St. Lucia	MoF	2021/22	1986	CG	C	CB	2020	BPM 6
St. Vincent and the Grenadines	MoF	2021	1986	CG	C	CB	2021	BPM 6
Sudan	MoF	2019	2001	CG	Mixed	CB	2019	BPM 6
Suriname	MoF	2021	1986	CG	Mixed	CB	2020	BPM 6

Table G. Key Data Documentation *(continued)*

		National Accounts					Prices (CPI)	
Country	Currency	Historical Data Source[1]	Latest Actual Annual Data	Base Year[2]	System of National Accounts	Use of Chain-Weighted Methodology[3]	Historical Data Source[1]	Latest Actual Annual Data
Sweden	Swedish krona	NSO	2021	2021	ESA 2010	From 1993	NSO	2021
Switzerland	Swiss franc	NSO	2021	2015	ESA 2010	From 1980	NSO	2021
Syria	Syrian pound	NSO	2010	2000	SNA 1993		NSO	2011
Taiwan Province of China	New Taiwan dollar	NSO	2021	2016	SNA 2008		NSO	2021
Tajikistan	Tajik somoni	NSO	2020	1995	SNA 1993		NSO	2021
Tanzania	Tanzanian shilling	NSO	2021	2015	SNA 2008		NSO	2021
Thailand	Thai baht	MEP	2021	2002	SNA 1993	From 1993	MEP	2021
Timor-Leste	US dollar	NSO	2020	2015	SNA 2008		NSO	2021
Togo	CFA franc	NSO	2020	2016	SNA 2008		NSO	2021
Tonga	Tongan pa'anga	CB	2020/21	2016/17	SNA 2008		CB	2020/21
Trinidad and Tobago	Trinidad and Tobago dollar	NSO	2021	2012	SNA 2008		NSO	2021
Tunisia	Tunisian dinar	NSO	2021	2015	SNA 1993	From 2009	NSO	2021
Türkiye	Turkish lira	NSO	2021	2009	ESA 2010	From 2009	NSO	2021
Turkmenistan	New Turkmen manat	IMF staff	2020	2006	SNA 2008	From 2007	NSO	2021
Tuvalu	Australian dollar	PFTAC advisors	2019	2016	SNA 1993		NSO	2020
Uganda	Ugandan shilling	NSO	2021	2016	SNA 2008		CB	2021
Ukraine	Ukrainian hryvnia	NSO	2020	2016	SNA 2008	From 2005	NSO	2021
United Arab Emirates	U.A.E. dirham	NSO	2020	2010	SNA 2008		NSO	2021
United Kingdom	British pound	NSO	2020	2019	ESA 2010	From 1980	NSO	2021
United States	US dollar	NSO	2021	2012	SNA 2008	From 1980	NSO	2021
Uruguay	Uruguayan peso	CB	2020	2016	SNA 2008		NSO	2021
Uzbekistan	Uzbek som	NSO	2021	2020	SNA 1993		NSO and IMF staff	2021
Vanuatu	Vanuatu vatu	NSO	2019	2006	SNA 1993		NSO	2020
Venezuela	Venezuelan bolívar digital	CB	2018	1997	SNA 1993		CB	2021
Vietnam	Vietnamese dong	NSO	2021	2010	SNA 1993		NSO	2021
West Bank and Gaza	Israeli new shekel	NSO	2021	2015	SNA 2008		NSO	2021
Yemen	Yemeni rial	IMF staff	2020	1990	SNA 1993		NSO, CB, and IMF staff	2020
Zambia	Zambian kwacha	NSO	2021	2010	SNA 2008		NSO	2021
Zimbabwe	Zimbabwe dollar	NSO	2019	2012	SNA 2008		NSO	2019

Table G. Key Data Documentation *(continued)*

	Government Finance					Balance of Payments		
Country	Historical Data Source[1]	Latest Actual Annual Data	Statistics Manual in Use at Source	Subsectors Coverage[4]	Accounting Practice[5]	Historical Data Source[1]	Latest Actual Annual Data	Statistics Manual in Use at Source
Sweden	MoF	2020	2001	CG,LG,SS	A	NSO	2021	BPM 6
Switzerland	MoF	2021	2001	CG,SG,LG,SS	A	CB	2021	BPM 6
Syria	MoF	2009	1986	CG	C	CB	2009	BPM 5
Taiwan Province of China	MoF	2021	2001	CG,LG,SS	C	CB	2021	BPM 6
Tajikistan	MoF	2020	1986	CG,LG,SS	C	CB	2020	BPM 6
Tanzania	MoF	2021	1986	CG,LG	C	CB	2021	BPM 6
Thailand	MoF	2020/21	2001	CG,BCG,LG,SS	A	CB	2021	BPM 6
Timor-Leste	MoF	2019	2001	CG	C	CB	2021	BPM 6
Togo	MoF	2020	2001	CG	C	CB	2020	BPM 6
Tonga	MoF	2020/21	2014	CG	C	CB and NSO	2020/21	BPM 6
Trinidad and Tobago	MoF	2020/21	1986	CG	C	CB	2021	BPM 6
Tunisia	MoF	2021	1986	CG	C	CB	2021	BPM 5
Türkiye	MoF	2021	2001	CG,LG,SS,other	A	CB	2021	BPM 6
Turkmenistan	MoF	2021	1986	CG,LG	C	NSO	2021	BPM 6
Tuvalu	MoF	2019	...	CG	Mixed	IMF staff	2019	BPM 6
Uganda	MoF	2021	2001	CG	C	CB	2021	BPM 6
Ukraine	MoF	2021	2001	CG,LG,SS	C	CB	2020	BPM 6
United Arab Emirates	MoF	2021	2001	CG,BCG,SG,SS	Mixed	CB	2021	BPM 5
United Kingdom	NSO	2021	2001	CG,LG	A	NSO	2021	BPM 6
United States	MEP	2021	2014	CG,SG,LG	A	NSO	2021	BPM 6
Uruguay	MoF	2021	1986	CG,LG,SS,NFPC, NMPC	C	CB	2020	BPM 6
Uzbekistan	MoF	2021	2014	CG,SG,LG,SS	C	CB and MEP	2021	BPM 6
Vanuatu	MoF	2020	2001	CG	C	CB	2020	BPM 6
Venezuela	MoF	2017	2001	BCG,NFPC,SS,other	C	CB	2018	BPM 6
Vietnam	MoF	2021	2001	CG,SG,LG	C	CB	2021	BPM 5
West Bank and Gaza	MoF	2021	2001	CG	Mixed	NSO	2021	BPM 6
Yemen	MoF	2020	2001	CG,LG	C	IMF staff	2020	BPM 5
Zambia	MoF	2021	1986	CG	C	CB	2021	BPM 6
Zimbabwe	MoF	2019	1986	CG	C	CB and MoF	2020	BPM 6

Note: BPM = *Balance of Payments Manual;* CPI = consumer price index; ESA = European System of National Accounts; SNA = System of National Accounts.
[1]CB = central bank; Customs = Customs Authority; GAD = General Administration Department; IEO = international economic organization; MEP = Ministry of Economy, Planning, Commerce, and/or Development; MoF = Ministry of Finance and/or Treasury; NSO = National Statistics Office; PFTAC = Pacific Financial Technical Assistance Centre.
[2]National accounts base year is the period with which other periods are compared and the period for which prices appear in the denominators of the price relationships used to calculate the index.
[3]Use of chain-weighted methodology allows countries to measure GDP growth more accurately by reducing or eliminating the downward biases in volume series built on index numbers that average volume components using weights from a year in the moderately distant past.
[4]BCG = budgetary central government; CG = central government; LG = local government; MPC = monetary public corporation, including central bank; NFPC = nonfinancial public corporation; NMPC = nonmonetary financial public corporation; SG = state government; SS = social security fund; TG = territorial governments.
[5]Accounting standard: A = accrual accounting; C = cash accounting; CB = commitment basis accounting; Mixed = combination of accrual and cash accounting.
[6]Base year deflator is not equal to 100 because the nominal GDP is not measured in the same way as real GDP or the data are seasonally adjusted.

Box A1. Economic Policy Assumptions Underlying the Projections for Selected Economies

Fiscal Policy Assumptions

The short-term fiscal policy assumptions used in the *World Economic Outlook* (WEO) are normally based on officially announced budgets, adjusted for differences between the national authorities and the IMF staff regarding macroeconomic assumptions and projected fiscal outturns. When no official budget has been announced, projections incorporate policy measures judged likely to be implemented. The medium-term fiscal projections are similarly based on a judgment about policies' most likely path. For cases in which the IMF staff has insufficient information to assess the authorities' budget intentions and prospects for policy implementation, an unchanged structural primary balance is assumed unless indicated otherwise. Specific assumptions used in regard to some of the advanced economies follow. (See also Tables B5–B9 in the online section of the Statistical Appendix for data on fiscal net lending/borrowing and structural balances.)[1]

Argentina: Fiscal projections are based on the available information regarding budget outturn, budget plans, and IMF-supported program targets for the federal government; on fiscal measures announced by the authorities; and on IMF staff macroeconomic projections.

Australia: Fiscal projections are based on data from the Australian Bureau of Statistics, the fiscal year FY2022/23 budget published by the Commonwealth government in March 2022, the FY2022/23 budget published by the respective state/territory governments (as of August 30, 2022), and the IMF staff's estimates and projections.

Austria: Fiscal projections are based on the 2022 budget, the Austrian Stability Programme, Austria's National Reform Programme, the NextGeneration European Union recovery funds, and the latest announcement on fiscal measures.

Belgium: Projections are based on the Belgian Stability Program 2022–25, the 2022 Budgetary Plan, and other available information on the authorities' fiscal plans, with adjustments for the IMF staff's assumptions.

Brazil: Fiscal projections for 2022 reflect the latest policy announcements.

Canada: Projections use the baseline forecasts from the Government of Canada's Budget 2022 and the latest provincial budgets. The IMF staff makes some adjustments to these forecasts, including those for differences in macroeconomic projections. The IMF staff's forecast also incorporates the most recent data releases from Statistics Canada's National Economic Accounts, including quarterly federal, provincial, and territorial budgetary outturns.

Chile: Projections are based on the authorities' budget projections, adjusted to reflect the IMF staff's projections for GDP, copper prices, depreciation, and inflation.

China: After a significant fiscal tightening in 2021, fiscal policy is projected to loosen considerably in 2022 based on the annual budget document released in March, subsequent announcements of additional fiscal support for the economy, and the fiscal outturn for the first seven months of 2022.

Denmark: Estimates for the current year are aligned with the latest official budget numbers, adjusted where appropriate for the IMF staff's macroeconomic assumptions. Beyond the current year, the projections incorporate key features of the medium-term fiscal plan as embodied in the authorities' latest budget. Structural balances are net of temporary fluctuations in some revenues (for example, North Sea revenue, pension yield tax revenue) and one-offs (COVID-19–related one-offs are, however, included).

[1] The output gap is actual minus potential output, as a percentage of potential output. Structural balances are expressed as a percentage of potential output. The structural balance is the actual net lending/borrowing minus the effects of cyclical output from potential output, corrected for one-time and other factors, such as asset and commodity prices and output composition effects. Changes in the structural balance consequently include effects of temporary fiscal measures, the impact of fluctuations in interest rates and debt-service costs, and other noncyclical fluctuations in net lending/borrowing. The computations of structural balances are based on the IMF staff's estimates of potential GDP and revenue and expenditure elasticities. (See Annex I of the October 1993 WEO.) Estimates of the output gap and of the structural balance are subject to significant margins of uncertainty. Net debt is calculated as gross debt minus financial assets corresponding to debt instruments.

Box A1 *(continued)*

France: Projections for 2022 onward are based on the 2018–22 budget laws, Stability Program 2022–27, and other available information on the authorities' fiscal plans, adjusted for differences in revenue projections and assumptions on macroeconomic and financial variables.

Germany: The IMF staff's projections for 2022 and beyond are based on the 2022 budget, the 2022 Stability Programme, the draft 2023 federal budget, the federal government's medium-term budget plan, and the data updates from the national statistical agency (Destatis) and the ministry of finance, adjusted for differences in the IMF staff's macroeconomic framework and assumptions concerning revenue elasticities.

Greece: Data since 2010 reflect adjustments in line with the primary balance definition under the enhanced surveillance framework for Greece.

Hong Kong Special Administrative Region: Projections are based on the authorities' medium-term fiscal projections for expenditures.

Hungary: Fiscal projections include the IMF staff's projections for the macroeconomic framework and fiscal policy plans announced in the 2022 budget.

India: Projections are based on available information on the authorities' fiscal plans, with adjustments for the IMF staff's assumptions. Subnational data are incorporated with a lag of up to one year; general government data are thus finalized well after central government data. IMF and Indian presentations differ, particularly regarding disinvestment and license-auction proceeds, net versus gross recording of revenues in certain minor categories, and some public sector lending. Starting with FY2020/21 data, expenditure also includes the off-budget component of food subsidies, consistent with the revised treatment of food subsidies in the budget. The IMF staff adjusts expenditure to take out payments for previous years' food subsidies, which are included as expenditure in budget estimates for FY2020/21.

Indonesia: The IMF staff's projections are based on moderate tax policy and administration reforms, some expenditure realization, and a gradual increase in capital spending over the medium term in line with fiscal space.

Ireland: Fiscal projections are based on the country's Budget 2022.

Israel: Projections assume spending will be below budget in 2022 given current trends but also assume more modest spending cuts over the medium term relative to the authorities' medium-term framework.

Italy: The IMF staff's estimates and projections are informed by the fiscal plans included in the government's 2022 budget and amendments. The stock of maturing postal bonds is included in the debt projections.

Japan: The projections reflect fiscal measures the government has already announced, with adjustments for the IMF staff's assumptions.

Korea: The forecast incorporates the overall fiscal balance in the 2022 annual budget and two supplementary budgets, the medium-term fiscal plan announced with the 2022 budget, and the IMF staff's adjustments.

Mexico: The 2020 public sector borrowing requirements estimated by the IMF staff adjust for some statistical discrepancies between above-the-line and below-the-line numbers. Fiscal projections for 2022 and 2023 are informed by the estimates in Criterios 2023; projections for 2024 onward assume continued compliance with rules established in the Fiscal Responsibility Law.

The Netherlands: Fiscal projections for 2022–27 are based on the IMF staff's forecast framework and are also informed by the authorities' draft budget plan and Bureau for Economic Policy Analysis projections.

New Zealand: Fiscal projections are based on the FY2022/23 budget (May 2022) and the IMF staff's estimates.

Portugal: The projections for the current year are based on the authorities' approved budget, adjusted to reflect the IMF staff's macroeconomic forecast. Projections thereafter are based on the assumption of unchanged policies.

Puerto Rico: Fiscal projections are informed by the Certified Fiscal Plan for the Commonwealth of Puerto Rico, which was prepared in January 2022, certified by the Financial Oversight & Management Board.

Box A1 *(continued)*

Russia: The fiscal rule has been suspended by the government in response to the sanctions imposed after the invasion of Ukraine. The projection assumes an increase in discretionary spending by the amount that would otherwise have been saved according to the fiscal rule, some borrowing, and a decline in revenues due to the projected recession.

Saudi Arabia: The IMF staff's baseline fiscal projections are primarily based on its understanding of government policies as outlined in the 2022 budget. Export oil revenues are based on WEO baseline oil price assumptions and the IMF staff's understanding of current oil policy under the OPEC+ (Organization of the Petroleum Exporting Countries, including Russia and other non-OPEC oil exporters) agreement.

Singapore: FY2020 figures are based on budget execution. FY2021 projections are based on revised figures based on budget execution through the end of 2021. FY2022 projections are based on the initial budget of February 18, 2022. The IMF staff assumes gradual withdrawal of the remaining pandemic-related measures and the implementation of various revenue measures announced in the FY2022 budget for the remainder of the projection period. These include (1) an increase in the Goods and Services Tax from 7 percent to 8 percent on January 1, 2023, and to 9 percent on January 1, 2024; (2) an increase in property taxes in 2023 for non–owner-occupied properties (from 10–20 percent to 12–36 percent) and for owner-occupied properties with an annual value in excess of $30,000 (from 4–16 percent to 6–32 percent); and (3) an increase of the carbon tax from S$5 per tonne to S$25 per tonne in 2024 and 2025 and S$45 per tonne in 2026 and 2027.

South Africa: Fiscal assumptions draw on the 2022 budget. Nontax revenue excludes transactions in financial assets and liabilities, as they involve primarily revenues associated with realized exchange rate valuation gains from the holding of foreign currency deposits, sale of assets, and conceptually similar items.

Spain: Fiscal projections for 2022 include COVID-19– and energy-related support measures, a legislated increase in pensions, and legislated revenue measures. Fiscal projections from 2023 onward assume no policy changes. Projections for 2021–24 reflect disbursements under the EU Recovery and Resilience Facility.

Sweden: Fiscal estimates for 2021 and 2022 are based on the authorities' Spring Fiscal Policy Bill and the Spring Amending Budget for 2022 and have been updated with the authorities' latest interim forecast. The impact of cyclical developments on the fiscal accounts is calculated using the 2014 Organisation for Economic Co-operation and Development elasticity[2] to take into account output and employment gaps.

Switzerland: The authorities' announced discretionary stimulus—as reflected in the fiscal projections for 2022—is permitted within the context of the debt brake rule in the event of "exceptional circumstances."

Türkiye: The basis for the projections is the IMF-defined fiscal balance, which excludes some revenue and expenditure items that are included in the authorities' headline balance.

United Kingdom: Fiscal projections are based on the latest GDP data published by the Office of National Statistics on August 12, 2022, and the forecasts by the Office for Budget Responsibility from March 23, 2022. Revenue projections are adjusted for differences between the IMF staff's forecasts for macroeconomic variables (such as GDP growth and inflation) and the forecasts for these variables assumed in the authorities' fiscal projections. Projections assume some additional fiscal consolidation relative to the policies announced to date starting in FY2023/24 with the goal of complying with the new fiscal rules announced at the time of the Autumn Budget and Spending Review on October 27, 2021, and

[2] Robert W. R. Price, Thai-Thanh Dang, and Yvan Guillemette, "New Tax and Expenditure Elasticity Estimates for EU Budget Surveillance," OECD Economics Department Working Paper 1174, Organisation for Economic Co-operation and Development, Paris, 2014.

Box A1 *(continued)*

securing public debt sustainability. The IMF staff's data exclude public sector banks and the effect of transferring assets from the Royal Mail Pension Plan to the public sector in April 2012. Real government consumption and investment are part of the real GDP path, which, according to the IMF staff, may or may not be the same as projected by the Office for Budget Responsibility. Data are presented on a calendar year basis.

United States: Fiscal projections are based on the July 2022 Congressional Budget Office baseline, adjusted for the IMF staff's policy and macroeconomic assumptions. Projections incorporate the effects of the Bipartisan Infrastructure Law and the Inflation Reduction Act. Fiscal projections are adjusted to reflect the IMF staff's forecasts for key macroeconomic and financial variables and different accounting treatment of financial sector support and of defined-benefit pension plans and are converted to a general government basis.

Monetary Policy Assumptions

Monetary policy assumptions are based on the established policy framework in each country. In most cases, this implies a nonaccommodative stance over the business cycle: official interest rates will increase when economic indicators suggest that inflation will rise above its acceptable rate or range; they will decrease when indicators suggest inflation will not exceed the acceptable rate or range, that output growth is below its potential rate, and that the margin of slack in the economy is significant. With regard to *interest rates*, please refer to the Assumptions section at the beginning of the Statistical Appendix.

Argentina: Monetary projections are consistent with the overall macroeconomic framework, the fiscal and financing plans, and the monetary and foreign exchange policies under the crawling-peg regime.

Australia: Monetary policy assumptions are based on the IMF staff's analysis and the expected inflation path.

Austria: Monetary growth projections are in proportion to nominal GDP growth.

Brazil: Monetary policy assumptions are consistent with the convergence of inflation toward the middle of the target range by the end of 2024.

Canada: Projections reflect monetary policy tightening by the Bank of Canada and increased long-term yields, in response to inflation significantly overshooting its target. It is expected that the Bank of Canada will continue to increase its key policy rate during 2022 and 2023. The economy is in excess demand, and the policy tightening is appropriate despite the worsening medium-term outlook.

Chile: Monetary policy assumptions are consistent with attaining the inflation target.

China: The overall monetary policy stance was moderately tight in 2021, but it is expected to be moderately accommodative in 2022.

Denmark: Monetary policy is to maintain the peg to the euro.

Euro area: Monetary policy assumptions for euro area member countries are in line with market expectations.

Greece: Broad money projections are based on monetary financial institution balance sheets and deposit flow assumptions.

Hong Kong Special Administrative Region: The IMF staff assumes that the currency board system will remain intact.

India: Monetary policy projections are consistent with achieving the Reserve Bank of India's inflation target over the medium term, despite a recent uptick in inflation that exceeded the upper target band.

Indonesia: Monetary policy assumptions are in line with inflation within the central bank's target band over the medium term.

Israel: Monetary policy assumptions are based on gradual normalization of monetary policy.

Italy: The IMF staff's estimates and projections are informed by the actual outturn from and policy plans by the Bank of Italy and the European Central Bank's monetary policy stance forecast from the IMF's euro area team.

Japan: Monetary policy assumptions are in line with market expectations.

Box A1 *(continued)*

Korea: Projections assume that the policy rate evolves in line with market expectations.

Mexico: Monetary policy assumptions are consistent with attaining the inflation target.

The Netherlands: Monetary projections are based on the IMF staff's estimated six-month euro London interbank offered rate projections.

New Zealand: Monetary projections are based on the IMF staff's analysis and expected inflation path.

Portugal: Monetary policy assumptions are based on the IMF staff's spreadsheets, given input projections for the real and fiscal sectors.

Russia: Monetary projections assume that the Central Bank of the Russian Federation is adopting a tight monetary policy stance. The IMF staff team regards this as the right policy stance given the hike in inflation.

Saudi Arabia: Monetary policy projections are based on the continuation of the exchange rate peg to the US dollar.

Singapore: Broad money is projected to grow in line with the projected growth in nominal GDP.

South Africa: Monetary policy assumptions are consistent with maintaining inflation within the 3–6 percent target band in the medium term.

Spain: Monetary growth projections are in proportion to nominal GDP growth.

Sweden: Monetary projections are in line with Riksbank projections.

Switzerland: Projections assume no change in the policy rate in 2022–23.

Türkiye: The baseline assumes that the monetary policy stance remains in line with market expectations.

United Kingdom: The short-term interest rate path is based on market interest rate expectations.

United States: The IMF staff expects the Federal Open Market Committee to continue to adjust the federal funds target rate in line with the broader macroeconomic outlook.

List of Tables[1]

[1] When countries are not listed alphabetically, they are ordered on the basis of economic size.

Table A1. Summary of World Output[1]

(Annual percent change)

	Average 2004–13	2014	2015	2016	2017	2018	2019	2020	2021	Projections 2022	2023	2027
World	**4.1**	**3.5**	**3.4**	**3.3**	**3.8**	**3.6**	**2.8**	**–3.0**	**6.0**	**3.2**	**2.7**	**3.2**
Advanced Economies	**1.6**	**2.0**	**2.3**	**1.8**	**2.5**	**2.3**	**1.7**	**–4.4**	**5.2**	**2.4**	**1.1**	**1.7**
United States	1.8	2.3	2.7	1.7	2.3	2.9	2.3	–3.4	5.7	1.6	1.0	1.9
Euro Area	0.9	1.4	2.0	1.9	2.6	1.8	1.6	–6.1	5.2	3.1	0.5	1.5
Japan	0.7	0.3	1.6	0.8	1.7	0.6	–0.4	–4.6	1.7	1.7	1.6	0.4
Other Advanced Economies[2]	2.7	3.0	2.2	2.3	2.9	2.5	1.9	–3.8	5.7	3.1	1.8	2.0
Emerging Market and Developing Economies	**6.4**	**4.7**	**4.3**	**4.4**	**4.8**	**4.6**	**3.6**	**–1.9**	**6.6**	**3.7**	**3.7**	**4.3**
Regional Groups												
Emerging and Developing Asia	8.5	6.9	6.8	6.8	6.6	6.4	5.2	–0.6	7.2	4.4	4.9	5.1
Emerging and Developing Europe	4.3	1.8	1.0	1.9	4.1	3.4	2.5	–1.7	6.8	0.0	0.6	2.2
Latin America and the Caribbean	4.0	1.3	0.4	–0.6	1.4	1.2	0.2	–7.0	6.9	3.5	1.7	2.4
Middle East and Central Asia	5.0	3.4	3.0	4.2	2.6	2.6	1.7	–2.7	4.5	5.0	3.6	3.7
Sub-Saharan Africa	5.6	5.0	3.2	1.5	3.0	3.3	3.2	–1.6	4.7	3.6	3.7	4.4
Analytical Groups												
By Source of Export Earnings												
Fuel	5.4	3.1	1.4	1.6	0.5	0.7	–0.1	–4.3	4.1	4.5	3.5	2.8
Nonfuel	6.6	5.0	4.7	4.8	5.3	5.1	4.0	–1.6	6.9	3.6	3.8	4.4
Of Which, Primary Products	4.8	2.2	2.9	1.9	2.9	1.9	1.2	–5.2	8.0	3.5	2.7	3.3
By External Financing Source												
Net Debtor Economies	5.4	4.5	4.2	4.1	4.8	4.5	3.3	–3.5	6.4	4.6	3.9	4.6
Net Debtor Economies by Debt-Servicing Experience												
Economies with Arrears and/or Rescheduling during 2017–21	4.6	3.1	2.1	3.4	4.0	3.7	3.6	–0.8	3.4	0.9	4.2	5.4
Other Groups												
European Union	1.2	1.7	2.5	2.1	3.0	2.2	2.0	–5.6	5.4	3.2	0.7	1.7
Middle East and North Africa	4.7	3.2	2.9	4.6	2.1	2.0	1.0	–3.1	4.1	5.0	3.6	3.6
Emerging Market and Middle-Income Economies	6.4	4.6	4.3	4.5	4.8	4.6	3.5	–2.2	6.8	3.6	3.6	4.1
Low-Income Developing Countries	6.1	6.1	4.8	3.9	4.9	5.1	4.9	1.1	4.1	4.8	4.9	5.7
Memorandum												
Median Growth Rate												
Advanced Economies	1.9	2.3	2.2	2.2	3.0	2.8	2.0	–4.2	5.3	3.1	1.5	1.9
Emerging Market and Developing Economies	4.7	3.8	3.3	3.4	3.7	3.5	3.1	–3.5	4.3	3.7	3.5	3.5
Emerging Market and Middle-Income Economies	4.1	3.4	3.0	3.0	2.9	2.9	2.4	–5.9	4.7	3.7	3.3	3.0
Low-Income Developing Countries	5.3	5.0	4.3	4.4	4.3	4.4	4.5	–0.5	3.7	3.7	4.4	5.0
Output per Capita[3]												
Advanced Economies	1.0	1.5	1.7	1.3	2.0	1.8	1.3	–4.9	5.1	2.2	0.9	1.4
Emerging Market and Developing Economies	4.7	3.2	2.8	2.9	3.3	3.3	2.3	–3.2	5.9	2.7	2.6	3.1
Emerging Market and Middle-Income Economies	5.0	3.3	3.0	3.2	3.6	3.6	2.5	–3.2	6.1	3.1	2.9	3.4
Low-Income Developing Countries	3.6	3.8	2.3	1.5	2.5	2.7	2.6	–1.2	2.5	2.5	2.6	3.4
World Growth Rate Based on Market Exchange Rates	**2.7**	**2.8**	**2.8**	**2.6**	**3.3**	**3.2**	**2.5**	**–3.4**	**5.8**	**2.9**	**2.1**	**2.8**
Value of World Output (billions of US dollars)												
At Market Exchange Rates	61,996	79,429	74,944	76,211	81,036	86,210	87,654	85,441	97,076	101,561	106,182	131,631
At Purchasing Power Parities	84,757	109,595	111,857	116,169	122,351	129,709	135,641	132,936	146,608	161,450	171,549	210,591

[1]Real GDP.
[2]Excludes euro area countries, Japan, and the United States.
[3]Output per capita is in international dollars at purchasing power parity.

Table A2. Advanced Economies: Real GDP and Total Domestic Demand[1]

(Annual percent change)

													Q4 over Q4[2]		
	Average									Projections				Projections	
	2004–13	2014	2015	2016	2017	2018	2019	2020	2021	2022	2023	2027	2021:Q4	2022:Q4	2023:Q4
Real GDP															
Advanced Economies	**1.6**	**2.0**	**2.3**	**1.8**	**2.5**	**2.3**	**1.7**	**–4.4**	**5.2**	**2.4**	**1.1**	**1.7**	**4.7**	**0.9**	**1.3**
United States	1.8	2.3	2.7	1.7	2.3	2.9	2.3	–3.4	5.7	1.6	1.0	1.9	5.5	0.0	1.0
Euro Area	0.9	1.4	2.0	1.9	2.6	1.8	1.6	–6.1	5.2	3.1	0.5	1.5	4.6	1.0	1.4
Germany	1.3	2.2	1.5	2.2	2.7	1.0	1.1	–3.7	2.6	1.5	–0.3	1.3	1.2	0.6	0.5
France	1.2	1.0	1.1	1.0	2.4	1.8	1.9	–7.9	6.8	2.5	0.7	1.4	5.0	0.4	0.9
Italy	–0.3	0.0	0.8	1.3	1.7	0.9	0.5	–9.0	6.7	3.2	–0.2	0.7	6.6	0.6	0.5
Spain	0.6	1.4	3.8	3.0	3.0	2.3	2.1	–10.8	5.1	4.3	1.2	1.7	5.5	1.3	2.0
The Netherlands	1.1	1.4	2.0	2.2	2.9	2.4	2.0	–3.9	4.9	4.5	0.8	1.5	6.2	2.6	1.2
Belgium	1.6	1.6	2.0	1.3	1.6	1.8	2.1	–5.7	6.2	2.4	0.4	1.2	5.7	0.5	1.2
Ireland	1.6	8.6	24.4	2.0	9.0	8.5	5.4	6.2	13.6	9.0	4.0	3.0	13.9	8.3	6.6
Austria	1.5	0.7	1.0	2.0	2.3	2.5	1.5	–6.7	4.6	4.7	1.0	1.7	6.4	1.9	3.7
Portugal	–0.1	0.8	1.8	2.0	3.5	2.8	2.7	–8.4	4.9	6.2	0.7	1.9	5.9	2.3	1.8
Greece	–1.7	0.5	–0.2	–0.5	1.1	1.7	1.8	–9.0	8.3	5.2	1.8	1.4	8.3	0.7	7.5
Finland	1.2	–0.4	0.5	2.8	3.2	1.1	1.2	–2.2	3.0	2.1	0.5	1.4	3.1	0.4	1.5
Slovak Republic	4.1	2.7	5.2	1.9	3.0	3.8	2.6	–4.4	3.0	1.8	1.5	2.8	1.2	1.1	2.4
Lithuania	3.3	3.5	2.0	2.5	4.3	4.0	4.6	–0.1	5.0	1.8	1.1	2.3	5.4	–0.7	3.4
Slovenia	1.5	2.8	2.2	3.2	4.8	4.5	3.5	–4.3	8.2	5.7	1.7	3.0	10.4	–0.4	3.7
Luxembourg	2.6	2.6	2.3	5.0	1.3	2.0	3.3	–1.8	6.9	1.6	1.1	2.5	4.9	–0.3	2.8
Latvia	2.7	1.9	3.9	2.4	3.3	4.0	2.5	–3.8	4.5	2.5	1.6	3.4	2.8	2.9	1.0
Estonia	2.6	3.0	1.9	3.2	5.8	3.8	3.7	–0.6	8.0	1.0	1.8	3.3	7.2	–0.1	1.8
Cyprus	1.3	–1.8	3.4	6.5	5.9	5.7	5.3	–5.0	5.6	3.5	2.5	2.9	6.2	–0.9	9.8
Malta	2.9	7.6	9.6	3.4	10.9	6.2	5.9	–8.3	10.3	6.2	3.3	3.4	11.6	2.4	5.6
Japan	0.7	0.3	1.6	0.8	1.7	0.6	–0.4	–4.6	1.7	1.7	1.6	0.4	0.5	2.1	0.9
United Kingdom	1.2	3.0	2.6	2.3	2.1	1.7	1.7	–9.3	7.4	3.6	0.3	1.5	6.6	1.0	0.2
Korea	4.0	3.2	2.8	2.9	3.2	2.9	2.2	–0.7	4.1	2.6	2.0	2.3	4.2	1.7	2.6
Canada	1.9	2.9	0.7	1.0	3.0	2.8	1.9	–5.2	4.5	3.3	1.5	1.7	3.2	2.2	1.3
Taiwan Province of China	4.2	4.7	1.5	2.2	3.3	2.8	3.1	3.4	6.6	3.3	2.8	2.0	4.9	2.5	2.2
Australia	3.0	2.6	2.3	2.7	2.4	2.8	2.0	–2.1	4.9	3.8	1.9	2.3	4.5	2.3	1.9
Switzerland	2.2	2.3	1.6	2.1	1.4	2.9	1.2	–2.5	4.2	2.2	0.8	1.2	3.9	0.4	1.5
Sweden	2.0	2.7	4.5	2.1	2.6	2.0	2.0	–2.2	5.1	2.6	–0.1	2.0	5.7	0.1	1.3
Singapore	6.7	3.9	3.0	3.6	4.7	3.7	1.1	–4.1	7.6	3.0	2.3	2.5	6.1	1.0	3.3
Hong Kong SAR	4.5	2.8	2.4	2.2	3.8	2.8	–1.7	–6.5	6.3	–0.8	3.9	2.8	4.7	2.1	1.5
Czech Republic	2.5	2.3	5.4	2.5	5.2	3.2	3.0	–5.5	3.5	1.9	1.5	2.5	3.5	–1.3	5.0
Israel	4.3	3.9	2.5	4.5	4.3	4.1	4.2	–1.9	8.6	6.1	3.0	3.5	10.4	1.6	3.4
Norway	1.6	2.0	2.0	1.1	2.3	1.1	0.7	–0.7	3.9	3.6	2.6	1.3	4.7	3.0	1.5
Denmark	0.9	1.6	2.3	3.2	2.8	2.0	1.5	–2.0	4.9	2.6	0.6	1.8	6.7	–0.4	1.0
New Zealand	2.1	3.8	3.7	4.0	3.5	3.4	2.9	–2.1	5.6	2.3	1.9	2.4	3.0	2.6	1.5
Puerto Rico	–0.7	–1.2	–1.0	–1.3	–2.9	–4.2	1.5	–3.9	2.7	4.8	0.4	0.0	...	...	...
Macao SAR	13.1	–2.0	–21.5	–0.7	10.0	6.5	–2.5	–54.0	18.0	–22.4	56.7	3.3	...	...	...
Iceland	2.7	1.7	4.4	6.3	4.2	4.9	2.4	–6.8	4.4	5.1	2.9	2.2	4.9	2.1	3.0
Andorra	–0.3	2.5	1.4	3.7	0.3	1.6	2.0	–11.2	8.9	6.6	2.0	1.5	...	...	...
San Marino	–1.7	–0.6	2.7	2.3	0.3	1.5	2.1	–6.7	5.4	3.1	0.8	1.3	...	...	...
Memorandum															
Major Advanced Economies	1.3	1.8	2.1	1.5	2.2	2.1	1.6	–4.8	5.1	2.0	0.8	1.5	4.4	0.6	0.9
Real Total Domestic Demand															
Advanced Economies	**1.4**	**2.0**	**2.6**	**2.0**	**2.5**	**2.3**	**2.0**	**–4.3**	**5.3**	**2.9**	**1.0**	**1.7**	**5.1**	**0.7**	**1.7**
United States	1.5	2.5	3.4	1.8	2.4	3.1	2.4	–3.0	6.9	2.3	0.6	1.8	6.2	0.3	0.7
Euro Area	0.5	1.3	2.3	2.4	2.3	1.8	2.4	–5.8	4.1	3.2	0.7	1.5	4.9	0.3	1.9
Germany	0.9	1.7	1.4	3.1	2.6	1.6	1.7	–3.0	1.9	3.2	0.0	1.4	2.4	1.6	1.2
France	1.3	1.5	1.4	1.4	2.5	1.4	2.1	–6.7	6.6	2.6	0.7	1.4	5.6	0.3	0.9
Italy	–0.7	0.1	1.2	1.8	1.8	1.3	–0.2	–8.5	6.8	3.6	–0.1	0.9	7.9	–0.9	1.5
Spain	0.1	1.9	4.1	2.1	3.3	3.0	1.6	–8.9	4.7	3.0	1.5	1.6	3.8	1.7	2.1
Japan	0.6	0.3	1.1	0.3	1.1	0.6	0.1	–3.8	0.6	1.9	1.3	0.4	0.5	1.9	1.1
United Kingdom	1.2	3.5	3.2	3.1	1.9	1.2	1.6	–10.1	8.5	4.6	0.3	1.5	4.8	–0.6	3.8
Canada	2.9	1.7	–0.2	0.4	4.1	2.5	1.2	–6.4	6.1	5.5	1.8	1.4	4.7	4.9	0.5
Other Advanced Economies[3]	3.0	2.8	2.6	2.9	3.6	2.7	1.5	–2.5	5.2	3.2	2.3	2.4	5.6	1.1	3.3
Memorandum															
Major Advanced Economies	1.2	1.9	2.4	1.7	2.2	2.2	1.7	–4.4	5.6	2.7	0.6	1.5	4.9	0.7	1.1

[1]In this and other tables, when countries are not listed alphabetically, they are ordered on the basis of economic size.
[2]From the fourth quarter of the preceding year.
[3]Excludes the Group of Seven (Canada, France, Germany, Italy, Japan, United Kingdom, United States) and euro area countries.

Table A3. Advanced Economies: Components of Real GDP

(Annual percent change)

	Averages										Projections	
	2004–13	2014–23	2014	2015	2016	2017	2018	2019	2020	2021	2022	2023
Private Consumer Expenditure												
Advanced Economies	**1.5**	**1.6**	**1.8**	**2.5**	**2.1**	**2.2**	**2.2**	**1.6**	**–5.8**	**5.3**	**3.5**	**1.2**
United States	1.8	2.3	2.7	3.3	2.5	2.4	2.9	2.2	–3.8	7.9	2.4	0.6
Euro Area	0.6	0.9	0.9	1.9	2.0	1.8	1.5	1.4	–7.7	3.7	3.8	0.8
Germany	0.7	0.9	1.1	1.9	2.4	1.4	1.5	1.6	–5.6	0.4	4.5	0.6
France	1.2	1.0	0.9	1.4	1.6	1.6	1.0	1.8	–6.8	5.3	2.7	1.3
Italy	–0.3	0.2	0.1	1.9	1.2	1.5	1.0	0.2	–10.6	5.2	2.8	–0.4
Spain	0.2	0.9	1.7	2.9	2.7	3.0	1.7	1.0	–12.0	4.6	3.0	1.7
Japan	0.9	–0.1	–0.9	–0.2	–0.4	1.1	0.2	–0.5	–5.2	1.3	2.8	1.1
United Kingdom	1.2	1.6	2.6	3.6	3.7	1.6	2.4	1.3	–10.6	6.2	5.5	0.7
Canada	2.9	2.5	2.6	2.3	2.1	3.7	2.6	1.4	–6.1	4.9	8.7	3.2
Other Advanced Economies[1]	2.9	2.1	2.5	2.9	2.6	2.8	2.8	1.8	–5.5	4.0	4.3	2.8
Memorandum												
Major Advanced Economies	1.4	1.6	1.7	2.4	2.0	2.0	2.1	1.5	–5.4	5.6	3.3	0.8
Public Consumption												
Advanced Economies	**1.3**	**1.6**	**0.6**	**1.7**	**2.0**	**0.8**	**1.5**	**2.3**	**1.8**	**3.4**	**0.9**	**0.7**
United States	0.5	0.9	–0.8	1.6	1.9	0.0	1.2	2.0	2.0	1.0	–0.9	0.9
Euro Area	1.3	1.5	0.8	1.3	1.9	1.1	1.0	1.7	1.1	4.2	1.8	0.2
Germany	1.5	2.4	1.7	2.9	4.0	1.7	0.8	2.6	4.0	3.8	3.3	–0.6
France	1.6	1.0	1.3	1.0	1.4	1.4	0.8	1.0	–4.0	6.4	1.6	–0.1
Italy	–0.2	0.1	–0.6	–0.6	0.7	–0.1	0.1	–0.5	0.5	0.6	1.3	–0.5
Spain	2.8	1.5	–0.7	2.0	1.0	1.0	2.3	2.0	3.3	3.1	–0.2	1.2
Japan	1.3	1.4	1.0	1.9	1.6	0.1	1.0	1.9	2.3	2.1	1.5	0.8
United Kingdom	1.6	1.7	2.0	1.3	0.5	0.6	0.4	4.2	–5.9	14.3	1.4	–0.8
Canada	1.8	2.0	0.6	1.4	1.8	2.1	3.2	1.7	0.0	5.8	1.7	1.6
Other Advanced Economies[1]	2.8	3.2	2.7	2.8	3.5	2.4	3.5	3.8	4.7	4.5	2.9	1.1
Memorandum												
Major Advanced Economies	0.9	1.2	0.2	1.6	1.8	0.4	1.0	2.0	1.1	3.1	0.5	0.5
Gross Fixed Capital Formation												
Advanced Economies	**1.0**	**2.4**	**3.4**	**3.6**	**2.6**	**3.8**	**3.0**	**3.0**	**–3.5**	**5.6**	**1.7**	**1.3**
United States	1.3	2.7	5.1	3.7	2.1	3.8	4.4	3.1	–1.5	6.1	0.5	–0.1
Euro Area	–0.2	2.6	1.4	4.7	4.0	3.9	3.1	6.9	–6.4	4.1	3.4	1.6
Germany	1.4	1.7	3.2	1.7	3.8	2.6	3.3	1.9	–2.3	1.2	0.8	0.9
France	1.0	1.9	0.0	0.9	2.5	5.0	3.2	4.2	–8.4	11.3	1.5	0.1
Italy	–2.5	3.0	–2.2	1.8	4.0	3.2	3.1	1.2	–9.1	17.0	10.3	3.1
Spain	–2.6	3.2	4.1	4.9	2.4	6.8	6.3	4.5	–9.5	4.3	7.5	2.2
Japan	–0.5	0.3	2.2	2.3	1.2	1.6	0.6	0.5	–4.9	–1.4	–1.2	2.7
United Kingdom	0.5	2.1	6.8	6.3	4.7	3.3	–0.1	0.5	–9.5	5.9	4.5	–0.6
Canada	3.8	0.6	2.3	–5.2	–4.7	3.3	2.5	0.0	–2.8	7.1	1.5	2.9
Other Advanced Economies[1]	3.4	2.6	2.6	2.3	3.0	4.9	2.0	0.7	–1.2	7.5	1.4	3.3
Memorandum												
Major Advanced Economies	0.8	2.1	3.7	2.8	2.2	3.4	3.2	2.3	–3.7	5.7	1.4	0.7

Table A3. Advanced Economies: Components of Real GDP *(continued)*

(Annual percent change)

	Averages										Projections	
	2004–13	2014–23	2014	2015	2016	2017	2018	2019	2020	2021	2022	2023
Final Domestic Demand												
Advanced Economies	**1.4**	**1.8**	**1.9**	**2.6**	**2.2**	**2.3**	**2.2**	**2.1**	**–3.9**	**5.0**	**2.6**	**1.1**
United States	1.5	2.2	2.7	3.1	2.3	2.4	3.0	2.4	–2.5	6.5	1.6	0.5
Euro Area	0.6	1.4	1.0	2.3	2.4	2.1	1.7	2.6	–5.6	3.9	3.2	0.9
Germany	1.0	1.4	1.7	2.1	3.1	1.7	1.8	1.9	–2.8	1.4	3.3	0.4
France	1.3	1.2	0.8	1.2	1.7	2.3	1.4	2.1	–6.5	6.9	2.1	0.7
Italy	–0.7	0.8	–0.4	1.4	1.6	1.5	1.2	0.3	–8.2	6.4	4.1	0.4
Spain	0.1	1.5	1.6	3.1	2.3	3.3	2.7	1.9	–8.5	4.2	3.2	1.7
Japan	0.6	0.3	0.1	0.8	0.3	1.0	0.5	0.2	–3.7	0.8	1.8	1.7
United Kingdom	1.1	1.7	3.2	3.6	3.3	1.7	1.6	1.7	–9.5	7.7	4.5	0.1
Canada	2.9	1.8	2.1	0.3	0.5	3.3	2.7	1.2	–4.1	5.6	4.9	2.2
Other Advanced Economies[1]	2.9	2.4	2.6	2.7	2.9	3.4	2.4	1.8	–2.5	4.9	3.1	2.6
Memorandum												
Major Advanced Economies	1.2	1.6	1.9	2.4	2.0	2.1	2.1	1.8	–3.9	5.3	2.3	0.7
Stock Building[2]												
Advanced Economies	**0.0**	**0.0**	**0.1**	**0.0**	**–0.2**	**0.2**	**0.1**	**–0.1**	**–0.4**	**0.3**	**0.3**	**–0.1**
United States	0.1	0.0	–0.1	0.3	–0.5	0.0	0.2	0.1	–0.5	0.3	0.7	0.1
Euro Area	–0.1	0.0	0.4	0.0	0.0	0.2	0.1	–0.2	–0.3	0.2	0.0	–0.2
Germany	–0.1	0.0	0.0	–0.7	0.0	0.9	–0.1	–0.1	–0.2	0.5	–0.1	–0.3
France	0.1	0.1	0.7	0.2	–0.3	0.2	0.0	0.0	–0.3	–0.3	0.5	0.0
Italy	0.0	0.0	0.5	–0.1	0.2	0.2	0.1	–0.5	–0.3	0.4	–0.4	–0.5
Spain	–0.1	–0.2	0.2	–1.5	–0.1	0.0	0.3	–0.2	–0.5	0.6	–0.4	–0.3
Japan	0.0	0.0	0.1	0.3	–0.1	0.1	0.2	–0.1	–0.1	–0.2	0.3	–0.1
United Kingdom	0.1	0.0	0.4	–0.1	–0.2	0.2	–0.5	0.2	–0.7	0.4	0.3	–0.2
Canada	0.1	0.0	–0.4	–0.5	0.0	0.9	–0.1	0.1	–1.3	0.9	0.9	–0.4
Other Advanced Economies[1]	0.0	0.1	0.3	–0.1	0.0	0.2	0.3	–0.2	0.0	0.2	0.1	–0.3
Memorandum												
Major Advanced Economies	0.0	0.0	0.1	0.1	–0.3	0.2	0.0	0.0	–0.5	0.3	0.5	–0.1
Foreign Balance[2]												
Advanced Economies	**0.2**	**–0.1**	**0.0**	**–0.3**	**–0.1**	**0.1**	**–0.1**	**–0.2**	**–0.1**	**–0.1**	**–0.4**	**0.2**
United States	0.2	–0.4	–0.3	–0.8	–0.2	–0.2	–0.3	–0.2	–0.3	–1.4	–0.7	0.4
Euro Area	0.4	0.0	0.1	–0.2	–0.4	0.4	0.0	–0.7	–0.5	1.3	0.0	–0.2
Germany	0.4	–0.2	0.7	0.3	–0.6	0.2	–0.6	–0.6	–0.8	0.8	–1.4	–0.2
France	–0.1	–0.3	–0.5	–0.4	–0.4	–0.1	0.4	–0.3	–1.0	0.0	–0.1	–0.1
Italy	0.4	–0.2	–0.1	–0.4	–0.5	0.0	–0.3	0.7	–0.7	0.0	–0.3	–0.1
Spain	0.6	–0.1	–0.5	–0.1	1.0	–0.2	–0.6	0.5	–2.2	0.5	1.3	–0.3
Japan	0.1	0.2	0.1	0.5	0.5	0.6	0.0	–0.5	–0.9	1.1	–0.1	0.3
United Kingdom	0.0	–0.2	–1.1	–0.4	–0.1	0.7	–0.1	0.1	1.0	–1.5	–1.1	0.0
Canada	–1.0	–0.2	1.2	0.8	0.4	–1.1	0.2	0.6	0.5	–2.0	–2.2	–0.4
Other Advanced Economies[1]	0.6	0.2	0.5	0.0	0.0	–0.2	0.2	0.6	0.7	0.5	–0.2	0.3
Memorandum												
Major Advanced Economies	0.1	–0.3	–0.1	–0.3	–0.1	0.0	–0.2	–0.2	–0.4	–0.7	–0.7	0.2

[1]Excludes the Group of Seven (Canada, France, Germany, Italy, Japan, United Kingdom, United States) and euro area countries.
[2]Changes expressed as percent of GDP in the preceding period.

Table A4. Emerging Market and Developing Economies: Real GDP

(Annual percent change)

	Average 2004–13	2014	2015	2016	2017	2018	2019	2020	2021	Projections 2022	2023	2027
Emerging and Developing Asia	**8.5**	**6.9**	**6.8**	**6.8**	**6.6**	**6.4**	**5.2**	**–0.6**	**7.2**	**4.4**	**4.9**	**5.1**
Bangladesh	6.1	6.1	6.6	7.1	6.6	7.3	7.9	3.4	6.9	7.2	6.0	6.9
Bhutan	7.9	4.0	6.2	7.4	6.3	3.8	4.4	–2.3	–3.3	4.0	4.3	5.8
Brunei Darussalam	0.7	–2.5	–0.4	–2.5	1.3	0.1	3.9	1.1	–1.6	1.2	3.3	3.4
Cambodia	7.9	7.1	7.0	6.9	7.0	7.5	7.1	–3.1	3.0	5.1	6.2	6.6
China	10.3	7.4	7.0	6.9	6.9	6.8	6.0	2.2	8.1	3.2	4.4	4.6
Fiji	1.6	5.6	4.5	2.4	5.4	3.8	–0.6	–17.0	–5.1	12.5	6.9	3.5
India[1]	7.7	7.4	8.0	8.3	6.8	6.5	3.7	–6.6	8.7	6.8	6.1	6.2
Indonesia	5.9	5.0	4.9	5.0	5.1	5.2	5.0	–2.1	3.7	5.3	5.0	5.1
Kiribati	1.4	–1.1	9.9	–0.5	–0.2	5.3	–0.5	–0.5	1.5	1.0	2.4	2.0
Lao P.D.R.	7.8	7.6	7.3	7.0	6.9	6.3	4.7	–0.4	2.1	2.2	3.1	4.3
Malaysia	5.0	6.0	5.0	4.4	5.8	4.8	4.4	–5.5	3.1	5.4	4.4	3.9
Maldives	5.0	7.3	2.9	6.3	7.2	8.1	6.9	–33.5	37.0	8.7	6.1	5.6
Marshall Islands	0.9	–1.0	1.6	1.4	3.3	3.1	6.8	–1.6	1.7	1.5	3.2	1.5
Micronesia	–0.5	–2.3	4.6	0.9	2.7	0.2	1.2	–1.8	–3.2	–0.6	2.9	0.6
Mongolia	8.6	7.9	2.4	1.5	5.6	7.7	5.6	–4.6	1.6	2.5	5.0	5.0
Myanmar	9.1	8.2	7.5	6.4	5.8	6.4	6.8	3.2	–17.9	2.0	3.3	3.6
Nauru	. . .	27.2	3.4	3.0	–5.5	5.7	1.0	0.7	1.6	0.9	2.0	1.8
Nepal	4.2	6.0	4.0	0.4	9.0	7.6	6.7	–2.4	4.2	4.2	5.0	5.3
Palau	0.0	4.7	8.4	0.4	–3.4	0.1	0.4	–8.9	–13.4	–2.8	12.3	3.2
Papua New Guinea	4.1	13.5	6.6	5.5	3.5	–0.3	4.5	–3.5	1.2	3.8	5.1	3.0
Philippines	5.4	6.3	6.3	7.1	6.9	6.3	6.1	–9.5	5.7	6.5	5.0	6.0
Samoa	1.8	0.7	3.9	8.0	1.4	–0.6	4.5	–3.1	–7.1	–5.0	4.0	2.6
Solomon Islands	5.2	1.2	1.7	5.6	3.1	2.7	1.7	–3.4	–0.2	–4.5	2.6	3.0
Sri Lanka	6.5	6.4	4.2	5.1	6.5	2.3	–0.2	–3.5	3.3	–8.7	–3.0	3.1
Thailand	4.0	1.0	3.1	3.4	4.2	4.2	2.2	–6.2	1.5	2.8	3.7	3.0
Timor-Leste[2]	5.3	4.5	2.8	3.4	–3.1	–0.7	2.1	–8.6	1.5	3.3	4.2	3.0
Tonga	0.1	2.0	1.2	6.6	3.3	0.2	0.7	0.5	–2.7	–2.0	2.9	1.8
Tuvalu	0.8	1.7	9.4	4.7	3.4	1.6	13.9	1.0	2.5	3.0	3.5	3.5
Vanuatu	3.5	3.1	0.4	4.7	6.3	2.9	3.2	–5.4	0.4	1.7	3.1	3.0
Vietnam	6.4	6.4	7.0	6.7	6.9	7.2	7.2	2.9	2.6	7.0	6.2	6.8
Emerging and Developing Europe	**4.3**	**1.8**	**1.0**	**1.9**	**4.1**	**3.4**	**2.5**	**–1.7**	**6.8**	**0.0**	**0.6**	**2.2**
Albania[1]	4.2	1.8	2.2	3.3	3.8	4.0	2.1	–3.5	8.5	4.0	2.5	3.4
Belarus	6.5	1.7	–3.8	–2.5	2.5	3.1	1.4	–0.7	2.3	–7.0	0.2	0.8
Bosnia and Herzegovina	3.0	1.1	3.1	3.1	3.2	3.7	2.8	–3.1	7.5	2.4	2.0	3.0
Bulgaria	3.3	1.0	3.4	3.0	2.8	2.7	4.0	–4.4	4.2	3.9	3.0	2.8
Croatia	0.8	–0.3	2.5	3.5	3.4	2.9	3.5	–8.1	10.2	5.9	3.5	2.5
Hungary	1.1	4.2	3.8	2.3	4.3	5.4	4.6	–4.5	7.1	5.7	1.8	3.2
Kosovo	4.2	3.3	5.9	5.6	4.8	3.4	4.8	–5.3	9.5	2.7	3.5	3.5
Moldova	4.5	5.0	–0.3	4.4	4.2	4.1	3.6	–8.3	13.9	0.0	2.3	5.0
Montenegro	3.1	1.8	3.4	2.9	4.7	5.1	4.1	–15.3	13.0	7.2	2.5	3.0
North Macedonia	3.4	3.6	3.9	2.8	1.1	2.9	3.9	–6.1	4.0	2.7	3.0	3.8
Poland	4.0	3.4	4.2	3.1	4.8	5.4	4.7	–2.2	5.9	3.8	0.5	3.1
Romania	3.7	3.6	3.0	4.7	7.3	4.5	4.2	–3.7	5.9	4.8	3.1	3.5
Russia	4.2	0.7	–2.0	0.2	1.8	2.8	2.2	–2.7	4.7	–3.4	–2.3	0.7
Serbia	3.8	–1.6	1.8	3.3	2.1	4.5	4.3	–0.9	7.4	3.5	2.7	4.0
Türkiye	5.9	4.9	6.1	3.3	7.5	3.0	0.8	1.9	11.4	5.0	3.0	3.0
Ukraine[1]	2.5	–6.6	–9.8	2.4	2.4	3.5	3.2	–3.8	3.4	–35.0	. . .	. . .
Latin America and the Caribbean	**4.0**	**1.3**	**0.4**	**–0.6**	**1.4**	**1.2**	**0.2**	**–7.0**	**6.9**	**3.5**	**1.7**	**2.4**
Antigua and Barbuda	1.3	3.8	3.8	5.5	3.1	6.9	4.9	–20.2	5.3	6.0	5.6	2.7
Argentina	4.9	–2.5	2.7	–2.1	2.8	–2.6	–2.0	–9.9	10.4	4.0	2.0	2.0
Aruba	0.6	0.0	3.6	2.1	5.5	5.3	0.6	–18.6	17.2	4.0	2.0	1.2
The Bahamas	0.4	1.8	1.0	–0.9	3.1	1.8	1.9	–23.8	13.7	8.0	4.1	1.5
Barbados	0.4	–0.1	2.4	2.5	0.5	–0.6	–1.3	–13.7	0.7	10.5	5.0	1.8
Belize	2.5	3.9	2.6	–2.3	–1.0	0.3	4.5	–13.7	16.3	3.5	2.0	2.0
Bolivia	4.9	5.5	4.9	4.3	4.2	4.2	2.2	–8.7	6.1	3.8	3.2	2.5
Brazil	4.0	0.5	–3.5	–3.3	1.3	1.8	1.2	–3.9	4.6	2.8	1.0	2.0
Chile	4.8	1.8	2.2	1.7	1.3	3.9	0.9	–6.1	11.7	2.0	–1.0	2.5
Colombia	4.8	4.5	3.0	2.1	1.4	2.6	3.2	–7.0	10.7	7.6	2.2	3.3

Table A4. Emerging Market and Developing Economies: Real GDP *(continued)*

(Annual percent change)

	Average									Projections		
	2004–13	2014	2015	2016	2017	2018	2019	2020	2021	2022	2023	2027
Latin America and the Caribbean (continued)	**4.0**	**1.3**	**0.4**	**–0.6**	**1.4**	**1.2**	**0.2**	**–7.0**	**6.9**	**3.5**	**1.7**	**2.4**
Costa Rica	4.5	3.5	3.7	4.2	4.2	2.6	2.4	–4.1	7.8	3.8	2.9	3.2
Dominica	1.9	4.8	–2.7	2.8	–6.6	3.5	5.5	–16.6	4.8	6.0	4.9	2.5
Dominican Republic	5.1	7.1	6.9	6.7	4.7	7.0	5.1	–6.7	12.3	5.3	4.5	5.0
Ecuador	4.9	3.8	0.1	–1.2	2.4	1.3	0.0	–7.8	4.2	2.9	2.7	2.8
El Salvador	2.1	1.7	2.4	2.5	2.3	2.4	2.4	–8.2	10.3	2.6	1.7	2.0
Grenada	0.9	7.3	6.4	3.7	4.4	4.4	0.7	–13.8	5.6	3.6	3.6	2.8
Guatemala	3.6	4.4	4.1	2.7	3.1	3.4	4.0	–1.8	8.0	3.4	3.2	3.5
Guyana	3.5	1.7	0.7	3.8	3.7	4.4	5.4	43.5	23.8	57.8	25.2	3.3
Haiti	2.0	1.7	2.6	1.8	2.5	1.7	–1.7	–3.3	–1.8	–1.2	0.5	1.5
Honduras[1]	4.1	3.1	3.8	3.9	4.8	3.8	2.7	–9.0	12.5	3.4	3.5	3.9
Jamaica	0.2	0.6	0.9	1.5	0.7	1.8	1.0	–10.0	4.6	2.8	3.0	1.6
Mexico	2.2	2.8	3.3	2.6	2.1	2.2	–0.2	–8.1	4.8	2.1	1.2	2.1
Nicaragua	4.0	4.8	4.8	4.6	4.6	–3.4	–3.8	–1.8	10.3	4.0	3.0	3.8
Panama	8.0	5.1	5.7	5.0	5.6	3.7	3.0	–17.9	15.3	7.5	4.0	4.5
Paraguay	4.5	5.3	3.0	4.3	4.8	3.2	–0.4	–0.8	4.2	0.2	4.3	3.5
Peru	6.4	2.4	3.3	4.0	2.5	4.0	2.2	–11.0	13.6	2.7	2.6	3.0
St. Kitts and Nevis	3.1	7.6	0.7	3.9	0.9	2.7	4.8	–14.0	–3.6	9.8	4.8	2.7
St. Lucia	2.0	1.3	–0.2	3.8	3.4	2.9	–0.7	–24.4	12.2	9.1	5.8	1.5
St. Vincent and the Grenadines	1.3	1.1	2.8	4.1	1.7	3.1	0.4	–5.3	0.5	5.0	6.0	2.7
Suriname	4.7	0.3	–3.4	–4.9	1.6	4.9	1.1	–15.9	–3.5	1.3	2.3	3.0
Trinidad and Tobago	3.4	–0.9	1.8	–6.3	–2.7	–0.7	–0.2	–7.4	–0.7	4.0	3.5	1.6
Uruguay[1]	5.6	3.2	0.4	1.7	1.6	0.5	0.4	–6.1	4.4	5.3	3.6	2.2
Venezuela	5.7	–3.9	–6.2	–17.0	–15.7	–19.7	–27.7	–30.0	0.5	6.0	6.5	. . .
Middle East and Central Asia	**5.0**	**3.4**	**3.0**	**4.2**	**2.6**	**2.6**	**1.7**	**–2.7**	**4.5**	**5.0**	**3.6**	**3.7**
Afghanistan[1]	8.9	2.7	1.0	2.2	2.6	1.2	3.9	–2.4	. . .	. . .	. . .	. . .
Algeria	3.2	3.8	3.7	3.2	1.4	1.2	1.0	–5.1	3.5	4.7	2.6	1.7
Armenia	5.9	3.6	3.3	0.2	7.5	5.2	7.6	–7.4	5.7	7.0	3.5	4.5
Azerbaijan	12.3	2.8	1.0	–3.1	0.2	1.5	2.5	–4.2	5.6	3.7	2.5	2.5
Bahrain	5.3	4.4	2.5	3.6	4.3	2.1	2.2	–4.9	2.2	3.4	3.0	3.0
Djibouti	4.4	7.1	7.5	7.1	5.5	4.8	5.5	1.2	4.8	3.6	5.0	6.0
Egypt	4.7	4.3	5.8	5.8	5.4	5.0	5.5	3.5	3.3	6.6	4.4	5.9
Georgia	5.9	4.4	3.0	2.9	4.8	4.8	5.0	–6.8	10.4	9.0	4.0	5.2
Iran	2.5	5.0	–1.4	8.8	2.8	–1.8	–3.1	3.3	4.7	3.0	2.0	2.0
Iraq	10.2	0.7	2.5	15.2	–3.4	4.7	5.8	–15.7	7.7	9.3	4.0	2.7
Jordan	5.5	3.4	2.5	2.0	2.1	1.9	2.0	–1.6	2.2	2.4	2.7	3.3
Kazakhstan	6.9	4.3	1.0	0.9	3.9	4.1	4.5	–2.6	4.1	2.5	4.4	2.7
Kuwait	4.3	0.5	0.6	2.9	–4.7	2.4	–0.6	–8.9	1.3	8.7	2.6	2.7
Kyrgyz Republic	4.5	4.0	3.9	4.3	4.7	3.5	4.6	–8.6	3.7	3.8	3.2	4.0
Lebanon[1]	5.3	2.5	0.5	1.6	0.9	–1.9	–6.9	–25.9	. . .	. . .	. . .	. . .
Libya[1]	–0.5	–23.0	–0.8	–1.5	32.5	7.9	–11.2	–29.5	28.3	–18.5	17.9	4.1
Mauritania	4.3	4.3	5.4	1.3	6.3	4.8	5.4	–0.9	2.4	4.0	4.8	4.8
Morocco	4.6	2.7	4.3	0.5	5.1	3.1	2.9	–7.2	7.9	0.8	3.1	3.4
Oman	4.9	1.3	5.0	5.0	0.3	1.3	–1.1	–3.2	3.0	4.4	4.1	2.7
Pakistan[1]	4.7	4.1	4.1	4.6	4.6	6.1	3.1	–0.9	5.7	6.0	3.5	5.0
Qatar	14.1	5.3	4.8	3.1	–1.5	1.2	0.7	–3.6	1.6	3.4	2.4	3.8
Saudi Arabia	4.5	3.7	4.1	1.7	–0.7	2.5	0.3	–4.1	3.2	7.6	3.7	3.0
Somalia	. . .	2.7	4.6	4.7	2.2	3.7	2.7	–0.3	2.9	1.9	3.1	4.1
Sudan[3]	0.7	4.7	4.9	4.7	0.8	–2.3	–2.5	–3.6	0.5	–0.3	2.6	6.0
Syria[4]	. . .	. . .	. . .	. . .	. . .	. . .	. . .	. . .	. . .	. . .	. . .	. . .
Tajikistan	7.3	6.7	6.0	6.9	7.1	7.6	7.4	4.4	9.2	5.5	4.0	4.0
Tunisia	3.7	3.1	1.0	1.1	2.2	2.5	1.4	–8.7	3.3	2.2	1.6	2.6
Turkmenistan	10.4	3.8	3.0	–1.0	4.7	0.9	–3.4	–3.0	4.6	1.2	2.3	1.7
United Arab Emirates	4.3	4.4	5.1	3.0	2.4	1.2	3.4	–4.8	3.8	5.1	4.2	4.2
Uzbekistan	7.7	6.9	7.2	5.9	4.4	5.4	5.7	1.9	7.4	5.2	4.7	5.0
West Bank and Gaza	7.7	–0.2	3.7	8.9	1.4	1.2	1.4	–11.3	7.1	4.0	3.5	2.0
Yemen	2.4	–0.2	–28.0	–9.4	–5.1	0.8	1.4	–8.5	–1.0	2.0	3.2	5.5

Table A4. Emerging Market and Developing Economies: Real GDP *(continued)*
(Annual percent change)

	Average									Projections		
	2004–13	2014	2015	2016	2017	2018	2019	2020	2021	2022	2023	2027
Sub-Saharan Africa	**5.6**	**5.0**	**3.2**	**1.5**	**3.0**	**3.3**	**3.2**	**–1.6**	**4.7**	**3.6**	**3.7**	**4.4**
Angola	8.4	4.8	0.9	–2.6	–0.2	–1.3	–0.7	–5.8	0.8	2.9	3.4	3.9
Benin	4.0	6.4	1.8	3.3	5.7	6.7	6.9	3.8	7.2	5.7	6.2	6.0
Botswana	3.3	5.7	–4.9	7.2	4.1	4.2	3.0	–8.7	11.4	4.1	4.0	4.0
Burkina Faso	5.9	4.3	3.9	6.0	6.2	6.7	5.7	1.9	6.9	3.6	4.8	5.3
Burundi	4.4	4.2	–3.9	–0.6	0.5	1.6	1.8	0.3	3.1	3.3	4.1	4.6
Cabo Verde	4.1	0.6	1.0	4.7	3.7	14.6	5.7	–14.8	7.0	4.0	4.8	4.5
Cameroon	3.7	5.8	5.6	4.5	3.5	4.0	3.4	0.5	3.6	3.8	4.6	4.9
Central African Republic	–1.5	0.1	4.3	4.7	4.5	3.8	3.0	1.0	1.0	1.5	3.0	3.7
Chad	7.8	6.9	1.8	–5.6	–2.4	2.4	3.4	–2.2	–1.1	3.3	3.4	3.5
Comoros	3.0	2.1	1.3	3.5	4.2	3.6	1.8	–0.3	2.2	3.0	3.4	4.4
Democratic Republic of the Congo	6.3	9.5	6.9	2.4	3.7	5.8	4.4	1.7	6.2	6.1	6.7	6.3
Republic of Congo	4.8	6.7	–3.6	–10.7	–4.4	–4.8	–0.4	–8.1	–0.6	4.3	4.6	3.3
Côte d'Ivoire	2.8	8.8	8.8	7.2	7.4	6.9	6.2	2.0	7.0	5.5	6.5	6.0
Equatorial Guinea	7.6	0.4	–9.1	–8.8	–5.7	–6.2	–5.5	–4.2	–3.2	5.8	–3.1	–1.1
Eritrea	1.8	30.9	–20.6	7.4	–10.0	13.0	3.8	–0.5	2.9	2.6	2.8	2.9
Eswatini	3.8	0.9	2.2	1.1	2.0	2.4	2.7	–1.6	7.9	2.4	1.8	2.3
Ethiopia	10.9	10.3	10.4	8.0	10.2	7.7	9.0	6.1	6.3	3.8	5.3	7.0
Gabon	2.8	4.4	3.9	2.1	0.5	0.8	3.9	–1.9	1.5	2.7	3.7	3.8
The Gambia	2.5	–1.4	4.1	1.9	4.8	7.2	6.2	0.6	4.3	5.0	6.0	5.0
Ghana	7.3	2.9	2.1	3.4	8.1	6.2	6.5	0.5	5.4	3.6	2.8	6.8
Guinea	3.6	3.7	3.8	10.8	10.3	6.4	5.6	4.9	3.8	4.6	5.1	5.2
Guinea-Bissau	3.5	1.0	6.1	5.3	4.8	3.8	4.5	1.5	5.0	3.8	4.5	5.0
Kenya	4.8	5.0	5.0	4.2	3.8	5.7	5.1	–0.3	7.5	5.3	5.1	5.5
Lesotho	3.6	2.1	3.3	1.9	–2.7	–0.3	0.0	–6.0	2.1	2.1	1.6	0.1
Liberia	7.4	0.7	0.0	–1.6	2.5	1.2	–2.5	–3.0	5.0	3.7	4.2	6.0
Madagascar	3.1	3.3	3.1	4.0	3.9	3.2	4.4	–7.1	4.3	4.2	5.2	5.0
Malawi	5.8	5.7	3.0	2.3	4.0	4.4	5.4	0.9	2.2	0.9	2.5	4.5
Mali	3.6	7.1	6.2	5.9	5.3	4.7	4.8	–1.2	3.1	2.5	5.3	5.0
Mauritius	4.0	3.7	3.6	3.8	3.8	3.8	3.0	–14.9	4.0	6.1	5.4	3.3
Mozambique	7.4	7.4	6.7	3.8	3.7	3.4	2.3	–1.2	2.3	3.7	4.9	13.2
Namibia	4.3	6.1	4.3	0.0	–1.0	1.1	–0.8	–8.0	2.7	3.0	3.2	2.5
Niger	5.3	6.6	4.4	5.7	5.0	7.2	5.9	3.6	1.3	6.7	7.3	6.0
Nigeria	7.3	6.3	2.7	–1.6	0.8	1.9	2.2	–1.8	3.6	3.2	3.0	2.9
Rwanda	8.0	6.2	8.9	6.0	4.0	8.6	9.5	–3.4	10.9	6.0	6.7	6.1
São Tomé and Príncipe	5.3	6.5	3.8	4.2	3.9	3.0	2.2	3.0	1.9	1.4	2.6	4.0
Senegal	3.2	6.2	6.4	6.4	7.4	6.2	4.6	1.3	6.1	4.7	8.1	5.2
Seychelles	4.4	4.7	5.6	5.4	4.5	3.2	3.1	–7.7	7.9	10.9	5.2	3.9
Sierra Leone	7.8	4.6	–20.5	6.4	3.8	3.5	5.3	–2.0	4.1	2.4	3.3	4.3
South Africa	3.3	1.4	1.3	0.7	1.2	1.5	0.3	–6.3	4.9	2.1	1.1	1.4
South Sudan	. . .	1.8	–0.2	–13.3	–5.8	–2.1	0.9	–6.5	5.3	6.5	5.6	4.4
Tanzania	6.5	6.7	6.2	6.9	6.8	7.0	7.0	4.8	4.9	4.5	5.2	7.0
Togo	3.0	5.9	5.7	5.6	4.3	5.0	5.5	1.8	5.3	5.4	6.2	6.5
Uganda	7.1	5.7	8.0	0.2	6.8	5.5	7.8	–1.4	6.7	4.4	5.9	6.8
Zambia	7.6	4.7	2.9	3.8	3.5	4.0	1.4	–2.8	4.6	2.9	4.0	5.0
Zimbabwe[1]	1.7	2.4	1.8	0.5	5.0	4.7	–6.1	–5.2	7.2	3.0	2.8	3.0

[1]See the country-specific notes for Afghanistan, Albania, Honduras, India, Lebanon, Libya, Pakistan, Ukraine, Uruguay, and Zimbabwe in the "Country Notes" section of the Statistical Appendix.
[2]Data for Timor-Leste exclude projections for oil exports from the Joint Petroleum Development Area.
[3]Data for 2011 exclude South Sudan after July 9. Data for 2012 and onward pertain to the current Sudan.
[4]Data for Syria are excluded for 2011 onward owing to the uncertain political situation.

Table A5. Summary of Inflation

(Percent)

	Average 2004–13	2014	2015	2016	2017	2018	2019	2020	2021	Projections 2022	2023	2027
GDP Deflators												
Advanced Economies	**1.6**	**1.4**	**1.3**	**1.0**	**1.5**	**1.7**	**1.5**	**1.5**	**2.9**	**5.5**	**3.7**	**1.8**
United States	2.1	1.9	1.0	1.0	1.9	2.4	1.8	1.2	4.2	7.1	3.6	1.9
Euro Area	1.6	0.9	1.4	0.9	1.1	1.5	1.7	1.7	2.1	4.3	4.4	1.9
Japan	–1.0	1.7	2.1	0.4	–0.1	0.0	0.6	0.9	–0.9	0.3	0.6	0.3
Other Advanced Economies[1]	2.0	1.3	1.1	1.2	1.9	1.7	1.2	1.8	3.4	6.3	4.3	1.9
Consumer Prices												
Advanced Economies	**2.0**	**1.4**	**0.3**	**0.8**	**1.7**	**2.0**	**1.4**	**0.7**	**3.1**	**7.2**	**4.4**	**1.9**
United States	2.4	1.6	0.1	1.3	2.1	2.4	1.8	1.2	4.7	8.1	3.5	2.0
Euro Area[2]	2.0	0.4	0.2	0.2	1.5	1.8	1.2	0.3	2.6	8.3	5.7	1.8
Japan	–0.1	2.8	0.8	–0.1	0.5	1.0	0.5	0.0	–0.2	2.0	1.4	1.0
Other Advanced Economies[1]	2.3	1.5	0.5	0.9	1.8	1.9	1.4	0.6	2.5	6.5	5.1	2.0
Emerging Market and Developing Economies[3]	**6.3**	**4.7**	**4.7**	**4.4**	**4.5**	**5.0**	**5.1**	**5.1**	**5.9**	**9.9**	**8.1**	**4.3**
Regional Groups												
Emerging and Developing Asia	5.0	3.5	2.7	2.8	2.5	2.7	3.3	3.1	2.2	4.1	3.6	2.8
Emerging and Developing Europe	8.1	6.5	10.6	5.5	5.6	6.4	6.6	5.3	9.5	27.8	19.4	6.7
Latin America and the Caribbean	4.9	4.9	5.4	5.5	6.3	6.6	7.7	6.4	9.8	14.1	11.4	5.7
Middle East and Central Asia	8.4	6.5	5.6	5.9	7.1	10.0	7.7	10.5	12.9	13.8	13.1	6.8
Sub-Saharan Africa	8.6	6.4	6.7	10.2	10.7	8.3	8.2	10.2	11.1	14.4	11.9	6.9
Analytical Groups												
By Source of Export Earnings												
Fuel	8.4	5.6	5.6	7.8	6.6	9.0	6.9	9.4	12.0	13.4	11.8	7.6
Nonfuel	5.9	4.6	4.6	3.9	4.2	4.5	4.9	4.7	5.2	9.5	7.6	3.9
Of Which, Primary Products[4]	6.6	7.3	5.7	6.6	11.6	13.8	16.8	18.3	22.0	26.9	23.4	9.8
By External Financing Source												
Net Debtor Economies	7.2	5.8	5.7	5.4	5.8	5.8	5.6	6.1	7.7	13.3	10.7	4.8
Net Debtor Economies by Debt-Servicing Experience												
Economies with Arrears and/or Rescheduling during 2017–21	9.9	9.1	13.4	11.0	16.8	15.8	12.7	15.3	19.4	20.5	16.9	6.5
Other Groups												
European Union	2.3	0.4	0.1	0.2	1.6	1.9	1.4	0.7	2.9	9.2	6.8	2.0
Middle East and North Africa	8.1	6.3	5.7	5.8	7.3	11.3	8.1	10.9	14.2	14.2	12.4	7.1
Emerging Market and Middle-Income Economies	6.0	4.5	4.6	4.0	4.1	4.6	4.8	4.6	5.3	9.5	7.7	4.1
Low-Income Developing Countries	9.7	7.2	6.5	8.3	9.2	8.8	8.3	11.3	13.0	14.2	12.0	6.1
Memorandum												
Median Inflation Rate												
Advanced Economies	2.3	0.7	0.1	0.5	1.6	1.8	1.4	0.4	2.5	7.5	4.5	2.0
Emerging Market and Developing Economies[3]	5.2	3.1	2.5	2.7	3.3	3.1	2.7	2.8	3.8	8.0	5.7	3.0

[1]Excludes the United States, euro area countries, and Japan.
[2]Based on Eurostat's harmonized index of consumer prices.
[3]Excludes Venezuela but includes Argentina from 2017 onward. See the country-specific notes for Argentina and Venezuela in the "Country Notes" section of the Statistical Appendix.
[4]Includes Argentina from 2017 onward. See the country-specific note for Argentina in the "Country Notes" section of the Statistical Appendix.

Table A6. Advanced Economies: Consumer Prices[1]

(Annual percent change)

													End of Period[2]		
	Average									Projections				Projections	
	2004–13	2014	2015	2016	2017	2018	2019	2020	2021	2022	2023	2027	2021	2022	2023
Advanced Economies	**2.0**	**1.4**	**0.3**	**0.8**	**1.7**	**2.0**	**1.4**	**0.7**	**3.1**	**7.2**	**4.4**	**1.9**	**5.2**	**7.0**	**3.2**
United States	2.4	1.6	0.1	1.3	2.1	2.4	1.8	1.2	4.7	8.1	3.5	2.0	7.4	6.4	2.3
Euro Area[3]	2.0	0.4	0.2	0.2	1.5	1.8	1.2	0.3	2.6	8.3	5.7	1.8	5.0	8.8	4.5
Germany	1.8	0.8	0.7	0.4	1.7	1.9	1.4	0.4	3.2	8.5	7.2	2.0	5.7	10.2	5.4
France	1.8	0.6	0.1	0.3	1.2	2.1	1.3	0.5	2.1	5.8	4.6	1.6	3.3	6.3	3.9
Italy	2.2	0.2	0.1	–0.1	1.3	1.2	0.6	–0.1	1.9	8.7	5.2	2.0	4.2	8.7	5.2
Spain	2.5	–0.2	–0.5	–0.2	2.0	1.7	0.7	–0.3	3.1	8.8	4.9	1.7	6.5	7.7	4.1
The Netherlands	1.8	0.3	0.2	0.1	1.3	1.6	2.7	1.1	2.8	12.0	8.0	2.0	6.3	12.8	3.4
Belgium	2.3	0.5	0.6	1.8	2.2	2.3	1.2	0.4	3.2	9.5	4.9	1.7	6.6	7.9	3.6
Ireland	1.3	0.3	–0.1	–0.2	0.3	0.7	0.9	–0.5	2.4	8.4	6.5	2.0	5.6	10.0	4.2
Austria	2.1	1.5	0.8	1.0	2.2	2.1	1.5	1.4	2.8	7.7	5.1	2.0	3.8	7.0	3.2
Portugal	2.0	–0.2	0.5	0.6	1.6	1.2	0.3	–0.1	0.9	7.9	4.7	2.0	0.0	12.5	4.0
Greece	2.6	–1.4	–1.1	0.0	1.1	0.8	0.5	–1.3	0.6	9.2	3.2	1.9	4.4	8.2	1.6
Finland	2.0	1.2	–0.2	0.4	0.8	1.2	1.1	0.4	2.1	6.5	3.5	1.8	3.2	6.6	3.5
Slovak Republic	3.1	–0.1	–0.3	–0.5	1.4	2.5	2.8	2.0	2.8	11.9	10.1	2.0	5.0	13.5	8.6
Lithuania	3.8	0.2	–0.7	0.7	3.7	2.5	2.2	1.1	4.6	17.6	8.4	2.3	10.7	16.5	5.0
Slovenia	2.7	0.2	–0.5	–0.1	1.4	1.7	1.6	–0.1	1.9	8.9	5.1	2.4	4.9	8.8	3.0
Luxembourg	2.8	0.7	0.1	0.0	2.1	2.0	1.7	0.0	3.5	8.4	3.7	2.0	5.4	7.5	3.0
Latvia	5.3	0.7	0.2	0.1	2.9	2.6	2.7	0.1	3.2	16.5	8.0	2.5	7.9	18.9	3.4
Estonia	4.4	0.5	0.1	0.8	3.7	3.4	2.3	–0.6	4.5	21.0	9.5	2.4	12.0	21.8	3.7
Cyprus	2.2	–0.3	–1.5	–1.2	0.7	0.8	0.5	–1.1	2.2	8.0	3.8	2.0	4.7	6.6	2.4
Malta	2.4	0.8	1.2	0.9	1.3	1.7	1.5	0.8	0.7	5.9	4.6	2.1	2.6	6.5	3.7
Japan	–0.1	2.8	0.8	–0.1	0.5	1.0	0.5	0.0	–0.2	2.0	1.4	1.0	0.5	2.4	1.2
United Kingdom	2.7	1.5	0.0	0.7	2.7	2.5	1.8	0.9	2.6	9.1	9.0	2.0	5.4	11.3	6.3
Korea	2.9	1.3	0.7	1.0	1.9	1.5	0.4	0.5	2.5	5.5	3.8	2.0	3.7	6.2	2.6
Canada	1.8	1.9	1.1	1.4	1.6	2.3	1.9	0.7	3.4	6.9	4.2	2.0	4.7	6.9	3.2
Taiwan Province of China	1.4	1.2	–0.3	1.4	0.6	1.3	0.6	–0.2	2.0	3.1	2.2	1.4	2.6	3.1	2.2
Australia	2.7	2.5	1.5	1.3	2.0	1.9	1.6	0.9	2.8	6.5	4.8	2.5	3.6	7.7	3.1
Switzerland	0.6	0.0	–1.1	–0.4	0.5	0.9	0.4	–0.7	0.6	3.1	2.4	1.0	1.5	3.8	1.6
Sweden	1.5	0.2	0.7	1.1	1.9	2.0	1.7	0.7	2.7	7.2	8.4	2.0	3.3	8.2	8.0
Singapore	2.7	1.0	–0.5	–0.5	0.6	0.4	0.6	–0.2	2.3	5.5	3.0	1.5	4.0	5.6	3.0
Hong Kong SAR	2.5	4.4	3.0	2.4	1.5	2.4	2.9	0.3	1.6	1.9	2.4	2.5	2.4	1.9	2.2
Czech Republic	2.5	0.3	0.3	0.7	2.5	2.1	2.8	3.2	3.8	16.3	8.6	2.0	6.6	20.0	4.0
Israel	2.1	0.5	–0.6	–0.5	0.2	0.8	0.8	–0.6	1.5	4.5	3.6	1.9	2.8	5.3	2.7
Norway	1.7	2.0	2.2	3.6	1.9	2.8	2.2	1.3	3.5	4.7	3.8	2.0	5.3	4.7	3.5
Denmark	1.9	0.4	0.2	0.0	1.1	0.7	0.7	0.3	1.9	7.2	3.8	2.0	3.4	7.2	3.8
New Zealand	2.6	1.2	0.3	0.6	1.9	1.6	1.6	1.7	3.9	6.3	3.9	2.1	5.9	5.1	2.9
Puerto Rico	3.1	0.6	–0.8	–0.3	1.8	1.3	0.1	–0.5	2.4	4.4	3.5	2.3	4.2	4.8	2.3
Macao SAR	4.6	6.0	4.6	2.4	1.2	3.0	2.8	0.8	0.0	2.5	2.4	2.2	1.0	2.5	2.4
Iceland	6.2	2.0	1.6	1.7	1.8	2.7	3.0	2.8	4.5	8.4	6.7	2.5	5.1	9.9	5.1
Andorra	2.2	–0.1	–1.1	–0.4	2.6	1.3	0.7	0.3	1.7	5.3	2.8	1.7	3.3	4.5	2.5
San Marino	2.3	1.1	0.1	0.6	1.0	1.8	1.0	0.2	2.1	6.9	4.5	1.8	2.1	6.9	4.5
Memorandum															
Major Advanced Economies	1.9	1.5	0.3	0.8	1.8	2.1	1.5	0.8	3.3	7.2	4.3	1.9	5.6	6.8	3.2

[1]Movements in consumer prices are shown as annual averages.
[2]Monthly year-over-year changes and, for several countries, on a quarterly basis.
[3]Based on Eurostat's harmonized index of consumer prices.

Table A7. Emerging Market and Developing Economies: Consumer Prices[1]

(Annual percent change)

													End of Period[2]		
	Average									Projections				Projections	
	2004–13	2014	2015	2016	2017	2018	2019	2020	2021	2022	2023	2027	2021	2022	2023
Emerging and Developing Asia	**5.0**	**3.5**	**2.7**	**2.8**	**2.5**	**2.7**	**3.3**	**3.1**	**2.2**	**4.1**	**3.6**	**2.8**	**3.0**	**4.7**	**3.0**
Bangladesh	7.7	7.3	6.4	5.9	5.4	5.8	5.5	5.6	5.6	6.1	9.1	5.5	5.6	7.6	8.5
Bhutan	6.3	9.6	6.7	3.3	4.3	3.7	2.8	3.0	12.6	7.7	6.6	4.0	9.2	6.2	7.0
Brunei Darussalam	0.7	–0.2	–0.5	–0.3	–1.3	1.0	–0.4	1.9	1.7	2.5	2.0	1.0	2.2	2.5	2.0
Cambodia	6.2	3.9	1.2	3.0	2.9	2.5	1.9	2.9	2.9	5.2	3.8	3.0	3.7	5.2	3.8
China	3.1	2.0	1.4	2.0	1.6	2.1	2.9	2.4	0.9	2.2	2.2	2.0	1.8	2.7	1.8
Fiji	4.1	0.5	1.4	3.9	3.3	4.1	1.8	–2.6	0.2	4.7	3.5	2.5	3.0	5.0	3.0
India	8.2	5.8	4.9	4.5	3.6	3.4	4.8	6.2	5.5	6.9	5.1	4.0	6.3	6.4	4.9
Indonesia	7.1	6.4	6.4	3.5	3.8	3.3	2.8	2.0	1.6	4.6	5.5	3.0	1.9	7.2	3.3
Kiribati	1.7	2.1	0.6	1.9	0.4	0.6	–1.8	2.5	3.0	5.6	3.3	1.6	3.2	5.4	3.1
Lao P.D.R.	6.0	4.1	1.3	1.6	0.8	2.0	3.3	5.1	3.8	15.0	9.0	3.0	5.3	15.0	9.0
Malaysia	2.5	3.1	2.1	2.1	3.8	1.0	0.7	–1.1	2.5	3.2	2.8	2.5	3.2	3.2	2.8
Maldives	6.7	2.4	1.4	0.8	2.3	1.4	1.3	–1.6	0.2	4.3	4.4	2.0	0.2	6.2	3.0
Marshall Islands	4.1	1.1	–2.2	–1.5	0.1	0.8	–0.1	–0.7	2.6	6.4	2.2	2.0	2.9	0.0	2.2
Micronesia	4.4	0.7	0.0	–0.9	0.1	1.1	2.2	0.9	2.1	5.8	3.0	2.0	2.1	5.8	3.0
Mongolia	11.2	12.3	5.7	0.7	4.3	6.8	7.3	3.7	7.1	14.8	12.1	6.5	13.5	14.2	10.1
Myanmar	10.6	5.7	7.3	9.1	4.6	5.9	8.6	5.7	3.6	16.2	13.3	7.8	7.3	19.4	11.1
Nauru	. . .	0.3	9.8	8.2	5.1	0.5	4.3	–6.6	1.2	2.0	2.0	2.0	1.2	2.6	1.7
Nepal	7.9	9.0	7.2	9.9	4.5	4.1	4.6	6.1	3.6	6.3	7.7	5.4	4.2	8.1	7.2
Palau	3.8	4.0	2.2	–1.3	1.1	2.0	0.6	0.7	0.4	12.2	8.1	0.9	4.6	15.0	6.2
Papua New Guinea	4.4	5.2	6.0	6.7	5.4	4.4	3.9	4.9	4.5	6.6	5.4	4.5	5.7	6.2	5.2
Philippines	4.6	3.6	0.7	1.2	2.9	5.3	2.4	2.4	3.9	5.3	4.3	3.0	3.1	5.8	3.7
Samoa	5.2	–1.2	1.9	0.1	1.3	3.7	2.2	1.5	–3.0	8.7	6.3	3.0	4.1	10.9	2.3
Solomon Islands	7.7	5.3	–0.6	0.5	0.5	3.5	1.6	3.0	–0.1	3.7	3.6	3.4	3.5	4.3	3.0
Sri Lanka	8.6	2.8	2.2	4.0	6.6	4.3	4.3	4.6	6.0	48.2	29.5	5.0	12.1	69.8	9.1
Thailand	3.1	1.9	–0.9	0.2	0.7	1.1	0.7	–0.8	1.2	6.3	2.8	2.0	2.2	7.3	0.3
Timor-Leste	6.3	0.8	0.6	–1.5	0.5	2.3	0.9	0.5	3.8	7.0	4.0	2.0	5.3	7.0	4.0
Tonga	6.0	2.3	0.1	–0.6	7.2	6.8	3.3	0.4	1.4	8.5	8.9	2.5	6.9	11.3	5.1
Tuvalu	2.4	1.1	3.1	3.5	4.1	2.2	3.5	1.6	2.9	5.7	4.0	2.9	2.9	5.7	4.0
Vanuatu	2.4	0.8	2.5	0.8	3.1	2.4	2.7	5.3	2.3	4.6	3.4	3.1	0.7	4.9	3.6
Vietnam	10.4	4.1	0.6	2.7	3.5	3.5	2.8	3.2	1.8	3.8	3.9	3.5	1.8	4.4	3.5
Emerging and Developing Europe	**8.1**	**6.5**	**10.6**	**5.5**	**5.6**	**6.4**	**6.6**	**5.3**	**9.5**	**27.8**	**19.4**	**6.7**	**15.0**	**28.3**	**13.9**
Albania[4]	2.7	1.6	1.9	1.3	2.0	2.0	1.4	1.6	2.0	6.2	4.3	3.0	3.7	5.8	3.3
Belarus	19.8	18.1	13.5	11.8	6.0	4.9	5.6	5.5	9.5	16.5	13.1	5.0	10.0	18.9	12.4
Bosnia and Herzegovina	2.6	–0.9	–1.0	–1.6	0.8	1.4	0.6	–1.1	2.0	10.5	4.5	2.1	1.8	9.5	4.1
Bulgaria[3]	5.0	–1.6	–1.1	–1.3	1.2	2.6	2.5	1.2	2.8	12.4	5.2	2.0	6.6	12.7	2.4
Croatia	2.9	–0.2	–0.5	–1.1	1.1	1.5	0.8	0.1	2.6	9.8	5.5	1.9	5.5	9.2	4.9
Hungary	4.8	–0.2	–0.1	0.4	2.4	2.8	3.4	3.3	5.1	13.9	13.3	3.2	7.4	20.1	6.7
Kosovo	2.4	0.4	–0.5	0.2	1.5	1.1	2.7	0.2	3.3	12.0	5.0	2.0	6.7	12.5	1.8
Moldova	8.5	5.1	9.6	6.4	6.5	3.6	4.8	3.8	5.1	28.5	13.8	5.0	13.9	30.0	8.0
Montenegro	3.5	–0.7	1.5	–0.3	2.4	2.6	0.4	–0.2	2.4	12.8	9.2	1.9	4.7	16.3	7.0
North Macedonia	2.4	–0.3	–0.3	–0.2	1.4	1.5	0.8	1.2	3.2	10.6	4.5	2.0	4.9	9.3	4.0
Poland	2.9	0.1	–0.9	–0.7	2.0	1.8	2.2	3.4	5.1	13.8	14.3	2.5	8.6	15.8	9.0
Romania	6.5	1.1	–0.6	–1.6	1.3	4.6	3.8	2.6	5.0	13.3	11.0	2.5	8.2	14.7	7.7
Russia	9.5	7.8	15.5	7.0	3.7	2.9	4.5	3.4	6.7	13.8	5.0	4.0	8.4	12.5	4.0
Serbia	9.6	2.1	1.4	1.1	3.1	2.0	1.9	1.6	4.1	11.5	8.3	3.0	7.9	12.5	6.0
Türkiye	8.3	8.9	7.7	7.8	11.1	16.3	15.2	12.3	19.6	73.1	51.2	15.0	36.1	73.5	36.9
Ukraine[4]	10.1	12.1	48.7	13.9	14.4	10.9	7.9	2.7	9.4	20.6	. . .	. . .	10.0	30.0	. . .
Latin America and the Caribbean[5]	**4.9**	**4.9**	**5.4**	**5.5**	**6.3**	**6.6**	**7.7**	**6.4**	**9.8**	**14.1**	**11.4**	**5.7**	**11.6**	**14.6**	**9.5**
Antigua and Barbuda	2.3	1.1	1.0	–0.5	2.4	1.2	1.4	1.1	1.6	8.5	4.5	2.0	1.2	10.5	2.7
Argentina[4]	8.9	. . .	. . .	. . .	25.7	34.3	53.5	42.0	48.4	72.4	76.1	32.2	50.9	95.0	60.0
Aruba	2.6	0.4	0.5	–0.9	–1.0	3.6	3.9	–1.3	0.7	6.0	5.5	2.8	3.6	7.7	3.0
The Bahamas	2.0	1.2	1.9	–0.3	1.5	2.3	2.5	0.0	2.9	5.7	5.3	2.4	4.1	7.2	3.4
Barbados	5.2	1.8	–1.1	1.5	4.4	3.7	4.1	2.9	3.1	9.9	8.2	2.4	5.2	10.0	6.7
Belize	2.3	1.2	–0.9	0.7	1.1	0.3	0.2	0.1	3.2	6.6	4.7	2.0	4.9	8.0	2.5
Bolivia	6.0	5.8	4.1	3.6	2.8	2.3	1.8	0.9	0.7	3.2	3.6	3.5	0.9	4.2	3.6
Brazil	5.5	6.3	9.0	8.7	3.4	3.7	3.7	3.2	8.3	9.4	4.7	3.0	10.1	6.0	4.7
Chile	3.1	4.7	4.3	3.8	2.2	2.3	2.3	3.0	4.5	11.6	8.7	3.0	7.1	12.2	6.2
Colombia	4.3	2.9	5.0	7.5	4.3	3.2	3.5	2.5	3.5	9.7	7.1	3.0	5.6	11.0	6.0

Table A7. Emerging Market and Developing Economies: Consumer Prices[1] *(continued)*

(Annual percent change)

	Average									Projections			End of Period[2]	Projections	
	2004–13	2014	2015	2016	2017	2018	2019	2020	2021	2022	2023	2027	2021	2022	2023
Latin America and the Caribbean (continued)[5]	**4.9**	**4.9**	**5.4**	**5.5**	**6.3**	**6.6**	**7.7**	**6.4**	**9.8**	**14.1**	**11.4**	**5.7**	**11.6**	**14.6**	**9.5**
Costa Rica	8.8	4.5	0.8	0.0	1.6	2.2	2.1	0.7	1.7	8.9	6.4	3.0	3.3	9.5	4.8
Dominica	2.1	0.8	–0.9	0.1	0.3	1.0	1.5	–0.7	1.6	5.3	4.7	2.0	3.5	3.5	4.9
Dominican Republic	9.7	3.0	0.8	1.6	3.3	3.6	1.8	3.8	8.2	9.0	5.7	4.0	8.5	8.0	4.9
Ecuador	4.0	3.6	4.0	1.7	0.4	–0.2	0.3	–0.3	0.1	3.2	2.4	1.0	1.9	3.8	1.4
El Salvador	3.4	1.1	–0.7	0.6	1.0	1.1	0.1	–0.4	3.5	7.3	2.7	1.2	6.1	6.0	2.0
Grenada	3.0	–1.0	–0.6	1.7	0.9	0.8	0.6	–0.7	1.2	4.5	3.5	2.0	1.9	5.4	2.3
Guatemala	6.1	3.4	2.4	4.4	4.4	3.8	3.7	3.2	4.3	6.4	5.6	4.0	3.1	8.0	4.6
Guyana	5.4	0.7	–0.9	0.8	1.9	1.3	2.1	1.2	3.3	7.6	7.6	3.5	5.7	9.4	6.0
Haiti	9.5	3.2	5.3	11.4	10.6	11.4	17.3	22.9	15.9	26.8	21.2	9.7	13.1	31.5	14.8
Honduras[4]	6.8	6.1	3.2	2.7	3.9	4.3	4.4	3.5	4.5	8.6	8.5	4.0	5.3	11.0	6.2
Jamaica	11.4	8.3	3.7	2.3	4.4	3.7	3.9	5.2	5.9	9.0	7.0	5.0	7.3	9.5	5.5
Mexico	4.2	4.0	2.7	2.8	6.0	4.9	3.6	3.4	5.7	8.0	6.3	3.0	7.4	8.5	4.8
Nicaragua	8.9	6.0	4.0	3.5	3.9	4.9	5.4	3.7	4.9	9.9	7.0	3.5	7.2	10.0	5.5
Panama	4.0	2.6	0.1	0.7	0.9	0.8	–0.4	–1.6	1.6	3.9	3.3	2.0	2.6	4.4	3.0
Paraguay	6.1	5.0	3.1	4.1	3.6	4.0	2.8	1.8	4.8	9.5	4.5	4.0	6.8	8.2	4.2
Peru	2.9	3.2	3.5	3.6	2.8	1.3	2.1	1.8	4.0	7.5	4.4	2.0	6.4	6.8	3.0
St. Kitts and Nevis	3.4	0.2	–2.3	–0.7	0.7	–1.0	–0.3	–0.6	0.2	3.8	2.8	2.0	1.9	3.4	2.2
St. Lucia	2.9	3.5	–1.0	–3.1	0.1	2.6	0.5	–1.8	2.4	6.4	2.7	2.0	4.1	5.5	2.3
St. Vincent and the Grenadines	3.4	0.2	–1.7	–0.2	2.2	2.3	0.9	–0.6	1.6	5.8	4.6	2.0	3.4	8.0	2.1
Suriname	8.5	3.4	6.9	55.5	22.0	6.9	4.4	34.9	59.1	47.6	27.2	5.0	60.7	35.2	22.9
Trinidad and Tobago	7.6	5.7	4.7	3.1	1.9	1.0	1.0	0.6	1.5	5.0	4.6	2.1	3.5	6.5	3.8
Uruguay	7.5	8.9	8.7	9.6	6.2	7.6	7.9	9.8	7.7	9.1	7.8	4.5	8.0	8.9	7.2
Venezuela[4]	24.1	62.2	121.7	254.9	438.1	65,374.1	19,906.0	2,355.1	1,588.5	210.0	195.0	. . .	686.4	220.0	150.0
Middle East and Central Asia	**8.4**	**6.5**	**5.6**	**5.9**	**7.1**	**10.0**	**7.7**	**10.5**	**12.9**	**13.8**	**13.1**	**6.8**	**12.7**	**15.6**	**10.8**
Afghanistan[4]	8.7	4.7	–0.7	4.4	5.0	0.6	2.3	5.6	. . .	. . .	. . .	. . .	. . .	. . .	. . .
Algeria	4.2	2.9	4.8	6.4	5.6	4.3	2.0	2.4	7.2	9.7	8.7	9.5	8.5	11.1	7.5
Armenia	5.1	3.0	3.7	–1.4	1.2	2.5	1.4	1.2	7.2	8.5	7.0	4.1	7.7	8.5	6.0
Azerbaijan	7.8	1.4	4.0	12.4	12.8	2.3	2.7	2.8	6.7	12.2	10.8	4.0	12.0	12.5	9.0
Bahrain	2.4	2.6	1.8	2.8	1.4	2.1	1.0	–2.3	–0.6	3.5	3.4	1.9	–0.4	3.0	1.8
Djibouti	4.2	1.3	–0.8	2.7	0.6	0.1	3.3	1.8	1.2	6.6	1.9	2.5	2.5	5.5	3.5
Egypt	9.8	10.1	11.0	10.2	23.5	20.9	13.9	5.7	4.5	8.5	12.0	7.0	4.9	13.1	9.2
Georgia	5.7	3.1	4.0	2.1	6.0	2.6	4.9	5.2	9.6	11.6	6.0	3.0	13.9	9.0	3.8
Iran	18.8	15.6	11.9	9.1	9.6	30.2	34.6	36.4	40.1	40.0	40.0	25.0	34.7	45.0	35.0
Iraq	. . .	2.2	1.4	0.5	0.2	0.4	–0.2	0.6	6.0	6.5	4.5	2.0	5.3	5.8	3.7
Jordan	4.7	3.0	–1.1	–0.6	3.6	4.5	0.7	0.4	1.3	3.8	3.0	2.5	2.3	4.4	3.0
Kazakhstan	8.4	6.7	6.7	14.6	7.4	6.0	5.2	6.8	8.0	14.0	11.3	5.3	8.4	16.4	9.0
Kuwait	4.0	3.1	3.7	3.5	1.5	0.6	1.1	2.1	3.4	4.3	2.4	2.5	4.1	3.2	2.6
Kyrgyz Republic	8.8	7.5	6.5	0.4	3.2	1.5	1.1	6.3	11.9	13.5	12.4	4.8	11.2	15.4	10.0
Lebanon[4]	4.1	1.1	–3.8	–0.8	4.5	6.1	2.9	84.9	. . .	. . .	. . .	. . .	. . .	. . .	. . .
Libya[4]	5.1	2.4	10.0	25.9	25.9	14.0	–2.9	1.5	2.8	5.5	4.0	3.1	3.7	5.8	2.6
Mauritania	6.6	3.8	0.5	1.5	2.3	3.1	2.3	2.3	3.8	7.1	7.8	5.7	5.7	8.5	7.0
Morocco	1.8	0.4	1.4	1.5	0.7	1.6	0.2	0.6	1.4	6.2	4.1	2.0	3.2	6.0	3.7
Oman	3.9	1.0	0.1	1.1	1.6	0.9	0.1	–0.9	1.5	3.1	1.9	1.9	3.8	1.7	0.8
Pakistan[4]	10.3	8.6	4.5	2.9	4.1	3.9	6.7	10.7	8.9	12.1	19.9	6.5	9.7	21.3	15.0
Qatar	5.4	4.2	0.9	2.7	0.4	0.3	–0.7	–2.7	2.3	4.5	3.3	1.5	5.9	3.1	3.5
Saudi Arabia	3.2	2.2	1.2	2.1	–0.8	2.5	–2.1	3.4	3.1	2.7	2.2	2.0	1.2	2.7	2.2
Somalia	. . .	1.3	0.9	0.0	4.0	4.3	4.5	4.3	4.6	9.0	3.9	3.2	5.7	8.3	3.8
Sudan[6]	16.5	36.9	16.9	17.8	32.4	63.3	51.0	163.3	359.1	154.9	76.9	8.1	318.2	129.5	49.4
Syria[7]	. . .	. . .	. . .	. . .	. . .	. . .	. . .	. . .	. . .	. . .	. . .	. . .	. . .	. . .	. . .
Tajikistan	9.3	6.1	5.8	5.9	7.3	3.8	7.8	8.6	9.0	8.3	8.1	6.5	8.0	8.5	7.6
Tunisia	3.9	4.6	4.4	3.6	5.3	7.3	6.7	5.6	5.7	8.1	8.5	4.8	6.6	9.4	8.2
Turkmenistan	6.4	6.0	7.4	3.6	8.0	13.3	5.1	7.6	15.0	17.5	10.5	8.0	21.0	14.0	7.0
United Arab Emirates	4.8	2.3	4.1	1.6	2.0	3.1	–1.9	–2.1	0.2	5.2	3.6	2.0	0.2	5.2	3.6
Uzbekistan	11.6	9.1	8.5	8.8	13.9	17.5	14.5	12.9	10.8	11.2	10.8	5.1	10.0	11.5	11.4
West Bank and Gaza	3.8	1.7	1.4	–0.2	0.2	–0.2	1.6	–0.7	1.2	4.9	3.4	2.0	1.3	5.7	3.8
Yemen	11.4	8.2	22.0	21.3	30.4	27.6	12.0	23.1	45.7	43.8	17.1	5.0	58.5	29.2	7.7

Table A7. Emerging Market and Developing Economies: Consumer Prices[1] *(continued)*
(Annual percent change)

	Average									Projections			End of Period[2]	Projections	
	2004–13	2014	2015	2016	2017	2018	2019	2020	2021	2022	2023	2027	2021	2022	2023
Sub-Saharan Africa	**8.6**	**6.4**	**6.7**	**10.2**	**10.7**	**8.3**	**8.2**	**10.2**	**11.1**	**14.4**	**11.9**	**6.9**	**11.5**	**15.5**	**10.2**
Angola	16.2	7.3	9.2	30.7	29.8	19.6	17.1	22.3	25.8	21.7	11.8	6.4	27.0	15.0	11.0
Benin	3.3	–1.1	0.2	–0.8	1.8	0.8	–0.9	3.0	1.7	5.0	1.8	1.6	1.7	5.0	1.8
Botswana	8.4	4.4	3.1	2.8	3.3	3.2	2.7	1.9	6.7	11.2	5.8	4.6	8.7	11.2	5.8
Burkina Faso	2.6	–0.3	1.7	0.4	1.5	2.0	–3.2	1.9	3.9	14.2	1.5	2.0	8.0	13.7	–3.5
Burundi	10.8	4.4	5.6	5.5	16.6	–2.8	–0.7	7.3	8.3	17.3	8.5	4.0	10.1	19.7	0.1
Cabo Verde	2.6	–0.2	0.1	–1.4	0.8	1.3	1.1	0.6	1.9	6.5	3.5	2.0	5.4	6.5	3.5
Cameroon	2.5	1.9	2.7	0.9	0.6	1.1	2.5	2.5	2.3	4.6	2.8	2.0	3.5	4.1	2.9
Central African Republic	3.3	17.8	1.4	4.9	4.2	1.6	2.8	0.9	4.3	6.5	6.3	2.5	2.7	11.0	3.3
Chad	2.6	1.7	4.8	–1.6	–0.9	4.0	–1.0	4.5	–0.8	4.9	3.1	3.0	1.0	5.2	2.5
Comoros	3.7	0.0	0.9	0.8	0.1	1.7	3.7	0.8	–0.2	11.4	8.4	1.9	7.1	16.3	0.9
Democratic Republic of the Congo	15.3	1.2	0.7	3.2	35.7	29.3	4.7	11.4	9.0	8.4	9.8	6.3	5.3	11.0	6.8
Republic of Congo	3.5	0.9	3.2	3.2	0.4	1.2	0.4	1.4	2.0	3.5	3.2	3.0	1.5	3.5	3.2
Côte d'Ivoire	2.2	0.5	1.2	0.6	0.6	0.6	0.8	2.4	4.2	5.5	4.0	2.0	5.6	6.4	2.7
Equatorial Guinea	4.4	4.3	1.7	1.4	0.7	1.3	1.2	4.8	–0.1	5.1	5.7	3.5	2.9	6.0	5.5
Eritrea	13.6	8.4	28.5	-5.6	-13.3	-14.4	1.3	5.6	6.6	7.4	6.4	5.0	6.7	8.2	4.5
Eswatini	6.7	5.7	5.0	7.8	6.2	4.8	2.6	3.9	3.7	4.9	4.2	4.4	3.5	4.9	4.2
Ethiopia	16.6	7.4	9.6	6.6	10.7	13.8	15.8	20.4	26.8	33.6	28.6	14.4	35.1	32.5	26.0
Gabon	1.2	4.5	–0.1	2.1	2.7	4.8	2.0	1.3	1.1	3.5	3.2	2.2	1.7	4.6	2.0
The Gambia	5.5	6.3	6.8	7.2	8.0	6.5	7.1	5.9	7.4	11.3	11.1	5.0	7.6	12.4	9.7
Ghana	11.2	15.5	17.2	17.5	12.4	9.8	7.1	9.9	10.0	27.2	20.9	6.5	12.6	31.7	17.4
Guinea	19.0	9.7	8.2	8.2	8.9	9.8	9.5	10.6	12.6	12.7	12.2	7.8	12.5	12.9	11.5
Guinea-Bissau	2.8	–1.0	1.5	2.7	–0.2	0.4	0.3	1.5	3.3	5.5	4.0	2.0	5.8	1.0	4.0
Kenya	9.0	6.9	6.6	6.3	8.0	4.7	5.2	5.3	6.1	7.4	6.6	5.0	5.7	8.1	6.0
Lesotho	6.0	5.4	3.2	6.6	4.4	4.8	5.2	5.0	6.0	8.1	6.2	5.5	7.2	7.4	5.0
Liberia	8.6	9.9	7.7	8.8	12.4	23.5	27.0	17.0	7.8	6.9	8.7	5.0	5.5	11.0	6.5
Madagascar	10.1	6.1	7.4	6.1	8.6	8.6	5.6	4.2	5.8	9.8	8.0	5.8	6.2	12.0	9.7
Malawi	12.9	23.8	21.9	21.7	11.5	9.2	9.4	8.6	9.3	18.4	16.5	6.5	11.5	20.6	15.2
Mali	2.6	0.9	1.4	–1.8	2.4	1.9	–3.0	0.5	3.8	8.0	3.0	2.0	8.8	4.0	3.0
Mauritius	5.6	3.2	1.3	1.0	3.7	3.2	0.5	2.5	4.0	10.2	6.1	3.6	6.8	9.7	6.4
Mozambique	9.1	2.6	3.6	17.4	15.1	3.9	2.8	3.1	5.7	11.3	8.6	5.5	6.7	15.4	8.2
Namibia	5.8	5.3	3.4	6.7	6.1	4.3	3.7	2.2	3.6	6.4	4.9	4.5	–0.8	6.9	4.4
Niger	2.6	–0.9	1.0	0.2	0.2	2.8	–2.5	2.9	3.8	4.5	3.0	2.0	4.9	4.8	3.0
Nigeria	11.5	8.0	9.0	15.7	16.5	12.1	11.4	13.2	17.0	18.9	17.3	11.5	15.6	21.0	15.1
Rwanda	8.3	1.8	2.5	5.7	4.8	1.4	2.4	7.7	0.8	9.5	8.0	5.0	1.9	8.7	6.5
São Tomé and Príncipe	16.6	7.0	6.1	5.4	5.7	7.9	7.7	9.8	8.1	15.0	11.2	5.0	9.5	16.7	6.8
Senegal	2.1	–1.1	0.9	1.2	1.1	0.5	1.0	2.5	2.2	7.5	3.1	2.0	3.8	7.0	0.6
Seychelles	8.1	1.4	4.0	–1.0	2.9	3.7	1.8	1.2	9.8	4.1	3.3	3.0	7.9	5.7	1.0
Sierra Leone	9.5	4.6	6.7	10.9	18.2	16.0	14.8	13.4	11.9	25.9	26.8	10.3	17.9	29.4	23.7
South Africa	5.5	6.1	4.6	6.3	5.3	4.6	4.1	3.3	4.6	6.7	5.1	4.5	5.4	7.0	4.5
South Sudan	. . .	1.7	52.8	322.7	213.0	83.4	49.3	24.0	30.2	17.6	21.7	8.0	2.4	28.4	15.0
Tanzania	8.8	6.1	5.6	5.2	5.3	3.5	3.4	3.3	3.7	4.0	5.3	4.1	4.2	4.4	5.4
Togo	2.7	0.2	1.8	0.9	–0.2	0.9	0.7	1.8	4.3	5.6	2.1	1.7	6.2	1.3	3.9
Uganda	9.2	4.3	3.7	5.2	5.6	2.5	2.1	2.8	2.2	6.4	6.4	5.0	2.9	8.4	6.8
Zambia	11.2	7.8	10.1	17.9	6.6	7.5	9.2	15.7	22.0	12.5	9.5	7.0	16.4	12.7	8.0
Zimbabwe[4]	5.0	–0.2	–2.4	–1.6	0.9	10.6	255.3	557.2	98.5	284.9	204.6	10.0	60.7	547.3	100.0

[1]Movements in consumer prices are shown as annual averages.
[2]Monthly year-over-year changes and, for several countries, on a quarterly basis.
[3]Based on Eurostat's harmonized index of consumer prices.
[4]See the country-specific notes for Afghanistan, Albania, Argentina, Honduras, Lebanon, Libya, Pakistan, Ukraine, Venezuela, and Zimbabwe in the "Country Notes" section of the Statistical Appendix.
[5]Excludes Venezuela but includes Argentina from 2017 onward. See the country-specific notes for Argentina and Venezuela in the "Country Notes" section of the Statistical Appendix.
[6]Data for 2011 exclude South Sudan after July 9. Data for 2012 and onward pertain to the current Sudan.
[7]Data for Syria are excluded for 2011 onward owing to the uncertain political situation.

Table A8. Major Advanced Economies: General Government Fiscal Balances and Debt[1]
(Percent of GDP, unless noted otherwise)

	Average 2004–13	2014	2015	2016	2017	2018	2019	2020	2021	Projections 2022	2023	2027
Major Advanced Economies												
Net Lending/Borrowing	–5.3	–3.6	–3.0	–3.3	–3.2	–3.3	–3.6	–11.9	–8.7	–4.4	–4.6	–4.9
Output Gap[2]	–2.3	–2.8	–2.0	–1.7	–0.8	–0.1	0.2	–3.4	–0.6	–0.3	–0.9	–0.1
Structural Balance[2]	–4.2	–2.5	–2.2	–2.7	–2.9	–3.2	–3.6	–8.2	–7.2	–4.3	–4.2	–4.7
United States												
Net Lending/Borrowing[3]	–6.5	–4.0	–3.5	–4.4	–4.6	–5.3	–5.5	–14.5	–10.9	–4.0	–5.7	–7.1
Output Gap[2]	–3.7	–4.0	–2.5	–2.1	–1.3	0.0	0.7	–3.2	0.5	0.0	–0.8	–0.3
Structural Balance[2]	–4.5	–2.7	–2.5	–3.6	–4.1	–5.1	–5.7	–10.8	–9.5	–4.0	–5.3	–6.8
Net Debt	60.6	81.1	80.9	81.9	80.3	81.2	83.0	99.1	99.6	94.7	96.9	112.0
Gross Debt	82.3	104.6	105.2	107.2	106.2	107.5	108.8	134.5	128.1	122.1	122.9	134.9
Euro Area												
Net Lending/Borrowing	–3.3	–2.5	–2.0	–1.5	–0.9	–0.4	–0.7	–7.0	–5.1	–3.8	–3.3	–2.5
Output Gap[2]	–0.5	–2.9	–2.3	–1.7	–0.6	–0.1	0.0	–4.5	–1.9	–0.3	–0.8	0.1
Structural Balance[2]	–3.0	–0.7	–0.5	–0.5	–0.5	–0.3	–0.5	–4.3	–3.8	–3.5	–2.9	–2.6
Net Debt	62.8	76.3	75.1	74.6	72.5	70.7	69.1	79.4	78.6	76.7	76.2	75.2
Gross Debt	78.2	93.1	91.2	90.4	87.9	85.9	83.8	96.9	95.3	93.0	91.3	87.8
Germany												
Net Lending/Borrowing	–1.7	0.6	1.0	1.2	1.3	1.9	1.5	–4.3	–3.7	–3.3	–2.5	–0.5
Output Gap[2]	–0.2	–0.4	–0.4	0.1	1.0	0.8	0.4	–3.0	–1.3	–0.5	–1.3	0.0
Structural Balance[2]	–1.3	1.2	1.2	1.2	1.1	1.6	1.3	–2.9	–3.0	–3.0	–1.8	–0.6
Net Debt	57.5	54.9	52.2	49.3	45.4	42.6	40.4	45.8	47.0	47.7	47.8	44.1
Gross Debt	72.3	75.3	71.9	69.0	64.6	61.3	58.9	68.0	69.6	71.1	68.3	59.7
France												
Net Lending/Borrowing	–4.4	–3.9	–3.6	–3.6	–3.0	–2.3	–3.1	–8.9	–6.4	–5.1	–5.6	–5.0
Output Gap[2]	–0.4	–2.2	–2.4	–2.7	–1.5	–0.8	0.0	–4.7	–1.9	–0.8	–1.2	–0.1
Structural Balance[2]	–4.1	–2.5	–2.1	–1.9	–1.9	–1.5	–2.1	–5.7	–5.1	–4.5	–4.8	–4.9
Net Debt	67.4	85.5	86.3	89.2	89.4	89.2	88.9	102.3	101.1	100.3	101.0	106.9
Gross Debt	77.1	94.9	95.6	98.0	98.1	97.8	97.4	114.7	112.6	111.8	112.5	118.5
Italy												
Net Lending/Borrowing	–3.4	–3.0	–2.6	–2.4	–2.4	–2.2	–1.5	–9.6	–7.2	–5.4	–3.9	–3.0
Output Gap[2]	–0.6	–4.1	–3.5	–2.7	–1.7	–1.2	–1.2	–6.2	–3.3	0.4	–0.6	0.6
Structural Balance[2]	–3.4	–1.0	–0.6	–1.2	–1.5	–1.6	–0.9	–6.0	–5.1	–5.7	–3.6	–3.3
Net Debt	104.3	121.4	122.2	121.6	121.3	121.8	121.7	141.8	138.3	135.4	135.6	132.3
Gross Debt	114.3	135.4	135.3	134.8	134.2	134.4	134.1	155.3	150.9	147.2	147.1	142.5
Japan												
Net Lending/Borrowing	–6.3	–5.6	–3.7	–3.6	–3.1	–2.5	–3.0	–9.0	–6.7	–7.9	–3.6	–2.6
Output Gap[2]	–2.1	–1.9	–1.5	–1.8	–0.3	–0.7	–1.2	–2.6	–2.5	–2.0	–1.1	0.0
Structural Balance[2]	–5.7	–5.5	–4.2	–4.0	–3.4	–2.5	–2.6	–8.2	–6.3	–7.3	–3.2	–2.6
Net Debt	115.7	145.1	144.6	149.6	148.1	151.0	151.5	162.6	168.1	172.6	172.4	175.1
Gross Debt[4]	195.1	233.5	228.4	232.5	231.4	232.3	236.3	259.4	262.5	263.9	261.1	263.4
United Kingdom												
Net Lending/Borrowing	–5.6	–5.5	–4.5	–3.3	–2.4	–2.2	–2.2	–12.8	–8.0	–4.3	–2.3	–1.0
Output Gap[2]	–1.1	–1.8	–1.0	–0.5	0.1	0.3	0.6	–3.5	–0.1	0.4	–1.0	0.0
Structural Balance[2]	–4.8	–3.9	–3.6	–2.8	–2.3	–2.4	–2.7	0.5	–3.2	–4.3	–1.7	–1.0
Net Debt	52.9	77.3	77.6	76.9	75.7	74.8	74.1	90.2	84.3	75.3	68.5	56.5
Gross Debt	59.1	85.5	86.0	85.8	85.1	84.5	83.9	102.6	95.3	87.0	79.9	68.0
Canada												
Net Lending/Borrowing	–1.0	0.2	–0.1	–0.5	–0.1	0.4	0.0	–11.4	–5.0	–2.2	–1.2	–0.5
Output Gap[2]	0.0	1.0	–0.1	–0.9	0.4	0.6	0.4	–3.4	–1.4	0.6	–0.1	0.0
Structural Balance[2]	–0.9	–0.6	0.0	0.1	–0.3	0.0	–0.2	–8.6	–4.0	–2.7	–1.2	–0.5
Net Debt[5]	26.5	28.5	28.6	28.5	25.8	25.7	23.1	33.6	31.6	30.5	30.3	27.3
Gross Debt	76.1	85.6	91.2	91.8	88.9	88.9	87.2	117.8	112.9	102.2	98.7	88.7

Note: The methodology and specific assumptions for each country are discussed in Box A1. The country group composites for fiscal data are calculated as the sum of the US dollar values for the relevant individual countries.

[1]Debt data refer to the end of the year and are not always comparable across countries. Gross and net debt levels reported by national statistical agencies for countries that have adopted the System of National Accounts 2008 (Australia, Canada, Hong Kong SAR, United States) are adjusted to exclude unfunded pension liabilities of government employees' defined-benefit pension plans.

[2]Percent of potential GDP.

[3]Figures reported by the national statistical agency are adjusted to exclude items related to the accrual-basis accounting of government employees' defined-benefit pension plans.

[4]Nonconsolidated basis.

[5]Includes equity shares.

Table A9. Summary of World Trade Volumes and Prices

(Annual percent change, unless noted otherwise)

	Averages										Projections	
	2004–13	2014–23	2014	2015	2016	2017	2018	2019	2020	2021	2022	2023
Trade in Goods and Services												
World Trade[1]												
Volume	5.4	2.8	3.8	2.9	2.3	5.7	4.1	0.9	–7.8	10.1	4.3	2.5
Price Deflator												
In US Dollars	4.1	0.4	–1.8	–13.3	–4.0	4.3	5.4	–2.4	–2.2	12.7	7.0	0.3
In SDRs	3.2	1.7	–1.7	–5.9	–3.4	4.5	3.2	0.0	–3.0	10.2	13.3	1.5
Volume of Trade												
Exports												
Advanced Economies	4.5	2.5	3.8	3.7	2.0	5.1	3.6	1.2	–9.0	8.7	4.2	2.5
Emerging Market and Developing Economies	7.4	3.2	3.4	1.9	2.8	6.4	4.3	0.5	–4.8	11.8	3.3	2.9
Imports												
Advanced Economies	3.7	3.0	4.0	4.7	2.5	4.8	3.8	2.1	–8.4	9.5	6.0	2.0
Emerging Market and Developing Economies	9.1	2.5	4.3	–0.6	1.6	7.5	5.2	–1.0	–7.8	11.8	2.4	3.0
Terms of Trade												
Advanced Economies	–0.4	0.3	0.3	1.8	1.1	–0.3	–0.4	0.3	0.9	0.6	–1.5	0.5
Emerging Market and Developing Economies	1.5	–0.6	–0.7	–4.4	–1.6	1.6	1.1	–1.5	–1.1	1.7	0.8	–1.7
Trade in Goods												
World Trade[1]												
Volume	5.3	2.7	3.0	2.3	2.1	5.7	3.9	0.2	–5.0	10.8	2.9	2.0
Price Deflator												
In US Dollars	4.2	0.3	–2.4	–14.6	–4.8	4.8	5.7	–3.0	–2.6	14.4	8.5	–0.4
In SDRs	3.4	1.6	–2.4	–7.3	–4.2	5.1	3.6	–0.7	–3.4	11.8	14.8	0.7
World Trade Prices in US Dollars[2]												
Manufactures	2.6	1.1	–0.5	–3.0	–5.2	0.1	2.0	0.4	–3.2	6.8	10.2	3.9
Oil	13.6	–1.9	–9.2	–46.0	–15.0	22.3	25.1	–7.5	–31.7	65.9	41.4	–12.9
Nonfuel Primary Commodities	8.3	1.4	–5.8	–17.0	–0.3	6.4	1.3	0.6	6.5	26.3	7.3	–6.2
Food	5.8	1.3	–1.6	–16.9	1.5	3.8	–1.2	–3.1	1.7	26.1	14.2	–5.8
Beverages	6.7	2.4	20.6	–7.4	–3.0	–3.8	–9.2	–5.7	2.4	22.4	16.5	–2.7
Agricultural Raw Materials	4.7	–1.2	–7.6	–11.3	–0.2	5.4	2.0	–5.4	–3.4	15.4	2.5	–6.9
Metal	13.1	0.3	–12.2	–27.3	–5.3	22.2	6.6	3.9	3.5	46.7	–5.5	–12.0
World Trade Prices in SDRs[2]												
Manufactures	1.8	2.4	–0.4	5.3	–4.6	0.3	–0.1	2.9	–3.9	4.4	16.6	5.1
Oil	12.7	–0.6	–9.1	–41.3	–14.4	22.6	22.6	–5.2	–32.2	62.2	49.8	–11.9
Nonfuel Primary Commodities	7.5	2.7	–5.7	–10.0	0.4	6.7	–0.8	3.1	5.7	23.5	13.6	–5.1
Food	4.9	2.7	–1.5	–9.8	2.2	4.1	–3.3	–0.7	0.9	23.3	20.9	–4.7
Beverages	5.8	3.8	20.7	0.5	–2.3	–3.5	–11.1	–3.4	1.6	19.7	23.3	–1.5
Agricultural Raw Materials	3.9	0.1	–7.6	–3.7	0.5	5.7	–0.1	–3.1	–4.1	12.8	8.5	–5.8
Metal	12.2	1.7	–12.1	–21.1	–4.7	22.5	4.4	6.4	2.6	43.4	0.1	–11.0
World Trade Prices in Euros[2]												
Manufactures	1.0	3.7	–0.5	16.2	–5.0	–1.9	–2.5	6.0	–5.0	3.0	23.3	7.2
Oil	11.8	0.7	–9.2	–35.3	–14.7	19.8	19.6	–2.3	–33.0	60.0	58.4	–10.2
Nonfuel Primary Commodities	6.6	4.0	–5.8	–0.7	0.0	4.3	–3.2	6.2	4.5	21.8	20.1	–3.3
Food	4.1	4.0	–1.6	–0.5	1.8	1.7	–5.6	2.3	–0.3	21.6	27.9	–2.9
Beverages	5.0	5.1	20.5	10.9	–2.7	–5.7	–13.2	–0.5	0.5	18.1	30.4	0.4
Agricultural Raw Materials	3.0	1.4	–7.7	6.3	0.1	3.3	–2.5	–0.2	–5.2	11.3	14.8	–4.0
Metal	11.3	3.0	–12.2	–12.9	–5.0	19.7	1.9	9.6	1.5	41.5	5.8	–9.3

Table A9. Summary of World Trade Volumes and Prices *(continued)*

(Annual percent change, unless noted otherwise)

	Averages										Projections	
	2004–13	2014–23	2014	2015	2016	2017	2018	2019	2020	2021	2022	2023
Trade in Goods *(continued)*												
Volume of Trade												
Exports												
Advanced Economies	4.3	2.3	3.0	3.0	1.7	5.1	3.0	0.3	–6.4	9.7	2.4	1.7
Emerging Market and Developing Economies	7.2	3.0	2.8	1.4	2.7	6.5	3.9	–0.4	–0.9	11.0	1.4	2.4
Fuel Exporters	4.9	0.3	–0.2	2.0	0.7	1.1	0.3	–4.3	–6.1	0.6	7.6	2.5
Nonfuel Exporters	7.9	3.5	3.7	1.3	3.1	7.5	4.6	0.4	0.0	12.4	0.5	2.3
Imports												
Advanced Economies	3.8	2.9	3.4	3.7	2.2	4.8	3.8	0.6	–5.8	10.8	5.3	1.5
Emerging Market and Developing Economies	9.0	2.7	2.7	–0.1	2.2	7.5	5.3	–0.1	–5.6	12.1	1.4	2.9
Fuel Exporters	10.0	–0.5	3.6	0.0	–6.8	–0.9	–3.0	2.4	–12.0	1.2	9.4	2.3
Nonfuel Exporters	8.9	3.2	2.5	–0.2	3.6	8.8	6.4	–0.3	–4.8	13.4	0.6	3.0
Price Deflators in SDRs												
Exports												
Advanced Economies	2.2	1.4	–1.8	–6.4	–2.2	4.1	2.7	–1.2	–2.2	10.1	11.5	1.0
Emerging Market and Developing Economies	6.2	1.8	–3.3	–9.1	–7.0	7.1	4.9	0.2	–5.8	15.9	19.2	0.3
Fuel Exporters	10.4	0.3	–7.9	–30.0	–10.7	15.5	13.9	–3.4	–22.0	38.8	37.4	–5.6
Nonfuel Exporters	5.0	2.3	–1.9	–3.6	–6.3	5.5	3.3	0.9	–2.9	12.8	16.4	1.5
Imports												
Advanced Economies	2.7	1.1	–2.0	–8.1	–3.5	4.5	3.4	–1.5	–3.3	9.5	13.3	0.8
Emerging Market and Developing Economies	4.4	2.3	–2.8	–5.2	–5.5	5.7	3.6	0.6	–2.9	13.9	17.4	0.7
Fuel Exporters	4.3	2.6	–2.6	–2.4	–3.6	3.4	1.3	2.6	–0.8	11.1	16.0	2.4
Nonfuel Exporters	4.4	2.2	–2.8	–5.7	–5.9	6.0	3.9	0.3	–3.2	14.3	17.6	0.5
Terms of Trade												
Advanced Economies	–0.4	0.3	0.2	1.9	1.3	–0.4	–0.7	0.3	1.1	0.6	–1.6	0.3
Emerging Market and Developing Economies	1.7	–0.4	–0.5	–4.1	–1.5	1.3	1.3	–0.4	–3.0	1.7	1.5	–0.4
Regional Groups												
Emerging and Developing Asia	–0.8	0.0	2.4	8.3	0.2	–3.2	–2.0	0.8	0.4	–5.6	–2.4	1.5
Emerging and Developing Europe	2.6	0.6	–0.4	–9.1	–5.4	3.3	4.2	0.4	–4.4	8.2	8.5	2.5
Latin America and the Caribbean	2.4	–0.8	–2.7	–9.0	0.9	4.4	–0.2	–0.6	0.6	4.2	–3.3	–1.9
Middle East and Central Asia	4.4	–1.7	–4.2	–24.1	–5.4	9.7	10.0	–4.6	–17.7	21.0	14.4	–6.5
Sub-Saharan Africa	4.6	–0.3	–3.6	–14.7	–1.5	9.4	4.8	–2.3	0.4	10.6	2.1	–5.5
Analytical Groups												
By Source of Export Earnings												
Fuel	5.8	–2.2	–5.5	–28.2	–7.3	11.7	12.5	–5.9	–21.4	24.9	18.5	–7.8
Nonfuel	0.6	0.1	1.0	2.2	–0.4	–0.4	–0.6	0.5	0.3	–1.3	–1.0	1.0
Memorandum												
World Exports in Billions of US Dollars												
Goods and Services	17,869	25,022	23,799	21,127	20,752	22,884	25,072	24,653	22,260	27,663	30,593	31,416
Goods	14,190	19,305	18,643	16,202	15,746	17,458	19,106	18,540	17,212	21,772	24,020	24,355
Average Oil Price[3]	13.6	–1.9	–9.2	–46.0	–15.0	22.3	25.1	–7.5	–31.7	65.9	41.4	–12.9
In US Dollars a Barrel	77.52	66.33	94.05	50.82	43.22	52.86	66.15	61.21	41.83	69.42	98.19	85.52
Export Unit Value of Manufactures[4]	2.6	1.1	–0.5	–3.0	–5.2	0.1	2.0	0.4	–3.2	6.8	10.2	3.9

[1]Average of annual percent change for world exports and imports.

[2]As represented, respectively, by the export unit value index for manufactures of the advanced economies and accounting for 82 percent of the advanced economies' trade (export of goods) weights; the average of UK Brent, Dubai Fateh, and West Texas Intermediate crude oil prices; and the average of world market prices for nonfuel primary commodities weighted by their 2014–16 shares in world commodity imports.

[3]Percent change of average of UK Brent, Dubai Fateh, and West Texas Intermediate crude oil prices.

[4]Percent change for manufactures exported by the advanced economies.

Table A10. Summary of Current Account Balances

(Billions of US dollars)

									Projections		
	2014	2015	2016	2017	2018	2019	2020	2021	2022	2023	2027
Advanced Economies	**225.5**	**273.0**	**369.3**	**489.3**	**398.6**	**379.3**	**179.9**	**339.4**	**–370.9**	**–170.2**	**236.6**
United States	–370.1	–408.5	–396.2	–361.0	–439.8	–446.0	–619.7	–846.4	–985.3	–822.9	–701.4
Euro Area	316.9	313.5	364.0	402.1	398.0	311.1	247.7	356.9	137.3	194.7	424.8
Germany	280.3	288.8	295.1	288.9	316.3	294.3	272.5	313.6	168.7	216.6	301.1
France	–27.3	–9.0	–12.0	–19.9	–23.2	14.0	–47.4	10.6	–35.1	–42.3	–9.1
Italy	41.0	26.4	48.9	50.7	52.9	64.8	70.9	51.3	–3.3	5.6	57.1
Spain	23.3	24.2	39.1	36.4	26.7	29.3	10.6	13.2	–2.4	–3.5	25.3
Japan	36.8	136.4	197.8	203.5	177.8	176.3	146.9	142.2	58.1	94.4	165.6
United Kingdom	–157.9	–152.7	–145.6	–98.1	–112.6	–76.8	–69.0	–82.5	–153.9	–157.9	–155.9
Canada	–41.9	–54.4	–47.2	–46.2	–41.0	–35.5	–29.4	0.9	11.6	–5.3	–51.9
Other Advanced Economies[1]	351.0	350.3	330.2	333.0	330.6	345.6	401.0	591.7	484.5	448.5	462.0
Emerging Market and Developing Economies	**161.4**	**–76.1**	**–99.4**	**–21.9**	**–55.4**	**–3.4**	**157.8**	**343.8**	**598.0**	**492.3**	**–108.2**
Regional Groups											
Emerging and Developing Asia	227.4	296.1	212.3	166.4	–51.3	93.2	319.8	250.2	191.6	166.9	–25.2
Emerging and Developing Europe	–10.9	34.2	–8.4	–19.9	66.1	50.1	0.4	71.0	131.9	131.5	–13.5
Latin America and the Caribbean	–189.9	–172.7	–102.3	–94.7	–142.1	–106.6	–8.7	–79.3	–97.6	–83.7	–98.2
Middle East and Central Asia	199.7	–140.8	–146.4	–39.0	111.8	17.3	–105.7	121.8	406.5	333.0	89.8
Sub-Saharan Africa	–64.9	–92.9	–54.6	–34.6	–40.0	–57.4	–48.0	–19.9	–34.6	–55.4	–61.2
Analytical Groups											
By Source of Export Earnings											
Fuel	252.0	–144.7	–99.4	41.0	201.3	72.9	–89.8	180.8	498.3	406.6	152.1
Nonfuel	–88.8	70.6	2.2	–60.7	–254.5	–74.5	249.4	164.5	101.6	87.4	–257.7
Of Which, Primary Products	–57.7	–65.0	–45.1	–57.7	–76.3	–48.5	–4.5	–19.0	–37.6	–36.7	–35.8
By External Financing Source											
Net Debtor Economies	–384.4	–353.3	–271.6	–306.0	–382.1	–299.2	–114.0	–294.5	–459.0	–430.2	–508.5
Net Debtor Economies by Debt-Servicing Experience											
Economies with Arrears and/or Rescheduling during 2017–21	–59.2	–72.7	–65.9	–59.5	–52.0	–52.5	–35.6	–40.0	–41.2	–51.1	–45.4
Memorandum											
World	**386.8**	**196.9**	**269.8**	**467.4**	**343.2**	**375.9**	**337.7**	**683.3**	**227.1**	**322.2**	**128.4**
European Union	451.8	443.2	472.3	502.2	509.1	467.7	418.7	571.6	190.5	262.3	541.2
Middle East and North Africa	191.5	–122.2	–121.1	–19.3	127.5	36.5	–90.2	128.9	399.4	321.3	112.8
Emerging Market and Middle-Income Economies	204.3	–1.0	–58.8	11.4	–0.7	54.2	209.2	418.9	690.8	583.7	–16.5
Low-Income Developing Countries	–42.9	–75.1	–40.6	–33.3	–54.7	–57.6	–51.4	–75.0	–92.8	–91.3	–91.7

Table A10. Summary of Current Account Balances *(continued)*
(Percent of GDP)

	2014	2015	2016	2017	2018	2019	2020	2021	Projections 2022	2023	2027
Advanced Economies	**0.5**	**0.6**	**0.8**	**1.0**	**0.8**	**0.7**	**0.4**	**0.6**	**–0.6**	**–0.3**	**0.3**
United States	–2.1	–2.2	–2.1	–1.9	–2.1	–2.1	–3.0	–3.7	–3.9	–3.1	–2.3
Euro Area	2.3	2.7	3.0	3.2	2.9	2.3	1.9	2.5	1.0	1.4	2.5
Germany	7.2	8.6	8.5	7.8	8.0	7.6	7.0	7.4	4.2	5.3	6.1
France	–1.0	–0.4	–0.5	–0.8	–0.8	0.5	–1.8	0.4	–1.3	–1.5	–0.3
Italy	1.9	1.4	2.6	2.6	2.5	3.2	3.7	2.4	–0.2	0.3	2.5
Spain	1.7	2.0	3.2	2.8	1.9	2.1	0.8	0.9	–0.2	–0.2	1.5
Japan	0.8	3.1	4.0	4.1	3.5	3.4	2.9	2.9	1.4	2.2	3.2
United Kingdom	–5.1	–5.2	–5.3	–3.6	–3.9	–2.7	–2.5	–2.6	–4.8	–4.5	–3.5
Canada	–2.3	–3.5	–3.1	–2.8	–2.4	–2.0	–1.8	0.0	0.5	–0.2	–1.9
Other Advanced Economies[1]	5.0	5.4	5.0	4.7	4.4	4.7	5.5	7.1	5.7	5.1	4.4
Emerging Market and Developing Economies	**0.5**	**–0.3**	**–0.3**	**–0.1**	**–0.2**	**0.0**	**0.5**	**0.8**	**1.3**	**1.0**	**–0.2**
Regional Groups											
Emerging and Developing Asia	1.5	1.9	1.3	0.9	–0.3	0.5	1.5	1.0	0.7	0.6	–0.1
Emerging and Developing Europe	–0.3	1.0	–0.3	–0.5	1.7	1.3	0.0	1.7	2.9	2.8	–0.2
Latin America and the Caribbean	–3.2	–3.4	–2.1	–1.7	–2.7	–2.0	–0.2	–1.6	–1.7	–1.4	–1.4
Middle East and Central Asia	4.9	–3.9	–4.1	–1.1	2.8	0.4	–2.5	2.3	6.5	5.2	1.2
Sub-Saharan Africa	–3.6	–5.7	–3.6	–2.1	–2.3	–3.3	–2.9	–1.1	–1.7	–2.5	–2.0
Analytical Groups											
By Source of Export Earnings											
Fuel	6.0	–4.2	–3.1	1.2	5.3	1.9	–2.4	3.8	8.4	6.7	2.1
Nonfuel	–0.3	0.3	0.0	–0.2	–0.8	–0.2	0.8	0.5	0.3	0.2	–0.5
Of Which, Primary Products	–2.8	–3.2	–2.3	–2.7	–3.6	–2.4	–0.2	–0.9	–1.6	–1.5	–1.2
By External Financing Source											
Net Debtor Economies	–2.7	–2.8	–2.1	–2.2	–2.6	–2.0	–0.8	–1.9	–2.7	–2.4	–2.1
Net Debtor Economies by Debt-Servicing Experience											
Economies with Arrears and/or Rescheduling during 2017–21	–4.8	–6.2	–5.7	–5.4	–4.5	–4.3	–2.9	–2.9	–3.1	–3.6	–2.4
Memorandum											
World	**0.5**	**0.3**	**0.4**	**0.6**	**0.4**	**0.4**	**0.4**	**0.7**	**0.2**	**0.3**	**0.1**
European Union	2.9	3.3	3.4	3.4	3.2	3.0	2.7	3.3	1.1	1.5	2.6
Middle East and North Africa	5.8	–4.2	–4.1	–0.6	3.9	1.1	–2.6	2.9	7.4	5.9	1.7
Emerging Market and Middle-Income Economies	0.7	0.0	–0.2	0.0	0.0	0.2	0.6	1.1	1.6	1.3	0.0
Low-Income Developing Countries	–2.1	–3.8	–2.1	–1.7	–2.5	–2.5	–2.2	–3.0	–3.4	–3.1	–2.1

Table A10. Summary of Current Account Balances *(continued)*
(Percent of exports of goods and services)

	2014	2015	2016	2017	2018	2019	2020	2021	Projections 2022	2023	2027
Advanced Economies	**1.5**	**2.0**	**2.7**	**3.4**	**2.5**	**2.4**	**1.3**	**2.0**	**–2.0**	**–0.9**	**1.0**
United States	–15.5	–17.9	–17.7	–15.1	–17.3	–17.5	–28.7	–33.1	–32.7	–26.3	–19.1
Euro Area	8.9	9.7	11.2	11.3	10.3	8.1	7.1	8.6	. . .	. . .	. . .
Germany	15.8	18.3	18.5	16.6	16.8	16.2	16.3	15.6	8.9	11.3	13.1
France	–3.1	–1.2	–1.5	–2.4	–2.5	1.6	–6.3	1.1	–3.2	–3.8	–0.7
Italy	6.5	4.8	8.9	8.4	8.1	10.2	12.7	7.5	–0.4	0.7	6.0
Spain	5.1	6.0	9.4	7.9	5.3	6.0	2.7	2.6	–0.4	–0.6	3.3
Japan	4.3	17.4	24.4	23.2	19.1	19.5	18.5	15.5	6.2	9.7	14.4
United Kingdom	–18.2	–19.0	–18.9	–12.1	–12.7	–8.6	–8.8	–9.6	–16.7	–15.7	–12.1
Canada	–7.3	–11.0	–9.8	–8.9	–7.4	–6.3	–6.1	0.1	1.6	–0.7	–6.5
Other Advanced Economies[1]	8.4	9.4	9.0	8.3	7.6	8.2	10.3	12.1	9.1	8.3	7.2
Emerging Market and Developing Economies	**2.0**	**–0.9**	**–1.3**	**–0.3**	**–0.7**	**–0.1**	**2.0**	**3.1**	**4.8**	**3.9**	**–0.8**
Regional Groups											
Emerging and Developing Asia	5.7	7.8	5.8	4.1	–1.1	2.1	7.3	4.5	3.1	2.6	–0.3
Emerging and Developing Europe	–0.7	2.9	–0.7	–1.5	4.3	3.3	0.0	4.0	7.0	6.7	–0.6
Latin America and the Caribbean	–15.3	–16.0	–9.7	–8.1	–11.2	–8.6	–0.8	–5.8	–6.2	–5.2	–5.3
Middle East and Central Asia	12.8	–10.5	–12.1	–3.3	6.5	0.9	–9.1	7.6	19.2	15.8	3.9
Sub-Saharan Africa	–14.3	–27.0	–17.1	–9.4	–9.4	–13.9	–14.2	–4.5	–6.6	–10.6	–9.8
Analytical Groups											
By Source of Export Earnings											
Fuel	14.8	–10.9	–8.3	2.8	12.3	4.8	–8.2	11.8	24.1	20.2	7.6
Nonfuel	–1.3	1.1	0.0	–0.9	–3.3	–1.0	3.5	1.8	1.0	0.8	–2.0
Of Which, Primary Products	–11.7	–15.3	–10.7	–12.2	–15.1	–9.7	–1.0	–3.2	–5.6	–5.3	–4.2
By External Financing Source											
Net Debtor Economies	–10.5	–11.0	–8.5	–8.4	–9.5	–7.4	–3.1	–6.4	–8.9	–8.0	–7.4
Net Debtor Economies by Debt-Servicing Experience											
Economies with Arrears and/or Rescheduling during 2017–21	–17.5	–27.4	–27.3	–21.7	–16.7	–16.7	–13.3	–11.9	–13.0	–16.0	–10.8
Memorandum											
World	**1.7**	**1.0**	**1.3**	**2.0**	**1.3**	**1.5**	**1.5**	**2.4**	**0.7**	**1.0**	**0.3**
European Union	6.3	6.9	7.2	7.0	6.4	6.0	5.8	6.6	2.1	2.8	4.6
Middle East and North Africa	13.9	–10.1	–11.0	–2.0	8.4	2.4	–8.8	9.0	21.2	17.3	5.7
Emerging Market and Middle-Income Economies	2.7	0.1	–0.8	0.1	–0.1	0.6	2.8	4.1	6.0	5.0	–0.2
Low-Income Developing Countries	–8.1	–15.6	–8.4	–5.9	–8.6	–8.4	–8.1	–10.1	–10.7	–10.0	–7.2

[1]Excludes the Group of Seven (Canada, France, Germany, Italy, Japan, United Kingdom, United States) and euro area countries.

Table A11. Advanced Economies: Current Account Balance
(Percent of GDP)

	2014	2015	2016	2017	2018	2019	2020	2021	Projections 2022	2023	2027
Advanced Economies	**0.5**	**0.6**	**0.8**	**1.0**	**0.8**	**0.7**	**0.4**	**0.6**	**–0.6**	**–0.3**	**0.3**
United States	–2.1	–2.2	–2.1	–1.9	–2.1	–2.1	–3.0	–3.7	–3.9	–3.1	–2.3
Euro Area[1]	2.3	2.7	3.0	3.2	2.9	2.3	1.9	2.5	1.0	1.4	2.5
Germany	7.2	8.6	8.5	7.8	8.0	7.6	7.0	7.4	4.2	5.3	6.1
France	–1.0	–0.4	–0.5	–0.8	–0.8	0.5	–1.8	0.4	–1.3	–1.5	–0.3
Italy	1.9	1.4	2.6	2.6	2.5	3.2	3.7	2.4	–0.2	0.3	2.5
Spain	1.7	2.0	3.2	2.8	1.9	2.1	0.8	0.9	–0.2	–0.2	1.5
The Netherlands	8.2	6.3	8.1	10.8	10.8	9.0	7.1	9.0	7.5	7.7	7.2
Belgium	0.8	1.4	0.6	0.7	–0.8	0.2	0.8	–0.4	–2.2	–0.9	0.7
Ireland	1.1	4.4	–4.2	0.5	4.9	–19.8	–6.8	14.2	12.2	9.8	7.1
Austria	2.5	1.7	2.7	1.4	0.9	2.1	1.9	–0.5	–2.6	–2.1	1.8
Portugal	0.2	0.2	1.2	1.3	0.6	0.4	–1.0	–1.2	–1.1	–0.4	–0.3
Greece	–2.4	–1.5	–2.4	–2.6	–3.6	–2.2	–7.3	–6.5	–6.7	–6.3	–3.9
Finland	–1.3	–0.9	–2.0	–0.8	–1.8	–0.3	0.6	0.9	–0.8	–0.2	–0.5
Slovak Republic	1.1	–2.1	–2.7	–1.9	–2.2	–3.4	0.3	–2.0	–3.7	–2.9	0.0
Lithuania	3.2	–2.8	–0.8	0.6	0.3	3.5	7.3	1.4	–1.6	–2.1	0.0
Slovenia	5.1	3.8	4.8	6.2	6.0	5.9	7.6	3.8	–0.1	0.4	0.6
Luxembourg	4.9	4.8	4.8	4.7	4.7	4.6	4.1	4.8	4.3	4.4	4.6
Latvia	–1.6	–0.6	1.6	1.3	–0.2	–0.7	2.9	–2.9	–3.3	–3.0	–1.0
Estonia	0.7	1.8	1.2	2.3	0.8	2.5	–0.3	–1.6	–0.2	0.1	0.6
Cyprus	–4.1	–0.4	–4.2	–5.1	–4.0	–5.7	–10.1	–7.2	–8.5	–7.2	–6.7
Malta	8.5	2.7	–0.6	5.9	6.4	5.0	–2.9	–4.9	–3.1	–2.2	2.0
Japan	0.8	3.1	4.0	4.1	3.5	3.4	2.9	2.9	1.4	2.2	3.2
United Kingdom	–5.1	–5.2	–5.3	–3.6	–3.9	–2.7	–2.5	–2.6	–4.8	–4.5	–3.5
Korea	5.6	7.2	6.5	4.6	4.5	3.6	4.6	4.9	3.2	3.5	4.4
Canada	–2.3	–3.5	–3.1	–2.8	–2.4	–2.0	–1.8	0.0	0.5	–0.2	–1.9
Taiwan Province of China	11.3	13.6	13.1	14.1	11.6	10.6	14.2	14.8	14.8	12.7	9.9
Australia	–3.0	–4.6	–3.3	–2.6	–2.2	0.4	2.4	3.1	2.1	0.7	–0.5
Switzerland	7.6	9.6	8.1	6.3	6.2	5.5	2.9	9.4	6.2	6.4	7.0
Sweden	4.2	3.3	2.4	3.0	2.7	5.5	5.9	5.4	3.8	3.5	3.2
Singapore	18.0	18.7	17.6	17.3	15.2	14.5	16.8	18.1	12.8	12.5	11.5
Hong Kong SAR	1.4	3.3	4.0	4.6	3.7	5.9	7.0	11.3	8.6	5.9	3.6
Czech Republic	0.2	0.4	1.8	1.5	0.4	0.3	2.0	–0.9	–4.3	–2.2	1.0
Israel	4.1	5.1	3.5	3.5	2.8	3.3	5.3	4.2	2.5	3.7	3.3
Norway	10.8	8.0	4.5	5.5	8.0	2.9	1.1	15.0	19.4	14.5	6.3
Denmark	8.9	8.2	7.8	8.0	7.3	8.5	8.0	8.8	8.2	7.4	7.2
New Zealand	–3.1	–2.8	–2.0	–2.8	–4.2	–2.9	–0.8	–6.0	–7.7	–6.0	–5.3
Puerto Rico	. . .	. . .	. . .	. . .	. . .	. . .	. . .	. . .	. . .	. . .	. . .
Macao SAR	32.7	23.3	26.5	30.8	33.0	33.8	15.2	13.8	–2.4	22.8	31.0
Iceland	4.4	5.6	8.1	4.2	4.1	6.5	1.9	–1.6	–2.0	–0.3	0.3
Andorra	. . .	. . .	. . .	. . .	. . .	18.0	14.6	15.9	16.7	17.3	19.1
San Marino	. . .	. . .	. . .	–0.4	–1.9	2.0	2.8	4.0	1.4	0.8	0.8
Memorandum											
Major Advanced Economies	–0.7	–0.5	–0.2	0.0	–0.2	0.0	–0.7	–1.0	–2.2	–1.6	–0.7
Euro Area[2]	3.0	3.4	3.6	3.6	3.5	3.1	2.7	3.7	1.5	1.9	3.1

[1]Data corrected for reporting discrepancies in intra-area transactions.
[2]Data calculated as the sum of the balances of individual euro area countries.

Table A12. Emerging Market and Developing Economies: Current Account Balance
(Percent of GDP)

									Projections		
	2014	2015	2016	2017	2018	2019	2020	2021	2022	2023	2027
Emerging and Developing Asia	**1.5**	**1.9**	**1.3**	**0.9**	**–0.3**	**0.5**	**1.5**	**1.0**	**0.7**	**0.6**	**–0.1**
Bangladesh	0.7	1.2	1.6	–0.5	–3.0	–1.3	–1.5	–1.1	–4.1	–3.8	–3.2
Bhutan	–27.1	–29.1	–30.1	–22.7	–18.4	–20.5	–15.8	–12.1	–24.5	–18.1	–3.7
Brunei Darussalam	30.7	16.7	12.9	16.4	6.9	6.6	4.3	4.6	11.2	9.7	13.6
Cambodia	–8.6	–8.7	–8.5	–7.9	–11.8	–15.0	–8.7	–47.9	–31.3	–17.0	–8.1
China	2.2	2.6	1.7	1.5	0.2	0.7	1.7	1.8	1.8	1.5	0.6
Fiji	–5.5	–4.3	–3.5	–6.6	–8.4	–12.6	–12.7	–13.7	–13.6	–13.6	–10.5
India	–1.3	–1.0	–0.6	–1.8	–2.1	–0.9	0.9	–1.2	–3.5	–2.9	–2.6
Indonesia	–3.1	–2.0	–1.8	–1.6	–2.9	–2.7	–0.4	0.3	2.2	1.1	–1.9
Kiribati	31.5	33.0	10.8	37.4	38.8	48.8	39.1	16.6	6.3	8.3	10.5
Lao P.D.R.	–23.3	–22.3	–11.0	–11.1	–13.0	–9.1	–4.5	–0.2	–2.5	–5.9	–7.9
Malaysia	4.3	3.0	2.4	2.8	2.2	3.5	4.2	3.8	1.6	2.2	2.0
Maldives	–3.7	–7.5	–23.6	–21.6	–28.4	–26.6	–35.5	–8.8	–15.0	–12.3	–6.9
Marshall Islands	2.0	15.6	13.5	5.0	4.0	–25.9	16.2	3.2	–4.0	–2.7	–3.9
Micronesia	6.1	4.5	7.2	10.3	21.0	14.5	3.7	1.0	0.4	–0.9	–5.5
Mongolia	–15.8	–8.2	–6.3	–10.1	–16.7	–15.2	–5.1	–12.8	–20.3	–17.5	–10.0
Myanmar	–4.5	–3.5	–4.2	–6.8	–4.7	–2.8	–3.4	–1.4	–1.7	–1.3	–1.9
Nauru	27.3	–19.1	4.1	12.3	8.0	4.9	2.8	4.1	–2.2	0.1	–0.1
Nepal	4.0	4.4	5.5	–0.3	–7.1	–6.9	–1.0	–7.9	–12.1	–6.3	–3.5
Palau	–19.4	–8.9	–13.4	–22.8	–19.4	–34.6	–41.7	–28.5	–43.2	–34.1	–15.4
Papua New Guinea	14.2	24.6	28.4	28.5	24.4	22.0	20.2	22.9	22.0	19.8	16.9
Philippines	3.6	2.4	–0.4	–0.7	–2.6	–0.8	3.2	–1.8	–4.4	–3.3	–1.8
Samoa	–8.6	–2.6	–4.2	–1.8	0.8	2.8	0.2	–14.5	–8.4	–7.4	–2.0
Solomon Islands	–3.8	–2.7	–3.5	–4.3	–3.0	–9.5	–1.6	–4.8	–10.1	–13.1	–9.4
Sri Lanka	–2.4	–2.2	–2.0	–2.4	–3.0	–2.1	–1.4	–3.8	–3.4	–2.0	–1.2
Thailand	2.9	6.9	10.5	9.6	5.6	7.0	4.2	–2.2	–0.5	1.9	3.3
Timor-Leste	75.6	12.8	–33.0	–17.5	–12.1	6.5	–16.2	1.8	–11.6	–39.4	–41.5
Tonga	–6.3	–10.1	–6.5	–6.4	–6.3	–0.9	–4.0	3.1	–6.0	–28.5	–10.9
Tuvalu	–3.7	–70.6	13.9	11.5	53.9	–16.9	–7.9	2.1	–5.9	0.5	–9.6
Vanuatu	7.8	0.3	3.4	–4.4	12.2	13.6	2.7	2.1	–9.0	–1.7	0.3
Vietnam	3.7	–0.9	0.2	–0.6	1.9	3.7	4.4	–2.0	0.3	1.0	0.6
Emerging and Developing Europe	**–0.3**	**1.0**	**–0.3**	**–0.5**	**1.7**	**1.3**	**0.0**	**1.7**	**2.9**	**2.8**	**–0.2**
Albania[1]	–10.8	–8.6	–7.6	–7.5	–6.8	–7.6	–8.7	–7.7	–8.6	–8.0	–7.4
Belarus	–6.6	–3.3	–3.4	–1.7	0.0	–1.9	–0.4	2.7	–1.5	–1.1	–0.2
Bosnia and Herzegovina	–7.4	–5.1	–4.8	–4.8	–3.3	–2.8	–3.8	–2.1	–4.3	–3.7	–3.2
Bulgaria	1.2	0.0	3.1	3.3	0.9	1.9	–0.1	–0.4	–0.9	–1.4	–0.1
Croatia	0.3	3.4	2.3	3.5	1.9	3.0	–0.1	3.4	2.2	2.0	2.5
Hungary	1.2	2.3	4.5	2.0	0.2	–0.7	–1.1	–3.2	–6.7	–3.0	0.7
Kosovo	–7.2	–8.8	–8.0	–5.5	–7.6	–5.7	–7.0	–8.8	–10.9	–8.7	–6.0
Moldova	–6.0	–6.0	–3.6	–5.8	–10.8	–9.5	–7.7	–11.6	–12.8	–12.4	–8.5
Montenegro	–12.4	–11.0	–16.2	–16.1	–17.0	–14.3	–26.0	–9.2	–13.8	–14.0	–12.9
North Macedonia	–0.5	–2.0	–2.9	–1.0	–0.1	–3.3	–3.4	–3.5	–6.7	–4.6	–3.9
Poland	–2.6	–0.9	–0.8	–0.4	–1.3	0.5	2.9	–0.7	–4.0	–3.3	–2.0
Romania	–0.3	–0.8	–1.6	–3.1	–4.6	–4.9	–5.0	–7.0	–8.4	–8.0	–6.1
Russia	2.8	5.0	1.9	2.0	7.0	3.9	2.4	6.9	12.2	11.1	3.3
Serbia	–5.6	–3.5	–2.9	–5.2	–4.8	–6.9	–4.1	–4.4	–8.4	–7.0	–4.8
Türkiye	–4.1	–3.2	–3.1	–4.8	–2.8	0.7	–4.9	–1.7	–5.7	–3.9	–2.6
Ukraine[1]	–3.9	1.7	–1.5	–2.2	–3.3	–2.7	3.3	–1.6	. . .	. . .	. . .
Latin America and the Caribbean	**–3.2**	**–3.4**	**–2.1**	**–1.7**	**–2.7**	**–2.0**	**–0.2**	**–1.6**	**–1.7**	**–1.4**	**–1.4**
Antigua and Barbuda	0.3	2.2	–2.5	–8.0	–14.5	–7.5	–18.4	–15.0	–19.0	–14.7	–11.2
Argentina	–1.6	–2.7	–2.7	–4.8	–5.2	–0.8	0.8	1.4	–0.3	0.6	0.5
Aruba	–4.8	3.9	4.6	1.0	–0.5	2.6	–13.0	1.4	2.9	3.3	0.6
The Bahamas	–19.6	–12.5	–12.4	–13.4	–9.4	–2.6	–24.5	–23.1	–18.2	–14.1	–7.7
Barbados	–9.2	–6.1	–4.3	–3.8	–4.0	–3.1	–6.9	–11.5	–10.0	–8.7	–4.3
Belize	–6.4	–7.9	–7.3	–7.0	–6.6	–7.8	–6.3	–6.7	–7.3	–7.1	–6.8
Bolivia	1.7	–5.8	–5.6	–5.0	–4.3	–3.3	–0.7	2.0	–1.4	–2.1	–3.6
Brazil	–4.1	–3.0	–1.4	–1.1	–2.7	–3.5	–1.7	–1.7	–1.5	–1.6	–2.0
Chile	–3.5	–2.8	–2.6	–2.8	–4.5	–5.2	–1.7	–6.7	–6.7	–4.4	–2.5
Colombia	–5.2	–6.4	–4.5	–3.2	–4.2	–4.6	–3.4	–5.7	–5.1	–4.4	–4.0

Table A12. Emerging Market and Developing Economies: Current Account Balance *(continued)*
(Percent of GDP)

	2014	2015	2016	2017	2018	2019	2020	2021	Projections 2022	2023	2027
Latin America and the Caribbean (continued)	**–3.2**	**–3.4**	**–2.1**	**–1.7**	**–2.7**	**–2.0**	**–0.2**	**–1.6**	**–1.7**	**–1.4**	**–1.4**
Costa Rica	–4.7	–3.4	–2.1	–3.6	–3.0	–1.3	–1.0	–3.3	–4.8	–4.4	–3.0
Dominica	–5.4	–4.7	–7.7	–8.9	–43.7	–34.4	–29.3	–32.5	–30.6	–28.1	–12.1
Dominican Republic	–3.2	–1.8	–1.1	–0.2	–1.5	–1.3	–1.7	–2.8	–3.3	–2.7	–2.9
Ecuador	–0.7	–2.2	1.1	–0.2	–1.2	–0.1	2.7	2.9	2.4	2.1	1.9
El Salvador	–5.4	–3.2	–2.3	–1.9	–3.3	–0.4	0.8	–5.1	–8.9	–3.9	–4.8
Grenada	–11.6	–12.5	–11.0	–14.4	–16.1	–14.6	–21.0	–24.2	–24.5	–19.8	–11.6
Guatemala	–3.3	–1.2	1.0	1.2	0.9	2.4	4.9	2.5	1.1	0.8	0.6
Guyana	–6.7	–3.4	1.5	–4.9	–29.0	–53.3	–16.4	–25.5	43.5	30.4	26.6
Haiti	–7.3	–5.1	–1.8	–2.2	–2.9	–1.1	1.1	0.5	0.8	–0.5	–1.2
Honduras[1]	–6.9	–4.7	–3.1	–1.2	–6.6	–2.6	2.8	–4.3	–4.6	–4.3	–3.5
Jamaica	–8.0	–3.0	–0.3	–2.7	–1.6	–2.2	–0.4	0.9	–6.0	–5.2	–2.2
Mexico	–1.9	–2.6	–2.2	–1.7	–2.0	–0.3	2.5	–0.4	–1.2	–1.2	–0.9
Nicaragua	–8.0	–9.9	–8.5	–7.2	–1.8	6.0	3.9	–2.3	–3.2	–2.8	–3.2
Panama	–13.4	–9.0	–7.8	–6.0	–7.6	–5.0	2.0	–2.2	–3.7	–3.3	–2.5
Paraguay	–0.1	–0.2	4.3	3.0	–0.2	–0.5	2.7	0.8	–3.8	–0.1	0.3
Peru	–4.5	–5.0	–2.6	–1.3	–1.7	–1.0	0.8	–2.5	–3.0	–2.1	–1.4
St. Kitts and Nevis	0.3	–8.3	–12.3	–10.5	–5.5	–2.2	–8.0	–5.0	–5.3	–4.0	–1.5
St. Lucia	–2.5	–0.7	–6.5	–2.0	1.4	5.7	–15.7	–11.0	–6.0	–0.1	0.5
St. Vincent and the Grenadines	–24.7	–14.7	–12.7	–11.7	–10.2	–3.1	–15.1	–22.6	–26.5	–27.6	–9.0
Suriname	–7.4	–15.3	–4.8	1.9	–3.0	–11.3	9.1	5.8	–2.0	–0.9	–1.2
Trinidad and Tobago	15.0	8.2	–3.5	6.1	6.8	4.3	–6.3	10.4	14.3	15.9	12.9
Uruguay	–3.0	–0.3	0.8	0.0	–0.4	1.6	–0.8	–1.8	–1.2	–1.9	–1.9
Venezuela	2.3	–12.8	–3.4	7.5	8.4	6.6	–8.0	–2.1	4.0	6.0	. . .
Middle East and Central Asia	**4.9**	**–3.9**	**–4.1**	**–1.1**	**2.8**	**0.4**	**–2.5**	**2.3**	**6.5**	**5.2**	**1.2**
Afghanistan[1]	6.5	3.7	9.0	7.6	12.2	11.7	11.2	. . .	. . .	. . .	. . .
Algeria	–4.4	–16.4	–16.5	–13.1	–9.6	–9.9	–12.9	–2.8	6.2	0.6	–3.8
Armenia	–7.8	–2.7	–1.0	–1.5	–7.0	–7.4	–3.8	–3.7	–5.5	–5.1	–4.9
Azerbaijan	13.9	–0.4	–3.6	4.1	12.8	9.1	–0.5	15.2	31.7	31.4	9.6
Bahrain	4.6	–2.4	–4.6	–4.1	–6.4	–2.1	–9.3	6.7	8.6	5.0	0.9
Djibouti	24.0	29.5	–1.0	–4.8	14.7	18.3	11.3	–0.7	–4.8	–3.2	1.7
Egypt	–0.9	–3.6	–5.7	–5.8	–2.3	–3.4	–2.9	–4.4	–3.6	–3.4	–1.6
Georgia	–10.1	–11.8	–12.5	–8.0	–6.8	–5.8	–12.5	–10.1	–7.2	–6.8	–5.3
Iran	2.9	0.3	2.9	3.1	5.1	–0.3	–0.1	0.7	1.6	1.5	0.3
Iraq	2.6	–6.4	–7.4	–4.7	3.0	0.4	–10.8	7.8	16.3	13.0	3.9
Jordan	–7.1	–9.0	–9.7	–10.6	–6.9	–1.7	–5.7	–8.8	–6.7	–4.8	–4.0
Kazakhstan	2.8	–3.3	–5.9	–3.1	–0.1	–4.0	–3.8	–2.9	3.0	1.8	–1.8
Kuwait	33.4	3.5	–4.6	8.0	14.4	12.5	3.2	16.3	29.1	23.0	16.1
Kyrgyz Republic	–17.0	–15.9	–11.6	–6.2	–12.1	–11.9	4.8	–8.7	–12.5	–9.6	–5.8
Lebanon[1]	–28.9	–19.9	–23.5	–26.4	–28.6	–28.2	–15.8	. . .	. . .	. . .	. . .
Libya[1]	–33.1	–18.9	–9.4	6.6	14.7	6.7	–8.5	18.1	16.6	24.5	10.6
Mauritania	–22.2	–15.5	–11.0	–10.0	–13.1	–10.3	–6.7	–9.4	–11.6	–9.1	–4.8
Morocco	–5.5	–2.0	–3.8	–3.2	–4.9	–3.4	–1.2	–2.3	–4.3	–4.1	–3.1
Oman	4.5	–13.9	–16.7	–13.4	–4.2	–4.5	–17.0	–6.1	6.2	3.6	1.5
Pakistan[1]	–1.1	–0.9	–1.6	–3.6	–5.4	–4.2	–1.5	–0.8	–4.6	–2.5	–2.4
Qatar	24.0	8.5	–5.5	4.0	9.1	2.4	–2.0	14.7	21.2	22.1	8.2
Saudi Arabia	9.8	–8.7	–3.7	1.5	8.8	4.8	–3.2	5.3	16.0	12.3	3.5
Somalia	–6.6	–6.3	–7.1	–7.8	–6.2	–10.4	–10.8	–17.1	–15.8	–14.1	–15.2
Sudan	–5.8	–8.5	–6.5	–9.4	–14.0	–15.6	–17.5	–7.4	–6.4	–7.5	–7.8
Syria[2]	. . .	. . .	. . .	. . .	. . .	. . .	. . .	. . .	. . .	. . .	. . .
Tajikistan	–3.4	–6.1	–4.2	2.1	–4.9	–2.2	4.1	8.4	3.8	0.0	–2.8
Tunisia	–9.3	–9.1	–8.8	–9.7	–10.4	–7.8	–5.9	–6.1	–9.1	–8.0	–5.2
Turkmenistan	–7.8	–17.3	–23.1	–11.1	4.9	2.8	–3.3	0.6	2.5	2.5	–1.6
United Arab Emirates	13.5	4.9	3.7	7.1	9.8	8.9	5.9	11.4	14.7	12.5	6.4
Uzbekistan	2.6	1.0	0.2	2.4	–6.8	–5.6	–5.0	–7.0	–3.3	–4.2	–5.0
West Bank and Gaza	–13.6	–13.9	–13.9	–13.2	–13.2	–10.4	–12.3	–8.2	–10.7	–8.9	–11.1
Yemen	–0.7	–6.2	–4.4	–1.4	–1.3	–3.8	–5.9	–5.1	–11.4	–8.2	0.0

Table A12. Emerging Market and Developing Economies: Current Account Balance *(continued)*
(Percent of GDP)

	2014	2015	2016	2017	2018	2019	2020	2021	Projections 2022	2023	2027
Sub-Saharan Africa	**–3.6**	**–5.7**	**–3.6**	**–2.1**	**–2.3**	**–3.3**	**–2.9**	**–1.1**	**–1.7**	**–2.5**	**–2.0**
Angola	–2.6	–8.8	–3.1	–0.5	7.3	6.1	1.5	11.2	11.3	5.4	–0.3
Benin	–6.7	–6.0	–3.0	–4.2	–4.6	–4.0	–1.7	–4.4	–6.0	–5.6	–5.5
Botswana	11.1	2.2	8.0	5.6	0.4	–7.0	–10.8	–0.5	2.0	2.5	4.9
Burkina Faso	–7.2	–7.6	–6.1	–5.0	–4.1	–3.3	4.3	0.2	–3.5	–3.4	–1.7
Burundi	–15.6	–11.5	–11.1	–11.7	–11.4	–11.6	–10.2	–13.4	–14.9	–14.1	–10.3
Cabo Verde	–9.1	–3.2	–3.8	–7.8	–4.9	0.2	–15.0	–11.2	–14.0	–6.2	–4.0
Cameroon	–3.9	–3.6	–3.1	–2.6	–3.5	–4.3	–3.7	–4.0	–2.3	–2.8	–3.0
Central African Republic	–13.3	–9.2	–5.5	–8.0	–7.9	–5.1	–8.6	–10.8	–14.1	–7.5	–5.6
Chad	–8.9	–13.8	–10.4	–7.1	–1.4	–4.4	–7.6	–4.5	0.8	–2.4	–6.7
Comoros	–3.8	–0.3	–4.4	–2.1	–2.9	–3.9	–3.0	–2.4	–10.5	–9.1	–5.5
Democratic Republic of the Congo	–4.8	–3.9	–4.1	–3.3	–3.5	–3.2	–2.2	–0.9	0.0	0.0	0.7
Republic of Congo	1.0	–39.0	–48.7	–6.0	–0.2	0.4	–0.1	12.6	19.1	11.1	1.5
Côte d'Ivoire	1.0	–0.4	–0.9	–2.0	–3.9	–2.3	–3.2	–3.8	–5.2	–5.0	–3.6
Equatorial Guinea	–4.3	–17.7	–26.0	–7.8	–2.1	–0.9	–4.2	–3.4	–1.6	–2.1	–7.0
Eritrea	17.7	22.4	13.4	24.8	15.7	13.1	14.6	13.5	12.2	10.8	9.3
Eswatini	11.6	13.0	7.9	6.2	1.3	3.8	6.7	2.5	–0.8	0.1	1.3
Ethiopia	–7.9	–11.5	–10.9	–8.5	–6.5	–5.3	–4.6	–3.2	–4.3	–4.4	–3.3
Gabon	7.6	–5.6	–11.1	–8.7	–4.8	–5.0	–6.9	–5.7	–1.4	–2.9	–2.7
The Gambia	–7.3	–9.9	–9.2	–7.4	–9.5	–6.2	–2.9	–8.1	–13.7	–11.7	–8.6
Ghana	–6.8	–5.7	–5.1	–3.3	–3.0	–2.7	–3.0	–3.2	–5.2	–4.4	–3.7
Guinea	–14.4	–12.5	–30.7	–6.7	–19.2	–11.5	–13.6	–1.3	–7.0	–8.0	–1.4
Guinea-Bissau	0.5	1.8	1.4	0.3	–3.5	–8.5	–2.7	–3.2	–6.5	–4.7	–4.0
Kenya	–9.3	–6.3	–5.4	–7.0	–5.4	–5.2	–4.7	–5.2	–5.9	–5.6	–5.0
Lesotho	–5.2	–4.2	–7.8	–4.2	–3.5	–1.7	–1.6	–5.0	–8.5	–8.7	–5.6
Liberia	–34.3	–28.5	–23.0	–22.3	–21.3	–19.6	–16.4	–17.7	–16.3	–16.5	–15.8
Madagascar	–0.3	–1.6	0.5	–0.4	0.7	–2.3	–5.4	–4.9	–5.4	–5.1	–3.2
Malawi	–7.0	–12.2	–13.1	–15.5	–12.0	–12.6	–13.8	–12.2	–12.1	–12.9	–10.5
Mali	–4.7	–5.3	–7.2	–7.3	–4.9	–7.5	–2.2	–10.0	–7.9	–7.1	–5.8
Mauritius	–5.4	–3.6	–4.0	–4.6	–3.9	–5.1	–9.2	–13.6	–13.0	–8.1	–5.0
Mozambique	–36.3	–37.4	–32.2	–19.6	–30.3	–19.1	–27.3	–22.9	–45.9	–39.6	–10.9
Namibia	–9.4	–13.6	–16.5	–4.4	–3.5	–1.7	2.6	–9.1	–8.0	–4.2	–3.4
Niger	–12.1	–15.3	–11.4	–11.4	–12.6	–12.2	–13.5	–13.8	–15.6	–13.9	–8.0
Nigeria	0.2	–3.1	1.3	3.4	1.5	–3.3	–4.0	–0.4	–0.2	–0.6	–0.2
Rwanda	–11.3	–12.7	–15.3	–9.5	–10.1	–11.9	–12.1	–10.9	–12.6	–11.7	–7.3
São Tomé and Príncipe	–20.7	–12.0	–6.1	–13.2	–12.3	–12.1	–11.0	–11.3	–13.9	–11.0	–7.2
Senegal	–7.0	–5.7	–4.2	–7.3	–8.8	–7.9	–10.9	–13.2	–13.0	–9.5	–5.0
Seychelles	–22.4	–18.1	–19.7	–19.1	–2.6	–3.2	–13.7	–10.5	–6.6	–7.7	–8.2
Sierra Leone	–9.4	–23.6	–7.6	–18.3	–12.4	–14.3	–6.8	–14.9	–8.5	–7.7	–6.0
South Africa	–4.8	–4.3	–2.7	–2.4	–2.9	–2.6	2.0	3.7	1.2	–1.0	–2.0
South Sudan	–1.2	1.7	16.8	4.8	7.3	1.5	–13.8	–2.7	8.6	2.1	–1.9
Tanzania	–9.8	–7.7	–4.2	–2.6	–3.1	–2.6	–1.8	–3.3	–4.4	–3.9	–2.6
Togo	–6.8	–7.6	–7.2	–1.5	–2.6	–0.8	–0.3	–1.9	–4.8	–5.7	–1.5
Uganda	–6.5	–6.0	–2.8	–4.8	–6.1	–6.6	–9.5	–8.3	–8.0	–10.2	–7.3
Zambia	2.1	–2.7	–3.3	–1.7	–1.3	1.4	12.0	7.6	–1.8	–3.7	3.8
Zimbabwe[1]	–12.0	–8.0	–3.4	–1.3	–3.7	4.0	2.9	1.1	0.6	0.3	0.5

[1]See the country-specific notes for Afghanistan, Albania, Honduras, Lebanon, Libya, Pakistan, Ukraine, and Zimbabwe in the "Country Notes" section of the Statistical Appendix.
[2]Data for Syria are excluded for 2011 onward owing to the uncertain political situation.

Table A13. Summary of Financial Account Balances

(Billions of US dollars)

	2014	2015	2016	2017	2018	2019	2020	2021	Projections 2022	Projections 2023
Advanced Economies										
Financial Account Balance	304.5	282.5	433.4	433.4	480.2	155.9	29.7	465.8	–307.8	–116.3
Direct Investment, Net	244.1	3.2	–246.5	355.4	–53.0	4.3	49.8	501.8	250.4	81.3
Portfolio Investment, Net	57.8	164.1	486.8	–10.1	506.7	57.3	183.2	288.5	–285.6	–198.9
Financial Derivatives, Net	1.8	–85.6	32.4	21.5	51.7	25.7	89.0	50.5	48.7	52.1
Other Investment, Net	–139.1	–25.6	–18.0	–178.6	–153.0	1.6	–650.0	–1,003.3	–342.8	–141.1
Change in Reserves	140.0	226.6	178.5	244.8	127.9	66.9	357.8	627.7	21.0	89.7
United States										
Financial Account Balance	–298.1	–386.4	–362.4	–373.2	–302.9	–565.5	–697.0	–740.6	–973.0	–825.2
Direct Investment, Net	135.7	–209.4	–174.6	28.6	–345.4	–209.1	122.9	–26.6	–47.3	–98.0
Portfolio Investment, Net	–115.9	–106.8	–193.8	–250.1	78.8	–244.9	–540.2	43.0	–245.7	–228.4
Financial Derivatives, Net	–54.3	–27.0	7.8	24.0	–20.4	–41.7	–5.1	–41.9	–6.4	–16.8
Other Investment, Net	–259.9	–37.0	–4.0	–174.1	–20.8	–74.5	–283.5	–829.1	–674.5	–482.0
Change in Reserves	–3.6	–6.3	2.1	–1.7	5.0	4.7	9.0	114.0	0.9	0.0
Euro Area										
Financial Account Balance	372.6	338.5	313.2	392.8	330.3	273.6	222.2	404.7	. . .	. . .
Direct Investment, Net	89.3	244.3	150.8	74.1	121.2	96.4	–229.2	345.6	. . .	. . .
Portfolio Investment, Net	87.0	133.5	529.8	402.6	272.6	–117.5	614.4	505.7	. . .	. . .
Financial Derivatives, Net	49.7	126.5	11.2	12.9	46.7	8.6	33.9	82.5	. . .	. . .
Other Investment, Net	142.2	–177.4	–395.7	–95.5	–140.0	279.3	–211.8	–683.1	. . .	. . .
Change in Reserves	4.4	11.6	17.1	–1.2	29.8	6.7	14.9	154.1	. . .	. . .
Germany										
Financial Account Balance	319.3	260.1	289.0	312.5	291.7	208.6	247.1	372.5	168.7	216.6
Direct Investment, Net	87.3	68.5	48.0	37.9	25.1	84.6	–4.0	120.5	65.9	59.9
Portfolio Investment, Net	179.9	210.5	220.0	229.6	181.2	78.0	48.9	301.9	86.4	119.0
Financial Derivatives, Net	51.2	33.7	31.7	12.6	26.8	27.5	109.9	72.2	2.9	29.1
Other Investment, Net	4.3	–50.2	–12.5	33.9	58.2	19.1	92.3	–159.8	13.5	8.6
Change in Reserves	–3.4	–2.5	1.9	–1.4	0.5	–0.6	–0.1	37.7	0.0	0.0
France										
Financial Account Balance	–10.3	–0.8	–18.6	–36.1	–28.4	–0.1	–61.9	3.6	–32.9	–40.2
Direct Investment, Net	47.2	7.9	41.8	11.1	60.2	30.7	6.3	–11.5	10.5	21.4
Portfolio Investment, Net	–23.8	43.2	0.2	30.3	19.3	–70.4	–37.8	–6.3	–25.7	–24.7
Financial Derivatives, Net	–31.8	14.5	–17.6	–1.4	–30.5	4.1	–27.2	21.0	6.8	0.3
Other Investment, Net	–2.9	–74.2	–45.4	–72.7	–89.7	32.3	–7.8	–26.7	–26.6	–40.7
Change in Reserves	1.0	8.0	2.5	–3.4	12.3	3.2	4.6	27.0	2.1	3.5
Italy										
Financial Account Balance	78.4	42.9	37.4	61.2	38.8	60.8	71.5	30.4	9.1	22.9
Direct Investment, Net	3.1	2.0	–12.3	0.5	–6.1	1.6	21.7	3.3	0.3	0.8
Portfolio Investment, Net	3.2	111.7	157.1	102.0	156.5	–58.0	123.8	146.6	–32.6	–15.8
Financial Derivatives, Net	–1.9	1.3	–3.6	–8.4	–3.3	2.9	–3.3	0.0	0.2	0.3
Other Investment, Net	75.2	–72.7	–102.5	–35.9	–111.5	110.6	–75.2	–144.0	41.2	37.6
Change in Reserves	–1.3	0.6	–1.3	3.0	3.1	3.6	4.6	24.5	0.0	0.0
Spain										
Financial Account Balance	22.8	31.8	39.2	40.0	38.3	28.3	20.2	34.1	22.2	19.8
Direct Investment, Net	14.2	33.4	12.4	14.1	–19.9	7.4	22.4	–15.6	4.7	4.8
Portfolio Investment, Net	–8.8	12.0	64.9	37.1	28.1	–53.5	90.9	38.8	15.0	11.6
Financial Derivatives, Net	1.3	4.2	2.8	8.7	–1.2	–8.5	–8.1	5.0	0.0	0.0
Other Investment, Net	10.9	–23.3	–50.1	–24.0	28.7	82.1	–84.6	–6.3	2.5	3.4
Change in Reserves	5.2	5.5	9.1	4.1	2.6	0.8	–0.4	12.2	0.0	0.0

Table A13. Summary of Financial Account Balances *(continued)*
(Billions of US dollars)

									Projections	
	2014	2015	2016	2017	2018	2019	2020	2021	2022	2023
Japan										
Financial Account Balance	58.9	180.9	266.5	168.3	183.9	228.3	129.2	99.3	55.4	91.5
Direct Investment, Net	118.7	133.3	137.5	155.0	134.6	218.9	84.5	122.6	122.8	122.2
Portfolio Investment, Net	–42.3	131.5	276.3	–50.6	92.2	87.4	38.5	–199.2	–68.6	–49.7
Financial Derivatives, Net	34.0	17.7	–16.1	30.4	0.9	3.2	7.8	22.1	22.1	22.1
Other Investment, Net	–60.0	–106.7	–125.6	10.0	–67.9	–106.7	–12.4	91.0	–40.9	–14.5
Change in Reserves	8.5	5.1	–5.7	23.6	24.0	25.5	10.9	62.8	20.0	11.5
United Kingdom										
Financial Account Balance	–141.6	–165.9	–159.9	–84.4	–102.9	–89.7	–56.1	–60.9	–156.7	–161.0
Direct Investment, Net	–176.1	–106.0	–297.4	46.1	–4.9	–51.6	–83.6	80.2	25.6	7.0
Portfolio Investment, Net	16.3	–231.7	–200.1	–120.1	–361.1	38.2	–17.3	–349.4	–173.5	–188.8
Financial Derivatives, Net	31.2	–128.6	29.3	13.3	11.2	11.3	39.0	–39.4	5.6	6.1
Other Investment, Net	–24.7	268.2	299.5	–32.4	227.2	–86.6	9.2	223.4	–14.3	14.8
Change in Reserves	11.7	32.2	8.8	8.8	24.8	–1.1	–3.3	24.4	0.0	0.0
Canada										
Financial Account Balance	–43.1	–51.8	–45.4	–44.2	–35.8	–38.3	–29.3	4.3	11.5	–5.3
Direct Investment, Net	1.3	23.6	33.5	53.4	20.4	29.2	23.4	38.0	36.3	39.7
Portfolio Investment, Net	–32.8	–36.2	–103.6	–74.9	3.4	–1.6	–67.8	–41.6	–29.2	–43.9
Financial Derivatives, Net	...	...	...	...	...	...	...	...	...	...
Other Investment, Net	–16.9	–47.8	19.1	–23.5	–58.2	–66.0	13.8	–12.2	4.4	–1.2
Change in Reserves	5.3	8.6	5.6	0.8	–1.5	0.1	1.3	20.2	0.0	0.0
Other Advanced Economies[1]										
Financial Account Balance	297.2	295.2	325.4	309.4	355.0	337.4	383.1	562.0	496.5	461.1
Direct Investment, Net	–6.1	–102.5	–79.7	–158.3	34.0	–42.5	60.6	–77.5	–88.8	–186.5
Portfolio Investment, Net	174.0	324.7	247.6	151.4	371.6	307.0	278.0	477.9	344.3	371.9
Financial Derivatives, Net	–22.4	–12.0	3.2	–5.6	31.9	20.0	–9.0	–20.7	–8.1	–15.6
Other Investment, Net	40.3	–90.9	3.9	108.4	–132.1	22.5	–269.3	–74.4	258.3	220.6
Change in Reserves	111.5	176.0	150.2	213.1	49.5	30.3	322.8	256.2	–9.8	70.2
Emerging Market and Developing Economies										
Financial Account Balance	–1.8	–313.0	–424.2	–284.3	–258.7	–146.0	57.7	152.2	653.8	522.3
Direct Investment, Net	–433.4	–345.2	–261.6	–311.4	–376.8	–367.0	–327.4	–514.9	–354.5	–351.8
Portfolio Investment, Net	–88.4	124.6	–57.4	–209.3	–102.0	–62.4	4.8	114.6	389.9	47.5
Financial Derivatives, Net	...	...	...	...	...	...	...	...	...	...
Other Investment, Net	408.0	479.5	384.8	62.3	104.1	119.8	275.4	36.0	719.5	467.1
Change in Reserves	94.2	–583.1	–481.1	189.9	127.0	169.0	83.3	523.6	–101.6	363.4

Table A13. Summary of Financial Account Balances *(continued)*
(Billions of US dollars)

	2014	2015	2016	2017	2018	2019	2020	2021	Projections 2022	2023
Regional Groups										
Emerging and Developing Asia										
Financial Account Balance	142.2	61.2	–37.8	–68.9	–270.6	–62.6	145.4	62.2	203.6	176.7
Direct Investment, Net	–201.0	–139.7	–26.2	–108.5	–170.5	–144.7	–164.8	–296.7	–217.8	–156.8
Portfolio Investment, Net	–124.6	81.6	31.1	–70.1	–100.3	–72.9	–107.5	–23.1	208.3	–45.6
Financial Derivatives, Net	0.7	0.7	–4.6	2.3	4.6	–2.6	15.9	18.1	17.8	18.3
Other Investment, Net	281.4	460.6	357.0	–80.3	–16.6	70.9	243.0	117.9	454.3	216.6
Change in Reserves	196.3	–333.0	–384.6	199.2	22.2	97.0	167.4	257.1	–246.6	156.1
Emerging and Developing Europe										
Financial Account Balance	–26.2	68.6	10.5	–23.0	109.9	63.1	11.7	95.7	170.2	150.5
Direct Investment, Net	0.5	–22.0	–45.4	–28.9	–25.4	–53.5	–37.8	–39.6	7.3	–29.4
Portfolio Investment, Net	23.8	53.5	–9.4	–34.5	11.1	–1.6	21.1	39.2	74.1	50.3
Financial Derivatives, Net	5.8	5.0	0.4	–2.5	–2.8	1.4	0.1	–6.2	–2.1	–2.5
Other Investment, Net	66.3	40.1	29.4	26.9	79.5	23.6	32.0	–32.7	160.8	139.0
Change in Reserves	–122.7	–7.9	35.5	16.2	47.6	93.3	–3.2	136.3	–69.6	–6.6
Latin America and the Caribbean										
Financial Account Balance	–196.2	–188.7	–106.5	–108.6	–160.5	–119.8	0.5	–93.3	–98.1	–85.4
Direct Investment, Net	–140.9	–133.4	–124.8	–121.2	–148.6	–114.7	–90.9	–97.8	–106.9	–116.5
Portfolio Investment, Net	–108.2	–50.8	–50.5	–39.3	–14.1	1.7	2.5	–1.7	–1.4	–1.7
Financial Derivatives, Net	6.8	1.4	–2.9	3.9	4.1	4.9	5.7	0.8	3.5	2.5
Other Investment, Net	6.5	22.8	50.6	30.6	–15.8	21.2	66.8	–43.7	–3.8	16.5
Change in Reserves	39.7	–28.8	21.0	17.1	13.8	–32.7	16.4	49.1	10.5	13.8
Middle East and Central Asia										
Financial Account Balance	156.9	–186.2	–225.5	–38.9	103.8	27.7	–78.8	98.4	401.2	326.0
Direct Investment, Net	–43.7	–12.4	–31.0	–15.4	–11.4	–23.5	–23.3	–11.2	–5.3	–8.8
Portfolio Investment, Net	129.3	61.8	–12.1	–41.5	5.8	29.2	86.4	55.5	103.5	40.0
Financial Derivatives, Net	. . .	. . .	. . .	. . .	. . .	. . .	. . .	. . .	. . .	. . .
Other Investment, Net	64.3	–52.6	–42.7	84.5	76.9	15.4	–63.8	6.3	95.3	104.7
Change in Reserves	–10.1	–196.8	–148.3	–58.4	38.6	5.2	–87.7	54.5	213.1	199.2
Sub-Saharan Africa										
Financial Account Balance	–78.5	–68.0	–64.8	–44.9	–41.3	–54.4	–21.1	–10.8	–23.2	–45.5
Direct Investment, Net	–48.2	–37.8	–34.3	–37.4	–20.9	–30.5	–10.6	–69.5	–31.8	–40.3
Portfolio Investment, Net	–8.6	–21.5	–16.6	–24.0	–4.5	–18.7	2.4	44.7	5.5	4.5
Financial Derivatives, Net	–1.5	–0.4	1.0	0.2	–0.5	0.3	0.7	–0.2	–0.3	–0.3
Other Investment, Net	–10.5	8.6	–9.4	0.5	–19.8	–11.3	–2.4	–11.7	13.1	–9.7
Change in Reserves	–9.1	–16.5	–4.6	15.9	4.7	6.2	–9.6	26.6	–9.0	1.0

Table A13. Summary of Financial Account Balances *(continued)*

(Billions of US dollars)

	2014	2015	2016	2017	2018	2019	2020	2021	Projections 2022	Projections 2023
Analytical Groups										
By Source of Export Earnings										
Fuel										
Financial Account Balance	180.0	–182.6	–189.7	12.0	173.9	67.9	–51.5	151.6	484.1	388.7
Direct Investment, Net	–29.5	–11.5	–20.6	11.4	12.1	–8.5	–11.2	1.6	12.9	9.7
Portfolio Investment, Net	137.2	67.7	–9.8	–35.9	7.1	28.0	86.1	71.9	85.8	55.5
Financial Derivatives, Net	. . .	. . .	. . .	. . .	. . .	. . .	. . .	. . .	. . .	. . .
Other Investment, Net	90.6	–18.5	–3.4	111.4	110.7	39.1	–46.7	28.3	154.9	148.4
Change in Reserves	–35.5	–234.4	–164.5	–66.9	49.9	7.8	–89.2	55.8	236.7	184.5
Nonfuel										
Financial Account Balance	–181.8	–130.4	–234.5	–296.3	–432.6	–213.9	109.2	0.7	169.7	133.6
Direct Investment, Net	–403.8	–333.8	–241.0	–322.8	–388.9	–358.5	–316.2	–516.5	–367.4	–361.5
Portfolio Investment, Net	–225.6	56.9	–47.5	–173.4	–109.1	–90.3	–81.3	42.7	304.1	–7.9
Financial Derivatives, Net	11.8	6.8	–6.1	4.0	5.4	4.0	22.3	12.4	19.0	18.2
Other Investment, Net	317.3	498.0	388.2	–49.1	–6.6	80.7	322.2	7.7	564.7	318.7
Change in Reserves	129.7	–348.7	–316.5	256.8	77.0	161.2	172.5	467.9	–338.2	178.9
By External Financing Source										
Net Debtor Economies										
Financial Account Balance	–388.9	–315.7	–277.2	–339.6	–367.9	–300.1	–92.9	–308.6	–413.8	–404.0
Direct Investment, Net	–284.4	–281.3	–292.1	–272.2	–313.3	–301.5	–249.2	–288.9	–298.9	–327.3
Portfolio Investment, Net	–211.3	–52.7	–63.5	–123.8	–35.9	–32.8	–44.2	–19.2	37.8	–36.1
Financial Derivatives, Net	. . .	. . .	. . .	. . .	. . .	. . .	. . .	. . .	. . .	. . .
Other Investment, Net	–11.3	38.5	25.3	–28.9	–14.1	–59.4	49.6	–204.3	–57.9	–94.7
Change in Reserves	120.6	–9.4	77.1	93.2	4.9	105.0	152.5	215.9	–89.3	60.7
Net Debtor Economies by Debt-Servicing Experience										
Economies with Arrears and/or Rescheduling during 2017–21										
Financial Account Balance	–49.9	–66.1	–70.3	–53.1	–46.1	–43.4	–21.1	–29.6	–30.0	–41.4
Direct Investment, Net	–22.9	–35.5	–27.8	–21.6	–25.9	–30.4	–20.1	–27.5	–23.4	–30.9
Portfolio Investment, Net	–6.1	–0.5	–10.3	–30.6	–18.7	–12.6	7.3	–21.6	15.0	–10.8
Financial Derivatives, Net	. . .	. . .	. . .	. . .	. . .	. . .	. . .	. . .	. . .	. . .
Other Investment, Net	–8.1	–26.1	–36.1	–11.0	–6.5	2.6	4.9	6.7	–11.3	–18.5
Change in Reserves	–12.9	–3.8	3.9	10.3	5.2	–3.0	–12.7	13.6	–10.9	18.6
Memorandum										
World										
Financial Account Balance	302.7	–30.5	9.2	149.1	221.5	9.8	87.4	618.0	346.0	405.9

Note: The estimates in this table are based on individual countries' national accounts and balance of payments statistics. Country group composites are calculated as the sum of the US dollar values for the relevant individual countries. Some group aggregates for the financial derivatives are not shown because of incomplete data. Projections for the euro area are not available because of data constraints.

[1]Excludes the Group of Seven (Canada, France, Germany, Italy, Japan, United Kingdom, United States) and euro area countries.

Table A14. Summary of Net Lending and Borrowing
(Percent of GDP)

	Averages								Projections		
											Average
	2004–13	2008–15	2016	2017	2018	2019	2020	2021	2022	2023	2024–27
Advanced Economies											
Net Lending and Borrowing	–0.5	0.0	0.8	1.0	0.7	0.6	0.3	0.7	–0.6	–0.2	0.2
Current Account Balance	–0.5	0.0	0.8	1.0	0.8	0.7	0.4	0.6	–0.6	–0.3	0.2
Savings	21.7	21.5	22.6	23.3	23.4	23.4	23.1	24.3	23.8	23.7	24.0
Investment	22.2	21.5	21.6	22.1	22.4	22.7	22.3	22.7	23.0	22.6	22.6
Capital Account Balance	0.0	0.0	0.0	0.0	–0.1	–0.1	0.0	0.1	0.1	0.1	0.0
United States											
Net Lending and Borrowing	–4.0	–2.8	–2.2	–1.8	–2.2	–2.1	–3.0	–3.7	–4.0	–3.2	–2.5
Current Account Balance	–4.0	–2.8	–2.1	–1.9	–2.1	–2.1	–3.0	–3.7	–3.9	–3.1	–2.5
Savings	16.9	17.2	18.9	19.5	19.6	19.4	19.2	20.1	21.1	21.5	21.9
Investment	20.9	19.8	20.6	20.8	21.1	21.4	21.2	21.4	22.0	21.8	21.8
Capital Account Balance	0.0	0.0	0.0	0.1	0.0	0.0	0.0	0.0	0.0	0.0	0.0
Euro Area											
Net Lending and Borrowing	0.2	0.8	3.1	3.0	2.6	2.1	1.9	2.8	. . .	. . .	. . .
Current Account Balance	0.1	0.7	3.0	3.2	2.9	2.3	1.9	2.5	1.0	1.4	2.3
Savings	22.7	22.5	24.3	24.9	25.4	25.9	25.0	26.6	24.7	24.5	25.0
Investment	21.8	20.8	20.7	21.3	21.9	22.9	22.3	23.0	23.2	22.5	22.2
Capital Account Balance	0.1	0.1	0.0	–0.2	–0.3	–0.2	0.0	0.3	. . .	. . .	. . .
Germany											
Net Lending and Borrowing	5.9	6.6	8.6	7.7	8.0	7.5	6.8	7.3	4.2	5.3	6.2
Current Account Balance	5.9	6.6	8.5	7.8	8.0	7.6	7.0	7.4	4.2	5.3	6.2
Savings	26.2	26.8	28.5	28.8	29.9	29.7	29.1	30.6	26.9	26.6	27.2
Investment	20.3	20.2	20.0	21.0	21.9	22.1	22.1	23.3	22.7	21.3	21.0
Capital Account Balance	0.0	0.0	0.1	–0.1	0.0	0.0	–0.2	0.0	0.0	0.0	0.0
France											
Net Lending and Borrowing	–0.3	–0.7	–0.4	–0.8	–0.7	0.6	–1.7	0.8	–1.2	–1.4	–0.6
Current Account Balance	–0.3	–0.7	–0.5	–0.8	–0.8	0.5	–1.8	0.4	–1.3	–1.5	–0.7
Savings	22.4	21.9	22.1	22.7	23.0	24.9	21.8	24.9	23.6	22.1	22.2
Investment	22.7	22.6	22.6	23.4	23.9	24.4	23.6	24.6	24.9	23.6	22.9
Capital Account Balance	0.0	0.0	0.1	0.0	0.1	0.1	0.1	0.5	0.1	0.1	0.1
Italy											
Net Lending and Borrowing	–1.4	–0.7	2.4	2.7	2.5	3.1	3.7	2.3	0.5	1.1	2.2
Current Account Balance	–1.4	–0.8	2.6	2.6	2.5	3.2	3.7	2.4	–0.2	0.3	1.7
Savings	19.0	18.2	20.0	20.7	21.0	21.4	21.4	22.3	22.4	23.1	23.1
Investment	20.4	18.9	17.6	18.1	18.5	18.2	17.7	20.0	21.9	22.0	20.9
Capital Account Balance	0.1	0.1	–0.2	0.1	0.0	–0.1	0.0	–0.1	0.6	0.9	0.5
Spain											
Net Lending and Borrowing	–4.3	–1.2	3.4	3.0	2.4	2.4	1.2	1.9	1.6	1.4	1.4
Current Account Balance	–4.8	–1.7	3.2	2.8	1.9	2.1	0.8	0.9	–0.2	–0.2	0.8
Savings	20.1	19.2	21.9	22.2	22.4	23.0	21.5	22.4	22.6	21.9	22.3
Investment	24.9	20.9	18.8	19.4	20.5	20.9	20.7	21.5	22.7	22.1	21.5
Capital Account Balance	0.5	0.5	0.2	0.2	0.5	0.3	0.4	0.9	1.8	1.6	0.6
Japan											
Net Lending and Borrowing	2.8	2.1	3.8	4.1	3.5	3.4	2.9	2.8	1.3	2.1	3.0
Current Account Balance	2.9	2.1	4.0	4.1	3.5	3.4	2.9	2.9	1.4	2.2	3.1
Savings	27.6	26.3	28.8	29.3	29.2	29.2	28.2	28.1	27.0	27.6	28.5
Investment	24.7	24.2	24.8	25.2	25.6	25.8	25.3	25.2	25.7	25.5	25.4
Capital Account Balance	–0.1	–0.1	–0.1	–0.1	0.0	–0.1	0.0	–0.1	–0.1	–0.1	–0.1
United Kingdom											
Net Lending and Borrowing	–3.1	–3.9	–5.4	–3.7	–4.0	–2.7	–2.6	–2.7	–4.9	–4.6	–3.8
Current Account Balance	–3.1	–3.8	–5.3	–3.6	–3.9	–2.7	–2.5	–2.6	–4.8	–4.5	–3.7
Savings	13.6	12.5	12.4	14.6	14.0	15.3	14.2	14.5	12.6	12.4	13.5
Investment	16.7	16.4	17.7	18.2	17.9	18.0	16.7	17.1	17.4	16.9	17.2
Capital Account Balance	0.0	–0.1	–0.1	–0.1	–0.1	–0.1	–0.1	–0.1	–0.1	–0.1	–0.1

Table A14. Summary of Net Lending and Borrowing *(continued)*

(Percent of GDP)

	Averages								Projections		
											Average
	2004–13	2008–15	2016	2017	2018	2019	2020	2021	2022	2023	2024–27
Canada											
Net Lending and Borrowing	–0.9	–2.7	–3.1	–2.8	–2.4	–2.0	–1.8	0.0	0.5	–0.2	–1.2
Current Account Balance	–0.9	–2.7	–3.1	–2.8	–2.4	–2.0	–1.8	0.0	0.5	–0.2	–1.2
Savings	22.6	21.3	19.7	20.7	21.0	21.0	20.5	23.8	23.8	22.8	22.6
Investment	23.5	24.0	22.8	23.6	23.4	23.1	22.3	23.7	23.3	23.0	23.8
Capital Account Balance	0.0	0.0	0.0	0.0	0.0	0.0	0.0	0.0	0.0	0.0	0.0
Other Advanced Economies[1]											
Net Lending and Borrowing	4.0	4.2	5.0	4.8	4.6	4.7	5.6	7.1	5.7	5.1	4.6
Current Account Balance	4.0	4.3	5.0	4.7	4.4	4.7	5.5	7.1	5.7	5.1	4.6
Savings	30.5	30.5	30.6	30.9	30.4	30.3	31.6	33.4	32.5	31.8	31.2
Investment	26.3	26.0	25.3	25.9	25.9	25.5	25.9	26.0	26.2	26.2	26.2
Capital Account Balance	0.0	–0.1	0.0	0.1	0.2	0.0	0.1	0.0	0.0	0.0	0.0
Emerging Market and Developing Economies											
Net Lending and Borrowing	2.4	1.2	–0.3	0.0	–0.1	0.1	0.6	0.9	1.3	1.0	0.2
Current Account Balance	2.4	1.1	–0.3	–0.1	–0.2	0.0	0.5	0.8	1.3	1.0	0.2
Savings	32.0	32.5	31.2	31.7	32.4	32.1	33.0	34.0	35.4	35.0	34.4
Investment	29.8	31.5	31.5	31.8	32.7	32.3	32.6	33.3	34.3	34.2	34.3
Capital Account Balance	0.2	0.1	0.1	0.1	0.1	0.1	0.1	0.1	0.1	0.1	0.0
Regional Groups											
Emerging and Developing Asia											
Net Lending and Borrowing	3.3	2.2	1.3	0.9	–0.3	0.5	1.5	1.0	0.7	0.6	0.2
Current Account Balance	3.2	2.2	1.3	0.9	–0.3	0.5	1.5	1.0	0.7	0.6	0.2
Savings	42.0	42.9	39.9	40.1	40.0	39.5	40.1	40.2	41.8	41.4	40.7
Investment	39.0	40.7	38.7	39.2	40.2	39.1	38.6	39.2	41.1	40.8	40.5
Capital Account Balance	0.1	0.0	0.0	0.0	0.0	0.0	0.0	0.0	0.0	0.0	0.0
Emerging and Developing Europe											
Net Lending and Borrowing	–0.4	–0.4	0.1	–0.2	2.2	1.8	0.7	2.2	3.3	3.2	1.1
Current Account Balance	–0.6	–0.7	–0.3	–0.5	1.7	1.3	0.0	1.7	2.9	2.8	0.7
Savings	23.2	23.3	23.5	24.1	25.5	24.2	23.8	25.8	27.0	26.4	25.4
Investment	23.6	23.8	23.7	24.6	23.6	22.9	23.7	24.2	24.1	23.7	24.7
Capital Account Balance	0.1	0.3	0.3	0.3	0.5	0.5	0.7	0.6	0.4	0.4	0.4
Latin America and the Caribbean											
Net Lending and Borrowing	–0.6	–2.1	–2.0	–1.7	–2.6	–2.0	0.0	–1.5	–1.7	–1.3	–1.3
Current Account Balance	–0.7	–2.2	–2.1	–1.7	–2.7	–2.0	–0.2	–1.6	–1.7	–1.4	–1.4
Savings	20.9	19.7	17.2	16.9	16.3	16.6	17.7	18.7	18.9	19.2	19.3
Investment	21.6	21.9	19.2	18.7	19.0	18.7	17.9	20.3	20.7	20.7	20.8
Capital Account Balance	0.1	0.1	0.0	0.0	0.0	0.1	0.2	0.0	0.0	0.0	0.0
Middle East and Central Asia											
Net Lending and Borrowing	9.0	6.3	–4.0	–1.3	2.3	0.4	–2.5	2.0	6.4	5.1	2.1
Current Account Balance	9.2	6.3	–4.1	–1.1	2.8	0.4	–2.5	2.3	6.5	5.2	2.2
Savings	36.1	33.9	23.6	26.2	28.8	27.8	26.3	30.2	33.9	33.0	30.5
Investment	27.2	27.4	26.9	27.1	26.2	27.8	29.1	28.4	27.8	28.3	28.5
Capital Account Balance	0.1	0.1	–0.1	–0.1	–0.2	0.0	0.0	–0.3	0.0	0.0	0.0
Sub-Saharan Africa											
Net Lending and Borrowing	1.5	–1.4	–3.2	–1.7	–1.9	–2.9	–2.4	–0.7	–1.3	–2.2	–2.0
Current Account Balance	0.2	–2.1	–3.6	–2.1	–2.3	–3.3	–2.9	–1.1	–1.7	–2.5	–2.3
Savings	20.8	19.5	17.7	18.4	19.2	19.6	19.8	23.1	18.9	17.9	17.4
Investment	20.7	21.6	21.0	20.5	21.2	22.9	22.6	24.0	20.5	20.4	19.6
Capital Account Balance	1.2	0.7	0.4	0.4	0.4	0.4	0.4	0.4	0.4	0.4	0.3

Table A14. Summary of Net Lending and Borrowing *(continued)*
(Percent of GDP)

	Averages								Projections		
	2004–13	2008–15	2016	2017	2018	2019	2020	2021	2022	2023	Average 2024–27
Analytical Groups											
By Source of Export Earnings											
Fuel											
Net Lending and Borrowing	12.0	8.0	–3.1	0.9	4.8	1.8	–2.4	3.3	8.3	6.5	3.1
Current Account Balance	12.2	8.0	–3.1	1.2	5.3	1.9	–2.4	3.8	8.4	6.7	3.3
Savings	38.8	35.5	25.5	28.4	31.2	30.4	28.9	34.2	36.5	34.7	31.2
Investment	27.0	27.4	27.4	26.9	26.0	28.9	31.6	31.1	28.6	28.6	28.2
Capital Account Balance	0.2	0.0	–0.2	–0.2	–0.3	0.0	0.0	–0.3	–0.1	–0.1	–0.1
Nonfuel											
Net Lending and Borrowing	0.9	0.1	0.1	–0.1	–0.7	–0.1	0.9	0.6	0.3	0.3	–0.2
Current Account Balance	0.7	0.0	0.0	–0.2	–0.8	–0.2	0.8	0.5	0.3	0.2	–0.2
Savings	30.9	32.0	31.9	32.1	32.6	32.3	33.4	34.0	35.2	35.1	34.8
Investment	30.3	32.0	32.0	32.3	33.4	32.6	32.7	33.6	35.0	34.9	35.0
Capital Account Balance	0.2	0.1	0.1	0.1	0.1	0.1	0.1	0.1	0.1	0.1	0.1
By External Financing Source											
Net Debtor Economies											
Net Lending and Borrowing	–1.7	–2.5	–1.9	–2.0	–2.4	–1.8	–0.5	–1.6	–2.5	–2.2	–2.0
Current Account Balance	–2.0	–2.8	–2.1	–2.2	–2.6	–2.0	–0.8	–1.9	–2.7	–2.4	–2.2
Savings	23.3	23.0	22.2	22.4	22.7	22.6	22.9	23.6	22.9	23.2	23.6
Investment	25.4	25.8	24.4	24.6	25.3	24.7	23.7	25.6	25.8	25.7	25.8
Capital Account Balance	0.3	0.3	0.2	0.2	0.2	0.2	0.3	0.2	0.2	0.2	0.1
Net Debtor Economies by Debt-Servicing Experience											
Economies with Arrears and/or Rescheduling during 2017–21											
Net Lending and Borrowing	–1.4	–3.6	–5.3	–4.9	–4.0	–3.8	–2.2	–2.4	–2.6	–3.2	–2.7
Current Account Balance	–2.4	–4.4	–5.7	–5.4	–4.5	–4.3	–2.9	–2.9	–3.1	–3.6	–3.0
Savings	19.9	18.1	15.1	15.9	17.3	16.4	14.7	15.2	. . .	. . .	. . .
Investment	22.4	22.3	21.0	21.7	21.5	21.4	18.0	18.5	. . .	. . .	. . .
Capital Account Balance	1.0	0.8	0.4	0.5	0.5	0.5	0.7	0.5	0.4	0.4	0.3
Memorandum											
World											
Net Lending and Borrowing	0.3	0.4	0.4	0.6	0.4	0.4	0.4	0.8	0.3	0.4	0.2
Current Account Balance	0.3	0.4	0.4	0.6	0.4	0.4	0.4	0.7	0.2	0.3	0.2
Savings	25.0	25.5	26.0	26.7	27.0	27.0	27.1	28.4	28.9	28.8	28.8
Investment	24.7	25.1	25.4	25.9	26.5	26.5	26.5	27.1	28.0	27.8	28.0
Capital Account Balance	0.1	0.0	0.0	0.0	0.0	0.0	0.0	0.1	0.1	0.1	0.0

Note: The estimates in this table are based on individual countries' national accounts and balance of payments statistics. Country group composites are calculated as the sum of the US dollar values for the relevant individual countries. This differs from the calculations in the April 2005 and earlier issues of the *World Economic Outlook*, in which the composites were weighted by GDP valued at purchasing power parities as a share of total world GDP. The estimates of gross national savings and investment (or gross capital formation) are from individual countries' national accounts statistics. The estimates of the current account balance, the capital account balance, and the financial account balance (or net lending/net borrowing) are from the balance of payments statistics. The link between domestic transactions and transactions with the rest of the world can be expressed as accounting identities. Savings (S) minus investment (I) is equal to the current account balance (CAB) (S – I = CAB). Also, net lending/net borrowing (NLB) is the sum of the current account balance and the capital account balance (KAB) (NLB = CAB + KAB). In practice, these identities do not hold exactly; imbalances result from imperfections in source data and compilation as well as from asymmetries in group composition due to data availability.
[1]Excludes the Group of Seven (Canada, France, Germany, Italy, Japan, United Kingdom, United States) and euro area countries.

Table A15. Summary of World Medium-Term Baseline Scenario

	Averages				Projections			
							Averages	
	2004–13	2014–23	2020	2021	2022	2023	2020–23	2024–27
				Annual Percent Change				
World Real GDP	**4.1**	**2.9**	**–3.0**	**6.0**	**3.2**	**2.7**	**2.2**	**3.3**
Advanced Economies	1.6	1.7	–4.4	5.2	2.4	1.1	1.0	1.8
Emerging Market and Developing Economies	6.4	3.8	–1.9	6.6	3.7	3.7	3.0	4.3
Memorandum								
Potential Output								
Major Advanced Economies	1.5	1.2	–1.2	2.1	1.7	1.4	1.0	1.4
World Trade, Volume[1]	**5.4**	**2.8**	**–7.8**	**10.1**	**4.3**	**2.5**	**2.1**	**3.6**
Imports								
Advanced Economies	3.7	3.0	–8.4	9.5	6.0	2.0	2.1	2.9
Emerging Market and Developing Economies	9.1	2.5	–7.8	11.8	2.4	3.0	2.1	4.8
Exports								
Advanced Economies	4.5	2.5	–9.0	8.7	4.2	2.5	1.4	3.2
Emerging Market and Developing Economies	7.4	3.2	–4.8	11.8	3.3	2.9	3.1	4.4
Terms of Trade								
Advanced Economies	–0.4	0.3	0.9	0.6	–1.5	0.5	0.1	0.3
Emerging Market and Developing Economies	1.5	–0.6	–1.1	1.7	0.8	–1.7	–0.1	–0.6
World Prices in US Dollars								
Manufactures	2.6	1.1	–3.2	6.8	10.2	3.9	4.3	1.7
Oil	13.6	–1.9	–31.7	65.9	41.4	–12.9	8.7	–4.5
Nonfuel Primary Commodities	8.3	1.4	6.5	26.3	7.3	–6.2	7.9	–0.2
Consumer Prices								
Advanced Economies	2.0	2.3	0.7	3.1	7.2	4.4	3.8	2.0
Emerging Market and Developing Economies	6.3	5.7	5.1	5.9	9.9	8.1	7.2	4.6
Interest Rates				*Percent*				
World Real Long-Term Interest Rate[2]	1.3	–0.7	–0.3	–2.5	–5.1	–1.1	–2.2	0.8
Current Account Balances				*Percent of GDP*				
Advanced Economies	–0.5	0.4	0.4	0.6	–0.6	–0.3	0.0	0.2
Emerging Market and Developing Economies	2.4	0.3	0.5	0.8	1.3	1.0	0.9	0.2
Total External Debt								
Emerging Market and Developing Economies	27.4	29.9	32.6	30.3	27.3	26.6	29.2	25.6
Debt Service								
Emerging Market and Developing Economies	9.2	10.8	11.4	10.6	9.8	9.6	10.3	9.3

[1]Data refer to trade in goods and services.
[2]GDP-weighted average of 10-year (or nearest-maturity) government bond rates for Canada, France, Germany, Italy, Japan, the United Kingdom, and the United States.

WORLD ECONOMIC OUTLOOK
SELECTED TOPICS

World Economic Outlook Archives

World Economic Outlook: Tensions from the Two-Speed Recovery—Unemployment, Commodities, and Capital Flows	April 2011
World Economic Outlook: Slowing Growth, Rising Risks	September 2011
World Economic Outlook: Growth Resuming, Dangers Remain	April 2012
World Economic Outlook: Coping with High Debt and Sluggish Growth	October 2012
World Economic Outlook: Hopes, Realities, Risks	April 2013
World Economic Outlook: Transitions and Tensions	October 2013
World Economic Outlook: Recovery Strengthens, Remains Uneven	April 2014
World Economic Outlook: Legacies, Clouds, Uncertainties	October 2014
World Economic Outlook: Uneven Growth—Short- and Long-Term Factors	April 2015
World Economic Outlook: Adjusting to Lower Commodity Prices	October 2015
World Economic Outlook: Too Slow for Too Long	April 2016
World Economic Outlook: Subdued Demand—Symptoms and Remedies	October 2016
World Economic Outlook: Gaining Momentum?	April 2017
World Economic Outlook: Seeking Sustainable Growth: Short-Term Recovery, Long-Term Challenges	October 2017
World Economic Outlook: Cyclical Upswing, Structural Change	April 2018
World Economic Outlook: Challenges to Steady Growth	October 2018
World Economic Outlook: Growth Slowdown, Precarious Recovery	April 2019
World Economic Outlook: Global Manufacturing Downturn, Rising Trade Barriers	October 2019
World Economic Outlook: The Great Lockdown	April 2020
World Economic Outlook: A Long and Difficult Ascent	October 2020
World Economic Outlook: Managing Divergent Recoveries	April 2021
World Economic Outlook: Uncharted Territory: Recovery during a Pandemic	October 2021
World Economic Outlook: War Sets Back the Global Recovery	April 2022
World Economic Outlook: Countering the Cost-of-Living Crisis	October 2022

I. Methodology—Aggregation, Modeling, and Forecasting

World Economic Outlook Downside Scenarios	April 2011, Box 1.2
Fiscal Balance Sheets: The Significance of Nonfinancial Assets and Their Measurement	October 2014, Box 3.3
Tariff Scenarios	October 2016, Scenario Box
World Growth Projections over the Medium Term	October 2016, Box 1.1
Global Growth Forecast: Assumptions on Policies, Financial Conditions, and Commodity Prices	April 2019, Box 1.2
On the Underlying Source of Changes in Capital Goods Prices: A Model-Based Analysis	April 2019, Box 3.3
Global Growth Forecast: Assumptions on Policies, Financial Conditions, and Commodity Prices	October 2019, Box 1.3
Alternative Evolutions in the Fight against COVID-19	April 2020, Scenario Box
Alternative Scenarios	October 2020, Scenario Box
Revised World Economic Outlook Purchasing-Power-Parity Weights	October 2020, Box 1.1
Scenario Box	April 2021

II. Historical Surveys

III. Economic Growth—Sources and Patterns

The Plucking Theory of the Business Cycle	October 2019, Box 1.4
Reigniting Growth in Low-Income and Emerging Market Economies: What Role Can Structural Reforms Play?	October 2019, Chapter 3
Countering Future Recessions in Advanced Economies: Cyclical Policies in an Era of Low Rates and High Debt	April 2020, Chapter 2
The Great Lockdown: Dissecting the Economic Effects	October 2020, Chapter 2
An Overview of the Literature on the Economic Impact of Lockdowns	October 2020, Box 2.1
Global Manufacturing: V-Shaped Recovery and Implications for the Global Outlook	April 2021, Box 1.1
After-Effects of the COVID-19 Pandemic: Prospects for Medium-Term Economic Damage	April 2021, Chapter 2
A Perfect Storm Hits the Hotel and Restaurant Sector	April 2021, Box 2.1
Research and Innovation: Fighting the Pandemic and Boosting Long-Term Growth	October 2021, Chapter 3

IV. Inflation and Deflation and Commodity Markets

Commodity Market Developments and Prospects	April 2011, Appendix 1.2
Oil Scarcity, Growth, and Global Imbalances	April 2011, Chapter 3
Life Cycle Constraints on Global Oil Production	April 2011, Box 3.1
Unconventional Natural Gas: A Game Changer?	April 2011, Box 3.2
Short-Term Effects of Oil Shocks on Economic Activity	April 2011, Box 3.3
Low-Frequency Filtering for Extracting Business Cycle Trends	April 2011, Appendix 3.1
The Energy and Oil Empirical Models	April 2011, Appendix 3.2
Commodity Market Developments and Prospects	September 2011, Appendix 1.1
Financial Investment, Speculation, and Commodity Prices	September 2011, Box 1.4
Target What You Can Hit: Commodity Price Swings and Monetary Policy	September 2011, Chapter 3
Commodity Market Review	April 2012, Chapter 1, Special Feature
Commodity Price Swings and Commodity Exporters	April 2012, Chapter 4
Macroeconomic Effects of Commodity Price Shocks on Low-Income Countries	April 2012, Box 4.1
Volatile Commodity Prices and the Development Challenge in Low-Income Countries	April 2012, Box 4.2
Commodity Market Review	October 2012, Chapter 1, Special Feature
Unconventional Energy in the United States	October 2012, Box 1.4
Food Supply Crunch: Who Is Most Vulnerable?	October 2012, Box 1.5
Commodity Market Review	April 2013, Chapter 1, Special Feature
The Dog That Didn't Bark: Has Inflation Been Muzzled or Was It Just Sleeping?	April 2013, Chapter 3
Does Inflation Targeting Still Make Sense with a Flatter Phillips Curve?	April 2013, Box 3.1
Commodity Market Review	October 2013, Chapter 1, Special Feature
Energy Booms and the Current Account: Cross-Country Experience	October 2013, Box 1.SF.1
Oil Price Drivers and the Narrowing WTI-Brent Spread	October 2013, Box 1.SF.2
Anchoring Inflation Expectations When Inflation Is Undershooting	April 2014, Box 1.3
Commodity Prices and Forecasts	April 2014, Chapter 1, Special Feature
Commodity Market Developments and Forecasts, with a Focus on Natural Gas in the World Economy	October 2014, Chapter 1, Special Feature
Commodity Market Developments and Forecasts, with a Focus on Investment in an Era of Low Oil Prices	April 2015, Chapter 1, Special Feature
The Oil Price Collapse: Demand or Supply?	April 2015, Box 1.1

Commodity Market Developments and Forecasts, with a Focus on Metals in the World Economy	October 2015, Chapter 1, Special Feature
The New Frontiers of Metal Extraction: The North-to-South Shift	October 2015, Chapter 1, Special Feature Box 1.SF.1
Where Are Commodity Exporters Headed? Output Growth in the Aftermath of the Commodity Boom	October 2015, Chapter 2
The Not-So-Sick Patient: Commodity Booms and the Dutch Disease Phenomenon	October 2015, Box 2.1
Do Commodity Exporters' Economies Overheat during Commodity Booms?	October 2015, Box 2.4
Commodity Market Developments and Forecasts, with a Focus on the Energy Transition in an Era of Low Fossil Fuel Prices	April 2016, Chapter 1, Special Feature
Global Disinflation in an Era of Constrained Monetary Policy	October 2016, Chapter 3
Commodity Market Developments and Forecasts, with a Focus on Food Security and Markets in the World Economy	October 2016, Chapter 1, Special Feature
How Much Do Global Prices Matter for Food Inflation?	October 2016, Box 3.3
Commodity Market Developments and Forecasts, with a Focus on the Role of Technology and Unconventional Sources in the Global Oil Market	April 2017, Chapter 1, Special Feature
Commodity Market Developments and Forecasts	October 2017, Chapter 1, Special Feature
Commodity Market Developments and Forecasts	April 2018, Chapter 1, Special Feature
What Has Held Core Inflation Back in Advanced Economies?	April 2018, Box 1.2
The Role of Metals in the Economics of Electric Vehicles	April 2018, Box 1.SF.1
Inflation Outlook: Regions and Countries	October 2018, Box 1.4
Commodity Market Developments and Forecasts, with a Focus on Recent Trends in Energy Demand	October 2018, Chapter 1, Special Feature
The Demand and Supply of Renewable Energy	October 2018, Box 1.SF.1
Challenges for Monetary Policy in Emerging Markets as Global Financial Conditions Normalize	October 2018, Chapter 3
Inflation Dynamics in a Wider Group of Emerging Market and Developing Economies	October 2018, Box 3.1
Commodity Special Feature	April 2019, Chapter 1, Special Feature
Commodity Market Developments and Forecasts	October 2019, Chapter 1, Special Feature
Commodity Market Developments and Forecasts	April 2020, Chapter 1, Special Feature
Commodity Market Developments and Forecasts	October 2020, Chapter 1, Special Feature
What Is Happening with Global Carbon Emissions in 2019?	October 2020, Chapter 1, Special Feature Box 1.SF.1
Commodity Market Developments and Forecasts	April 2021, Chapter 1, Special Feature
House Prices and Consumer Price Inflation	October 2021, Box 1.1
Commodity Market Developments and Forecasts	October 2021, Chapter 1, Special Feature
Inflation Scares	October 2021, Chapter 2
Core Inflation in the COVID-19 Crisis	October 2021, Box 2.2
Market Developments and the Pace of Fossil Fuel Divestment	April 2022, Special Feature
Dissecting Recent WEO Inflation Forecast Errors	October 2022, Box 1.1
Market Power and Inflation during COVID-19	October 2022, Box 1.2
Commodity Market Developments and Food Inflation Drivers	October 2022, Special Feature

V. Fiscal Policy

Separated at Birth? The Twin Budget and Trade Balances	September 2011, Chapter 4
Are We Underestimating Short-Term Fiscal Multipliers?	October 2012, Box 1.1
The Implications of High Public Debt in Advanced Economies	October 2012, Box 1.2
The Good, the Bad, and the Ugly: 100 Years of Dealing with Public Debt Overhangs	October 2012, Chapter 3
The Great Divergence of Policies	April 2013, Box 1.1
Public Debt Overhang and Private Sector Performance	April 2013, Box 1.2
Is It Time for an Infrastructure Push? The Macroeconomic Effects of Public Investment	October 2014, Chapter 3
Improving the Efficiency of Public Investment	October 2014, Box 3.2
The Macroeconomic Effects of Scaling Up Public Investment in Developing Economies	October 2014, Box 3.4
Fiscal Institutions, Rules, and Public Investment	October 2014, Box 3.5
Commodity Booms and Public Investment	October 2015, Box 2.2
Cross-Border Impacts of Fiscal Policy: Still Relevant	October 2017, Chapter 4
The Spillover Impact of U.S. Government Spending Shocks on External Positions	October 2017, Box 4.1
Macroeconomic Impact of Corporate Tax Policy Changes	April 2018, Box 1.5
Place-Based Policies: Rethinking Fiscal Policies to Tackle Inequalities within Countries	October 2019, Box 2.4

VI. Monetary Policy, Financial Markets, and Flow of Funds

Financial Conditions Indices	April 2011, Appendix 1.1
House Price Busts in Advanced Economies: Repercussions for Global Financial Markets	April 2011, Box 1.1
International Spillovers and Macroeconomic Policymaking	April 2011, Box 1.3
Credit Boom-Bust Cycles: Their Triggers and Policy Implications	September 2011, Box 1.2
Are Equity Price Drops Harbingers of Recession?	September 2011, Box 1.3
Cross-Border Spillovers from Euro Area Bank Deleveraging	April 2012, Chapter 2, Spillover Feature
The Financial Transmission of Stress in the Global Economy	October 2012, Chapter 2, Spillover Feature
The Great Divergence of Policies	April 2013, Box 1.1
Taper Talks: What to Expect When the United States Is Tightening	October 2013, Box 1.1
Credit Supply and Economic Growth	April 2014, Box 1.1
Should Advanced Economies Worry about Growth Shocks in Emerging Market Economies?	April 2014, Chapter 2, Spillover Feature
Perspectives on Global Real Interest Rates	April 2014, Chapter 3
Housing Markets across the Globe: An Update	October 2014, Box 1.1
U.S. Monetary Policy and Capital Flows to Emerging Markets	April 2016, Box 2.2
A Transparent Risk-Management Approach to Monetary Policy	October 2016, Box 3.5
Will the Revival in Capital Flows to Emerging Markets Be Sustained?	October 2017, Box 1.2
The Role of Financial Sector Repair in the Speed of the Recovery	October 2018, Box 2.3
Clarity of Central Bank Communications and the Extent of Anchoring of Inflation Expectations	October 2018, Box 3.2
Can Negative Policy Rates Stimulate the Economy?	April 2020, Box 2.1
Dampening Global Financial Shocks in Emerging Markets: Can Macroprudential Regulation Help?	April 2020, Chapter 3
Macroprudential Policies and Credit: A Meta-Analysis of the Empirical Findings	April 2020, Box 3.1
Do Emerging Markets Adjust Macroprudential Regulation in Response to Global Financial Shocks?	April 2020, Box 3.2
Rising Small and Medium-Sized Enterprise Bankruptcy and Insolvency Risks: Assessment and Policy Options	April 2020, Box 1.3

VII. Labor Markets, Poverty, and Inequality

VIII. Exchange Rate Issues

Exchange Rate Regimes and Crisis Susceptibility in Emerging Markets	April 2014, Box 1.4
Exchange Rates and Trade Flows: Disconnected?	October 2015, Chapter 3
The Relationship between Exchange Rates and Global-Value-Chain-Related Trade	October 2015, Box 3.1
Measuring Real Effective Exchange Rates and Competitiveness: The Role of Global Value Chains	October 2015, Box 3.2
Labor Force Participation Rates in Advanced Economies	October 2017, Box 1.1
Recent Wage Dynamics in Advanced Economies: Drivers and Implications	October 2017, Chapter 2
Labor Market Dynamics by Skill Level	October 2017, Box 2.1
Worker Contracts and Nominal Wage Rigidities in Europe: Firm-Level Evidence	October 2017, Box 2.2
Wage and Employment Adjustment after the Global Financial Crisis: Firm-Level Evidence	October 2017, Box 2.3

IX. External Payments, Trade, Capital Movements, and Foreign Debt

Unwinding External Imbalances in the European Union Periphery	April 2011, Box 2.1
International Capital Flows: Reliable or Fickle?	April 2011, Chapter 4
External Liabilities and Crisis Tipping Points	September 2011, Box 1.5
The Evolution of Current Account Deficits in the Euro Area	April 2013, Box 1.3
External Rebalancing in the Euro Area	October 2013, Box 1.3
The Yin and Yang of Capital Flow Management: Balancing Capital Inflows with Capital Outflows	October 2013, Chapter 4
Simulating Vulnerability to International Capital Market Conditions	October 2013, Box 4.1
The Trade Implications of the U.S. Shale Gas Boom	October 2014, Box 1.SF.1
Are Global Imbalances at a Turning Point?	October 2014, Chapter 4
Switching Gears: The 1986 External Adjustment	October 2014, Box 4.1
A Tale of Two Adjustments: East Asia and the Euro Area	October 2014, Box 4.2
Understanding the Role of Cyclical and Structural Factors in the Global Trade Slowdown	April 2015, Box 1.2
Small Economies, Large Current Account Deficits	October 2015, Box 1.2
Capital Flows and Financial Deepening in Developing Economies	October 2015, Box 1.3
Dissecting the Global Trade Slowdown	April 2016, Box 1.1
Understanding the Slowdown in Capital Flows to Emerging Markets	April 2016, Chapter 2
Capital Flows to Low-Income Developing Countries	April 2016, Box 2.1
The Potential Productivity Gains from Further Trade and Foreign Direct Investment Liberalization	April 2016, Box 3.3
Global Trade: What's behind the Slowdown?	October 2016, Chapter 2
The Evolution of Emerging Market and Developing Economies' Trade Integration with China's Final Demand	April 2017, Box 2.3
Shifts in the Global Allocation of Capital: Implications for Emerging Market and Developing Economies	April 2017, Box 2.4
Macroeconomic Adjustment in Emerging Market Commodity Exporters	October 2017, Box 1.4
Remittances and Consumption Smoothing	October 2017, Box 1.5
A Multidimensional Approach to Trade Policy Indicators	April 2018, Box 1.6
The Rise of Services Trade	April 2018, Box 3.2
Role of Foreign Aid in Improving Productivity in Low-Income Developing Countries	April 2018, Box 4.3
Global Trade Tensions	October 2018, Scenario Box
The Price of Capital Goods: A Driver of Investment under Threat?	April 2019, Chapter 3
Evidence from Big Data: Capital Goods Prices across Countries	April 2019, Box 3.2
Capital Goods Tariffs and Investment: Firm-Level Evidence from Colombia	April 2019, Box 3.4
The Drivers of Bilateral Trade and the Spillovers from Tariffs	April 2019, Chapter 4

X. Regional Issues

XI. Country-Specific Analyses

XII. Climate Change Issues

Topic	Issue
The Price of Manufactured Low-Carbon Energy Technologies	April 2019, Box 3.1
What's Happening with Global Carbon Emissions?	October 2019, Box 1.SF.1
Mitigating Climate Change—Growth and Distribution-Friendly Strategies	October 2020, Chapter 3
Glossary	October 2020, Box 3.1
Zooming in on the Electricity Sector: The First Step toward Decarbonization	October 2020, Box 3.2
Who Suffers Most from Climate Change? The Case of Natural Disasters	April 2021, Box 1.2
Jobs and the Green Economy	October 2021, Box 1.2
Clean Tech and the Role of Basic Scientific Research	October 2021, Box 3.2
Commodity Market Developments and Forecasts	October 2021, Chapter 1 Special Feature
A Greener Labor Market: Employment, Policies, and Economic Transformation	April 2022, Chapter 3
The Geography of Green- and Pollution-Intensive Jobs: Evidence from the United States	April 2022, Box 3.1
A Greener Post-COVID Job Market?	April 2022, Box 3.2
Near-Term Macroeconomic Impact of Decarbonization Policies	October 2022, Chapter 3
Near-Term Implications of Carbon Pricing: A Review of the Literature	October 2022, Box 3.1
Political Economy of Carbon Pricing: Experiences from South Africa, Sweden, and Uruguay	October 2022, Box 3.2
Decarbonizing the Power Sector While Managing Renewables' Intermittence	October 2022, Box 3.3

XIII. Special Topics

Topic	Issue
Getting By with a Little Help from a Boom: Do Commodity Windfalls Speed Up Human Development?	October 2015, Box 2.3
Breaking the Deadlock: Identifying the Political Economy Drivers of Structural Reforms	April 2016, Box 3.1
Can Reform Waves Turn the Tide? Some Case Studies Using the Synthetic Control Method	April 2016, Box 3.4
A Global Rush for Land	October 2016, Box 1.SF.1
Conflict, Growth, and Migration	April 2017, Box 1.1
Tackling Measurement Challenges of Irish Economic Activity	April 2017, Box 1.2
Within-Country Trends in Income per Capita: The Cases of Brazil, Russia, India, China, and South Africa	April 2017, Box 2.1
Technological Progress and Labor Shares: A Historical Overview	April 2017, Box 3.1
The Elasticity of Substitution between Capital and Labor: Concept and Estimation	April 2017, Box 3.2
Routine Tasks, Automation, and Economic Dislocation around the World	April 2017, Box 3.3
Adjustments to the Labor Share of Income	April 2017, Box 3.4
Smartphones and Global Trade	April 2018, Box 1.1
Has Mismeasurement of the Digital Economy Affected Productivity Statistics?	April 2018, Box 1.4
The Changing Service Content of Manufactures	April 2018, Box 3.1
Patent Data and Concepts	April 2018, Box 4.1
International Technology Sourcing and Knowledge Spillovers	April 2018, Box 4.2
Relationship between Competition, Concentration, and Innovation	April 2018, Box 4.4
Increasing Market Power	October 2018, Box 1.1
Sharp GDP Declines: Some Stylized Facts	October 2018, Box 1.5
Predicting Recessions and Slowdowns: A Daunting Task	October 2018, Box 1.6
The Rise of Corporate Market Power and Its Macroeconomic Effects	April 2019, Chapter 2
The Comovement between Industry Concentration and Corporate Saving	April 2019, Box 2.1
Effects of Mergers and Acquisitions on Market Power	April 2019, Box 2.2
The Global Automobile Industry: Recent Developments, and Implications for the Global Outlook	October 2019, Box 1.1
Measuring Subnational Regional Economic Activity and Welfare	October 2019, Box 2.1

IMF EXECUTIVE BOARD DISCUSSION OF THE OUTLOOK, SEPTEMBER 2022

The following remarks were made by the Chair at the conclusion of the Executive Board's discussion of the Fiscal Monitor, Global Financial Stability Report, *and* World Economic Outlook *on September 29, 2022.*

Executive Directors broadly agreed with staff's assessment of the global economic outlook, risks, and policy priorities. They broadly concurred that high inflation and associated tightening financial conditions resulting from policy normalization; the effects of Russia's war in Ukraine, particularly on food and energy prices; and the lingering COVID-19 pandemic, with its related supply chain disruptions, have all contributed to a weakening in global economic prospects. Directors recognized that risks to the outlook are unusually high. They agreed that the most prominent risks—including policy divergence and cross-border tensions, further energy and food price shocks, an entrenchment of inflation dynamics and a de-anchoring of inflation expectations, and debt vulnerabilities in some emerging markets—tilt the distribution of likely growth outcomes to the downside. Moreover, Directors recognized that the current environment of high inflation, slowdown in growth, and heightened uncertainty about the economic and policy outlook poses particularly difficult tradeoffs and challenges for policymakers, making the likelihood of a policy mistake higher than usual.

Against this backdrop, Directors agreed that the appropriate policy responses differ across countries, reflecting their local circumstances, their inflation and growth outlooks, and differences in trade and financial exposures. For most economies, they considered that tighter monetary and fiscal policies are necessary to durably reduce inflation. At the same time, they emphasized that these policies should be accompanied by structural reforms that improve productivity, expand economic capacity, and ease supply-side constraints. Directors recognized that many emerging market and developing economies (EMDEs) face tougher policy choices, as higher food and fuel prices, the need to support the recovery and vulnerable populations, and rising costs of market financing from tighter global financial conditions and US dollar appreciation can pull in different directions, necessitating a difficult balancing act.

Directors stressed that monetary authorities should act decisively and continue to normalize policy to prevent inflationary pressures from becoming entrenched and avoid an unmooring of inflation expectations. They agreed that central banks in most advanced economies and EMDEs would need to continue tightening the monetary policy stance to bring inflation credibly back to target and to anchor inflation expectations. Directors stressed that maintaining central bank independence and policy credibility will be essential to secure price stability. They also emphasized the importance of continuing to assess the impact of the simultaneous monetary tightening by central banks and, in particular, its implications for EMDEs. Directors stressed that clear communication of both policy functions and the unwavering commitment to achieve price objectives is crucial to preserve credibility and avoid unwarranted market volatility. They considered that, should global financial conditions tighten in a disorderly manner, EMDEs could face capital outflows and should be ready to use all available tools, including foreign exchange interventions and capital flow management measures, guided when appropriate by the Integrated Policy Framework and in line with the Institutional View on the Liberalization and Management of Capital Flows and without substituting for exchange rate flexibility and warranted macroeconomic adjustments.

Directors concurred that fiscal policy is operating in a highly uncertain environment of elevated inflation, slowdown in growth, high debt, and tightening borrowing conditions. They stressed that, where inflation is elevated, a tighter fiscal stance would send a powerful signal that policymakers are aligned in their fight against inflation. Such a signal would, in turn, reduce the size of required interest rate increases to keep inflation expectations anchored and would help keep borrowing costs lower. Directors emphasized that fiscal support to address the surge in cost of living from high food and energy prices should primarily focus on targeted support to the most vulnerable segments, given the criticality of preserving price incentives to promote energy conservation. Some Directors considered that additional but temporary energy policies may be needed in countries that face exceptionally high and volatile energy prices owing to Russia's war in Ukraine.

Directors broadly agreed that fiscal policy has a role in protecting people against loss in real incomes in moments of large adverse shocks, but that requires healthy public finances. Building on the experience of the pandemic, they considered that governments should invest in social safety nets and develop policy strategies and tools that can be readily deployed under various scenarios. Directors concurred that a sound and credible medium-term fiscal framework, including spending prioritization and efforts to raise revenues, can help manage urgent needs from high food and energy prices, rebuild fiscal buffers to cope with future crises, and make progress in long-term development needs, such as investment in renewable energy and health care, which can also foster economic resilience.

Directors noted that, although no material systemic event has materialized so far, financial stability risks have risen along many dimensions, which highlights the importance of containing a further buildup of financial vulnerabilities. Being mindful of country-specific circumstances and near-term economic challenges, they agreed that selected macroprudential tools may need to be adjusted to tackle pockets of elevated vulnerabilities. Directors noted, however, that striking a balance between containing the buildup of vulnerabilities and avoiding procyclicality and a disorderly tightening of financial conditions is important given heightened economic uncertainty and the ongoing policy normalization process.

Directors reiterated their urgent call for global cooperation and dialogue, which are essential to defuse geopolitical tensions, avoid further economic and trade fragmentation, and respond to challenges in an interconnected world. They agreed on the criticality of multilateral actions to respond to existing and unfolding humanitarian crises, end Russia's war in Ukraine, safeguard global liquidity, manage debt distress, mitigate and adapt to climate change, and end the pandemic. Noting that many countries are contending with tighter financial conditions, high debt levels, and pressures to protect the most vulnerable from surging inflation, Directors called on the multilateral institutions to stand ready to provide emergency liquidity to safeguard essential spending and contain financing crises. They also called for greater debt transparency and better mechanisms to produce orderly debt restructurings—including a more effective Common Framework—in those cases where insolvency issues prevail. Acknowledging that recent energy and food price shocks may have undermined the green transition, Directors stressed that achieving energy security and addressing the climate agenda go hand-in-hand, including by addressing the significant climate financing needs of EMDEs and investing in renewable energy and energy efficiency. Even though the COVID-19 pandemic is starting to fade, Directors called for decisive actions to address the continued inequity in access to health care and vaccinations worldwide and reduce the threat of future pandemics.